THE SHAME GAME

For anyone who has ever known what it feels like to be poor.

This book is dedicated to the memory of my dear friend, Jennifer Kearney, her son Arthur, and to the memory of Harry Leslie Smith, an extraordinary advocate for social justice and equality.

This book is for the incredible young women who are my goddaughters: Carrie Birch, Lucy Morson and Katie Tarrant.

"Overcoming poverty is not a gesture of charity. It is the protection of a fundamental human right, the right to dignity and a decent life."

Nelson Mandela

Shame (Verb): A Definition (MacMillan Dictionary)

1. to make someone feel guilty or embarrassed;
2. to cause yourself or someone else to lose respect or a good reputation.

Stigma (Noun): A Definition (Merriam Webster Dictionary)
: a mark of shame or discredit

Bullying (Noun): A Definition (Merriam Webster Dictionary)
: abuse and mistreatment of someone vulnerable by someone stronger, more powerful, etc.

> *Narratives are often described as a collection or system of related stories that are articulated and refined over time to represent a central idea or belief.*
> **The Narrative Initiative, *Toward New Gravity*[1]**

THE SHAME GAME
Overturning the Toxic Poverty Narrative

Mary O'Hara

First published in Great Britain in 2020 by

Policy Press
University of Bristol
1-9 Old Park Hill
Bristol
BS2 8BB
UK
t: +44 (0)117 954 5940
pp-info@bristol.ac.uk
www.policypress.co.uk

North America office:
Policy Press
c/o The University of Chicago Press
1427 East 60th Street
Chicago, IL 60637, USA
t: +1 773 702 7700
f: +1 773 702 9756
sales@press.uchicago.edu
www.press.uchicago.edu

British Library Cataloguing in Publication Data
A catalogue record for this book is available from the British Library.

Library of Congress Cataloging-in-Publication Data
A catalog record for this book has been requested.

ISBN 978-1-4473-4926-6 paperback
ISBN 978-1-4473-4928-0 ePub
ISBN 978-1-4473-4927-3 ePdf

Cover design and cover image credit: blu inc, Bristol

Contents

Acknowledgements   x

Foreword by Danny Dorling   xiii

Introduction   1

PART I: The inconvenient truth: poverty is real   **15**

A short prologue   18

1   Who are these 'poor' people anyway? Being on the breadline in Britain   21

2   What? There are poor people in the richest nation on earth?   52

PART II: Turning the screw on poor people: shame, stigma and cementing of a toxic poverty narrative   **83**

3   A twisted tale: evolution of the poverty narrative   88

4   Lights, camera, vilification: the narrative in action   129

5   The games we play: weaponising the narrative   151

6   Shame on you: making the toxic narrative stick   173

PART III: Flipping the script: challenging the narrative war on the poor   **193**

7   Feeling it: the truth about living in poverty   197

8   Changing times: fighting poverty, not the poor   221

9   New generation: young people writing their own script   251

10   Altered images: constructing a new narrative   272

Notes   307

Selected further reading   354

Index   357

Acknowledgements

A book is always a collaboration but for one like this, which is part of a much larger multi-platform initiative, and where so many people contributed their time, support, expertise, insights and advice, it is especially true. To every single person who helped me with Project Twist-It and this book, in any way, I couldn't have done it without you and I thank you from the bottom of my heart.

I owe a debt of gratitude to the people who worked directly on the production of this book and who were instrumental in making Project Twist-It a reality: to Ali Shaw and her team at Policy Press; and Abigail Scott Paul and the team at JRF for having faith in and championing this work, including Paul Brook who very kindly gave us permission to use his illustrations. My thanks also to copywriter and all-round production whizz Alexis Harvey, Think Nation founder Lizzie Hodgson, Linsay Rousseau, Chris Kaboli, Sam Kieffer, Dann Galucci, Sandra Barron, Jessica Rae Huber, Jessica Samson and Billie J.D. Porter, who in so many wonderful ways brought Project Twist-It to life.

To everyone to who worked with PTI and Think Nation on making films or who was involved in our live event in Canterbury, England, including the team at the Gulbenkian Theatre, Louisa Roach, Dr Heejung Chung, Educational Life CIC, Sarah Jones, Chris Duncan, Possibility People, Art31, Wigan Youth Zone and Imago.

Sincere thanks also to June Cigar, Kerry Hudson, Natasha Carthew, Sarah Smarsh, Linda Tirado, Vince Wallace Junior, Dominic Gwinn, Kayleigh Garthwaite, Mahsuda Snaith, Kat Woods, Shaun Glanville, Jonathan Wakeham, Conrad Murray, Cash Carraway, Paul Sng, Pete McKee, Chuck Collins, Mark Brown, Holly Walsh and Janet Owen-Driggs, and Mary Bisbee-Beek, my US publicist. To Jameela Jamil, Wale Shittu, Anna

Miles, Nadine Shah, Aoife Lennon, Tim Whittaker and the kids and volunteers at Mighty Writers, JJ Tatten and Mez Green from The Warren in Hull and all the amazing youngsters who agreed to be interviewed including Jodie Langford and Andrew Gooch, who took part in PTI Live, and all the incredible young people from Battersea Arts Centre's Beatbox Academy who brought so much creativity and energy to the project and to PTI Live.

My gratitude also to Rebecca Vallas, Alice Wong and her colleagues working on #CripTheVote for organising a powerful and impactful livestream on disability and poverty on Twitter, Frances Ryan, Kwame Boateng, Sarah Anderson, Christine Riccione, George W. Hopkins, Kieton Saunders-Browne, Olivia Chumacero, Sylvia Hernandez, Antonio Rodriguez, Hayk Makhmuryan, Peter Stefanovic, the Poor People's Campaign team including Reverend Dr William Barber, Reverend Dr Liz Theoharis, and grassroots volunteers including Joyce Brody, Lenny Brody and Sheilah Garland. To Shane Pangburn, Howard Read, Tim Molina, Karen Dolan, Diana Skelton and the team at ATD Fourth World including the people with lived experience who added their voices, Andrea Levere, Kat Calvin, Poverty2Solutions, Ruth Patrick and the Dole Animators, Thrive Teesside, Bev Skeggs, Imogen Tyler, Stephen Hinshaw, Gray Brechin, Simon Duffy, Maria Mansfield, Maurice Lim-Miller, Trevor Davis, Eric Trules, Jude Habib of Sound Delivery and those working on Being the Story, Leeds Poverty Truth Commission, Jacqui Roberts and the team at Shoreditch Trust, Kate Walz, Michael Sheen, Sean McAllister, Brian Pelan, Una Murphy, Jo Unwin, Zita Holbourne, Beth Johnson, Gee Sinah, Nat Kendal Taylor, Skylinn Landry, Carol Bostridge, Garry Greenland, Dr Adi Jaffe, Rachel Broady, all the women I met in South Carolina who talked to me about the links between domestic violence and poverty, the US army veterans who shared their experiences, and Dr Jonathan Tomlinson and the patients in his surgery in London, who told me their stories. Thanks also to Bird La Bird, Mairi Ryan at the RSA, Paul Scates, Ian Jones, and to the people who put time in to sharing the mission and content of PTI across social media.

I owe a great debt to the people on both sides of the Atlantic who read and critiqued early drafts of this book and shored me up when I needed it most. Their feedback and encouragement helped me see the wood for the trees and made this a better book than it otherwise would have been. So, heartfelt thanks to Colin Anderson, Saba Salman, Danny Dorling, Mark Blyth and Renee Colvert. And to my friends Felicity Wren and Rick Tucker who were always there to lend an ear. I'd also like to thank Talia and Luis at The Hatchery in Larchmont Village, Los Angeles. They have created a wonderful space for writers that is more than conducive, it's a community. Writing there, and being around other writers with shared challenges, made an enormous amount of difference on my most difficult writing and research days.

Finally, I need to thank people in my life as I was growing up without whom I don't know how things might have turned out. The people who taught me, who invested in me, and helped me find a route out of poverty. My teachers, including the late great Sister Genevieve O'Farrell, Frances Egan, Gerard Devlin and Mairead O'Halloran, all of whom mentored, championed and advised me, and my extraordinary childhood friends Michelle and Mary Ward, Madeline Maxwell, Aine Linden and Joanne Dowd who got me through some of the toughest periods of my early life along with my sister, Lisa.

Foreword

Danny Dorling

Shame is how they get away with it. Shame is the weapon they use. Shame is the weapon you use on yourself that makes you feel so useless. And those who are shamed most often and most deeply, made to feel ashamed for so much of their life, are the poorest among us.

When others say that they are disappointed in you, they are trying to inflict shame on you. They are attempting to make you contrite and silent. To force shame upon you. The poor are the most common targets of shaming because the rich are not ashamed of how they became rich and use shame as a weapon to control those they most harm.

Shame beats you down. Shame is an ancient form of control. Shame is the mechanism used to control behaviour. Most of us are capable of feeling shame for our own actions without anyone else having to shame us. However, those who play the specific and cruel 'shame game' outlined in this book – a public and prolific shaming that targets the poorest among us and a mechanism that has been used with incredible effectiveness to 'keep the poor in their place' – are rarely ever ashamed of themselves .

In this book, Mary O'Hara shows why the 'shame game' being played out against poorer people in the US and the UK is so destructive and effective. She dissects how it works to help keep the poor, poor – through blaming and shaming. She outlines why, for people who have lived in poverty, the impact of being shamed can be devastating, and how those who do the shaming do so by turning a blind eye to the experiences and the voices of the poor.

For the players of the shame game – the rich and the powerful who consolidate their power and vast wealth at the expense of others – shaming people is a way of affirming how great they are. And, they constantly need to feed that affirmation. They tell us they are 'wealth creators' while ignoring the role of inherited fortunes or that it is in fact workers, often paid a pittance, who generate wealth. They claim they are successful because of their own talents and efforts, rather than having benefited from ever-growing social and economic inequities – divisions they created.

Poverty is inflicted on millions in the US and the UK, and especially on the young, on women, on people who are differently abled or labelled as belonging to a lower race or class. But to inflict poverty on huge numbers of people in an affluent nation state is far from easy, it takes hard work. Those who play the shame game have to work tirelessly to maintain their fabricated mantra that the poor are feckless and idle, stupid and undeserving because, as this book demonstrates, it is essential that the poor feel ashamed if the rich are to keep getting richer at the expense of others.

Those with the most power use the fear of being cast out to incite people to join in the shaming of those just beneath them on the social scale. The implicit message conveyed by the rich and powerful is that there will always be wide divisions. Their core message is: you may never be as rich as us, but by joining in our bullying, you can insure yourself against falling into poverty.

'Work hard,' people are told, 'as hard as you possibly can, and one day you, or one of your children or grandchildren, could join us at the very top.' The rich call this 'equality of opportunity'.

Those who believe in inequality, who, as an act of faith, think that only a few should ever have most of what we all could have, use powerful messages and mechanisms – including the media – to spread their lies. However, this is not a debate. It is not a reasoned argument. It is abuse. The rich are trying to use your pride and your fear to control you. They are telling you that you are better than those people with just a little less than you, but simultaneously that they are much better than you, because they have so much more money than you. They are wrong.

As this book so clearly shows, the USA and the UK are the most economically unequal states of all the large rich nations because the shamers have, for now, won, while those who endure poverty every day are shamed into silence. These two states are outliers. They are unusual among the rich nations. They are examples of what happens when inequality and poverty become entrenched and when a false narrative about the causes of poverty prevails.

This book will show you the true scale of poverty and deprivation in today's America and Britain. Children are growing up stunted in the US and the UK today. More babies died in 2018 than in the previous year, and the year before, and the year before that. More children and adults are going hungry amid the riches. More and more are forced to beg for food at soup kitchens and foodbanks. More are forced to take yet longer and longer hours of lowly paid, insecure work from a series of jobs, while the shamers have the gall to cry out how low unemployment now is. Growing millions are forced to sleep outside on the street or live in constant fear of eviction from their homes. Many people living on the street have jobs.

More elderly people are dying earlier. Life expectancy has peaked in both the UK and the US (in 2014 in both cases). It is now falling. Nowhere else in the rich world is suffering such absolute immiseration because nowhere else have the greedy allowed the shame game to be played so effectively. Shame on us.

It has not always been this way. And, as this book argues with facts and the insights of people who have actually been on the receiving end of the shame game, it doesn't have to continue.

Do what has worked in the past and what works in the majority of nations today, where both poverty and inequality are falling. Help those who might succumb to playing the shame game to see how they are being used. Respect those who are the victims of the gamesters. Whenever you hear the words 'skiver' and 'shirker', 'feckless' and 'burden', 'sponger' or 'taker' applied to people who have the least – think. Think, just for a minute, about how in the most unequal of rich states the powerful are trying to take you for a ride.

Think about who shirk their responsibilities to others, who are dismissive of the lives of others, who are the real burdens on us all, who sponge off the vast majority to grow their riches – and who take the most. Expose them. Call them out for their role in creating the poverty and staggering levels of inequality we live with today. Shine a light on the absurdity of their claims to 'deserve' their vast fortunes while others work for poverty wages and struggle to feed their kids.

So, stand up, stand proud and don't play their game any more. Read this book to educate yourself. Read this book to hear from the people who are being shamed, whose voices are rarely heard, and who aren't standing for it any more. Call out the shame game whenever and wherever you see it. Don't be ashamed. When they can no longer shame you, they lose.

Danny Dorling,
Halford Mackinder Professor of Geography,
University of Oxford

The question below was sent by the author to the Twittersphere in late 2018:

Why, when the structural causes of #poverty are well documented, are people who are poor blamed for their circumstances? Why is there so much shame associated with struggling to get by or living on a low income?

Below are some of the replies. All of them inform this book.

Because victim blaming is how the rich and powerful live with themselves. The less powerful finger pointers like to imagine they are a cut above.

It is politically expedient by the privileged to believe in a meritocracy, to reject inequality, & to claim welfare is unaffordable.

Psychology. Partly it's fear, we shun what we fear esp if we're afraid it could happen to us. People want to associate with what they aspire to. Blaming the poor helps us feel in control & believing we'll be OK if we don't make their mistakes.

I find the British have a very odd relationship with poverty. There's a covert snobbery in how poverty as a social issue is framed. Last week I saw a mother of 4, sneered & mocked on here as the bank had issues with their mobile app.

Simple answer is that if people/culture were to admit that poverty isn't a choice then all of those other things we 'choose' will all seem shaky too.

I would wager that part of it is that we don't want to admit to ourselves that poverty can happen to anyone, including us. We also don't want to admit that there are systemic inequalities that we've bought into. To deny is to absolve ourselves.

People are lazy. We like to think in simplistic terms. Thus it's easier to blame the poor than the circumstances that create them. By blaming the poor we also disassociate ourselves from the idea that we might be part of the problem.

I've often heard people who grew up in deprived areas say that they managed to 'get out' and become successful and therefore it's something that everyone can do. The assumption being that people who don't didn't try hard enough.

It's divide and rule, if you can remove empathy for the poor as they are 'undeserving'.

People with inherited wealth or privilege propagate the mantra that their wealth is solely down to their hard work and their ability. This is to stop society redistributing their wealth through progressive taxation.

Introduction

"True individual freedom cannot exist without economic security and independence. People who are hungry and out of a job are the stuff of which dictatorships are made."
US President Franklin D. Roosevelt, 1944 State of the Union Address[1]

"The history of the poor is a history of attitudes towards the poor, since the voices of poor people have generally gone unheard."
Jeremy Seabrook, *Pauperland*, p 1[2]

This book is about a 'shame game' that is being played out against millions of the poorest people in Britain[3] and America. It tells the story of how a pervasive toxic narrative that shames and blames the poor has secured a stranglehold on our collective understanding of poverty and it asks how we might bring this to an end. Drawing on interviews with people in both countries who have first-hand experience of poverty, this book documents how a narrative – a powerful story – plays a pivotal role in sustaining and justifying high levels of poverty[4] and inequality by repeatedly misrepresenting, and stigmatising, people who are poor. It examines how we can shift perceptions and work towards building a consensus on how to tackle poverty and improve people's lives.

For a long time in the US and the UK, two of the wealthiest yet most unequal nations on earth, the primary story told about poverty has been that it is the fault of the individual and is the result of personal flaws or 'bad life decisions' rather than policy choices or economic inequality. If only people worked harder, if only they 'pulled themselves up by their bootstraps' or got 'on their bikes', as the one-time Conservative Secretary for Education Norman Tebbit once declared,[5] they too could find a job, they too could 'make it', the story goes. In fact, some people believe poverty doesn't[6] exist (or barely) in America and Britain, while others argue that we have no choice but to accept that 'the poor' will always be with us.

For years the poor have been portrayed as a drain on society, while attempts to counter this false impression have fallen on deaf ears. Those in our societies who are caught in poverty's clutches – including children – have been framed as a 'problem' through demeaning rhetoric and mendacious epithets. All the while, their own voices, their stories, and their views about poverty (and most anything) have been marginalised or ignored – even by many of those who profess to support helping people out of poverty.

This destructive poverty narrative, which dehumanises and dismisses the poorest people in our societies, is promoted by politicians and the media and across the culture with incredible frequency and has become deep-rooted in the minds of the public. This multi-faceted poverty narrative has proven to be a huge barrier to building support for positive policy action. As the British poverty expert and academic Ruth Lister said in a keynote address to a conference at the Organisation for Economic Cooperation and Development in Paris in May 2019:[7]

> **"**If the non-poor fail to perceive people in poverty as fellow human beings with similar needs, aspirations, and dreams, it's all too easy to ignore them.**"**

This erroneous poverty narrative endures despite the realities of low pay, insecure work, high housing costs, discrimination, and insufficient social safety nets that plunge people into poverty, or keep them there. It persists despite soaring inequalities[8] that render the contemporary notion of 'meritocracy' little more than a fantasy.[9] It remains dominant even though we know that in America and Britain the top jobs in politics, business, the media and law are disproportionately filled with privately educated individuals from well-off backgrounds educated at elite universities who pass on their privilege, locking out people from less well-off beginnings from having the same chances to succeed.[10] Wealthy donors pump money into 'think tanks' that reproduce the narrative's core messages of the poor as 'dependent' in reports and in the media: denigrating rhetoric that 'others' those who are struggling reinforces structural inequalities to the benefit of the already well off.[11]

Ask yourself why it is that we have so many dismissive and degrading labels casually applied to poorer people while the rich are widely eulogised? Ask yourself why, even when, as was happening by the end of 2019, the excessive wealth of billionaires was under sustained attack from progressive politicians including Democratic Party presidential contenders Elizabeth Warren and Bernie Sanders in the US, the billionaire PR machines went into overdrive saying, among other things, that Warren 'vilifies successful people'.[12] Think about words such as 'scrounger' and 'skiver', which became inescapable in the press and in everyday language when the UK government deployed them to justify savage and unnecessary austerity following the financial crash of 2008.[13] Or think of the term 'welfare queen' in the US, a racist stereotype popularised by Ronald Reagan that equated needing public assistance with a universal trope of being a black, single woman who supposedly lived the life of Riley by fleecing the benefits system. A concoction that, research shows, was bought hook, line and sinker by the wider population.[14] And what about the 'underclass', a ubiquitous and denigrating catch-all term that first gained currency in the US (later in Britain) and which became shorthand for dismissing entire groups of people from poorer areas as (among other things) feckless, anti-social criminals?[15]

The poorest, and especially people in receipt of assistance from government unemployment benefits or anti-poverty programmes in Britain and America, have been easy targets for those who would paint them as undeserving of help. Even though research shows that well-designed social safety net programmes – including many across the world – can transform people's lives for the better and help lift people out of the poverty trap,[16] these same programmes have been labelled as ineffective and lavish.

Exploiting myriad negative stereotypes associated with poorer people, those who advocate for cutting (even eradicating) social safety nets persistently paint programmes established to help the poorest as exorbitantly wasteful of valuable 'taxpayers' money, when, in reality, in both America and Britain, they account for a fraction of national public spending.[17] So often do these purveyors of the narrative repeat this fallacy as if fact that the British and American public consistently and vastly overestimate the spend, reach and defrauding of welfare programmes.

A political choice is being exercised when it comes to poverty: a choice to pillory the poor for scrabbling for mere scraps from the table, while taxes are cut for the rich and for corporations, and wealth shoots up towards the top rather than 'trickling' down. Meanwhile the stigma and shame of poverty are rarely acknowledged or spoken of in any meaningful way, despite the deep emotional and psychological imprint impoverishment produces, preventing people from realising their potential.

There is a long history of the poorest being shunned and shamed and 'kept in their place', but there is also a history of these practices being challenged with genuine successes – from grassroots protests and union organising to landmark legislation that pushed for, and delivered, social justice. The forming of the Welfare State and the National Health Service in Britain in the aftermath of World War II attacked poverty at its core and transformed lives. President Franklin D. Roosevelt's 'New Deal' and President Lyndon Johnson's slate of progressive laws in the 1960s were in large part the products of collective pressure for change. The fight to tackle poverty is ongoing.

However, nothing is guaranteed. When Boris Johnson won the UK General Election in December 2019 by a landslide, it was after almost a decade of austerity policies that had left millions impoverished, had seen homelessness soar, and which introduced drastic cuts to social benefits that inflicted extraordinary and avoidable suffering on people with disabilities – and cost thousands of lives. Those policies were ushered in with the help of a turbo-charged poverty narrative that vilified the poorest and, even as the facts of the harm austerity had done became ever clearer, it wasn't enough to get people to vote to end it. The same month, the Trump administration unveiled yet another attack on one of the most important types of assistance left for families and individuals in need in America, food stamps. An estimated 700,000 people were set to lose one of the few remaining protections against hunger under new plans. Again, this was made possible because recipients of such public assistance are routinely denigrated as being part of a 'handouts' culture.

Inequality and poverty are rampant in today's America and in Britain and, as this book attests, we cannot afford to underestimate the role that the dominant poverty narrative plays in this. This is no time for complacency.[18]

When I began to research and write this book there were millions of children, women and men (tens of millions in the case of the US) either living below or hovering on the breadline, or who were homeless, on the verge of it, or reduced to living in substandard, expensive or temporary accommodation. As the UN Special Rapporteur on Extreme Poverty and Human Rights, Professor Philip Alston, reported after visiting Britain in 2018 to assess the impact of almost a decade of austerity cuts, some 14 million Britons live in poverty; while the Institute for Fiscal Studies (IFS) reported in June 2019 that the country had seen a huge jump in the number of 'working poor'.[19] Meanwhile, according to the Resolution Foundation think tank, child poverty was predicted to reach a record high by 2023.[20]

In the US, where Professor Alston also visited on a similar fact-finding tour to assess levels of poverty, he reported:

> "About 40 million [Americans] live in poverty, 18.5 million in extreme poverty, and 5.3 million live in Third World conditions of absolute poverty. It has the highest youth poverty rate in the Organization for Economic Cooperation and Development (OECD)."

At the same time, in both countries, millions of people who were working long hours for low pay – sometimes even two or more jobs at a time – to make ends meet watched as their wages stagnated while executive pay soared[21] (the average executive at an S&P 500 company took home 287 times the median worker's pay in America in 2018 according to one analysis of federal data) and saw valuable state support and anti-poverty programmes culled or cut back. All of this while taxes on the rich and corporations were being slashed, avoided or evaded.[22]

Huge swathes of the populace in Britain and America have had little or no opportunity to move beyond poverty or a low-income existence. The prospect of greater long-term economic security has been nothing more than a pipe dream.[23] The choices of people struggling to get by have been curtailed and cut off by political, economic and benefit systems that increasingly prevent them having a reasonable standard of living – or a chance for the kind of stable future previous generations took for granted. Even college graduates weren't guaranteed stable, well-paid employment,[24] while at the same time they were drowning in record levels of student debt, particularly in the US.[25]

This is what the toxic poverty narrative has helped to perpetuate. The structural causes of poverty and the actions that give rise to these are shrugged off or minimised. It is a situation all of us with a commitment to a fairer society should be profoundly concerned about – and be determined to change.

Make no mistake, as this book demonstrates, people in poverty *feel* the impact of being ritually disparaged. They understand that shame and extreme financial difficulty go hand in hand – and that the dominant narrative helps keep people poor. As the British actor Jameela Jamil, who spent her childhood in poverty, told me: "Shame has never helped anyone, it only holds you back."[26]

I understand that it might be profoundly discomforting for many people who are well off, who have never had to live in poverty, or who are fortunate enough to be financially secure to even begin to grapple with the idea that the system, along with the narrative that shores it up, stacks life's deck in your favour. We all want to believe that our individual efforts reap just rewards. We are continually told after all that hard work alone will bring success. It's a tantalising notion. But it is far from the full picture. In all likelihood, if you are well off in America or Britain, you have never lived close to, been educated alongside, or socialised with poorer and low-income people. That is a reflection of how our societies and our economies are structured to divide and discriminate. It means that opportunities to speak to one another are significantly diminished and that leaves us more open to fear, suspicion and preconceptions.

I hope that this book prompts you to at least consider the possibility that the messages you absorb day in, day out about people in poverty are not a reflection of reality. In particular, I hope that you take on board the words of people with first-hand experience of life at the sharp end of poverty and think twice before you accept stereotypes as the truth. Ultimately, finding solutions to poverty, including ending the blaming and shaming of the poorest among us, rests with all of us. As former First Lady, Eleanor Roosevelt advised:

> "We must wipe out any feeling ... of intolerance, of belief that any one group can go ahead alone. We all go ahead together or we go down together."

Why focus on the US and the UK?

The first answer to this question is that these are the countries that I have lived and worked in during my professional life. The second is that they are the focus of my regular column in *The Guardian*, 'Lesson From America', where I frequently cover poverty, inequality and other intersecting social issues including disability, health and criminal justice.

The third answer, related to this, is that through my journalism as well as through studying American and British politics over the years I've learned how these two countries, while very different in so many ways, share a number of important similarities, especially when it comes to how poverty is perceived and portrayed, that make them quite unique among the Western wealthy nations.

As the first two decades of the 21st century were coming to a close, these were places of raging inequalities not seen since the most unequal period in modern times, the 'Gilded Age' at the turn of the 20th century when 'Robber Barons' and child labour were the norm.[27]

Britain and America are set apart from their wealthy counterparts. It's not as if similar developed nations don't have their own problems with poverty and inequality – nor that they are devoid of examples where the poor are shamed[28] – but the US and, increasingly, the UK[29] are outliers in a number of ways. In 2019 the Nobel Prize-winning economist Sir Angus Deaton warned that the UK was coming precipitously close to the US in terms of inequality of wealth, pay and health.[30] Deaton, who, along with the IFS, was leading a five-year review of inequality in Britain, said it was necessary to "make sure the UK is inoculated from some of the horrors that have happened in the US". At an event to launch the review, the IFS said the work would "point to the risk of the UK following the US" in terms of extreme inequality.

Danny Dorling, Halford Mackinder Professor of Geography of the School of Geography and the Environment of the University of Oxford and a global expert on inequality, put it this way to me when I interviewed him:[31]

> "The US and the UK are remarkably similar in terms of inequality and in terms of poverty. Amongst the richest countries in the world, these two are the largest countries that have the highest rates of inequality. They are almost like twins.
>
> If you look at the incomes on which the poorest people are living, compared to the average, these are the two countries where you are really living a parallel, separate life if you are in the bottom 20 or 30 per cent. You are not like average people, and average people are not like better off people, and better off people are not like the [top] 1 per cent."

Dorling pointed out that while the UK's "residual" Welfare State, which includes universal healthcare in the form of the NHS, is a fundamental distinction between the two in terms of the vulnerability of the poorest, he notes that a steady undermining of the NHS in recent years – including by Conservatives pushing privatisation[32] – has been propelling Britain even further away from its European neighbours and towards a US-style system. "Health is crucial," Dorling says.

"Thankfully in the UK we have a universal health system, which insures you, which doesn't cost. If you are seriously hurt, injured or get a disease you will be treated without cost. But that is under incredible attack by the current government who would like to have an American system where you have to be able to insure yourself. And even then, unless you have an enormous amount of money, if you get seriously ill you are in trouble."

Britain and America, as political leaders in both have often touted, have long seen themselves as having a 'special relationship'.[33] While this tends to refer to diplomacy, it stretches much further and deeper and it is reflected in their approaches to welfare policies directed at the poor. Indeed, British politicians (especially Conservatives but also New Labour after it was elected in a landslide in 1997) have often looked to the US for policy inspiration, including on social policy, driving what some have called 'The Americanisation of the British Welfare State',[34] which ultimately has weakened it. Brits, but especially Americans, also tend towards the belief that individual effort and talent is what brings success in life – that there is a meritocracy – even while the evidence shows they are both failing on this measure.[35] The American Dream, the idea that anyone can make it in the US, is woven into the very fabric of national life.

Finally, it is far from insignificant that a UN rapporteur on extreme poverty has only conducted tours probing poverty in three wealthy nations in a 20-year period. One was the UK, another was the US (twice), and Ireland, the third (which was visited in 2011), received nothing like the censure of Alston's reports. Ordinarily the rapporteur's mandate is to investigate countries with very high levels of deprivation, so they tend to be developing nations. The fact that America and Britain were visited – and that the reports were so damning – speaks volumes to their status as outlier nations on poverty and treatment of the poor.

Alston's conclusions about the proliferation of poverty – but also about the narrative that is employed to rationalise it – are remarkably, and pertinently similar.

On the UK and its pursuit of austerity, Alston's report said:

> The Government has made no secret of its determination to change the value system to focus more on individual responsibility, to place major limits on government support and to pursue a single-minded focus on getting people into employment.
>
> British compassion has been replaced by a punitive, mean-spirited and often callous approach apparently designed to impose a rigid order on the lives of those least capable of coping, and elevate the goal of enforcing blind compliance over a genuine concern to improve the well-being of those at the lowest economic levels of British society.

And on the US, he concluded:

> Some politicians and political appointees with whom the special rapporteur spoke were completely sold on the narrative of such scammers sitting on comfortable sofas, watching cable television or spending their days on their smartphones, all paid for by welfare. As a result, money spent on welfare is money down the drain. If the poor really want to make it in the United States they can easily do so: they really can achieve the American Dream if only they work hard enough.
>
> In thinking about poverty, it is striking how much weight is given to caricatured narratives about the purported innate differences between rich and poor that are consistently peddled by some politicians and the media. The rich are industrious, entrepreneurial, patriotic, and the drivers of economic success. The poor are wasters, losers and scammers.

Background to this book

As well as growing up in poverty I've been writing about it and how it affects people's lives for a decade and a half. As part of this, six years ago I wrote a book about the damage austerity was doing to the UK, including to the poorest and most vulnerable populations.[36] During that time people all over Britain told me about the harm that austerity policies and cuts to vital public services were unleashing and how they were being thrust into poverty that could have been avoided as a result of far-reaching changes to the benefits system. I reported how foodbanks were popping up like mushrooms to cater for people who couldn't feed their families properly, and how local councils' budgets had been cut so savagely that essential services for the elderly and for disabled people were disappearing

But my austerity journey was about more than chronicling the immediate and dire impact. A fundamental part was the realisation that a specific austerity 'narrative' was constructed by the politicians implementing the cuts that convincingly framed these as unavoidable (they weren't – austerity was a political choice) and which demonised people in need of state help so effectively that many believed it was ok if the poorest suffered while the better off were left untouched. It was, I came to realise, a very powerful version of the bigger 'meta' poverty narrative that I have encountered in the US and the UK as a reporter.

In 2018, partly as a response to what I had been learning from people I interviewed about how stigma related to poverty materially, socially and psychologically impacted their lives, I set up the multi-platform anti-poverty initiative, Project Twist-It, as a counter to the narrative.[37] Project Twist-It became a hub for people to tell their own stories about poverty, to challenge stereotypes, and to make concrete suggestions for how we might realistically fight poverty and the narrative simultaneously. Over a two-year period I interviewed scores of people with lived experience of poverty as well as researchers, activists, NGO workers, writers and artists who were involved in anti-poverty action across America and Britain. The longer the project ran, the more people approached me asking if they could be a part of it.

One of the most important things I learned from the process was that the fight to overturn the poverty narrative had already begun.

Structure of this book

This book is partly a product of the work of Project Twist-It. By harnessing not just statistics or research but the insights of people in poverty, as well as my personal and professional experience, it tries firstly to unpick where we currently stand when it comes to poverty levels and the dominant narrative, but secondly it also explores where we might find the solutions we so desperately need. It asks how we can overturn the narrative once and for all.

Part I of this book looks in some detail at the nature, scale and reality of contemporary poverty in America and Britain and at its direct impact on individuals, families and communities. It explores the extent of the problem and shows how, while many groups in society are experiencing ever-growing hardship, the dominant narrative has been deployed with incredible effectiveness to dismiss them and to deny the problems they face.

Part II assesses how the poverty narrative over the past half-century has become entrenched. It asks: What exactly is the poverty narrative? What are its specific functions? How does it manifest in our politics, society and culture? In what ways does it shame the poor? How does it affect the lives, self-perceptions and opportunities of people in poverty? Who benefits from this narrative and from keeping people poor? With a focus on first-person testimonies from people with lived experience this section looks at the political and cultural forces that have shaped our misunderstanding of who 'the poor' are and how they got there – and what the true human cost of this is.

Part III chronicles how a burgeoning fightback against the toxic narrative gives us hope for the future. In this section people with lived experience, writers, artists, musicians, activists, academics and the younger generation explain their ideas for how the narrative can be challenged. It documents how activists and organisations in the US and the UK are already building the foundations of a movement to challenge the toxic narrative head-on. From the leveraging of personal stories about poverty and presenting alternative narratives (including by some wealthy individuals arguing against the mantra of individualism) to efforts focused on re-framing the entire discourse around poverty, to young people speaking up, it argues how the overturning of the toxic poverty narrative could, finally, be within our grasp.

Scope of this book

This book is not intended to be a comprehensive (or comparative) history of poverty in the US or the UK. Nor is it an historical, sociological or psychological analysis of the shame and stigma associated with poverty, which is complex and multi-tiered. I am not an academic, so this book isn't written for an academic audience – but for a wider one. That said, I hope this book does appeal to researchers, and throughout the book and in the notes section you will find numerous references to reports and works of scholarship, including some excellent books which I hope you will find useful for further research if that's your goal.

I am first and foremost a journalist, but I am also a person who has known poverty (as a child and adolescent) and I draw on both of these experiences throughout the book. I write this book as someone trying to make sense of why it has been so damn hard to take down the dominant narrative around poverty.

I include my personal story and observations, which I hope will help illuminate the very profound impact poverty can have. In my work I have endeavoured always to elevate the voices of people with lived experience of the topics I cover – be that mental health, youth justice, poverty or other social justice issues. My almost 20 years as a writer and journalist have convinced me of the vital importance of this for reporting and for broader discussions relating to policy affecting these groups.

For this reason, I have included the views, insights and stories of as many people as possible throughout this book. Due to limitations of space there are many that don't make it on to these pages. I wish it were otherwise. However, each and every one of these people informed what I have written and the way this book unfolded as well as the conclusions it has reached. And, thanks to the internet, you can find them and listen to their stories for yourself either via my journalism or on projecttwistit.com where so many people across Britain and America shared their stories with me through blogs, video, audio, poetry and more. It has been my privilege to provide a platform for people who are so often shunned and unheard – for the people at whom the toxic poverty narrative is directed yet who respond with dignity in the face of scorn, and with a determination to see it gone forever.

A word of caution. This book was conceived and written against a backdrop of terrible and incredible social, economic and political turmoil. Poverty, inequality, joblessness, economic insecurity, technological transformation and a cynicism about mainstream politicians, politics and the media were giving rise to tensions across Europe, America and elsewhere. Nativism and right-wing populism were responding by manipulating and capitalising on the very real worries – financial and otherwise – that people expressed. Trump in America and Brexit in Britain were among the most visible and risible manifestations of these developments. There was pushback, of course, with progressive social movements and politicians fighting to hold back the tide. However, this is no time for complacency, including around the impact of poverty on individuals and society. The quote at the top of this introduction from Franklin D. Roosevelt is as relevant now as it was when, as US president, he picked America up off its knees after the catastrophe of the Great Depression.

Poverty isn't just the problem of those living it; it is a problem for us all.

Finally, it would be a mistake to assume that when people are dealing with poverty it is the same as misery. As hard as it can be to be poor and to talk about the difficulties people face, there was also plenty of dark humour and even some laughter in the course of researching and writing this book and while working on Project Twist-It – just as there was during my own childhood even with all the challenges we faced. It's a survival mechanism many of us are familiar with and grateful for. Every person's experience of poverty is different, but there are shared struggles – and even with the odds stacked against us, there can be some triumphs along the way.

This book explores the poverty narrative, its impact, and what can be done about it. First, however, we need to examine what constitutes poverty in contemporary Britain and America. We need to understand *who* the poor are and how they are treated. We need to understand how many people are affected by poverty – and in what ways. We need to understand poverty – because poverty is real.

I
The inconvenient truth: poverty is real

"Narratives from people who have experienced poverty first-hand are crucial."
Sarah Smarsh, author of *Heartland*, talking to Project Twist-It

"For the first time that any of us can remember, the safety net is not now the Welfare State but charity – and the lifeline for families in need is not social security but foodbanks."
Former UK Labour Prime Minister Gordon Brown, October 2018[1]

The pity party

When I was a kid I loved to dance. Anywhere. Almost as much as I loved to read. I danced in the street, on my way to school, in the local shop and at the back of the smoke-filled bingo hall where I tagged along every Thursday night with a neighbour who had no kids of her own.

Old women on their doorsteps would shout small encouragements as I counted out beats with my toes to tunes only I could hear and as I lunged left or right, pointing my hands towards the sky and gazing earnestly upwards. Every now and then, I'd convince my friends to allow me to choreograph them. (Until they became bored of being directed a bit too enthusiastically.)

I was seven or eight when I knew for sure I wanted to do more than dance in the street. One Saturday afternoon I asked my mum and dad if I could go to dance lessons. I'd heard about them on the TV. Someday, maybe, they told me. There just wasn't the money for luxuries like that.

I couldn't let it go, so when I heard disco dancing classes had started for 10p every Tuesday night at the church hall, there was no stopping me. It was exactly the amount I got in pocket money of a Friday when my dad came home from working on the building site. Each week until my early teens I walked the mile to the church hall where I handed it over and danced my heart out for 90 minutes to the records played by Sammy and Peggy, two old-time ballroom champions.

'Can You Feel It', 'Stayin' Alive', 'Don't Stop 'Till You Get Enough' sent me into paroxysms of concentrated delight.

Peggy said I was good. I should enter the regional disco dancing championships, she advised when I was ten. I ran home to tell my mum who was peeling a bag of potatoes in the living room as she watched the TV, a baby and a toddler. As usual my other siblings were out in the street playing. Sorry, love, mum said, we just can't afford it. Its only 50p to enter, I countered, but she said nothing and looked back with sad eyes.

The pity party

A week later I won £1.50 at the bingo. I gave my parents a pound and kept the rest. That Saturday I put on my best red blouse under the denim dungarees I practically lived in but which were an inch too short, and laced up my one pair of decent shoes after polishing the toes with the cloth my dad used to shine his best boots for Mass on Sundays.

At 2pm precisely I began the three-mile walk in the rain to the big convention centre on the other end of the city, not telling anyone where I was going. That might bring bad luck.

I'd never been to that side of town with its big houses and manicured gardens. It was like another world.

The convention centre was vast. Multicoloured lights suspended from the ceiling swept around the huge room where the competition was to be held. The wooden floor shone in a way I didn't think wood could. Groups of girls began piling in, giggling and sparkling in the most incredible outfits I had ever laid eyes on. A posse of mothers followed the girls, all carrying little pink or powder blue coloured cases. They checked for creases, applied blusher, fixed bows and clips in their daughters' hair.

I approached the long table at the front of the room, my hair still wet from the rain, where I handed over my 50p entrance fee and a middle-aged man gave me a white, square piece of paper with the number 11 on it. He asked if I was ok in a way that made me think the man thought I was in the wrong place. It would be fine, he assured me, before patting my shoulder and turning to talk to a woman nearby who then glanced over and shook her head slowly.

A bouncy older woman in a sequinned jumpsuit at the front of the room made announcements over a microphone. Girls, clucking loudly and preening, raced to the floor and took up spaces. One by one they edged me towards the back. Mothers stared at me from the side lines. Not in a bad way, but with a look I would soon come to understand was a combination of pity and disdain. My presence seemed to make them uncomfortable. I was out of place.

My eyes filled with water but I willed the tears back. I pinned the number card to my chest and pushed out my chin as I waited for the opening beats of the music. One, two, three, four.

A short prologue

Being poor

The incident at the dance competition is the first memory I can recall of when I felt the sting of other people's pity and when I think I realised, on a visceral level, that being from a poor background came (though I certainly hadn't heard of the concept yet) with a stigma attached to it. Being poor or 'on welfare' was a source of shame.

Over the years there would be many other incidents that sharpened my understanding of the intersection of poverty, pity and shame. Like realising our first home, the one I lived in until we were re-housed when I was seven into new, public housing, was nothing short of a slum. Our first house had just two tiny bedrooms for eight people, and was perpetually damp. Rats were so commonplace they may as well have been members of the family. (A shovel was kept handy in the living room for when one appeared.) There was no bathroom, indoor toilet or central heating and the kitchen was a makeshift scullery with a plastic corrugated roof. Having a fridge or washing machine was unimaginable. My mum kept it immaculately clean and looking as nice as possible, but there's only so much make-up you can put on a pig.

As I got a bit older and my dad became unemployed there was the realisation that claiming the 'dole' (unemployment benefits) as my father had to do for long periods of time, was a source of humiliation, even within a community where many people were in the same situation. And there was the knowledge that relying on state assistance to get by was not something that everyone had to face and was seen by some people as a sign of parental failure. There was the awareness too that while the food in our cupboards mostly met our daily needs (we had to borrow from neighbours when things got really tight) and that even though we had occasional treats (often paid for by going into debt with loan sharks), this was not how everyone lived.

West Belfast, which was also one of the main flashpoints during Northern Ireland's sectarian conflict[1] in the 1970s and 1980s, was among the most deprived areas in the whole of Western Europe[2] – but even if I had known this, I doubt it would have made my younger self feel any better about how much we had to struggle or how much shame there was at not being able to afford what others could.

I'd seen enough TV to know that there were people who were well off or rich. I knew my teachers were better off. I'd just never really been anywhere near a wealthier part of town and interacted with people who lived there. I'd never met anybody from that background in any intimate way. Like most poorer families – and this is true today in Britain and America[3] – we lived our lives in the poorer parts of town. We didn't have middle-class friends. But, when I first began to understand that we were looked down upon or pitied by many more financially fortunate people, the undercurrent of shame stayed with me for a long time. I wrote about the looks from the women at the dance competition in my childhood diary. Those looks, and how I was dressed compared to the other girls, stayed with me.

Anyone who has grown up poor will have similar stories to tell: those small or large experiences or encounters that force you to register that your family is not just lacking in material things (as hard as that may be), but that as a kid you are set apart from other children. Maybe it's your first day at a new school when you look around and realise that the kids whose parents have jobs, or better-paid ones than yours do, have pocket money or nicer clothes. Maybe a teacher tells you that the best you can hope for in life is a minimum-wage job at a fast-food chain and not to set your sights too high. Perhaps it's watching a parent struggle to make sure there's enough food on the table or warmth in the room when you have a new friend round whose family don't seem to have the same financial hardships.

Or maybe you don't ever ask friends to come to your house because there's nothing in the cupboard to offer them. It could be that you overheard a conversation where someone commented on how scruffy you and your siblings look or criticised your parents for failing to take 'proper' care of you. If you're female, you may have experienced the humiliation and discomfort during adolescence of not being able to afford sanitary products and having to improvise while spending the day fretting that it might not work.

If you didn't grow up in poverty, these sorts of indignities most likely will not have affected you, and you will be unaware of the enduring impact they can have on a young person. You might never have thought much about the reasons people end up trapped by poverty or the dearth of opportunities that keep them there. If you have never lived on the breadline, it's probably difficult to grasp, for example, that for many people, no matter how hard they work at their minimum-wage precarious job/s, they just never have enough to make the rent, eat nutritious food every day, or buy a much-needed new pair of shoes for their kids or a warm winter coat. You might not have thought about what it feels like to have no choice but to swallow your pride and go to a foodbank to stock up on essentials because you don't qualify for state assistance – or what you do qualify for falls far short of what you actually need to survive and help you get back on your feet. Yet, every single day, people all over the US and the UK live with the gross injustice that is being poor and with the humiliation of being blamed for circumstances beyond their control.

It doesn't have to be this way. It really doesn't.

As someone who directly benefited from the structural redistribution in the UK that followed the Second World War including the founding of the Welfare State, affordable council housing, the National Health Service and free school meals, I know that where there is a will, we can provide a springboard to better things for the poorest among us. A fairer, more equitable society where we don't blame and shame the poor is not beyond the reach of wealthy nations like Britain and America. It's an honourable, gettable goal.

1

Who are these 'poor' people anyway? Being on the breadline in Britain

"There comes a point where we need to stop just pulling people out of the river. We need to go upstream and find out why they're falling in."
Desmond Tutu

"When I look at the world today, the first thing that enters my head is that I've seen all this before. There is no safety for any of us unless we form a society whereby we respect each other. A government should be for the majority of the people, not for the already endowed."
Harry Leslie Smith, author and anti-poverty advocate, talking to Project Twist-It

The poverty trap: struggling to get by in contemporary Britain

It's November 2018. Perhaps the most important mid-term elections in a generation have just taken place in the US in one of the most divisive periods in recent history. In the UK, there is chaos as the deadline for a deal to exit the European Union nears, with that country also riven by profound socio-political fissures. But, in the UK, there is one political story that is somehow managing to break through the thicket of wall-to-wall Brexit coverage to muster some significant headlines.[1] The United

Nations Special Rapporteur on Extreme Poverty and Human Rights, Philip Alston,[2] has just submitted a scathing preliminary report[3] on the disastrous impact[4] of almost a decade of austerity in the UK on the poorest and most vulnerable.[5]

Following a two-week fact-finding tour of the UK[6] – where he listened carefully to the stories and experiences of people living in financial hardship and who had borne the brunt of the austerity regime introduced by the Coalition government and the gutting of the country's safety net – law professor Alston, with a track record for holding power to account from Saudi Arabia to the UN itself,[7] delivered an unequivocal rebuke of the politicians and policies responsible:

> "The experience of the United Kingdom, especially since 2010, underscores the conclusion that poverty is a political choice."

In a statement almost tailor-made to put the politicians behind austerity and rising impoverishment on the defensive, he said there was a "complete disconnect" between the government's assessments of poverty levels and the experiences of the people he encountered. In another comment that was sure to send bristles of hypersensitivity through the corridors of Conservative Westminster, he added: "Austerity could easily have spared the poor, if the political will had existed to do so", a conclusion I had reached four years earlier, in my book *Austerity Bites*.[8]

The 24-page preliminary report appeared to unnerve the government. It had no grey areas. Rather it incorporated an abundance of data and uncompromising analysis. It's worth highlighting key passages for how they contextualise the wilful impoverishment – or 'great misery', as the report puts it – of so many in one of the richest nations on earth. This scathing report, rooted in the stories and insights of the people most affected by poverty and austerity (the very people typically not consulted about the policies affecting them), tells us much about not only the nature of contemporary poverty in the UK, but also the extent of it, what drives it and the role of the politicians who have made poverty worse.

The UN report states:

The UK is the world's fifth largest economy, it contains many areas of immense wealth, its capital is a leading centre of global finance, its entrepreneurs are innovative and agile, and despite the current political turmoil, it has a system of government that rightly remains the envy of much of the world. It thus seems patently unjust and contrary to British values that so many people are living in poverty.

This is obvious to anyone who opens their eyes to see the immense growth in foodbanks and the queues waiting outside them, the people sleeping rough in the streets, the growth of homelessness, the sense of deep despair that leads even the government to appoint a minister for suicide prevention and civil society to report in-depth on unheard of levels of loneliness and isolation.

And local authorities, especially in England, which perform vital roles in providing a real social safety net have been gutted by a series of government policies. Libraries have closed in record numbers, community and youth centres have been shrunk and underfunded, public spaces and buildings including parks and recreation centres have been sold off...."

The report continues:

The results? 14 million people, a fifth of the population, live in poverty. Four million of these are more than 50 per cent below the poverty line, and 1.5 million are destitute, unable to afford basic essentials. The widely respected Institute for Fiscal Studies predicts a 7 per cent rise in child poverty between 2015 and 2022, and various sources predict child poverty rates of as high as 40 per cent.

For almost one in every two children to be poor in twenty-first century Britain is not just a disgrace, but a social calamity and an economic disaster, all rolled into one.

Lambasting those in power, the report gets right to the heart of how poverty is framed and discussed:

> In the area of poverty-related policy, the evidence points to the conclusion that the driving force has not been economic but rather a commitment to achieving radical social re-engineering.
>
> Successive governments have brought revolutionary change in both the system for delivering minimum levels of fairness and social justice to the British people, and especially in the values underpinning it…. The government has made no secret of its determination to change the value system to focus more on individual responsibility, to place major limits on government support, and to pursue a single-minded, and some have claimed simple-minded, focus on getting people into employment at all costs….
>
> British compassion for those who are suffering has been replaced by a punitive, mean-spirited, and often callous approach apparently designed to instil discipline where it is least useful, to impose a rigid order on the lives of those least capable of coping with today's world, and elevating the goal of enforcing blind compliance over a genuine concern to improve the well-being of those at the lowest levels of British society.

And then, topping it all off:

> A just and compassionate UK can ensure these people are able to escape the restrictions of poverty. More and more working people are trapped in poverty by a rising tide of low pay, debt and high living costs…

So, who exactly were the people identified as bearing the brunt of government cuts and risk of poverty?

- Children
- Women
- Lone parents
- Minorities[9]
- Disabled people[10]
- Families with children
- Asylum seekers and migrants
- Rural dwellers
- Those reliant on public services like social care, children's centres or emergency welfare funds.

With all of this so clearly put, the UK central government in London had nevertheless, Alston concluded, "remained determinedly in a state of denial", with ministers insisting – in the face of overwhelming evidence of poverty and destitution and their culpability for it – that everything was well and "running to plan".

When staring the facts in the face, it's hard to believe anyone would argue things were going to plan.

Following publication of the preliminary report Alison Garnham at the charity Child Poverty Action Group (CPAG) was crystal clear in her assessment of its significance saying it should be a 'wake-up call'. She was right. The effects of high levels of poverty on children should have been embarrassing for any government.

In November 2018 Garnham said in a statement:[11]

> Child poverty isn't only happening elsewhere, it's here in the UK and it's rising. It's in families where parents can't work because of illness or disability but mostly it's in families who work for low wages while costs are rising.
>
> Teachers report working with children who look 'grey' from lack of nourishment. Doctors talk about not being able to discharge well children from hospital, because of unsuitable housing conditions at home. Rhetoric about burning injustices isn't enough. The poverty that the Rapporteur has

reported is not inevitable in the UK today. We now need a strategy with targets to eradicate poverty – the UK's children deserve nothing less.

On 28 June 2019, when the rapporteur was scheduled to present his full report to the UN Human Rights Council, 50 leading UK poverty and inequality groups, including Just Fair, the Equality Trust, and the Women's Budget Group, signed an open letter to the government demanding change in light of the rapporteur's report.[12]

Missing the point: the politics of poverty

Significantly, if the UK government had acknowledged the problems highlighted by the UN report, there would have been a better chance of addressing them. But, true to form, instead of engaging with Alston's analysis and recommendations, the blowback was fast, fierce and furious. Rather than take Alston's gauntlet and do something constructive with it, there came a steady volley of knee-jerk reactions and condemnation.

Amber Rudd, former Home Secretary[13] and newly appointed Secretary of State for Work and Pensions (DWP) (the department responsible for designing and implementing most of the egregious reforms to the benefits system that had caused so much misery since 2010),[14] declared the tone of Alston's report "highly inappropriate".[15] It was interesting (bearing in mind the rapporteur's reflections on poverty as a political issue) that Rudd condemned Alston for "the extraordinary political nature of his language", saying it "discredited a lot of what he was saying".[16]

Meanwhile one government spokesman told *The Guardian*[17] ministers "completely disagreed" with Alston's findings – as if by dismissing the report outright its arguments could be simply wished away. And, junior Brexit Minister Kwasi Kwarteng replied dismissively that he "didn't know who this UN man is".[18]

In the week following the report's publication an episode of the BBC radio show Moral Maze,[19] which invites guests to advocate on and debate subjects deemed to present a moral quandary – often with a devil's advocate dynamic, the rapporteur's conclusions took centre stage. The programme was reflecting on whether the report was politically motivated and incendiary.

Melanie Phillips (a controversial columnist, including when it comes to people on benefits[20]), while conceding that poverty does exist in Britain, accused the report of using a definition of poverty that "exaggerates it in a quite disgraceful way", while the former Conservative minister Michael Portillo declared the report inappropriate because the UK "doesn't have extreme poverty".

Of course, people on the frontline of austerity and those confronted with the hardship of poverty in their everyday lives – people Alston took the time to listen to – offered a very different take on the report and its findings.

One woman, Tracey Whitenstall, a mother of three who was on Universal Credit[21] (one of the most contentious of the government's so-called welfare 'reforms', which merged six existing welfare benefits) had met with the rapporteur at an advice centre in Newcastle in the North East of England. She gave her verdict[22] of Rudd's reaction as "absolutely appalling." Whitenstall said of ministers:

> "They should get out of their [chauffeur-driven] cars. They are turning a blind eye. If they are going to ignore the facts, I don't see any way out of poverty and foodbanks."

A youth leader, also from the North East, interviewed for the same article, said ministers were "not living in the real world. They are people who have no idea what is going on". He added:

> "Poverty is political. When you are suffering, you are going to get angry about it.... These people shield themselves form the anger and suffering."

One young mother of two interviewed for Channel 4 News,[23] who was describing being left with almost nothing to live on while waiting for Universal Credit benefits to come through – choosing, as she put it, between "bread and bus fare" – was asked how important she thought the UN mission was. Like those who turned up to the open sessions held by Alston around the country, the very fact of being heard mattered profoundly. She said: "I think it's important for people like me that someone is fighting a little bit in your corner."

A damning poverty picture

Progressive commentators and publications reacted to the report, declaring that poverty in contemporary Britain was "shameful".[24] Charity leaders, including Alison Garnham of CPAG, were quick to point[25] out that yes, poverty was real; yes, people were suffering all over the country; and yes, millions of children were living lives with multiple (fixable) hurdles in the way of escaping poverty. In fact, just one month prior to the UN report a new study by the Social Metrics Commission[26] (SMC) mapped out a pretty damning picture of UK poverty.

THE SMC MEASURE OF POVERTY

The Social Metrics Commission is an independent commission set up to develop a new approach to poverty measurement 'that both better reflects the nature and experiences of poverty that different families in the UK have, and can be used to build a consensus around poverty measurement and action in the UK', with a poverty indicator that goes beyond a simple measure of people's relative income, taking into account core living costs such as housing, childcare and the extra costs of disability, and people's wider resources, such as savings, in assessing whether they can be defined as in poverty.[27]

The existing poverty measure, which sets the poverty line at 60 per cent of median UK income, was abolished as an official measure in 2015 by the Conservative government (although it has been retained in Scotland, Wales and Northern Ireland).[28] That there is no officially agreed poverty measure for the whole of the UK can make comparing the four nations difficult.

The SMC measure sets a poverty threshold of 55 per cent of median total available resources – in effect creating a poverty line relative to what the median family has available to spend. A key principle of the measure is that poverty 'should be related to the extent to which people have the resources to engage adequately in a life regarded as the norm in society'.

The top-line findings on poverty in the UK by the SMC included:

More than **14 million people**, including **4.5 million children** (about 33 per cent) are living in poverty.

Lone parent families are **twice as likely** to live in poverty as couples with children.

Twelve per cent of the UK population are in 'persistent poverty'.[29]

Twenty-eight per cent of families in London [despite all the city's enormous wealth] are living in poverty.

One year later, in July 2019, the Commission would release yet another report, this time showing that 4.5 million Brits were more than 50 per cent below the poverty line. It also highlighted that groups, such as pensioners and children, who had been doing better on poverty rates for over a decade between 2000/01 and 2014/15 were seeing the progress made (progress driven by anti-poverty measures introduced by New Labour governments prior to 2010) begin to go into reverse.

On publication, the chair of the SMC, Philippa Stroud, commented: "Decisions made by policymakers can have a significant impact on who is in poverty and how deep and persistent that poverty is."

A couple of weeks prior to the UN preliminary report in 2018, the independent analysis organisation, the Institute for Fiscal Studies (IFS),[30] forecast that:

> **Thirty-seven per cent** of UK children will be in relative poverty by 2022, undoing any progress in the past 20 years and constituting the highest percentage since modern records began in 1961.
>
> This translates to a record **5.2 million** children.
>
> The increase in relative child poverty would increase across all regions.
>
> The gap between rich and poor would widen further.

> **"In our projection, the majority of children who either have a single parent; are in larger families; are in a household where no-one is in work; or live in private or social rented housing, will be in poverty by 2023–24."**
> Resolution Foundation, Key Findings from *The Living Standards Outlook 2019*

In addition, in February 2019, the Resolution Foundation, an independent think tank, issued a bleak forecast that made despairing reading for anyone hoping for a shard of light at the end of the tunnel. According to the Foundation, Britain risked the proportion of children living in poverty reaching a record high[31] by 2023–24, with an unprecedented number of parents predicted to be in poverty by the same date. Against a backdrop where the outlook for household incomes overall is weak – as it has been since the financial crisis – the Foundation's report reaches these stark conclusions:

> The outlook for typical incomes is worse for some groups, such as families with children, single adults, social renters and mortgagors. With a new stagnation coming on top of the financial crisis and (for many) a pre-crisis slowdown, income growth over the entire

20 years from 2003–04 to 2023–24 is currently projected to be close to zero for some groups – including low to middle income working households.

The report continues:

> Child poverty is projected to rise by a further 6 percentage points by 2023–24, which (on existing data) would mark a record high, even surpassing the highs of the 1990s. The proportion of parents living in poverty is also forecast to hit a record high.
>
> In our projection, the majority of children who either have a single parent; are in larger families; are in a household where no-one is in work; or live in private or social rented housing, will be in poverty by 2023–24. But poverty rates for other groups are also projected to rise. The child poverty rate for working households averaged 20 per cent between 1996–17 and 2013–14, but is projected to increase to 29 per cent by 2023–24, while the poverty rate for children living with two parents may have already hit a record high in 2017–18 or 2018–19.

Moreover, according to another, earlier, report[32] from social change non-profit, the Joseph Rowntree Foundation (JRF), over one and a half million people in the United Kingdom – including 365,000 children – were already destitute in 2017. This analysis of the situation in 2017 showed that, to a large degree, the high levels of destitution – while lower than in 2015 when benefits sanctions were ubiquitous – were by design, because of a direct link with harsh welfare penalties and ongoing sanctions.[33] Multiple reports[34] underscored the extent to which poverty and changes to the benefits system are intertwined.

THE JOSEPH ROWNTREE FOUNDATION'S DEFINITION OF DESTITUTION[35]

People were defined as destitute in the study if they or their children have **lacked two or more of the following six essentials** over the past month because they cannot afford them, or their income is so low – less than £10 per day for a single person (excluding housing costs) – that they have been unable to purchase them for themselves:

- **Shelter** (have slept rough for one or more nights)
- **Food** (have had fewer than two meals a day for two or more days)
- **Heating their home** (have been unable to do this for five or more days)
- **Lighting their home** (have been unable to do this for five or more days)
- **Appropriate clothing and footwear**
- **Basic toiletries** (soap, shampoo, toothpaste, toothbrush)

The main factors tipping people into destitution were, according to the report:

- Low benefit levels, delays in receiving benefits and sanctions
- Harsh and uncoordinated debt-recovery practices by public authorities and utility companies
- Pressures caused by poor health or disability
- High costs for housing and other essentials.

Reality check

One of the most vivid examples of the reality of poverty for families all over Britain came from the soaring number of foodbanks,[36] a phenomenon singled out by the Rapporteur. Unlike the US, where foodbanks and pantries have long been an essential plank of anti-poverty efforts due to the lack of an equivalent to the welfare states of Europe, foodbanks were almost unheard of at the beginning of the century in Britain. Yet, following years of austerity and systematically regressive benefits changes, they have spread at a galloping pace,[37] with demand continuing to increase year-on-year.

Between 1 April 2018 and 31 March 2019, the Trussell Trust's foodbank network distributed 1.6 million three-day emergency food supplies to people in crisis, a 19 per cent increase on the previous year. More than half a million of these went to children.[38]

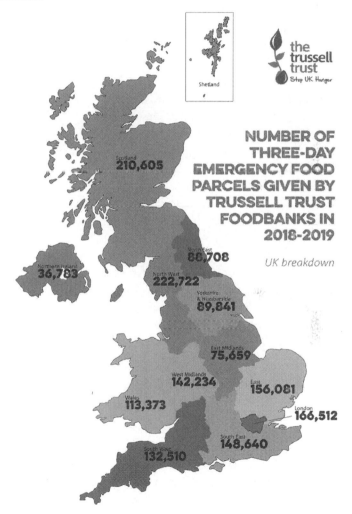

Such was the extent of food insecurity in the UK by the beginning of 2019 that MPs were urging the government to appoint a 'minister for hunger' for the first time in British history The House of Commons Environmental Audit Committee urged the move, stating that one in five of the UK's children were experiencing food insecurity.[39] The committee accused the government of 'turning a blind eye' to the hunger on their doorstep, citing evidence that the UK had some of the worst levels of food insecurity in Europe, with a third of the poorest households skipping meals.[40] In addition, according to the committee, almost two million people in the UK may be undernourished, including up to a third of people admitted to hospital.

The mushrooming of foodbanks in Britain – and the decades of entrenchment in the US – was highlighted in a scathing letter to newspapers signed by signatories including a UN former Special Rapporteur on the right to food, Professor Olivier de Schutter,[41] criticising the corporatisation and 'institutionalisation' of foodbanking and decrying claims of poverty alleviation.

The letter read that charitable food aid

> ... is a sticking plaster on a gaping wound of systemic inequalities in our societies. On both sides of the Atlantic, the elimination of food poverty demands social and economic justice. At the heart of this approach must be a guarantee of the human right to adequate food and nutrition: living wages, income security and a fit-for-purpose welfare system, not 'leftovers' for 'left behind people'.

The foodbank workers and volunteers

With its tightly packed redbrick houses, the street in Forest Hill, South London looked just like any other when I arrived early one morning in September. So mundanely familiar was it in fact, and already such a standard feature of communities across Britain, that at first I walked right past the foodbank sign on the building on the corner.

I've visited a number of foodbanks since 2012 around Britain, when they began to proliferate in the wake of austerity, speaking mostly to people in need of their services. When I interviewed foodbank users, they would often tell me how shameful it was that this was becoming normalised in Britain but how it was increasingly something about which they had no choice if they wished to feed their families. I wanted to learn more this time from people on the ground working and volunteering about what it's like on the frontline of food poverty after years of people struggling in the face of low-wage jobs and benefits overhauls. The comedian and writer Holly Walsh, an early supporter of Project Twist-It, had told me how she felt volunteering was something practical that she could do in response to the growing demand. As a first-time volunteer she told me of how moved she had been when she heard stories of people who had been helped by foodbanks returning with donations themselves once back on their feet.

Sipping mugs of tea before they begin preparing to welcome the foodbank's visitors that day, Reverend Carol Bostridge, the chief operating officer of Lewisham foodbank's four branches, and Forest Hill branch manager, Garry Greenland, who worked alongside Holly at the branch, reflected on their experiences. The political rhetoric since 2010 may have tried to paint people who were struggling as 'scroungers' or deadbeats, but this was far from the reality on the ground, they said.

Carol talked about meeting former clients determined to give back:

> **"**I remember, particularly, the couple I met in Tesco's, because Tesco's allow us once a year to be in store and ask for donations. This couple came up, with a trolley, and said, oh no the whole lot is for you. And wow. They then told me their story. The husband had had a heart attack or some illness problem, which meant they suddenly had got no income coming in and it was taking too long to sort it, and she said with great reticence they came to the foodbank feeling quite ashamed that this had happened. [The] foodbank helped them out, loved them, gave them food for two or three weeks, gave them some support. They're back on their feet now, he's back at work, she's doing all right, so they wanted to give back.**"**

Later, the couple wrote to Carol:

"We were desperate. My husband suffered a massive heart attack and was hospitalised for ten weeks. We could not get benefits as he didn't fit any category. We eventually had to resort with some trepidation, and humiliation at having to come to the foodbank. The volunteers were amazing and kind. Only because of the generosity of others were we able to survive. It has been two long years and thank God [for] friends and the foodbank.**"**

Garry and Carol talked of how rapidly demand had grown since the first Lewisham branch opened six years earlier. "On average we will see about 100 people come through the doors each week and that means giving away 50 tonnes of food a year," Carol explained. "I've compared the first eight months of 2018 with the first eight months of 2017 and that's a 20 per cent increase just on that year. The trajectory is upwards, and has continued to be upwards." She added: "It always gets me when people phone up. They sometimes tell me what's in the cupboard. Literally, they are telling me about the six tins [of food] that are left."

Garry observed that a key characteristic of this new normal of foodbanks is that people are often nervous or embarrassed when they first turn up in need. Even when they are desperate, people tend to feel ashamed of asking for help so publicly. "They don't want to be here. They might turn around and walk away," he said. On why so many people are in need of help, he added: "A lot of people have been sanctioned. We're getting more people with letters from the Benefits Office coming here. You wouldn't have got that a couple of years ago." Carol added: "I would say for a lot of people what we do as much as give them food, is we listen without judgement or prejudice to what they need."

For Holly, who says she has an inexplicable passion for "stacking things" and relishes working at organising the supplies cupboard, doing something even once a week at a foodbank made her "feel a little bit less hopeless" in the face of the poverty hidden in plain sight. It was also a reality check.

"I'm an incredibly privileged person, who's had a lovely easy life. I'd like to say I have read and thought a lot about it before, but it just doesn't come into your world if you don't have to worry about money and you can just go to the supermarket and buy your cereals and everything without thinking about it. So, it completely altered my view because I realised the need. I think the big thing for me, the thing I find most shocking, is that the people who come through the door could be my friends."

"At Christmas we had a woman come in," she continues, recalling an encounter that left an intense impression,

"I was probably eight months pregnant and a woman came in with a two-week-old baby and she reminded me so much of a really good friend of mine. We just sat and chatted. …I walked away from that just thinking: "Why is a woman with a two-week-old baby standing in a queue waiting for food?" That just doesn't make any sense to me. You get to meet a ton of people from a ton of different situations that could easily happen to you, and they are amazing, interesting, lovely people. I find that the best and worst bit of it."

What safety net?

In addition to growing demand for food staples, foodbanks and other charitable organisations across the UK were being forced by 2018/19 to adapt to shifts in demand for other essentials needed for everyday life as the number of people struggling to get by, including the working poor, swelled.

In February 2019, the BBC reported that Baby Banks[42] – yes, *for babies* in a country with a supposed safety net – were seeing more users than ever. At the time there were over 100 operating in the UK, providing essentials such as nappies, wipes and cots, for needy families with newborns.

These 'banks' began to take into account, for example, that women facing impoverishment couldn't afford sanitary products or other hygiene essentials for themselves or their children.

Initiatives emerged to fill the widening gaps in the safety net, including 'Beauty Banks' to cater to hygiene needs.[43] Even the Girl Guides were involved, launching a nationwide 'Period Poverty' badge scheme to shine a spotlight on the fact that one in ten girls in the UK couldn't afford sanitary products (which, it should be said, were taxed as if luxury items).[44] Other schemes – such as Bloody Big Brunch, which had been campaigning for an end to period poverty and holding events around the country, and Big Red Box, which was advocating for free sanitary products in schools[45] – pointed out, among other things, that supplying products through schools could play a huge part in addressing the problem.

By February 2019 the issue of period poverty had gained so much traction that the government was pressed into announcing something resembling concrete action. As well as saying they would make £2 million available to tackle the problem internationally, acknowledging that for women and girls in poverty around the globe a lack of access to suitable products was widespread, the government set up a £250,000 'task force' in Britain, pooling resources from government departments, charities and business to come up with ideas to deal with it.[46] The following month, in his Spring Statement, the Chancellor of the Exchequer even pledged to provide free sanitary products in schools,[47] while the NHS committed to offering free tampons and towels.[48]

In Lewisham, Carol's experience reflected this trend. The foodbank branches had seen "an ever-increasing demand" for products like "shower gel, nappies, sanitary products, cleaning materials, other things like that".

Even as demand for foodbanks continued to escalate, as austerity pushed ever more people to desperation, someone in the Conservative Party thought it would be a good idea if ministers who had backed the policies that caused the problem in the first place posed for smiley photo ops at foodbank venues around the country. They were quickly branded as shameless hypocrites.[49]

There were a lot of choices and the government chose to balance the budget on the backs of poorest.
Professor Jonathan Portes, economist

A particularly potent report[50] published towards the end of 2018 by the Equality and Human Rights Commission (EHRC) concluded that the government's cuts to public services and its roll-out of benefits changes had disproportionately hit the poorest hardest, reinforcing a rapidly expanding pool of evidence that poverty was being exacerbated by those in power. In its damning diagnosis, the equalities watchdog said the government was actually in breach of its human rights obligations. The poorest 20 per cent of people in England lost an average 11 per cent of their incomes as a result of austerity compared with zero losses for the top fifth, the report found.

By the end of November 2019, just before this book was about to go to press, the policies that were aggravating already deep poverty were highlighted in yet another unsettling report. *The State of Hunger* report, which detailed the results of research by Heriot-Watt University for the Trussell Trust,[51] found that government austerity policies such as the Bedroom Tax and Universal Credit were key factors in rising demand at foodbanks and the re-emergence of extreme poverty.

As Patrick Butler wrote in *The Guardian*: 'According to the research, there is "clear and robust evidence" that people struggling on the lowest rungs of the income ladder are pushed rapidly into destitution when their already tight budgets are broken by benefit payment delays, cuts, deductions or sanctions.'[52]

The study, which estimated that 1 in 50 UK households used a foodbank in 2018–19, found that five key welfare policies had 'sizable and significant effects' on rising demand for food parcels. The five key policies – all flagship austerity policies – were:

- Increases in benefits sanctions
- Bedroom Tax
- Universal Credit
- The benefits freeze
- The withdrawal of disability benefits.

And, again as this book was going to press, yet another slew of statistics from the Trussell Trust revealed[53] that the upward trend in food parcel distribution had reached new heights. Some 823,000 emergency food parcels were handed out by the charity in just six months between April and September 2019 – a leap of 23 per cent on the same time the previous year – and including more than 300,000 for children.

Number of three-day emergency food supplies given by Trussell Trust Foodbanks

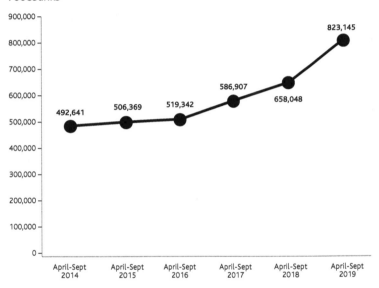

Emma Revie, the charity's chief executive, said on the figures:[54] "What's really concerning us is the steepness of the increase – 23% compared with the same period last year is such a step up. We're really worried about what the coming winter is going to look like. Our benefits system is supposed to protect us all from being swept into poverty, but currently thousands of women, men and children are not receiving sufficient protection from destitution."

It's hard to overestimate the damage wrought by austerity in Britain. I documented this in *Austerity Bites*[55] as the policies driving it tightened their grip over just 10 years. But ever since first publication in 2014 the scale of the harm inflicted has been dramatically unfolding, and worsening rapidly, like a terrible story with no end.[56] One of the most appalling examples is the number of additional deaths related to austerity.[57] A shocking report in 2017, for example, concluded that austerity was costing tens of thousands of lives. One of the report's authors even called it 'economic murder'. The paper, published in the *British Medical Journal*,[58] estimated that billions of pounds of cuts since 2010 – including to social care, upon which many elderly, disabled people and vulnerable groups depend and which was dramatically undermined by swingeing austerity policies – could be linked to around 45,000 deaths by 2014, with tens of thousands more possible by 2020.

In May 2019, a study by the Institute for Public Policy Research (IPPR) concluded that 130,000 deaths in the UK since 2012 could have been prevented if austerity cuts had not stalled improvements in public health over the previous two decades.[59]

While there is clearly an important difference between cause and correlation, the number of lives being caught in the headwinds of government cuts to vital public programmes and care provision was without doubt an extraordinary and exceptionally brutal experience for such a rich nation to unleash on its most vulnerable citizens.

According to the EHRC, the decision to burden the least well-off groups with the weight of austerity contravened the non-discrimination principles to which the UK is signed up under international human rights law.[60] Summing up the findings, economist and professor at King's College London and co-author of the report, Jonathan Portes, said:

> "There were a lot of choices and the government chose to balance the budget on the backs of poorest."

The unprecedented growth of the 'working poor', homelessness and child poverty

Yet another important manifestation of impoverishment more generally in recent years, and one stressed by JRF, was high levels of 'in-work' poverty.[61] The organisation demonstrated over a series of reports that, however much politicians say that employment is a route out of poverty,[62] a combination of wages stagnating for decades, a lower than sufficient minimum wage and the rise of precarious employment practices is relegating families where people are in work to impoverishment. The organisation pointed out in an October 2018 note, for example, that two thirds of children in poverty in the UK (around three million) were in working families.[63]

Putting this in context, the note summed it up this way:

> As a society, we believe work should provide a route out of poverty. Yet despite record employment rates in the UK, the number of people trapped in poverty in working families has risen by over one million in the three years to 2016/17.

In addition, it pointed out that five in every six people in low-paid work fail to escape low pay over ten years.[64] By the time JRF published its 2018 UK poverty report[65] as that year drew to a close, examining poverty trends the situation was stark.

The JRF report found:

> The number of UK workers in poverty hit **4 million** in 2017, which translates as **one in eight** workers.

> More than **14 million** people overall are struggling in poverty – **one in five** of the population.

> **Half a million** more children have become trapped in poverty over a five-year period, bringing the total to **4.1 million**.

> Parents stuck in low-wage jobs in sectors like retail and hospitality were among the key drivers of the upwards trend.

> Positives from increases to the National Living Wage[66] were outweighed by changes to tax credits and benefits.[67]

As the end of 2018 gave way to another year, it seemed increasingly the case that a sort of national complacency around poverty had taken root. It was as if the wider public had become so desensitised to people in dire need – or had had its attention consumed by Brexit and become numbed by nearly a decade of austerity propaganda – that no number of shocking figures were enough to trigger widespread outrage. The JRF's 2018 report[68] found that the number of children in working families in poverty had risen more steeply than at any time in the past 20 years. Another report projected that a million youngsters under the age of ten in Scotland and England would be experiencing 'Dickensian' levels of deprivation over the festive season.[69]

At the same time, the homelessness charity Shelter estimated that 130,000 kids would be living in temporary or inadequate accommodation over Christmas 2018.[70] In fact, homelessness – both 'rough sleepers' on the streets and people without a permanent place to live – rocketed under austerity in Britain.[71] Along with foodbanks, it was one of the single most visible exemplifications of the misery induced by cuts. Prior to austerity, and following three Labour governments, street homelessness was all but disappearing in the UK. By the end of 2019 youth homelessness charity Centrepoint was estimating that more than 22,000 young people could be homeless or at risk of being made homeless in England by Christmas.[72]

I remember walking regularly around parts of London like The Strand which, when I first arrived to work in the capital in 1991, had homeless people huddled in almost every doorway. By the mid-2000s, the numbers of visible homeless people had reduced markedly, but as austerity took hold the figures rose again – a fact which would have been impossible to deny if you lived in a major city or spent time in a town centre. I recall in 2015 an American friend of mine who is a frequent visitor to the UK calling me up in shock on a trip back when, after an absence of a year, he was appalled by what he saw. "For a moment I thought I was back in San Francisco!" He told me of the numbers of people he encountered sleeping on the streets, in tube station entryways and in tunnels.

One of the more disturbing characteristics of the austerity era in Britain, and which can in part be attributed to the demonising rhetoric deployed by politicians and the press to justify the cuts that thrust ever more people into poverty, was a growing pervasiveness in the culture of a casual, cruel dehumanisation of homeless people[73] – an easy target among the poorest and most vulnerable already being scapegoated. As the number of homeless people rocketed in the UK during austerity – research by the charity Crisis suggested that 12,300 people were sleeping rough on the streets of Britain and that the number had risen by 98 per cent since 2010 – so too did both verbal and physical attacks.[74]

One headline in *The Guardian* from December 2018 summed up what was increasingly becoming commonplace tragedy: 'Beaten, harassed, set alight: rough sleepers tell of horrific rise in violence'.[75] One 42-year-old homeless man in Cardiff, Wales, told the paper he suffered burns after his tent was set on fire with him, his partner and dog in it. "I've had my tent destroyed twice and there's always groups of drunk lads trying to make me the butt of some nasty joke. A lot of people are looking for someone to take their rage out on and homeless people are an easy target," the man said. "It definitely makes you more wary, but I've seen people dragged out of their tents by their feet before."

Six months later, an article with the headline: '"Homeless" man dies and another fighting for life after tent "set on fire".'[76]

In another article, a homeless man in Liverpool told of how someone had tried to set his sleeping bag alight, while other kinds of abuse, including being spat on, are common.[77] (Police reported that attacks on homeless people in the city had doubled in a year to more than 200.) In a separate incident, this time outside a railway station in London, a video by a member of the public captured rail staff casually pouring dirty water over a man sleeping rough.[78] Meanwhile members of Oxford University's exclusive Bullingdon Club[79] – whose past members include the former UK Prime Minister and Chancellor of the Exchequer responsible for austerity, David Cameron and George Osborne – were reported as burning a £50 note mockingly in front of a homeless person as part of their exclusive club's initiation process.[80] In the spring of 2019, a particularly worrisome incident occurred in North Wales when it was reported that a 55-year-old homeless woman was sentenced to prison for begging in a town centre in what campaigners called a result of a wider shift to 'remove poverty from the streets'.[81] There was no evidence of criminal behaviour, homelessness campaigners pointed out. Jon Glackin, a former homeless person and a founder of a grassroots homeless organisation, told reporters:

> "This is happening more and more across the UK. We should be addressing the issues of why people are there on the streets, not to move them with the punishment of criminalisation ..."

Meanwhile, as reports of people living on the streets being attacked mushroomed, a kind of twisted dystopian response[82] emerged when in the spring of 2019 it was announced that parts of the UK had plans in place to issue homeless people with protective clothing. What on the surface could look like a practical, immediate response to an urgent problem – coats that turn into sleeping bags – could also be read as a tacit acceptance that the high numbers of homeless people are here to stay. And, just when you think it couldn't be worse, the coats would be 'non-flammable' and 'stab-proof'. Again, by one interpretation, a pragmatic reaction to attacks on homeless people, but it suggests acquiescence to the abuse rather than confronting the belief systems that foster the sort of degrading violence homeless people were being subjected to. In October 2019 new official figures published by the Office for National Statistics revealed that in 2018 the number of deaths among homeless people in England and Wales rose by a record 22% year-on-year to 726.[83]

Professor Andrew Hayward of University College London commented: 'The unprecedented numbers of homeless deaths reported by the Office for National Statistics should be considered a national public health emergency. These deaths are driven by poverty and represent a failure of our society to protect the most vulnerable. Whilst drug-related deaths are important, homeless people are also much more likely than the general population to die of common treatable conditions such as respiratory disease, heart disease and cancer.'[84]

The 10 years of spending cuts and the consequent shrinking of the state that have fuelled rising child poverty are not the consequences of forces beyond our control, forces furthermore that we have not been able to confront because of Brexit.
The Observer newspaper editorial, March 2019

Throughout 2019, yet more warning flares were flying around poverty in general – and child poverty in particular.[85] The government's own figures showed that the number of kids in absolute poverty jumped by 200,000 in 2017/18. Relative poverty also increased, before housing costs, according to the Department for Work and Pensions. There was a leap too in pensioner absolute and relative poverty, and an increase in inequality was also confirmed, thanks to rising incomes for the wealthiest workers and as the government's brutal benefits freeze entered its fourth year, hitting families really hard.[86]

According to the Resolution Foundation, the increases recorded for child poverty were driven by government cuts to working age benefits (which help subsidise low earnings for many working families) and were exacerbated by a rise in inflation. Adam Corlett, a senior economic analyst at the Foundation, said:

> "The political conversation around austerity may have shifted but the lived experience of it hasn't for millions of families. Reducing child poverty needs to return to near the top of the government's priority list."

Needless to say, anti-poverty organisations lambasted the government for presiding over such an unsettling situation, while ministers, true to form, said it was taking the figures 'extremely seriously'. It *was* taking it extremely seriously – if extremely seriously means tumbling down a Brexit rabbit hole at the expense of such an important domestic policy and failing to address the fact that, as a direct result of government actions, children across the country would needlessly suffer.

While people were preoccupied with an increasing political mess surrounding Brexit, poverty statistics all but disappeared into the ether.

As one editorial in *The Observer* newspaper pointed out:[87]

> It's nothing short of a national disgrace yet these figures merited hardly a mention in last week's parliamentary debates. The 10 years of spending cuts and the consequent shrinking of the state that have fuelled rising child poverty are not the consequences of forces beyond our control, forces furthermore that we have not been able to confront because of Brexit. Instead, the factors that have recreated this reservoir of poverty are the result of longstanding political choices, first made by David Cameron and George Osborne then later embraced enthusiastically by [Theresa] May and Philip Hammond.

Bearing in mind that the figures followed a plethora of previous signals of just how bad things were getting – and would continue to get – the lack of widespread outrage was telling.[88] Even the repeatedly upsetting alarm bells raised by teachers[89] about students turning up for school hungry and with inadequate clothing seemed to just come and go in a roundabout of terrible, normalised stories.[90]

In the summer of 2018, the issue of children going hungry during school holidays came to the fore[91] when the Trussell Trust highlighted that when children were off school, demand at foodbanks spiked. Without access to the free school meals many families depended on, they struggled to provide for the nutritional needs of children.

If you've never relied on free school meals it's difficult to fully appreciate the role they play. For many youngsters they are the only nutritional meal they receive most days. When I was a kid, the summer holidays in Northern Ireland lasted nine long weeks. The strain this put on family budgets was enormous. Imagine – we went from five days a week of meat and two veg plus dessert every lunchtime free of charge to our parents suddenly having to magic up food from a budget that hadn't altered. For me, a lot of the summer entailed making packets of chicken noodle soup to stretch as far as possible at lunchtime with some bread to bulk it out. Sometimes lunch was bread and butter with sugar sprinkled on top to give the illusion of it being a treat. Occasionally friends whose parents had a bit more would share their crisps or fruit, or a neighbour would help out.

A step too far

In April 2019 when it emerged that another indicator of the impact of poverty was potentially on the rise – newborn deaths among the country's less well off were increasing – it barely made a brief blip on the media dial.[92] The independent MP Frank Field called for a government investigation after figures obtained by his office seemed to suggest a worrying shift in infant mortality among poorer social groups in 2015/16 – the rate of which had been decreasing or steady for the previous eight to ten years. In 2016, Field found, among four out of five groups (all but the most affluent), infant mortality had risen.

Also in 2019, researchers from the University of Liverpool, University of Leeds and Newcastle University published the results of a time trend analysis of rising infant mortality in England in the British Medical Journal Open (BMJO).[93] The objective of the study, titled 'Assessing the impact of rising child poverty on the unprecedented rise of infant mortality in England, 2000–2017' was: 'To determine whether there were inequalities in the sustained rise in infant mortality in England in recent years and the contribution of rising child poverty to these trends.' The researchers wrote:

> The sustained and unprecedented rise in infant mortality in England from 2014 to 2017 was not experienced evenly across the population. In the most deprived local authorities, the previously declining trend in infant mortality reversed and mortality rose, leading to an additional 24 infant deaths per 100,000 live births per year (95% CI 6 to 42), relative to the previous trend. There was no significant change

from the pre-existing trend in the most affluent local authorities. As a result, inequalities in infant mortality increased, with the gap between the most and the least deprived local authority areas widening by 52 deaths per 100 000 births (95% CI 36 to 68).

They concluded:

This study provides evidence that the unprecedented rise in infant mortality disproportionately affected the poorest areas of the country, leaving the more affluent areas unaffected. Our analysis also linked the recent increase in infant mortality in England with rising child poverty, suggesting that about a third of the increase in infant mortality from 2014 to 2017 may be attributed to rising child poverty.

And, by the summer of 2019, serious concerns were being raised when it was reported that life expectancy in the UK was faltering, with Britons living shorter, less healthy lives compared to the recent past, breaking a century of upward trends in life expectancy. Many experts believed that austerity was a key factor.[94]

In yet one more unsettling development, an increasingly common term thought long-since irrelevant in Britain came up once again when the joint general secretary of the National Education Union Mary Bousted said the reality on the ground painted a "Dickensian picture" of life for many children: "The government is out of touch with the distressing new reality of children's daily lives," Bousted said, "with what it means to live without enough money for basics such as food, shoes and adequate clothing. Children can't escape the poverty trap without an urgent change to national policies."

When Action for Children chief executive Julie Bentley also used the term 'Dickensian'[95] it was jumped upon by one newspaper as an outright exaggeration. But it is possible, and understandable, that campaigners were so exasperated by the level of poverty being ignored they felt the need to apply an adjective the wider population might understand.

Exasperation was the order of the day when in late spring 2019 Alston published his final report.[96] While in substance it reflected the preliminary publication, ministers latched on to some of his more pointed judgements. Alston accused ministers of 'systematic immiseration of a significant part of the British population'. He compared government welfare policies to the creation of 19th-century workhouses and, referencing the British philosopher Thomas Hobbes, warned that should austerity continue, the future facing the country's poorest would be: 'solitary, poor, nasty, brutish and short'. He probably didn't do himself any favours with the workhouse comment, opening the report's conclusions to accusations of hyperbole, but the fact remains that his conclusion will have come as no shock whatsoever to anyone who has felt the pain of austerity first-hand or, like myself, conducted in-depth research about it.

As the journalist Frances Ryan who has written extensively on the impact of austerity, especially on disabled people,[97] succinctly put it to Project Twist-It: "I've spoken to many hundreds of people who are struggling in poverty in recent years, often as a direct result of government policy."

Right on cue upon the report's release Amber Rudd responded. The government declared the report 'barely believable'[98] (people on the receiving end of cuts to benefits may have begged to differ), while Rudd decried the report, saying she planned to lodge a formal complaint on account of Alston's "bias".[99] Alston hit back. As *The Guardian* reported, he 'said the government response amounted to "a total denial of a set of uncontested facts" and that when he first read its public comment, "I thought it might actually be a spoof".'[100]

As the second decade of the century came to a close, the Conservative government did make a number of moves to mitigate the fallout of some policies since 2010. For example, when he was Chancellor of the Exchequer, Philip Hammond put back almost £2 million into Universal Credit – a policy first mooted as simplifying the benefits system, but which had been plagued with problems during its rollout – to better fund the new system. The Conservatives also reiterated right at the start of the 2019 General Election campaign a pledge to end the benefits freeze.[101]

Nevertheless, austerity policies and other reforms, as well as other issues such as wage stagnation in the wake of the financial crisis had fuelled poverty and financial insecurity for a sizeable proportion of the population. Even the Murdoch press ran campaigns highlighting in-work poverty.

During a visit to a foodbank in Scotland just before Christmas 2018 the former Labour Prime Minister and Chancellor of the Exchequer, Gordon Brown – whose policies while in power in the pre-austerity era actively contributed to reductions in pensioner and child poverty – summed up the state of UK poverty as well as anybody could.[102]

Brown told a reporter:

> "It makes me angry. I'm seeing poverty I didn't think I'd ever see again in my lifetime. Slum housing was a feature of my childhood in the 1950s and 1960s and I thought we had finally got over the worst of child poverty."

Pinpointing one of the core components of the toxic poverty narrative this book is seeking to understand, he added:

> "The government is trying to analyse this as people who are too lazy to get into work. But the problem is that people can't earn enough to stay out of poverty."

2

What? There are poor people in the richest nation on earth?

"Poverty, or poor, or working-class – whatever level of not enough you're at – you feel it in a million tiny ways. Sometimes it's the condescension, sometimes it's that you're itchy."
Linda Tirado, in *Hand to Mouth: Living in Bootstrap America*

"What poor Americans have usually demanded (when they have demanded anything at all) is not charity or welfare but a safe job and a decent wage. What they have had to settle for (when they could get anything at all) was paltry and demeaning aid work with wages so low that they still remained poor."
Stephen Pimpare, *A People's History of Poverty in America*, p 9

A price to pay: the human cost of poverty in America

Dogs bark excitedly as we approach Christine Riccione's apartment in a public housing complex on the north side of Charleston, South Carolina. It's a typical soupy hot Carolina summer afternoon and once myself and George, a professor of history and a local activist, are inside, Christine apologises for the noise of a portable air conditioner positioned on the floor that rattles furiously against the fierce heat. Once the two dogs are dispatched to the bedroom, it's marginally quieter and Christine settles into the sofa to tell her story.

Like so many in her situation living on the breadline who I spoke to while working on Project Twist-It and this book, Christine told us she was determined to talk about her experiences and what she had learned along the way because stories like hers often remain untold or are misunderstood or misrepresented.

> **"**Tic, tac, toe. We were like dominoes being flushed down, you know?**"**

Once we are all seated Christine describes how, after a series of car troubles three or so years before (she doesn't recall the exact dates) she lost her minimum-wage job delivering pizza near Columbia, the state capital. Around the same time, the other earner in the family and also a delivery driver, her brother-in-law, saw his car written off in an accident.

They'd just about been holding it together until then, making payments on her car and the trailer they lived in. "My car would not run no more. I couldn't get it to run," Christine says, explaining that the car was essential to the job. "I had a time loan on it so they came and repossessed it. We lived in a county where the nearest grocery store was six miles away. The whole road is nothing but dirt and sand. Walmart was like 30 minutes to drive so walking there wasn't an option." With no car, Christine was let go by her employer. "I'm a dime a dozen," she explains of how quickly she went from employed to not. "They could hire any driver they want."

> **"[People] look at me or they look at the homeless and they say, why bother, they're homeless because they want to be. No. Homelessness is not a disease, it's a problem in society where people – they're living paycheck to paycheck."**
> Christine Riccione, former homeless person

Christine is in the small apartment she now shares with her boyfriend (they were lucky to get it, she says, thanks to his status as an army vet). It's a cramped space made to feel even smaller by the mementos, knick-knacks and pictures distributed around, but it feels like home and it's a huge step up from before when losing a car and a job meant destitution. Back before they had the apartment, and after her brother-in-law lost his job, things had gone from bad to worse and the three of them, Christine, her boyfriend and brother-in-law found themselves moving to chase down work, ending up in another trailer they couldn't afford the rent for, then a shabby hotel.

> "We had no money coming in except the foodstamps. Food stamps can't pay for electric, they can't pay the land payment [on the trailer]. If you own property, welfare won't help you financially. They'll help you with foodstamps – up to a point. So, I ended up not having a job, losing the land and the trailer. We ended up selling everything we owned. We didn't have three cents between us to rub together."

Within a few months all three ended up on a campsite but even that proved unstable when a massive flood meant they lost most of their few remaining possessions. "It was like one extreme to the next," Christine recalls.

Stints scrabbling for temporary work did nothing to offer a sustainable way out of the poverty trap each of them was now in. "The temp service, they pay you by the day but they work you like a dog. Then they pay you minimum wage," Christine says. They felt disposable.

> "I think everybody should be treated equally, rich or poor. But when you have nothing, you don't treat people who have nothing like they are nothing – they already feel low. It's like trying to pick yourself up the ladder and somebody pushes it out from under you, you know? And you pick it back up and you get back up again, and it falls. Two steps forward, four steps back."

At rock bottom as 2016 turned to 2017, Christine, her brother-in-law and her boyfriend – who was out of work too, having been dealing with depression and addiction – ended up living downtown in a tent. Finding a job and a way out from those circumstances isn't something people can easily understand the challenges of, Christine says:

> "You don't have a home, you don't have a phone so there's no way for [employers] to call you for that job interview. And there's no home where you can take a shower and get dressed.
>
> [People] look at me or they look at the homeless and they say, why bother, they're homeless because they want to be. No. Homelessness is not a disease, it's a problem in society where people – they're living paycheck to paycheck. And everybody's one paycheck away from being homeless. I don't need money to be rich or happy. I just want enough money to have a roof over my head, food in my cupboard and my refrigerator and clothes. If you've never had to worry about being hungry, try it sometime. Go downtown, go somewhere near a highway, sit there for three days. See what it feels like to really be homeless and hungry. And tell me, do you really think I wanted that?"

After a few months on the streets of downtown Charleston, Christine, her boyfriend and brother-in-law made their way to a shelter short term and during their stay managed to find the kind of support that helped them begin to get back on their feet. Christine's brother-in-law was helped into shared housing while her boyfriend, an army veteran, found work installing equipment. "They got me my disability," she explains, describing how as well as living with post-traumatic stress disorder from "deep-rooted" childhood trauma, she suffers with chronic back pain and emphysema. "I've been fighting for that for years."

The home Christine and her boyfriend moved into in April 2017 after he was helped to claim assistance as a veteran is modest but she chokes up when explaining what it means after so much time without a permanent place to live.

"I don't have to worry about when the wind blows, my walls move. I don't have to worry about the rain [or if] the ceiling's going to cave in. I can go to the bathroom any time I want. I don't have to be in the elements or the weather. My dogs have a place to run and play.**"**

Letting out a throaty, acerbic chuckle, Christine adds:

"I'm a survivor. They can't destroy [what's] in me. They can take away material things. But if the person does not lay down and die, you can't take away their pride.**"**

Christine Riccione's story could be the story of many thousands of people across the US.

Putting the record straight

While spending some time over a weekend in late 2018 with Philip Alston, *The Guardian* columnist Aditya Chakrabortty asked the UN Rapporteur whether he saw any echoes in the British experience from the testimonies he had heard while investigating Donald Trump's America less than a year before.[1] Alston's response might have surprised people who still believed that significant vestiges of the founding collectivism and safety net of the Welfare State[2] in Britain remained in place and would protect them from the worst vagaries of a US-like system. It might also have come as a shock to US activists and campaigners – many of whom I interviewed for this book – who have been fighting increased attacks[3] on what's left of their threadbare welfare safety net in America.

"In many ways," Alston told Chakrabortty, "you in the UK are far ahead of the US." The Republicans would be "ecstatic" to have pushed through the kind of austerity measures the UK had endured over the past few years, he said.

That a UN Rapporteur on Extreme Poverty and Human Rights was investigating the UK and the US[4] was not insignificant. (As Patrick Kingsley pointed out in *The New York Times*,[5] because of their mandate to investigate countries with high levels of deprivation, rapporteurs tend to focus on developing nations.) The UK was only the rapporteur's second mission to a Western European country this century (the other was Ireland in 2011),[6] and America has the dubious honour of being visited twice since 2000. The rapporteur's remit includes assessing the extent to which government policies and programmes targeting extreme poverty align with human rights obligations. It also involves making recommendations. Both the UK and US reports drew on a wealth of available research around poverty and policy, as well as crucial interviews with people whose lives were impacted by the experience of being poor and of policy changes.

About *40 million* [Americans] live in poverty, *18.5 million* in extreme poverty, and *5.3 million* live in Third World conditions of absolute poverty.
Philip Alston, UN Special Rapporteur on Extreme Poverty and Human Rights

If the UN Rapporteur's verdict on the UK in November 2018 was a biting indictment, the one presented in Alston's full report to the UN Human Rights Council in the summer of the same year on the US following a similar fact-finding mission at the end of 2017, was excoriating.[7] And, as Chakrabortty's question to Alston intimated, the benefits systems may differ in many fundamental respects, but when it comes to systematic efforts to undermine and discredit the safety net, there are indeed echoes of like-minded policy thrusts – and political rationalisations for these – aggravating poverty further. Many of these tendencies come through loud and clear in the UN assessment of poverty in both countries. The similarities were both in substance and in rhetoric.

However, when it comes to the US's record on poverty and inequality there was no beating about any bush in the rapporteur's report's core conclusion.[8] It was damning. He wrote:

> About 40 million [Americans] live in poverty, 18.5 million in extreme poverty, and 5.3 million live in Third World conditions of absolute poverty. It has

the highest youth poverty rate in the Organization for Economic Cooperation and Development (OECD), and the highest infant mortality rates among comparable OECD states. Its citizens live shorter lives compared to those living in all other rich democracies, eradicable tropical diseases are increasingly prevalent, and it has the world's largest incarceration rate, one of the lowest levels of voter registration among OECD countries and the highest obesity levels in the developed world.

The American Dream is rapidly becoming the American Illusion.
Philip Alston, UN Special Rapporteur on Extreme Poverty and Human Rights

And on it goes:

> The United States already leads the developed world in income and wealth inequality, and it is now moving full steam ahead to make itself even more unequal. High child and youth poverty rates perpetuate the intergenerational transmission of poverty very effectively, and ensure that the American dream is rapidly becoming the American illusion.

Taking direct aim at the Trump administration and the Republican congressional obsession with tax cuts for the rich,[9] while attacking the safety net for the poor, the report said:

> The $1.5 trillion in tax cuts in December 2017 overwhelmingly benefited the wealthy and worsened inequality. The consequences of neglecting poverty and promoting inequality are clear.

The report also highlighted policies pursued by Republicans over the course of 2018 that would directly and negatively affect the poorest, especially multiply marginalised groups such as people with disabilities. Among these was restricting eligibility for many government assistance programmes even further, attempting to 'add over 20 million poor and middle-class persons to the ranks of those without health insurance', and pushing for further 'work requirements'[10] to qualify for Medicaid, something that would disproportionately impact disabled adults and children who rely on additional support.[11]

The report continued:

> The policies pursued over the past year seem deliberately designed to remove basic protections from the poorest, punish those who are not in employment and make even basic health care into a privilege to be earned rather than a right of citizenship.

When interviewed at the time of his report,[12] Alston directed his ire (just as he did with the UK equivalent report) towards the patent cruelty of what he concluded was a politically designed systematic attack on welfare provision. He said in the interview:

> **"**This systematic attack on America's welfare program is undermining the social safety net for those who can't cope on their own. Once you start removing any sense of government commitment, you quickly move to cruelty.**"**

Referring to government proposals that targeted basic provision – including assistance with buying food, healthcare access and housing supplements – for cuts and more stringent qualifying criteria,[13] he went on: "If foodstamps and access to Medicaid are removed, and housing subsidies cut, then the effect on people living on the margins will be drastic."

This is a conclusion people who have fallen foul of a low-wage, insecure jobs market with minimal safety net or who live with a disability – people like Christine Riccione – understand only too well. Project Twist-It spoke to a number of US army veterans, all of whom identified similar challenges to Christine. This, from Marquis Davis, was typical:

"A lot of Americans, we're just above the line where if we don't receive a paycheck, we will not be eating.**"**

Alston visited four states – California, the nation's wealthiest and most populous, Alabama, Georgia and West Virginia, which has some of the worst pockets of poverty in the country and was a Trump heartland in the 2016 election – as well as Washington DC and the US territory of Puerto Rico. The trip began just as the Senate voted for highly contentious tax cuts,[14] estimated at the time by the independent Center on Budget and Policy Priorities to cost $1.5 trillion over ten years while further exacerbating income inequality between those at the very top and everyone else. It also came just one year after the Stanford Center on Poverty and Inequality's *State of the Union: The Poverty and Inequality Report 2016*[15] ranked the US at the bottom of its international table of ten well-off countries (the UK was ranked seventh) for income and wealth inequality.[16] The report noted that: 'the United Kingdom has a poverty and inequality profile that, among the Anglophone countries, comes closest to that of the US'.

Set against some data on those at the bottom – America's most needy – the value of a UN intervention is even more apposite. At the very least, as the US Senator for New Jersey and presidential hopeful Corey Brooker said of the rapporteur's conclusion, while "disturbing," it was "unfortunately not surprising".[17]

Blowback: poverty denial in the Trump era

An escalating antagonism between the Trump administration and the UN Human Rights Council, which hit a nadir when in June 2018 the US withdrew from the world's most important human rights body,[18] puts some context perhaps on why Nikki Haley, the then US Ambassador to the UN, dismissed Alston's report, accusing its methodology of vastly overstating the extent of deep poverty.[19] The report was politically motivated and exaggerated, she concluded. The administration suggested that rather than the 18.5 million people the UN estimated were living in extreme poverty, the figure was more like 250,000.[20]

A written statement from the US Mission to the UN[21] declared that:

> ... accusations that the United States shows 'contempt and hatred' for the poor, including accusations of a criminal justice system designed to keep low income persons in poverty while generating public revenue, are inaccurate, inflammatory, and irresponsible.

Haley went so far as to say it was "patently ridiculous for the UN to examine poverty in America". In a not dissimilar rebuttal to that seen from the Conservatives in Britain to Alston's analysis of the UK, the report was dismissed as 'inaccurate, inflammatory and irresponsible' by the administration.[22]

Bearing in mind the state of US politics generally by the time the summer of 2018 came around when the Trump administration declared in June that year that there was no such thing as extreme poverty in America, people could be forgiven for not even batting an eyelid at the calculated absurdity of it.

The UN report so enraged the Trump administration's (and its fans'[23]) apparently newly discovered sensibilities to the plight of the poor that it pronounced the 'War on Poverty' initiated by President Lyndon B. Johnson in 1964 in his State of the Union Address[24] – an historic milestone in anti-poverty drives in US history, including creating Medicare and Medicaid – was all but over – dealt with, done.

In apparent self-contradiction, an administration that – like many administrations before it – regarded government programmes and policies assisting the poor as wasting money, encouraging so-called 'welfare dependency' and ultimately ineffective because of this,[25] was now attempting to justify making it even harder to qualify for assistance because they now deduced that the anti-poverty programmes had worked after all.

This is how the poverty podcast *Off-Kilter* at the Center for American Progress (CAP) summed up the farcical situation:[26]

"Move over, climate change. Late last week, the White House issued a sweeping denial[27] of poverty. A major report released by Trump's Council of Economic Advisers brazenly declared the War on Poverty 'largely over and a success.' ... the report is literally page after page of gaslighting the very real hardship faced by tens of millions of Americans struggling to afford food, housing, health care and more – all for the purpose of justifying Trump's quest to dismantle Medicaid, nutrition assistance, and other programs that help families get by (to pay for his millionaire tax cuts)."

Guesting on the podcast, CAP's director of anti-poverty advocacy, Jeremy Slevin, hit the absurd nail on the head when he concluded:

"They literally said, and I quote, that the war on poverty is quote, "largely over and a success", end quote. And notably, this after for years conservatives try[ing] to say the War on Poverty was a failure, now they say it's done, we can move on. And the message of this report ... is basically that poverty in essence does not exist and is not a major problem in America today and therefore we can begin rolling back all of these programs that help people, whether it's help people get health care through Medicaid or help people access food through SNAP[28] or whether it's housing assistance, but that is the broad frame of the report."

Rebecca Vallas, the show's host and a long-standing anti-poverty advocate and a lawyer, expressed the farcicality of the administration's statistical gymnastics with pointed precision. Vallas said:

"There are pages and pages of all kinds of statements about how, for example, homelessness isn't really a meaningful problem in this country. They try to do these funny things with stats where they're like, well, I don't know, doesn't seem like a problem because throughout the year, 99.6 per cent of people won't spend a single night in a homeless shelter. That is literally their case; that's the evidence that they mount. Just, you know, erasing the plight over half a million Americans without shelter on any given night, which I will note includes 58,000 families with children, but hey, you guys are not the majority of people so I guess you don't count. That's basically the logic."

Vallas goes on:

"And it does the same thing with hunger ... the report literally says sorry to you folks who are hungry, that's not good enough for us. We think you should actually be starving in a way that might put [you] in a commercial that would be asking for money for a third world country that's trying to erase say child hunger with distended bellies ... it's basically treating poverty like this administration has treated climate change: if you just deny that it's really a problem, then that justifies your agenda, which in the case of poverty is trying to dismantle the programs that ... help people have health care and food and everything else."

After disseminating the report via Twitter, Vallas noted:

"The number of people I had reaching out to me and saying thank you for acknowledging that what we experience every day really is actually happening, that is what this White House doesn't want to do. It wants to whitewash it, it wants to erase it."

By May 2019, in another blatant attack on the country's most financially vulnerable, the administration was floating drastic changes to the poverty measure that would,[29] according to an analysis by the Center on Budget and Policy Priorities (CBPP), 'reduce or eliminate assistance to millions of low-income Americans'.[30] Senior Fellow Sharon Parrott warned at the time:[31]

> "The Trump Administration yesterday floated a proposal to use a lower measure of inflation when adjusting the poverty line each year. Consistent with other policies the Administration has pursued, this policy would over time cut or take away entirely food assistance, health, and other forms of basic assistance from millions of people who struggle to put food on the table, keep a roof over their heads, and see a doctor when they need to. If the poverty line is altered in this fashion, fewer individuals and families will qualify over time for various forms of assistance, including many who work hard but are paid low wages.[32]"

Incidentally, not long after the administration produced its Council of Economic Advisors' response to the UN report, it emerged that the economics consultants asked to consult on a draft rebuttal had actually flagged some of the content up as problematic. Internal state department documents obtained by *Foreign Policy* magazine and Coda Story[33] reported on how the public had been misled.

Foreign Policy magazine wrote:

> Their [consultants'] comments, typed into the margins of the draft or included in emails, were either watered down or ignored altogether. As a result, the statement the administration issued in June [2018] included misleading data and painted an overly optimistic picture of the American economy.[34]

In his essay titled 'Donald Trump's Poverty Denial'[35] in the summer of 2018 for *The Atlantic*, the journalist Vann R. Newkirk II offered a searing and pointed assessment of the contemporary political landscape around poverty in light of the rapporteur's damning appraisal. Writing that Alston's recommendations for addressing poverty in the US, including rolling back mass incarceration and redistribution of wealth via progressive taxation, were 'deeply ideological by nature, tied to a number of progressive critiques of capitalism and white supremacy over the years', he concluded that in the context of poverty in the US, the topic is 'necessarily partisan'. Trump and his congressional enablers were failing to contribute to a serious conversation on poverty reduction.

Newkirk II wrote:

> Indeed, if it must be judged solely by its results, Trumpian policy is designed to increase the ranks of the impoverished, and to hasten the declining economic prospects of people at the margins in America. The president wants to obliterate the Affordable Care Act and its Medicaid expansion, which studies indicate have saved thousands of people from bankruptcy. In that Medicaid program and in other means-tested welfare programs, the administration has rolled out work requirements and a growing list of restrictions that will only serve to kick people off assistance, and will create a new subclass of even poorer people who are ineligible for public assistance.

He continues:

> The White House has also proposed a government reshuffle that experts believe will make means-tested programs like foodstamps more vulnerable to cuts, and has rolled out a proposed budget that does that cutting. And from its tax policy to its endorsement of a plan to hike rental rates of people living in public housing, the Trump administration has espoused a poverty plan that simply rejects that the government has a major role in reducing poverty.

Hardest hit: life at the coal face of American poverty

It's late spring in 2018 and I'm sitting in a hotel lobby in Culver City, California with anti-poverty and civil rights advocate, Reverend Dr William Barber III[36] when he points out something that, in a nutshell, puts the place of poverty within the broader American consciousness in perspective.

> "What we've seen over the last 50 years is a removal of poverty even from the political discourse. And when it does [make it in] the Republicans, they talk about blame – basically poor people are on some kind of glorified vacation. Two years ago, we go through a presidential election, 26, by my count, maybe more maybe a bit less, presidential debates...and not one hour on [the] poverty and low wealth ... that is impacting 43.5 per cent of our country."

Barber, who came to prominence as a pastor, president of the North Carolina NAACP, and indefatigable architect of the Forward Together Moral Monday movement,[37] which mobilised record numbers of demonstrators against state policy in North Carolina, was traversing the country to promote the latest anti-poverty effort he helped establish with another reverend, Liz Theoharis, and supporters around the country.

The Poor People's Campaign: A National Call for Moral Revival[38] (PPC) was inspired by the original Poor People's Campaign launched by Martin Luther King Junior 50 years earlier. The latest incarnation was, as Barber explained to me, "a movement" led by a "fusion" of activists, clergy and people with lived experience of poverty. It was about time, he told me, that the reality and scale of poverty and low income in America be brought to national attention.

"Down in Lyles County, Alabama, which is barely 15 miles from Independence Bridge where Congress people come every year to talk about how great people were in the past ... we saw a grandfather and a mother in two different locations, where their homes, in the back of their yards is literally raw sewage."
Reverend Dr William Barber III, the Poor People's Campaign

In May 2018, not long after Reverend Barber and I met, and after two years of preparation and grassroots coalition-building, the PPC kick-started a social justice effort with six weeks of peaceful direct action in state capitals around the US.[39] The intention of the campaign was to construct a broad, citizen-led movement that challenges the shocking and avoidable scale of poverty and the structural pillars that reinforce it, including 'systemic racism, ecological devastation, and the war economy'. Thousands of people, including many who had never been activists, signed up.

Importantly, Barber pointed out, the weeks of action came after months of 'deep' research in multiple states to ascertain the ways poverty was impacting people and to explore ways to expose how the 'story' characterising the poor as lazy and irresponsible that shored up this poverty was being deployed with reverberations felt far and wide. Barber, and others across the movement, were convinced that this long-entrenched negative narrative and poisonous rhetoric surrounding poverty and poorer people was making it harder to advocate for policy changes that would assist poorer people. If poverty were to be properly fought, he argued, the narrative had to be upended.

The PPC's research culminated in an 'audit' of poverty on the 50th anniversary of Reverend King's campaign launch. A report, 'The Souls of Poor Folk: Auditing America 50 years after the Poor People's Campaign'[40] was published by the Institute for Policy Studies (IPS) think tank in Washington DC in the spring of 2018. By the summer of 2019, the PPC would acquire considerable media attention, including for its protests in state capitals and, when Democratic contenders were vying for the party's presidential nomination,[41] the movement's figureheads met with candidates.[42] Along with the IPS, it published a 'Moral

Budget'.[43] About the PPC's travels around the country, Barber told me this:

> ⁶⁶So down in Lyles County, Alabama, which is barely 15 miles from Independence Bridge where Congress people come every year to talk about how great people were in the past … we saw a grandfather and a mother in two different locations, where their homes, in the back of their yards is literally raw sewage. Where children and grandchildren have to play. And we saw where the political operatives worked to get sewage [systems] up to where the businesses were, but would not bring it to those homes.⁹⁹

Visiting the homes of native Americans – for a long time among the very poorest in the country[44] – PPC activists witnessed a myriad of devastating poverty-related problems.

> ⁶⁶We've seen on the Apache Nation in Arizona. We went there and saw how their burial grounds are being destroyed by multinational companies, that have been given permission by United States senators to drill down for copper, though they know that 98 per cent of what comes up is unusable and will turn into airborne toxins that cause cancer. I went to Alaska and met with the tribes there who are going to suffer because of … the opening up of the wildlife refuge and the way in which the Alaskan people – the natives particularly – are treated and the level of poverty they face and the way in which their culture is destroyed.⁹⁹

Barber continued:

> ⁶⁶We have been to Detroit and we've seen the people who've kept the fight alive, the welfare rights workers, but also looking at communities that look like they have been bombed.⁹⁹

Reflecting on the 'water contamination crisis' in Flint, Michigan which, when brought to national attention, exposed a cavalcade of abuses of power over a number of years so bad that people were dying as a result of exposure to the city's water supply,[45] he said:

> "I went to Flint [Michigan] and looked into that black water and saw it and talked to people who have been poisoned by that water.
>
> We've seen up at Gray's Harbor in Washington, a whole community of white millennials, adults, but millennials living homeless in the middle of the city, where politicians don't even come. Dying. People who are veterans who fought in this country.
>
> You look at it and it's not even third world – it's fourth world. We met Amy who came out of the hills of West Virginia, who came to testify about being a woman with a degree but having to work a poverty level job and how she was upset because when the teachers wanted a pay increase, the government played the teachers against poor people by saying 'we are going to give the teachers a raise, but we're going to cut Medicaid and stop SNAP programs [to pay for it]'. We went to Dallas and found that in Dallas – with all of its tall buildings – has the largest population of poor children in the country. These are just some of the stories."

The nationwide battle with poverty

The IPS report, 'The Souls of Poor Folk', which challenged racism, poverty, the war economy/militarism and national morality,[46] laid bare the degree to which people across the US were suffering and struggling to get by. It makes for stark reading as it chronicles the structural underpinnings of contemporary impoverishment spanning a low-wage, de-unionised economy, systemic racism, voter suppression, and erosion of the social safety net.

Here's a summary of some of the IPS report's key points:

- Nearly **41 million** Americans are living below the federal poverty line.[47]
- People of colour are disproportionately impacted by poverty, influenced by historical and enduring systemic racism, education policy, housing discrimination, health systems, criminal justice, immigration and voter suppression.
  - While in absolute terms, more White people are poor, the proportion of White people who are poor is **11%**, while for Black people the proportion is **22%**, for Latinx it's **19.4%** and for Asian Americans it's **10.1%**.
  - The highest poverty rate for any group is for Native Americans and Alaskan natives, with more than a quarter **(26.2%)** affected.
- Nearly **140 million** people across the US (**43.5%**) are either poor or low-income under the alternative Supplemental Poverty Measure (SPM).
- Almost **four in ten children** spend at least one year of their lives in poverty.[48]
- The country's richest and biggest state, California, has the highest poverty rate.
- In 2016, households led by single mothers comprised almost **30%** of families with incomes below the poverty line.[49]
- Housing, higher education, and healthcare costs have increased significantly. Over the past 30 years, rents have gone up faster than incomes in nearly every urban area in the country.
- Cuts in federal housing assistance and affordable, subsidised housing since the 1970s have contributed to rising structural homelessness.[50]

The same month that the IPS released its report, another study highlighted the fact that millions of Americans were struggling to afford a basic 'middle-class life'.[51] The United Way Alice Project (ALICE)[52], which researches low-income communities, reported that 51 million US households – including 34.7 million lower-income families not officially defined as 'poor' – don't make enough to afford a monthly budget that covers basics like housing, food, childcare, healthcare, transportation and a mobile phone. Many of these were people in low-paid jobs such as home health aides and store clerks.

The study's conclusions about the financial fragility of households around the country[53] were acutely reflected in the January 2019 US government shutdown triggered by Donald Trump's demands that funding be released for his 'border wall'. Huge numbers of furloughed government workers, and others such as contractors who depended on government contracts, had to work without pay as a result of the shutdown. Many were in a position where being without pay for a single month meant hardship or moonlighting to get by,[54] exposing the fact that even federal workers in steady employment were far from financially secure. For contractors, the fallout brought its own additional problems, with one estimate suggesting that 10,000 companies were affected to the tune of around $200 million a week.

At the end of January 2019, figures released by the advocacy group Prosperity Now, after crunching Census data, revealed that millions of ordinary Americans – not just the very poorest – were in fact just one paycheck away from poverty, with 40 per cent considered 'liquid asset poor',[55] meaning they are one emergency away from financial ruin.

The furlough may have drawn attention towards the plight of federal workers in otherwise supposedly secure employment, but it was a mere surface scratch of a deeper problem. Regardless of the positive numbers on unemployment by early 2019 (though even these 'positive' numbers were problematic),[56] millions of households were, as CBS News put it: "on thin financial ice".

Putting some of the statistics – and how they are used – into context, Rebecca Vallas had this to say:

> "The official poverty rate for a family of four in the United States is a little over $24,000. That's how poor you have to be to be considered poor by the United States government, and therefore the media and everybody else who uses those statistics. But guess what it actually costs to achieve a basic but adequate standard of living for the same family? It's

actually more than twice that. It's more than $50,000 a year. When you look at measures of hardship in this country you find that somewhere between one third and half of Americans are actually living paycheck to paycheck, or struggling to make ends meet. Compare that to the 12 per cent (and change) who are officially considered poor in this country. **"**

The economic status of most Americans – not just the poorest – was a fragile one in 2019 despite a 'booming' economy. On the face of it, the official unemployment figure was low going into 2019 but for all too many of those in work, living paycheck to paycheck was the norm. Millions of Americans – 40 per cent – didn't even have enough spare cash to pay for an unexpected emergency expense of just $400.[57] Numerous other reports and analyses were also showing that, clearly, too many Americans were struggling to get by. One analysis by researchers at the Center on Poverty and Social Policy at Columbia University published towards the end of 2019, 'The Costs of Being Poor',[58] looked at a phenomenon called: 'inflation inequality', 'where prices have risen more quickly for people at the bottom of the income distribution', an implication of which is that levels of poverty and inequality are potentially being underestimated. The report says: 'Our adjusted inflation index indicates that 3.2m more people are classified as living in poverty in 2018, and that real household income for the bottom 20 percent of the income distribution actually declined by nearly 7% since 2004.'

The thrust of findings from the IPS, ALICE and other research dovetails with Alston's analysis. Pulling together a considerable body of contemporary research on poverty in America, Alston's conclusions provided a blistering summation of key systemic and structural drivers of poverty in the world's richest nation that have been long documented by anti-poverty advocates – and yet are persistently undermined politically by rhetoric that frames people who are struggling as universally personally responsible for their predicament. In what was an unambiguous counter-argument to the dominant poverty narrative in America – that impoverishment is a sign of personal failure or individual flaws – some of the areas highlighted were:

'**Structural racism** keeps a large percentage of non-whites in poverty or near poverty', including housing discrimination[59] and large disparities in wages[60] and wealth.

Increasing gaps between rich and poor.

The US has the **highest rate of child poverty** among the world's most advanced (OECD) economies while it is also home to **more billionaires** than any other country.[61]

The impact of the **criminal justice system** in generating and sustaining poverty.

The role of **health problems** experienced by the poorest.

The hardest hit by poverty in America, and by the relentless undermining of programmes designed to assist them, are (broadly) the same groups hit hardest on the other side of the Atlantic in Britain:

- Children
- Women
- Lone parents
- Minorities and indigenous people
- Disabled people
- Families with children
- Asylum seekers and migrants
- Rural dwellers
- Those reliant on public assistance programmes like Medicaid and foodstamps.

For millions of Americans, even with some provision through foodstamps (SNAP), going hungry is a fact of life. According to the US Department of Agriculture, **11.1%** of American households were food insecure during 2018. For households with children, the proportion was even higher, with a national figure of **13.9%**. For Hispanic households the percentage stood at **16.2%** while for black (non-Hispanic) households more than a fifth – **21.2%**. And for households headed by a single woman? More than a quarter: **27.8%**.[62]

Millions of Americans turn to foodbanks and pantries to put food on the table.[63] As the organisation Feeding America has pointed out, many households don't qualify for government nutrition programmes and – as increasingly also the case in the UK, as we have already seen – are left with little choice but to turn to charity.[64]

The shame of child impoverishment and the shedding of a safety net

The state of poverty in the United States, particularly among children, is abhorrent and scandalous, putting America, the richest and most powerful country in the world, in a shameful light.
Alon Ben-Meir, Senior Fellow, the Center for Global Affairs, NYU

The US Census figures for 2017 showed that **17.5%** of children were officially in poverty – **12.8 million** in total. Children are **62%** more likely than adults in the US to live below the poverty line.
The Shriver Brief [65]

In the case of children, the levels and nature of poverty tolerated in so rich a country are nothing short of extraordinary. As Alon Ben-Meir, senior fellow at the Center for Global Affairs at NYU, wrote in a 2017 *Huffington Post* article entitled: 'Child Poverty in America is Indefensible':[66]

> The state of poverty in the United States, particularly among children, is abhorrent and scandalous, putting America, the richest and most powerful country in the world, in a shameful light. Black and Hispanic children are disproportionately suffering from poverty – one in three and one in four respectively. Successive

American administrations are guilty of outrageous negligence toward poor children and have inflicted incalculable damage to millions who continue to suffer, causing a tremendous loss of human resources and productivity to the country. There is no part of the country that does not experience intense poverty from which children suffer the most.

As Ben-Meir also points out, this is not an aberration. This 'heart-wrenching' set of conditions is down to a system that creates it, fails to mitigate it and fosters a climate in which it is tolerated. All of this, as we'll see in subsequent chapters of this book – and as Ben-Meir recognises – is buttressed by an entrenched and dominant poverty narrative.

Citing the attacks on the safety net by the Trump administration straight off the bat in the administration's first budget (which saw even worse to come later)[67] that would directly impact children, Ben-Meir continues:

The most saddening truth of the situation is that these children were *born* into a mentally, emotionally, and physically oppressive system. These Americans are unable to rely on the support of any community, as they are often assigned a stigma by those more privileged and must hide what little they *do* have from others who are equally desperate and hungry. For them, the American dream is a living nightmare which is heightened by Trump's ill-conceived budget.

And, talking of budgets, two years after Ben-Meir offered these words of warning, the budget proposed by Trump in February 2019 contained a veritable profusion of cruel cuts that would, if introduced, directly harm poorer children and their families by making it even more difficult to receive essential assistance. White House budgets are proposals, as John Cassidy succinctly put it in *The New Yorker*, 'extended wish lists, which the spending authorities on Capitol Hill often set aside, especially when the government is divided',[68] but as he also underscored, the signals they send about policy priorities are critical.

The 2019 budget proposal spoke volumes about who was under attack in Trump's America: the very poorest. Never mind that he had pledged on the campaign trail to not cut Medicaid or Medicare.[69] On the table was an unprecedented slashing of the very things he said he would protect, including Medicaid and Medicare programmes, while also wiping billions from federal housing subsidies and foodstamps, and pushing for another ratcheting up of 'work-requirements' for recipients and squeezing of eligibility criteria. And, these were being mooted while huge spending increases were proposed for, among other things, the military. People with disabilities meanwhile were in the firing line on multiple fronts, with a raft of agencies that served Americans with disabilities set for a slew of cuts by 2020 that would, if implemented, leave a huge hole in the resources needed to assist with, for example, job-seeking, independent living and assistive technology programmes.[70]

The budget was roundly lambasted for its scope and mendacity. Bernie Sanders, a member on the Senate budget committee and who had recently thrown his hat in the ring to run for president in 2020, said:

> "The Trump budget is breathtaking in its degree of cruelty and filled with broken promises. This is a budget for the military industrial complex, for corporate CEOs, for Wall Street and for the billionaire class. It is dead on arrival."

The 2019 Trump budget was not so much hammer-to-crack-a-nut but more bulldozer. As Stacy Dean, president for food assistance at the Center on Budget and Policy Priorities, put it to *The Washington Post*: "This budget proposes taking away food assistance from millions of low-income Americans – and on the heels of a tax cut that favored the wealthy and corporations. It doesn't reflect the right values."[71]

In the summer of 2019 something happened that suggested a disturbing contempt for the poor. When the President announced that it should be tougher for immigrants who might access benefit programmes to get into the country, acting director of US Citizenship and Immigration Services, Ken Cuccinelli, proposed a new interpretation of one of the most famous pieces of writing associated with America. Apparently, he suggested in media interviews, the line 'Give me your tired, your poor, your huddled masses yearning to breathe free', which adorns the Statue of Liberty should be changed. What to? To this: '... and your poor who can stand on their own two feet and who will not become a public charge...'

Cuccinelli faced a swift blowback – as did Trump's recently announced decision to make it harder for less well-off immigrants to apply for a Green Card and which Cuccinelli was doing media interviews to defend. However, for all the protestations, this contentious deployment of a favourite metaphor from the poverty narrative playbook, 'stand on your own two feet', was yet another highly visible example of the narrative in action.

The special case of healthcare

In his recommendations at the end of the UN report Alston wrote something that many in America who rage against what tends to be framed as 'socialised medicine' would be inclined to balk at.[72] He said that the *right* to healthcare should be recognised, stressing that 'the civil and political rights of the middle class and the poor are fundamentally undermined if they are unable to function effectively, which includes working, because of a lack of access to healthcare that every human being needs'. In the context of the gigantic cuts proposed by Trump, the analysis took on even more prescience. Healthcare should be regarded as a human right, Alston concluded.

Healthcare provision – and attitudes towards it – is a glaring difference between the UK and the US. That Britain's safety net has been rooted in a philosophy that healthcare is available to all – regardless of employment or financial status – lies in stark contrast to the US's enduring (and expensive) attachment to avoiding this very thing. Even in my own childhood, where poverty was all around me, I and others in the same position had the right to access the National Health Service (NHS) for medical problems and emergencies, including dental and eye care. The same goes for today. When I or my family are ill, that illness is the primary worry – not whether we can afford to have it treated. Every time I speak to someone who is battling to stay afloat in the US when a loved one is ill and the bills are drowning them, it still shocks me that this is somehow a system that is tolerated.

Even at a time when the NHS is facing huge financial challenges, there are no 'co-pays', no 'deductibles', no demands to see insurance documents while your loved one is rushed to the emergency room, as there are in the US.[73] And accessing healthcare won't lead to bankruptcy.[74]

Talking to photographer and journalist Vince Wallace Junior for Project Twist-It, he said of the rhetoric around healthcare in the US:

> "What I hear from younger people especially is, for a long time the rhetoric has been, 'oh, you want public healthcare – that's socialism.' But at this point, all of these policies [that undermine welfare] are having such visible effects in people's lives that people are kind of saying, 'I guess I want socialism then'."

Conservative government failures to properly fund the NHS[75] (while acting as a cloak for partial US-style privatisation[76]), plus the fallout of cuts to social care that should help prevent health crises among the most vulnerable but can't do it without the resources, have taken a toll without doubt. Wait times at Accident and Emergency departments and for cancer treatments have got worse, for example,[77] while Brexit has produced a shortage of staff as EU workers leave.[78] But there remains widespread support for a health system accessible to all. It is the most vital kind of safety net for the poorest.[79]

In the US, by contrast – even with the existence of government programmes like Medicare[80] and Medicaid[81] that help support millions of Americans who need health and other assistance, and despite the introduction of an extension to health insurance ushered in by the Affordable Care Act under President Obama[82] (as Alston correctly points out) – there are still millions of uninsured Americans.[83] Getting sick, in addition to often being a side effect of poverty, can propel people who were otherwise getting by into destitution almost overnight.[84] There are even hospitals that actively sue poorer people who can't pay their bills.[85]

Healthcare has (to the bafflement of people in other rich nations) been a political lightning rod[86] in America for decades – and one that has a major bearing on poverty. The very fact that politicians would actively work to undo the landmark shift towards wider access under Obama – one of the most notable attempts being to reverse progress on access for people with pre-existing conditions[87] – would mystify many outside the US. It advertises their lack of concern for citizens who can't otherwise afford (increasingly expensive) insurance.

As Alston observed: "The Affordable Care Act was a good start, although it was limited and flawed from the outset." Referring to the multiple efforts by Republicans to undo the progress, he went on: "Undermining it by stealth is not just inhumane and a violation of human rights, but an economically and socially destructive policy aimed at the poor and the middle class."

Interplay between healthcare and poverty

Some of the key data on healthcare access, costs and outcomes in the US illustrate the significance of the interplay between healthcare and poverty – and risk of poverty. For example:

- According to the Center for Disease Control (CDC) 2017 National Health Interview Survey, **28.9 million** people under the age of 65 had no health insurance even after the Affordable Care Act had been rolled out. That's **10.7%** of the under-65 population.[88]

- In 2017, US healthcare costs were $3.9 trillion and accounted for an incredible **17.9% of GDP**. Americans pay far more for healthcare than their equivalents in other developed nations[89] and costs have risen faster than in other countries[90] (yet the US system performs much worse on many measures of health). Infant mortality in the US[91] is extraordinarily high for such a rich country.

- Bankruptcies as a result of unforeseen or larger medical bills affect hundreds of thousands of Americans annually.[92] Medical debt is the number one cause of personal bankruptcy filings, with an estimated **40%** of Americans taking on debt because of medical issues.[93]

- While there had been a steady fall in the number of uninsured children (helped in recent years by the Affordable Care Act and the expansion of provision through Medicaid and CHIP (Children's Health Insurance Programme) which together cover nearly four in ten American kids – 39%), under Trump the figure rose for the first time in a decade.[94] According to one Georgetown study published in late 2018, the number of kids without insurance rose by 275,000 in 2017 – up from 4.7% to 5% of children on the previous year. A report published in October 2019 from the Georgetown University Center for Children and Families estimated, after analysing Census Bureau data, that the numbers of uninsured children had ballooned between 2016 and 2018 with in the region of 400,000 new youngsters added to the list. Around **4.1 million** children were uninsured in 2018, up from a low of 3.6 million in 2016, according to the research.[95]

Any reduction in coverage from programmes like Medicaid and CHIP – which has been sought by Republicans in numerous guises – would affect the poorest children most.[96] Approximately two thirds of children from low-income families (66 per cent) and 76 per cent of children in poor families get healthcare through just these two programmes.[97]

The 'special relationship'

While healthcare is a pronounced difference between America and Britain, the two countries share considerable similarities in their approach to poverty and their depictions of the poor – especially since 2010 when Conservatives in the UK were cutting vital programmes by attacking the social safety net and sought to emulate the US conservatives' preference for punitive approaches to social assistance from government programmes, including making it harder to qualify and expecting charities and churches to pick up the pieces.

These shared ideas, selling welfare 'reforms' as reducing the supposed 'dependency' of the poorest on the state, are promoted by a narrative that labels the poor as 'undeserving' of help. Sometimes, as austerity in the UK illustrated all too clearly,[98] cuts have been cleverly framed and sold as 'necessary' to reduce deficits (they weren't and they didn't).

On this fundamental aspect of poverty Alston was, to use an apposite euphemism, right on the money. He concluded that, in the US and the UK, the persistence of extreme poverty: "is a political choice made by those in power".

In order for high levels of poverty to endure in wealthy nations like Britain and America, it has to be a choice. In order to preserve the incredible redistribution of income and wealth over the past half-century from the bottom up, protecting the interests of those who benefit from it – the top 1 per cent (or as Danny Dorling has pointed out, the top 1 per cent of the 1 per cent) – another group has to lose out. The (shrinking) middle class have not been unscathed, of course, but they still wield a modicum of influence in that they vote in higher numbers. No, it is those least able to exercise any power who must take the hit as billionaires multiply and corporations garner yet more tax breaks.

The poverty narrative, especially in recent years, has had to do some seriously heavy lifting. Something has to be at play to present this appalling situation as if it's acceptable, or at the very least, tolerable, or even inevitable.

A prevailing, powerful narrative that blames the poor for their misfortune, shames them for being poor, and which distorts and distracts from the structural causes of poverty and the actions required to overcome it is exactly what's at play.

To differing degrees, the wilful blaming and shaming of the poor occurs across cultures, countries and time,[99] but there is considerable evidence that it has become hyper-normalised in America and Britain. The demonisation of the least well off by politics, the media and wider culture as undeserving, lazy and personally culpable for their poverty – in contrast with an adulation of wealth (including inherited wealth) and consumerism – compounds people's misery. It affects how poorer people see themselves and how others see them.

None of this is inevitable. Neither poverty nor the distorted story we are fed about the people who experience it should be acceptable. There are solutions – even for entrenched poverty[100] and high rates of child poverty.[101] There are ways to challenge the toxic poverty narrative. There *are* answers to the question: 'What can we do about it?'

I was not poor as a child in inner-city Belfast because I had done something 'wrong'. Christine Riccione was not poor and living on the streets of Charleston because she enjoyed working minimum-wage jobs with zero employment security and couldn't care less if she lost her home. The people in desperate need swallowing their pride to turn up on the doorsteps of foodbanks in the fifth richest nation on earth or relying on foodstamps in the richest nation are not doing so because they are flawed, failed people.

To win the battle against the very real, destructive poverty that surrounds us we must first win the war of words. To win that, we need to communicate the truth about poverty in a way that the public can understand and relate to. We need to know what exactly the toxic poverty narrative is, how it functions and what (and who) sustains it. Only then can we learn how to fight it.

As Reverend Barber told me in Culver City:

> **"**We have to shift the narrative. But you can't do that without shifting the narrators.**"**

II

Turning the screw on poor people: shame, stigma and the cementing of a toxic poverty narrative

"Throughout history, philosophers and political figures have sought to distinguish between the deserving and the undeserving poor; or, to put it another way, between those whose poverty is caused by outside forces and thus merits society's sympathy and those whose poverty is the result of poor life decisions, or communal dysfunction and thus merits our scorn."

Sasha Abramsky, in *The American Way of Poverty*

Shop till you drop

FRIDAY

Peter came every Friday night to our new council house. Like clockwork. At six o'clock when the knock on the door came, the living room atmosphere would take on a sudden air of anxiety. Without waiting for anyone to answer the knock, Peter made his way down the hallway and hovered at the living room door while he retrieved a small black notebook from his pocket and a fancy fountain pen he kept clipped to his jacket lapel. He was well groomed, clean-shaven, with a heavy head of thick rusty-coloured hair carefully combed in a side parting. He was tall and wore a suit and tie and white shirt. In winter he wore a beige mac on top.

We moved out of our slum property and into a new council house when I was seven and a half years old. A slum clearance and rehousing programme saw to it that we had a brand-new house with a spacious kitchen, four bedrooms and a small front and back garden. We had our first indoor toilet and a bathroom. Rent levels were controlled by local government agencies. There were no rats. It smelled of freshly cut wood. We still didn't own a fridge, but that house felt like a precious piece of possibility.

"Hiya Peter. How are ya doin'?" one of my parents would ask with a flustered obsequiousness reserved only for Peter, usually after he'd been hovering for an awkward minute or two. He'd reply with some vague small talk about the weather and everyone would agree it was miserable. Clinging to the banknotes in her hand as if willing him not to take them from her, my mum would chat for an uncomfortably extended length of time.

Peter came to our house on the day the dole money arrived. And by the time he left he'd taken most of it with him. We didn't know his surname. We only knew that he would lend money to people with no bank account and that the total amount owed after interest was so far in excess of what was borrowed that it was never – ever – paid off. Most of what he loaned us was for Christmas or emergencies. We had nowhere else to turn for that kind of money.

I hated Friday nights. I hated watching my parents kowtow to this man we didn't know who took what little money we had away from us. I hated Peter and his sinister civility. I hated him because the next day was the main grocery shopping day and there was never enough for what we actually needed. It was my responsibility to make the money stretch as far as possible.

At 9am every Saturday from the age of 11, I left for the supermarket with £20 in my pocket. This £20, equivalent to around £100 in 2019,[1] had to get the family – all nine of us – through to Tuesday when the 'Family Allowance', a weekly child benefit, arrived.[2] Each week I would repeat my ritual walk up and down the aisles and then go to the checkout. If it was the owner on the till, he would look at me with undisguised disdain. After paying for the shopping, I packed the items into a box and paid 50 pence so that it was delivered to our door. From time to time a friend would come with me and we'd pocket the 50 pence and carry the heavy shopping bags for the mile home.

SATURDAY

Grocery list
2 loaves of (local) bread
1 packet of (local) Irish Soda Bread
1 packet of (local) Irish Potato Bread
2 tomatoes
2 small chickens or a pound of minced meat for Sunday dinner
1 box (Tetley) tea bags
1 bag of vegetables for Sunday dinner (range: Brussels sprouts/ cauliflower)
1 bag of potatoes for Sunday and Monday dinner
2 large cans of (Heinz) beans
2 large cans of (Bigga) peas
2 large cans of (Heinz) spaghetti
1 2lb bag of sugar
1 bottle of (Saxa) salt
2lb of (Kerrygold) butter
1 block of (any kind of) lard
1 large box of (Kellogg's) cornflakes
1 large box of (Quaker) sugar puffs
2 jars of (Hartley's) jam
1 bottle of (Heinz) ketchup

1 bottle of (HP) brown sauce
1 packet of (Bisto) gravy or Oxo cubes
1 bottle of (Fairy) washing-up liquid
1 bottle of (Harpic) bleach
1 bottle of Dettol (disinfectant)
1 bar of (Fresh) soap
1 bottle of bubble bath
8 slices of streaky bacon
6 sausages
12 eggs
1 large packet of (McVitie's) chocolate digestives
1 packet of (Club) fruit or orange biscuits (substitute Taxis or
    Breakaways)
1 packet of Garibaldi biscuits (or equivalent)

The list was identical each week with some allowance for special occasions and in the summer months when we needed extra bread and soup for lunches in the absence of school dinners. Milk was delivered courtesy of the milkman on a daily basis. For two months in the run-up to Christmas I would be dispatched with £2 extra each week to put 'on account' at the butcher to cover 'extras' including the turkey. The brand names were important to my family. To buy non-branded products was seen as advertising your poverty. So, rather than make the limited cash go a little bit further with 'own' brands, to save face the more expensive equivalents were deemed 'essentials'. Also, branded biscuits were a sacrosanct indulgence – like sticking two fingers up to poverty.

TUESDAY

When we left for school of a Tuesday morning there was usually nothing left in the cupboard to eat. BUT – when we got back from school after the Family Allowance had been collected from the Post Office we were in for a treat. First, some cakes from the local bakery would be gobbled down the minute any of us kids entered the house after school. Second, dinner came from the local chip shop. Everyone got a bag of chips. My dad would get two sausages because he didn't like chips. As always, I was the designated shopper and at 4.30pm I would stand in line at Fusco's chippie. Albert, a jovial Irish Italian and the brother of the owner, greeted me with a warm smile and as he handed over the family's many bags of chips gave me a separate package. My own chips came with free curry sauce. "There ya go, Maureen," – my Irish name – Albert would say, without a hint of pity. "Good job."

THURSDAY

The Family Allowance money was gone. Our neighbour Margaret bought jam, bread and a few other essentials, out of her own pocket. She and her husband didn't make much money (Margaret was a home helper for older people and Eddie worked in the public toilets at the local park) but she also paid for our family's dinner each Thursday. Sometimes I went to the shops with her – "You're like my shadow," she told me each week as if it were the very first time she'd said it. She would buy the extras I needed for school or for the plays and musicals I was in too. I don't know what we, or I, would have done without her.

3

A twisted tale: evolution of the poverty narrative

"It is almost certainly the case that more is known about how much poverty there is than about what it means to be poor."
Robert Walker, *The Shame of Poverty*, p 31

"There are folks who fall out of ... their stable lives into poverty and can't handle it. You know, because of the narrative that what you get, that it's your fault."
Sheilah Garland-Olaniran, community advocate, Chicago Poor People's Campaign, talking to Project Twist-It

The games we play: targeting the poor and most vulnerable

In the 1980s the British satirical TV show *Spitting Image*, in which puppets resembling the biggest political and cultural figures of the day poked fun at their real-life counterparts, there was a regular segment called: 'The President's Brain is Missing'. Each time the segment appeared, a presidential lackey would rummage around desperately trying to find the puppet president's brain (roughly the size of a walnut) in time to prevent Puppet Ronald Reagan doing something socially good. In Episode 2 of the first series in 1984[1] (after the brainless president uncharacteristically called for cooperation with the Russians on nuclear disarmament) this is what happened:

Lackey: Delves under the bedclothes in an attempt to locate the tiny brain.

Puppet President Reagan: Sitting up in bed looking dopey declares: "Together with our Soviet allies we must fight poverty and injustice ... We must all, Americans and Soviets, reach out our hands to poor people everywhere. And, when they reach forward to grasp our hands, we must..."

Lackey: Finds and hastily reinserts the brain, exclaiming: "Back to normal!"

Puppet President Reagan: Continues: "... knee 'em in the nuts. Yes, my friends, God gave us poor people for only two reasons:

1. To work all week for practically nothing.
2. To give us something to laugh at on Sundays."

Poverty, as one of the many people I interviewed for Project Twist-It succinctly put it, "stinks". Poverty is a desperate, humiliating, degrading, gruelling position to find yourself in. Poverty is not noble. Poverty is not, as some would have us believe, a 'pathology', a sickness or about being 'dumb'.[2] Poverty is trying to walk up an escalator that's racing down. Poverty is attempting to stay afloat in a boat full of holes when someone has taken away your oars and shouts at you from the security of a distant shore to paddle a bit harder.

No matter that you are a child, are ill, or have a serious disability. No matter if you fall on hard times because an employer who was already paying you next to nothing for working your fingers to the bone lays you off at a moment's notice leaving you with bills you can't pay and rent you can't make. No matter that the welfare benefits you once relied on to plug the gap in your meagre earnings have been cut or capped. No matter that you've been sanctioned and fined because the government's new system of benefits requires you to fill in impenetrable forms online when you have no access to a computer and the local library, where you used to be able to use a computer for free, has shut because of government cutbacks.

No matter that no amount of frantic, pointless paddling on your own is going to keep you from sinking.

You see, according to what we are told in Britain and America about the poorest among us – and especially those who deign to seek help from the state in the form of welfare assistance or other support – you alone are to blame. And, because you alone are to blame, you will be publicly shamed.

The dominant poverty narrative in Britain and America as it currently stands is a two-pronged beast. When stripped down it is, in essence, **this**:

THE DOMINANT POVERTY NARRATIVE (UK AND US)	
The poor are to blame for their own predicament because of bad life choices and if only they would take some 'personal responsibility', show some 'self-reliance', stop expecting government to support them, and work hard like everyone else they would be 'productive' members of society who contributed their 'fair share'.	The well off and wealthy are so because of their own hard work, talents, skills and determination and they should be admired and respected for it.

On the right side, the narrative is anchored in a tantalising proposition (that is also central to the 'American Dream'[3]): 'You too could be rich if only...!' But, on the left side, it is predominantly a cautionary tale: 'If you don't pull those bootstraps up you will be doomed to a life of penury, and it's entirely your own fault for being lazy!'

This framing of poverty sustains a misguided commitment to a belief in meritocracy[4] and opportunity for all, yet all the while contributing to keeping poorer people down. It reduces empathy for their predicament by solely equating human worth with work, conspicuous consumption and the accumulation of wealth. It provides cover for those with power to systematically pillory people who are struggling and – crucially – offers convenient justification for policies and practices predicated on a notion of 'individual responsibility = worthy and empowering' that are, in reality, barriers to betterment.

The poverty narrative is a form of bullying. It is used as a means to 'punch down', to humiliate and to cower people who are vulnerable or regarded as unable to fight back.

According to the poverty narrative's nakedly reductive worldview of the poorest, but especially of those who are regarded as 'undeserving' for relying on government assistance at some point, you are a 'skiver' rather than a 'striver'; 'feckless' as opposed to 'productive'; a 'burden' instead of an 'asset'. You are a 'taker' rather than a 'maker'.[5] The role of the state is not to help you when you are down; it is to kick you out of your supposed 'entitled' complacency.

The satirical vignette from 1984 at the top of this chapter perfectly encapsulates a toxic orthodoxy of attitudes towards the poorest people in British and American society.

The poverty narrative with its malignant, reinforcing stereotypes[6] and ritualistic rhetoric, this spin, this fabricated distortion is so confoundingly effective in its finger-pointing framing, simplicity, determined dissemination, and daunting assimilation within the culture, that it's as if it has seeped through the collective consciousness. This story, deployed with disarming deftness and frequency in a relentless shame game by politicians and the media alike, is enabled by a Pick-n-Mix of prevalent and corrosive representations and stereotypes about people in poverty – thematic micro-myths recycled in political and wider discourse that have ensured its power and endurance.

In no particular order here are some of the common stereotypes.

POVERTY STEREOTYPES

- It's your own fault if you are poor – due to your moral or personal failings.

- You are lazy and most likely stupid and inarticulate too.

- You actively fail to take personal responsibility.

- You are unemployed/under-employed/unemployable by choice.

- You lack ambition and drive.

- You are living the life of Riley while others go out to work and pay taxes.

- You are a drain on tax revenues because you claim (particular) types of state assistance.

- If you receive welfare benefits you are also likely to be defrauding the system.

- You don't care about the well-being of your children.

- You've probably got 'too many' children.

- You actively choose to eat bad-quality food, have rotten teeth and wear cheap clothes.

- You are going to get sick and become more of a drain due to your unsavoury 'lifestyle choices'.

- You are most likely a person of colour.

- You are probably part of a family of multi-generational poverty and are also part of something called a 'culture of welfare dependency'.

- You are highly likely to be a single mum (who got pregnant deliberately to get benefits/public housing).

- You are a criminal/potential criminal, violent – or both.[7]

- You are mentally deficient/an addict – or both.

- You attract disparaging and pejorative labels because they are an accurate reflection of who and what you are: inferior. These pejorative labels might include (depending on the time, place and how the cultural winds that popularise them are blowing), but are not limited to:

  - scrounger
  - chav
  - welfare queen
  - entitled
  - dependent
  - sponger
  - benefits cheat
  - underclass

  - idle
  - workshy
  - indolent
  - workless
  - skiver
  - grifter
  - failure
  - feral

- There may be a few of you who are 'deserving' because you go out to work at a minimum wage job/s (although don't get too excited because it's still despicable that you sometimes get help from the state to subsidise your paltry wages rather than just suck it up).

- Mostly you're an 'undeserving', lumpen, homogenous mass of layabout riff-raff who prefer daily humiliation to dignity and respect.

The dominant narrative about poverty is the mirror image of the dominant narrative justifying great wealth. If I were to summarize it on a bumper sticker it would be: People are (economically) where they deserve to be.
Chuck Collins, author and activist

Take a brief moment away from this book and type this short phrase into Google: 'things poor people do'.

Done it?

Good. Unless something very odd has happened in the world since I was writing this, what you'll find is a selection of unedifying links to pieces espousing what great decision makers rich people are compared to poorer people. Grist for the mill of the poverty narrative and available online to anyone who buys into the dominant poverty stereotypes.

For example, this one:[8]

MORE POVERTY STEREOTYPES

Poor people:

- Always see the problem ahead, never the solution

- Often have a lot of advice, but never any experience to share

- Spend money that they don't have

- Focus on what they can buy, not how great they can be

- Are excited about work–life balance, not work

- Always have a story or excuse why they haven't made it yet

- Have great ideas but do nothing about them other than talk about them

- Surround themselves with stupid so that they don't feel bad

- Believe that others should help them reach the top

- Ask for feedback but never listen.

This sort of ready-made, casual castigation comes in video and text formats, taking full advantage of the online world's special capacity for identifying new nadirs of human behaviour. It is just one of many ways the culture has adapted to upholding and reinforcing the toxic poverty narrative.

As with other murky corners of the internet, trolls love to have a pop at poorer people who dare to open up about their circumstances.

TYPICAL SOCIAL MEDIA EXCHANGE

Troll
||||||||||

You are fat because you eat too much. You are broke because you spend too much and don't earn enough. You are weak because you don't challenge yourself. You are lower energy because you don't move. You're tired because you don't sleep. Your life is your fault.

Response from a disabled person
||||||||||||||||||||||||||||||||||||||||||||||||||||||||||||||||||||||||||||||||

My weight is determined by how much food my PTSD will let me eat. I am poor because I made about $10,000 last year and have thousands in out-of-pocket medical expenses. I'm not fit because I don't have enough money to keep my body uninjured. I'm tired because of PTSD & insomnia.

There are any number of ways that these various stereotypes are crystalised in the culture as a 'poverty narrative' – the prevailing story of who and what the poor are – but the American scholar, anti-poverty activist and co-editor of Inequality.Org,[9] Chuck Collins, offers one of the best distillations, which, while focused on the US,[10] hits the nail firmly on the head for the UK as well.

Collins writes:[11]

> The dominant narrative about poverty is the mirror image of the dominant narrative justifying great wealth. If I were to summarize it on a bumper sticker it would be, 'People are (economically) where they deserve to be.' In other words, people possess wealth because they work hard, take risks, have greater creativity and intelligence – they have greater

virtues such as grit, etc. And the shadow corollary to that story: people are poor because of individual deficiencies.

He continues:

> Of course, there are individual differences in effort, skills, etc. And these might account for differentials in rewards. But such relatively minor differences should not be deployed to explain deep and systemic inequalities. The narrative of individual 'deservedness' has the effect of taking big systemic causes and individualizing them or personalizing them. The implication is, therefore, to fix poverty we must 'fix the individual' or fix the 'delivery mechanism' of access to education services. Without these simplistic narratives, we would have to address the underlying systemic roots of inequality, including historical barriers to ownership, wealth, land.

My own understanding that there was a powerful, erroneous narrative – one that frames poverty and the poor in a negative light in order to shore up policies that benefit the rich at the poor's expense – goes back to my late teens, and I have been observing it ever since.

In 1987, when I turned 17, my father had been out of work for almost a decade. There were serious health issues in the family that contributed to his lack of employment. And, times were tough. Unemployment in Northern Ireland was among the worst in Europe and far higher than in the rest of the UK.[12] Putting it bluntly, there is no way we would have been able to get by without state assistance, including unemployment and child benefits, public housing (by this time we were living in our new council house), free school meals, and free healthcare through the NHS. As an almost-adult in 1987, certain material realities of poverty were coming sharply into focus. I couldn't go on school trips unless they were day trips and local, for example, while I relied on a family friend to buy me some of the essentials I needed for school and a second pair of shoes. However, what struck me specifically around this time, especially as a student of politics and sociology, was *the way* people from my background were being painted by politicians.

I had been studying British and American politics for three years when something hit with lightning-force: it wasn't merely the case that poverty was as hard as hell or that it was embarrassing to admit or talk about on a personal level, I became aware that powerful people were painting the poorest in society – people like us – as a form of parasite feeding off the supposedly hard-earned wealth of others. In this framing, someone like my father, who had worked for many years on building sites, was skilled, and had paid his fair share of taxes, the moment he became unemployed somehow magically morphed into a welfare freeloader. That unemployment was through the roof, that there were family health issues that could not be sidestepped, had absolutely nothing to do with his situation apparently.

It's all about the money, money, money: there's no such thing as society

In 1987, Margaret Thatcher made a statement that defined the era. "There is no such thing as society," she declared in an interview with the weekly lifestyle magazine *Woman's Own*.[13] The statement would come to be emblematic of Thatcher's political mission to shrink the state generally[14] and her wish to dismantle the UK's Welfare State by undermining vital supports for the poorest that had been a foundation of the country's post-Second World War rebuilding and political consensus.[15] This was a legacy that would be wholeheartedly embraced by the Conservative-led governments from 2010 to well into 2019 under austerity – arguably doing more damage than Thatcher ever did.[16]

Dr Heejung Chung of the University of Kent in England, who studies benefits systems internationally and was interviewed for Project Twist-It,[17] points out that the groundwork laid by Reagan and Thatcher helped to reshape thinking about poverty and welfare. There is a long history of denigrating the poor – for example, the notion of a 'deserving' versus 'underserving' poor has deep historical roots in many countries – but the ferocity of the recent narrative in the UK and the US owes much of its lasting impact to the 1980s. During the Reagan and Thatcher era a desire to "dismantle the welfare state and benefits systems" became a focal point, Chung says, sending a clear-as-day signal that being a citizen no longer meant you were eligible for some state help when times were tough. Instead, "you don't have the right to a decent living. You have to show that you're going to be working for it."

Thatcher's 1987 statement cemented a political mission[18] to champion individualism over social solidarity,[19] advocate slashing taxes for the rich, privatise public assets, choke the supply of affordable council housing, promote unfettered wealth accumulation over equitable distribution and deregulate the financial system.[20] These were all objectives that had been bubbling for the previous few decades[21] and were upending the post-war collectivism that had birthed an unparalleled era of wealth and income redistribution and equality in the UK and the US.[22] They were the turbo-charged engine of the structural inequalities that thrust millions of people into poverty – including the working poor. They were also objectives that would rely on a potent narrative – a creed – to uphold them.

As the writer and activist George Monbiot would later succinctly explain in *The Guardian* in 2016,[23] the core doctrine to which Thatcher and Reagan were tethered went like this:

> Attempts to limit competition are treated as inimical to liberty. Tax and regulation should be minimised, public services should be privatised. The organisation of labour and collective bargaining by trade unions are portrayed as market distortions that impede the formation of a natural hierarchy of winners and losers. Inequality is recast as virtuous: a reward for utility and a generator of wealth, which trickles down to enrich everyone. Efforts to create a more equal society are both counterproductive and morally corrosive. The market ensures that everyone gets what they deserve.

And, he goes on:

> We internalise and reproduce its creeds. The rich persuade themselves[24] that they acquired their wealth through merit, ignoring the advantages – such as education, inheritance and class – that may have helped to secure it. The poor begin to blame themselves for their failures, even when they can do little to change their circumstances.

"I think we have gone through a period when too many children and people have been given to understand: "I have a problem, it is the government's job to cope with it. I am homeless, the government will house me," and so they are casting their problems on society."
Former UK Conservative Prime Minister, Margaret Thatcher

I observed how Thatcher espoused her philosophy in tandem with President Ronald Reagan's drive for rolling back the state, reducing banking regulation, and undermining unions in the US (and which would become a major factor in the conditions that precipitated the 2008 financial crisis three decades later, along with some deregulatory help from Bill Clinton,[25] further propelling inequality).[26] Thatcher's 'No Such Thing as Society' statement crowned a career that first made inroads into the public consciousness years before she became Prime Minister by (literally) taking milk from the mouths of babes. As Secretary of State for Education she was decried as 'Thatcher, Thatcher, Milk Snatcher' by the Labour Opposition for presiding over the Department of Education during the removal of a popular anti-poverty nutritional programme – free school milk for 7- to 11-year-olds.

Almost a decade later Thatcher told her *Woman's Own* interviewer:

> "I think we have gone through a period when too many children and people have been given to understand: 'I have a problem, it is the government's job to cope with it. I am homeless, the government

will house me,' and so they are casting their problems on society."

In her customary supercilious fashion, she told the interviewer: "… people have got the entitlements too much in mind without the obligations …" A system that was supposed to help the "unfortunate" somehow, she argued, had instead become something people were "manipulating" for personal gain.

It was a mantra that would be picked up and regurgitated with terrifying effectiveness as austerity took hold after 2010.[27]

Set aside for a moment that the evidence clearly shows that defrauding the benefits system (then and now) is miniscule in reality.[28] Set aside also the absurdity of suggesting that children possess a level of political sophistication that translates to understanding 'the State' to be a kind of social saviour, Thatcher's supposition was an explicit pronouncement that people in receipt of government assistance – people like me, my family and friends – were defined by a number of unacceptable, if not repellent, characteristics. According to Thatcher and her ilk, we were undeserving, entitled, a drain, swindlers. By implication, people like us needed to be reminded in no uncertain terms that the jig was up and we'd be told to change our 'pov-like' ways.

While this tale of supposed wanton irresponsibility and rapacity by the poorest was cavalierly pushed across the culture, pundits and politicians were simultaneously proselytising about greed and conspicuous consumption as laudable attributes that were the barometer for individual 'success'. Just as my eyes were being opened to the poverty narrative in political discourse, the broader cultural backdrop of 1987 was dispatching clear signals of where we were headed in the 1990s and beyond. Images of swaggering City Bankers in London with gigantic mobile phones and fat cigars quaffing champagne from bottles were ubiquitous, while something called 'Yuppies'[29] had emerged, who were 'gentrifying' working-class areas – pushing up house prices and forcing locals out. In the same year the bestselling book *Bonfire of the Vanities*, with its 'Master of the Universe'[30] moneyed Manhattan protagonist, and the box office hit movie *Wall Street*[31] (Gordon – 'Greed is Good' – Gekko) were embellishing the Thatcher/Reagan era as one of worshipping excessive wealth while those at the bottom were being hung out to dry. Investment bankers on six-figure salaries were even reporting anxiety that they weren't making enough cash.[32]

I can say this as someone who for years each week saw the look of barely suppressed anguish on my father's face as he walked the mile to the dole office to 'sign on' (he absolutely always wore his Sunday Best and polished his shoes to make that trip with at least some semblance of dignity): far from revelling in 'handouts' from the state (as the right-wing press in particular love to characterise it[33]), signing on for assistance is an obligatory and ritualistic humiliation – and this is even more the case today as eligibility criteria have been severely tightened or restricted.

For me, every day of my teenage years involved at least one micro reminder of our breadline status. As with many poorer people, if you'd asked any of us if we were poor we would have said 'no'. Any word but *poor*. Yet for much of the time, no matter what we called it, it was our reality. Something as mundane as putting a penny in the charity collection every morning at school was a source of abject mortification. I never had the penny. At secondary school when it was break time I never had any money to spend on a snack from the 'tuck shop' and, even though I wasn't the only one in a school that drew its pupils from one of the most deprived areas of Europe, I felt embarrassed. However, whenever as a young teenager I passed the dole office with my youngest brother, a toddler, it was with a particular kind of shame. As we went past, he'd lift his hand and point at the grey building and say: "Look! There's my daddy's Bru."[34] If people heard, I would hang my head and rush along.

"I think that you cannot really have a discussion about poverty in this country without talking about racism. Because in this country, poverty is tantamount to being black, and if you're poor, you're black. Poverty impacts us all."
Sheilah Garland-Olaniran, community activist, Chicago, 2018

'Welfare queens': fabricating myths to suit the narrative

If people like my father were the butt of ridicule, women were specifically targeted as objects of scorn. You couldn't swing a cat when I was a teenager without witnessing a parade of morally loaded judgements being lobbed at single mothers. A favourite trope touted repeatedly in the UK was that if you were a single mother you were so by choice; you were a one-dimensional, morally irresponsible sponger who got pregnant (early) to get a council house/flat.[35] At the same time, if you were a single mother in the US you were a morally irresponsible black woman living off 'welfare' and splurging your great fortune on luxuries and travel.[36] The single mother, especially if young or teenage, was a totem, a proxy, for all that was supposedly dysfunctional[37] and burdensome about the impoverished.[38]

In the early 1980s in the UK, for example, the then Education Secretary, Sir Keith Joseph, suggested to the then Conservative Prime Minister, Margaret Thatcher, that young girls should be shown films to frighten them out of becoming pregnant.[39] Joseph's proposals might have been at the extreme end of the scale, but they were laden with the kind of pejorative assumptions that blamed and shamed, and it all came down to bad character. For example, he said: "the young concerned tend to be ... from the least good homes". They "embark on parenthood casually" and those most at risk tend not to "restrain themselves". This from a politician whose speech eight years earlier warning that young single mums from the lower classes were a threat to "our human stock" had been received with such outrage that his career prospects were blighted.[40]

The political rhetoric has problematised lone parenthood.
Dr Miyang Jun, University of York, England

In tandem with the Thatcher era's framing[41] of single mothers as a moral problem to be strongly dealt with, it was clear to me that they were also regular fare for the British tabloids, with teenagers in particular being decried as promiscuous, irresponsible scroungers.[42] To varying degrees it continues today, including approbation for how much young single mums supposedly 'cost the state' in benefits, even as their numbers have fallen dramatically.[43]

In a 2015 paper examining the position of lone parents in Britain over recent decades, Dr Miyang Jun of the University of York in England offers a good summation:

> Over the last few decades, therefore, lone parenthood has been at the centre of the British political rhetoric. [Lone parents] have been conceptualised as a social threat that is associated with various social problems, including poverty, unemployment, child abuse/maltreatment, and low levels of health and education. The political rhetoric has problematised lone parenthood in (largely) two ways. Firstly, it has created a moral crisis, since lone parents are reported as actively choosing to be dependent on state benefits... This moralistic discourse links to underclass theories of poverty. The theory positions the poor as inhabiting a different and dangerous culture to the rest of society, and one which poses a moral threat to society and to itself, through the 'transmission' of poverty and immoral rationality down the generations.[44]

The media portrayal of single mums, and especially younger, poorer single mums, has since the 1980s at times taken on the aura of public spectacle. They are an easy target for ridicule, bullying and punching down, as all vulnerable groups tend to be.[45] In a 2017 paper[46] examining class tensions in the UK in relation to media and entertainment portrayals of young single mums, researcher Hetty Frampton from the School of Humanities and Cultural Industries at Bath Spa University in England pointed out that stigmatising this group has a long history. But, she argued, in recent years with the rising potency of the notion of a 'feckless underclass' and derogatory 'chav' terminology it has taken on fresh force. Frampton writes:

> These evident changes to our own phraseology and cultural disposition – and the ease with which

we tend to accept these alterations – indicate the inherent power which everyday discourses have upon the representation and construction of class in contemporary media formats, emphasised through social panic and anxiety.

She continues:

The intense preoccupation with class in society can be recognised in a range of contemporary media portrayals which deal with the issue of teenage pregnancy; these include reality television, film, documentary, comedy sketch-shows and investigative journalism. For instance, the plethora of BBC productions concerning young mothers and underage pregnancy are hard to ignore: from reality programmes such as *Young Mums' Mansion* (2008), to documentaries following teenage mothers-to-be in *Underage and Pregnant* (2009) and the girls who are feeling broody in *Pregnancy: My Big Decision* (2009), we are constantly confronted by the issue of teenage pregnancy in different media forms.

Indeed, the contempt with which single mothers from the working class were held by some came to the fore during the December 2019 UK General Election campaign. Prime Minister Boris Johnson, known for pejorative insults towards all kinds of groups, including Muslim women, was on the campaign trail when journalists dug out some of his more concerning columns from the time when he was a 'journalist' himself. Writing in *The Spectator* magazine in 1995, as voters were reminded, Johnson had declared single mothers to be 'uppity' and 'irresponsible' for getting pregnant. He had called working-class fathers 'feckless' and referred to children of single mums as 'ill-raised, ignorant, aggressive and illegitimate'. He opined that there was 'an appalling proliferation of single mothers'. Just in case all of this wasn't enough, he drummed his point home, arguing that 'cuts to the safety net' which could reduce women to 'destitution' on a Victorian scale might encourage them not to reproduce.[47]

A decade after *The Spectator*'s piece in 2006, just before he became mayor of London, he was at it again. In a series of essays (again dug up during the 2019 election campaign) he'd called the children of lower income working mothers 'unloved and undisciplined' and more likely to 'mug you on the street corner'.[48]

In the US, the story has been another version of the same demonisation. In an article in *The New York Times* in the autumn of 2018,[49] sociologists David Brady, Ryan M. Finnigan and Sabine Hubgen refer to how 'no group is as linked to poverty in the American mind as single mothers'. The authors, comparing the US with other rich nations, point out that first of all the proportion of households headed by a single mother was a small subset of those headed with working-age adults – 8.8 per cent – while a defining characteristic of policy in relation to this group is how they are treated compared to other, similar nations.

> What really differentiates rich democracies is the penalty attached to single motherhood. Our political choices result in families headed by single mothers being 14.3 per cent more likely to be poor than other families. Such a severe penalty is unusual. Common, knee-jerk reaction against generous social policies for single mothers is that they pose a moral hazard and encourage more single motherhood. The problem with this argument is that it is overwhelmingly contradicted by social science.

When it comes to teenage parenthood there has been a special level of shaming and stigmatising – especially for the girls involved (it is almost always the girls who contend with being vilified, not the boys/men). Some of this even happens within schools.[50] There was the North Carolina teen who was told her picture wouldn't appear in the high school yearbook because apparently having her son in it with her would promote teenage pregnancy. Then there were the two Michigan high schoolers banned from having their pregnant bellies in the yearbook pictures because it went against the school's 'abstinence' approach to sexual health, while in some instances pregnant teenagers have been banned from attending classes on campus.[51] Not all pregnant teens are living in poverty, but a large proportion are and, as Tara Culp-Ressler wrote in an article in 2013 for Think Progress titled: 'Too often teen mothers receive shame instead of support',[52] the wider structural factors at play, including access to robust sexual health education and other resources, are often conveniently ignored in favour of blaming and shaming.

Culp-Ressler writes:

> ... the situation in Michigan also illustrates the pervasive negativity that Americans associate with teenage pregnancies. That attitude ultimately creates an environment that punishes, stigmatizes and shames young mothers – many of whom are subject to much larger structural issues that are out of their control, like the type of sex education they received in school or the level of poverty they were born into.

The significance of 'the media' in transmitting the poverty narrative generally, including on lone parents, is not in doubt. As this report from the specialist journalism analysis outfit Nieman Lab at Harvard University concludes:[53]

> Thirty or so years of communications research shows that the media can influence what issues people pay attention to (their agenda-setting role). How the media highlight issues can lead readers and viewers to make judgments about politicians and policies (their so-called 'priming' role). And finally, it is clear that qualitative aspects of news reporting determine how people think about public problems and their remedies (their 'framing' role). In short, as we all recognize, news coverage influences public opinion.

In relation to the evolution of poverty and welfare policy in the US since the 1960s, the same report summarises research that concluded the myth of the welfare queen had 'assumed the status of common knowledge'. It says:

In the midst of this evolving political landscape on which new debates about welfare ensued, the news media played—and continues to play—a critical role in the public's understanding of what 'welfare' ought to be.

And, when the author of the report, Franklin D. Gilliam Jr, explains his findings on the 'narrative script' on the so-called 'welfare queen', he writes:

> The welfare queen script has two key components— welfare recipients are disproportionately women, and women on welfare are disproportionately African-American. What I discovered is that among white subjects, exposure to these script elements reduced support for various welfare programs, increased stereotyping of African-Americans, and heightened support for maintaining traditional gender roles.

Thatcher and Reagan, the political backdrop to some of my family's most challenging financial years, opened my eyes to the fact that poverty is a political choice. Policy – good and bad – affects change. Just as Margaret Thatcher presided over mass unemployment that swelled the lines at dole offices across the country and thrust families into poverty, a future New Labour government introduced policies and programmes that pulled many out of the poverty trap – including millions of pensioners and children.

Within the US political landscape during my teenagehood the overarching messages about wealth and poverty were in a similar 'them and us' vein to the UK, albeit with some distinctly American characteristics, including the discredited mantra of 'trickle down' economics,[54] where apparently if the rich paid less tax the benefits would filter down to everyone else's wallet via investment and jobs (spoiler – they didn't). In June 2019, Trump was widely rebuked for giving the presidential medal of freedom to the economist who advised Ronald Reagan on 'supply side economics' and trickle down in the 1980s.[55] Reagan, despite his reputation as a sunny optimist who injected some hope back into a country still rocked by ruptures like the Vietnam War, a corrupt Republican President and the economic upsets of the 1970s,[56] became synonymous with feeding the entrenched perception that poor person = failure and/or cheat. This was made manifest with the incredibly potent and racist stereotype of the 'welfare queen' which took previous moral panics around single mothers to an entirely new, myth-inducing level.[57] (Reagan first used the term 'welfare queen' in 1976 at a campaign rally conflating one woman's actions – "She used 80 names, 30 addresses, 15 telephone numbers to collect foodstamps, Social Security, veteran's benefits for four non-existent deceased veteran husbands, as well as welfare" – with an entire section of society, and then deployed the racially coded allusions while president.)[58]

This emblematic creation was embodied by a single (black) woman who supposedly lived the life of Riley at the taxpayer's expense. The stereotype would endure right through to (and reinforce) Bill Clinton's welfare 'reforms' of the 1990s when he infamously promised to end "welfare as we know it" and in the process managed to catapult legions of single mothers into low-paid jobs that would trap them in 'working poverty'.[59] Clinton's near-total eradication of welfare for the poorest in the US – under a dog-whistle legislative title, if ever there was one: 'of the Personal Responsibility and Work Opportunity Reconciliation Act' – as highlighted by anti-poverty advocates and researchers, among other things,[60] placed time limits on eligibility for core government assistance programmes and enabled later attacks on programmes by Republicans.[61]

Significantly, as Rachel Black and Aleta Sprague explain in their 2016 *New America* article, 'The Rise and Reign of the Welfare Queen',[62] this pernicious myth of 'poor = black' (especially single women) didn't appear in a vacuum in the US.[63] For example, the civil rights movement's 'rhetoric about dignity, opportunity and justice and amplifying broader calls for economic justice', alongside advocacy for poor black women, 'triggered a new wave of backlash against welfare recipients and intensified racialised criticisms of the "undeserving" poor', they argue. By the time the Clinton reforms were implemented in the US, Black and Sprague point out, the public were long primed 'for a face to be attached to the perceived waste, fraud, and abuse they saw as enabled by indulgent government programs' that were supposedly 'absent accountability'. By 1989 '64 per cent of Americans felt that welfare benefits make poor people dependent and encourage them to stay poor', providing a fairly substantial chunk of the populace ready to buy the Kool-Aid on welfare 'reform' being necessary to root out dependency.

"Thatcher, in the '80s, during her reforms had this rhetoric of: There Is No Alternative – TINA. Well there is. You look at other countries and you see that this is not, in any way, the only way."
Dr Heejung Chung, University of Kent

As Dr Chung explained to me, the twin philosophies of Thatcher and Reagan consolidated the poverty narrative using the single mother, or 'welfare queen', as a proxy:

> "[The welfare queen] doesn't actually exist in the US but they used that imagery to make sure that people, the voters, were ok with the state dismantling the benefits and services at that time, to really penalise some of those small, very deprived groups. I think that's exactly what happened in the UK as well. It was through policy, through the discourse of politicians, but also the media. Because in media you always get this image ... of welfare scroungers."

The "dehumanising" and demonisation, especially of people on benefits, "does not happen to that extent in other countries", Chung points out.

However, if Reagan and Thatcher helped lay the groundwork for the version of the poverty narrative we have in America and Britain today, then in the following decade President Bill Clinton constructed the scaffolding. As Black and Sprague explain,[64]

> ... rather than eliminating the myth of the welfare queen, these reforms codified it by shaping policy choices around the prevention of wilful idleness and

criminal behaviour. As a result, welfare reform created a system that expects the worst from families seeking assistance, and in so doing entrenches a presumed link between poverty and poor character in popular discourse.

It seemed clear to me – even back in 1987 and into the 1990s when as a university graduate I was able to begin a career and support myself, and as I observed the malevolent narrative gymnastics used to justify policy that harmed the least well off – who the truly 'entitled' people were. It certainly wasn't the single mother so desperate they needed foodstamps in the US, or a jobless father claiming the dole in Britain.

When I went to university in England in 1988 (I was the first in my extended family to attend university and the first from my working-class school to go to 'Oxbridge') I was surrounded by people from extremely privileged backgrounds for the first time in my life. It was an eye-opening experience. I learned a valuable lesson: the degree to which entitlement is integral to the identity and behaviour of many people from wealthy backgrounds. I asked myself time and again: how come these aren't the people being labelled as entitled? How come it's people like me, who have next to nothing? Most of the students from wealthy backgrounds that I encountered simply *knew* that they were headed for a bright – and financially lucrative – future in banking or law or another profession their fathers and grandfathers had enjoyed. It was a given. Their insouciance was mind-blowing. Even if their exam results were mediocre, it turned out it didn't matter that much, they would get where they wanted to go regardless.

It wasn't uncommon that if you came from my background and raised the issues of privilege and entitlement, you would be dismissed as having 'a chip on your shoulder'. You were envious, apparently. The idea that you may actually have an insight into structural inequities – including in the UK the conveyor belt of the public school system to powerful positions across society – was unthinkable. For many people from working-class backgrounds (very few from the very poorest ever make it to Cambridge), their accent was an assumed indicator of class and social status. A friend of mine who went to Oxford a decade after I went to Cambridge told me of how, at a meet-and-greet function not long after she started, other students assumed she was 'staff' and ordered her to fetch them drinks. This kind of behaviour was not a rarity.

The numbers of people from fee-paying school backgrounds at the very top of the professions provide a clear barometer of the fast track from privilege to yet more privilege, but studies also show that it's not just what your father did or which school or college you went to that gets you there. Social codes and class behavioural expectations play a huge part. From how you speak to how you dress. Something as apparently mundane as wearing brown shoes when going for a job in banking in the City of London is enough to disqualify a job applicant at interview.[65]

It wasn't until I was at university that I understood (although I didn't know this term at the time) that 'social capital' existed. That I excelled academically was almost moot if I didn't have the necessary connections or knowledge of the social codes, or years of inculcated confidence needed to get a foothold in tough-to-enter industries such as the media and if I wasn't part of networks developed since boarding school. (Especially in a recession, as was the case when I graduated.) I simply didn't know the terrain. And, while I fought the shame and stigma of poverty during this time with everything I had – and while I would never have let anyone who tried to belittle me see that their comments had made so much as a dent – the impact on my self-esteem remained powerful.

Three decades on from the late 1980s and the framing of the poor – and especially those who need assistance from government programmes at some point – as society's weak links worthy only of vilification and ill-informed abuse has very deep roots indeed. Three decades later, against a backdrop of extraordinarily binary political divisions and disturbing right-wing populism in Britain and America (and beyond), the toxic poverty narrative is well and truly embedded into the fabric of our collective discourse.

A toxic tale for the times

The journalists John Harris and John Domokos have a regular video series in Britain called *Anywhere but Westminster*.[66] Over a few years they've travelled the length and breadth of the UK talking to people on the ground about the biggest issues of the day, but especially austerity and Brexit. The series stands out for doing what so many news outlets don't – consistently puts people at the centre who aren't the power brokers and asks them what they think. As the pressure was building towards Brexit in March 2019 the two visited the northern English town of Wigan. While ostensibly about Brexit, the Wigan film featured two women at a food recycling centre that helps local people in need of a meal. The women spontaneously turned the conversation towards poverty, and the shame, blame and stigma that goes with it. In a short sequence, these two women illuminate the pathos at the core of the toxic poverty narrative and the shame it facilitates, illustrated by their evident urge to not overtly label their work as 'a poverty' project.

Here they are, bustling about their work in the kitchen at the food centre:

"**Woman 1:** We're definitely not a poverty project. We're an environmental project. And there's a reason for that. Everybody's got pride.

Woman 2: You can't be resilient if you're hungry. Something's gone very wrong.

Woman 1. We've developed an acute talent for blaming the victims. I can't stand it when I see programmes like *Benefits Street* and all that. The people who are to blame are the people at the top who've got more than they need.

Women 2: And they won't stop that blame because it serves to blame. I think people do feel shame about the position they find themselves in but they don't know a way out of it. So, then they get defensive. Nobody asks those people, do they? They point to them, they have *a story about* them that they don't really know. But then don't actually talk to them."

When conducting interviews for Project Twist-It I found the sentiments expressed by these two women to be deeply felt by many people and across generations. Variations of the women's observations were repeated over and over again by interviewees and contributors. There was an acute awareness that the labelling of people struggling to get by had penetrated the broader consciousness – and that it was fundamentally and morally wrong.

Two people with chronic illnesses from East London I interviewed for Project Twist-It who relied for a time on state benefits as a result were typical. They explained how the rhetoric and stereotypes around welfare so prevalent across society, and the way these intersect with applying for help, penetrate at an individual level.

> "**Steve:** It's sort of like hiding. You just want to hide away.

> **Toni:** It's shameful, isn't it. It is very isolating.... You're a number. That's the bottom line. It really does fuck your head up. It really, really does."

The safety net is one of the biggest cultural problems we've got.
Rush Limbaugh, conservative pundit on his radio show, 2012[67]

For people living in poverty, exposure to the blame and shame transmitted by the narrative is part and parcel of being on the breadline in a culture where maligning the poor is tolerated. People are aware of how they are portrayed. They are aware of the narrative as a mechanism for shaming people – sometimes as a dog whistle and other times, not so much. Take this from Rush Limbaugh on his US radio show: "The safety net is one of the biggest cultural problems we've got."

That's the problem with all of society anyway; we have to label everything.
Jimmy Wood, US army veteran

Jimmy Wood is another person who articulated how the narrative infiltrates a person's everyday existence. Jimmy is a US army veteran who grew up in poverty. When he spoke with Project Twist-It he was acutely cognizant of how he and others like him are depicted by politicians and wider society. Brought up by a single mum, he recalled that "she busted her ass every day" for him and his brother. "She never caught a break. Getting out of that slump is hard because when you've got two or three kids, you're a single parent, you're working two or three jobs trying to make ends meet, it's a never-ending cycle. It's the hardest thing."

Jimmy offered his views on the reality of poverty but wanted to address not just the hardship familiar to anyone with experience of it, but also the issue of *what it feels like* to be misrepresented and demeaned. He wanted to say something to the politicians and pundits who denigrate poorer people for political gain – even people like him who have fought for their country. He wanted his voice heard.

"The misnomer is usually [people] are lazy, they need to get a job, they need to stop living off the system," he says of the portrayal of people struggling.

> "Most of [the people who say this] don't know what it's like to live in poverty, most of them don't know what it's like to wonder what's going to be for supper or if you're going to have enough gas to get to town the next day, or how many bills you can pay with this check, or if your kids are going to be able to have lunch money. They don't get it. They don't know. They need to actually show people that have struggled, [who] didn't ask for it. If you really knew how it was, you would not say the things you do about that class of people. That's the problem with all of society anyway; we have to label everything."

Veterans all too often end up in poverty – many homeless – after leaving the armed services. Despite some notable efforts to reduce the number on the streets or in shelters,[68] 39,000 'vets' were nevertheless homeless in 2016[69] in the US, with many more experiencing food insecurity and poverty. According to the Center on Budget and Policy Priorities, around 1.4 million are in receipt of foodstamps (now known as SNAP) – the very programme that Republicans have taken renewed aim at decimating since 2016. For Jimmy, the cold facts of poverty for vets and other groups tell only one part of the story.

in reality, the poor are overwhelmingly those born into poverty, or those thrust there by circumstances largely beyond their control, such as physical or mental disabilities, divorce, family breakdown, illness, old age, unliveable wages or discrimination In the job market.
Philip Alston, UN Special Rapporteur

Philip Alston directly addressed the nature and role of the narrative surrounding poverty in his reports. In a section titled 'Who are the Poor?' in the 2017 US report,[70] he delivers a sharp appraisal of what this narrative is, how it is disseminated and by whom, as well as how it impacts on policy decisions that affect people's lives and livelihoods.

Alston observes:

> In thinking about poverty, it is striking how much weight is given to caricatured narratives about the purported innate differences between rich and poor that are consistently peddled by some politicians and the media. The rich are industrious, entrepreneurial, patriotic, and the drivers of economic success. The poor are wasters, losers and scammers. As a result, money spent on welfare is money down the drain. If the poor really want to make it in the United States they can easily do so: they really can achieve the American Dream if only they work hard enough.

He also pinpoints the invidious role of racism in a poverty narrative that rests on manufactured stereotypes for people of colour that:

1. reinforces a notion that: Poor = Lazy + Black;
2. rests on the myth that Poor = Black Woman = Single Parent/welfare queen.

In fact, there are millions more white people in the US living in poverty or close to the official poverty line. In 2017 the proportion of African Americans in poverty was 21.2 per cent (9 million people) which was two and a half times higher than for Whites (8.7 per cent), while the rate was more than double for Hispanics (18.3 per cent). However, in terms of sheer numbers, 17 million white people fell below the poverty line.[71] A similar racial pattern occurs when looking at child poverty but with even starker racial proportional variations.[72]

On the racial poverty stereotyping Alston writes:

> In imagining the poor, racist stereotypes are usually not far beneath the surface. The poor are overwhelmingly assumed to be people of colour, whether African Americans or Hispanic 'immigrants.' The reality is there are 8 million more poor Whites than there are poor Blacks. The face of poverty in America is not only black or Hispanic, but also White, Asian and many other backgrounds.

Alston also identifies people in need of welfare assistance as coming in for particular opprobrium (the working poor are, to some degree, regarded as more 'deserving') and that politicians all too readily buy into the narrative of this group being especially lazy and irresponsible. Stating that there were 'anecdotes aplenty' of the stereotypes but little evidence to support the premise of the narrative, he said:

> Similarly, large numbers of welfare recipients are assumed to be living high on 'the dole'. Some politicians and political appointees with whom the

special rapporteur spoke were completely sold on the narrative of such scammers sitting on comfortable sofas, watching cable television or spending their days on their smartphones, all paid for by welfare.

The special rapporteur wonders how many of those politicians have ever visited poor areas, let alone spoken to those who dwell there. There are anecdotes aplenty, but little evidence. In every society there are those who abuse the system, as much in the upper income levels as in the lower. But in reality, the poor are overwhelmingly those born into poverty, or those thrust there by circumstances largely beyond their control, such as physical or mental disabilities, divorce, family breakdown, illness, old age, unliveable wages or discrimination in the job market.

Stephen Pimpare, author of *A People's History of Poverty in America*,[73] who has researched poverty over the span of US history, writes in his book:

> Some of our long-standing resistance to generous programs of public welfare can be in part traced to the pernicious myth of the lazy (black or immigrant) poor who are supposedly glad to live off the dole and ready to exploit any effort by government (or private charity) to offer food, cash, or shelter. As with any good myth, it persists despite the lack of evidence to support it.

The journalist, scholar and author of *The American Way of Poverty: How the Other Half Still Lives*,[74] Sasha Abramsky, argues that to some extent it is the simplicity of the rhetoric, language, labels and semantic ploys – the narrative's linguistic girders, if you will – directed at poorer people that renders it so pervasive and persuasive.

It is much easier to blame an individual for something that is, in reality, extremely complex, than to engage with a level of complexity and intricate structural inequalities that might undermine your preconceived prejudices, or mean you actually have to think seriously and with an open mind about it.

Abramsky writes:

> Because we use such simplistic language to explain poverty we oftentimes find it easier to pile blame on the poor for their plight rather than look for ways to tackle poverty. After all, it's easier to castigate someone; it's much harder to truly understand his or her circumstances.

In the context of America, he writes: 'Both major political parties have been guilty of this sleight of hand in recent decades, though the Republicans and their talk radio allies, have taken it to new levels – turning verbal denigration of the poor into something of an art form.'

Foodstamps, to which those who are really desperate must turn, are a case in point as something regularly under attack from the right (as if they were some sort of indulgence for feeding idleness rather than hungry bellies). Abramsky, writing about the early post-financial crises years, has this to say:

> … as tens of thousands have come to rely on foodstamps to avoid hunger and malnutrition, political figures such as Newt Gingrich and Rick Santorum have accused those on foodstamps of no longer possessing the American will to success, of having become permanent charity cases…. For Gingrich, poverty represented not a societal failing, but an individual one.

And, as he also astutely observed, castigating the poorest is frequently a convenient political ploy that avoids the real problems. 'Precisely why so many tens of millions of Americans were poor enough to qualify for foodstamps … didn't concern these presidential hopefuls.' Indeed, Gingrich managed to suggest in a speech at Harvard in 2011 – a century and a half after the first great wave of the child labour reform movement in the country[75] – that a relaxation of child labour laws should be considered as a way to help children "entrapped" by poverty.

Poverty propaganda

The toxic, demeaning, rhetoric around poverty favoured by some corners of the media and politicians is something of an art form in Britain too. There are plenty of incidences of poor-blaming and dog-whistling across the political spectrum,[76] but, as it is with conservatives in the US, in Britain it's primarily the purview of the Conservative Party and its media co-dependants performing a similar function to Fox News pundits and partisan talk radio.

The notion that there exists a deviant, recalcitrant underbelly of society has come to so infect perceptions of poverty and disadvantage that more accurate depictions and understandings of poverty and its causes and consequences are all but drowned out.
Tracy Shildrick, researcher and author

Among the most erudite on the topic is the researcher Tracy Shildrick. In her book *Poverty Propaganda: Exploring the Myths*,[77] Shildrick makes a powerful case for why the current prevailing narrative around poverty, especially in the wake of the UK's brutal austerity cuts since 2010 (and what she conceptualises as multi-faceted propaganda), is especially potent. Shildrick points out:

> The idea that segments of the population experience poverty because of their own failings is nothing new, but poverty propaganda is so powerful and pervasive in the current context that all poverty and related disadvantages are generally believed to be deserved in one way or another. [These are] narratives about poverty and people who are disadvantaged in various ways that deliberately misrepresent both the causes and the consequences of poverty in contemporary Britain. Such is the power and influence of poverty propaganda in the current context that many people

– even those experiencing deep poverty themselves – tend to distance themselves from the condition and the maligned and stigmatised populations that are so readily associated with it.

The notion that there exists a deviant, recalcitrant underbelly of society has come to so infect perceptions of poverty and disadvantage that more accurate depictions and understandings of poverty and its causes and consequences are all but drowned out.

Another British researcher with a focus on stigma and the benefits system is Ruth Patrick of the University of Liverpool. Examining the poverty narrative in the age of austerity, Patrick drew a direct line between the 'scrounger' and 'striver' rhetoric that took hold after 2010 and the problematised nature of 'welfare' in the US, especially its role in 'othering' the jobless. She also demonstrated how pervasive the narrative became as some politicians adopted rhetoric that systematically denigrated people who were struggling and claiming benefits.

In a journal paper from 2016 Patrick writes:[78]

In the UK, a dominant narrative operates to stereotype and stigmatise out-of-work benefits claimants as inactive welfare dependants who require activation if they are to enter paid employment and behave responsibly. During the 2015 general election, politicians from all the main parties competed to be seen as *the* party prepared to stand up and deliver for the 'hard-working majority,' families 'doing the right thing' by engaging in the formal labour market. By contrast, those in receipt of 'welfare' – a popular, Americanised shorthand for out-of-work-benefits – were problematised. The politicians' positioning is reflective of a contemporary climate that sees longstanding divisions between 'deserving' and 'undeserving' populations reinvigorated and recast as a dichotomous distinction between 'strivers' and 'shirkers', between those engaging in paid employment and the most visible non-workers.

Pinpointing the atomising potency of the work/welfare axis of the contemporary narrative, Patrick has this to say:

> In the UK, it is possible today to speak of a 'framing consensus on welfare' that sees widespread political and media support for efforts to correct and address the supposedly problematic behaviours of out-of-work benefit claimants. Structural and systemic causes of poverty are neglected and even concealed, through an approach that foregrounds individualised 'pathways to poverty': namely worklessness, family breakdown, addiction, low education and debt. Today, out-of-work benefit receipt is often seen as inherently and necessarily problematic, with almost all claimants – except an ever-smaller number of those deemed most 'vulnerable' – expected to be on a journey from 'welfare dependence' to a fetishized 'independence' via participation in paid employment.

Karen Dolan is a poverty expert at the Institute for Policy Studies in Washington DC. Talking to Project Twist-It about how the blaming and shaming of poorer people builds upon deep-rooted political preoccupations and belief systems to give credence to regressive policy moves in the US, she argues that the narrative's deployment actively entrenches poverty. Far from being just one instrument in the political toolbox, she says, the narrative plays a fundamental role in the nature of contemporary poverty and inequality.[79]

> "[Something] that is really surprising is that narrative, which has existed since the founding of the country … that people who suffer have brought it upon themselves through a lack of character or through being lazy. Given what we know is true, it's rather shocking that the narrative is still so persistent today, when it is very clear that you can look at the last

50 years and see that this narrative as it persists (and some would argue that it has grown since [Trump's election in] 2016) is fundamentally false. It is provably false, because you can see the ways in which policy decisions have created and perpetuated the conditions of poverty and the lack of access to power and [including through voter suppression and criminalisation] the lack of access to democracy even."

"When 70 per cent of Americans are going to need to turn to at least one means-tested safety net program like Medicaid or foodstamps at some point in their lives. That's not a 'them'. That's an 'us'."
Rebecca Vallas, Center for American Progress

Rebecca Vallas, at the Center for American Progress, has been challenging and monitoring the intersection between the poverty narrative and the real-life consequences of the policies it is used to justify. Vallas told me:

"I think the dominant narrative about poverty in America, which has for a long time been really heavily reinforced by right-wing media – I'm thinking in particular about Fox News – is this conception of poverty and of people who are struggling to make ends meet, as people who are sitting on a couch eating bonbons waiting for a check from the government Republicans in this country have come to use and to rely on and to stoke at every chance to try to diminish support for programs that they want to cut. Programs like Medicaid, like nutrition assistance, like affordable housing. All these programmes are incredibly popular, people understand that they are there for them in their time of need. But, that conception of that lazy person on the couch who just doesn't want to work is really core to how Republicans in the country need poverty to be viewed so that they can advance their agenda."

Vallas continued:

"The thing that is so fundamentally problematic about the discussion about poverty in the United States is how much it is framed as an 'us and them' situation, as opposed to the 'us' that is really borne out by the research. Where nearly half of Americans are going to be poor or really close to poor at some point in their lives for a year. When 70 per cent of Americans are going to need to turn to at least one means-tested safety net program like Medicaid or foodstamps at some point in their lives. That's not a 'them'. That's an 'us'."

Karen Dolan concurs. Since the election of Donald Trump in 2016, which, as anyone who has so much as switched on a television channel (other than Fox News) will know, brought with it an escalation in the demonising of marginalised groups including immigrants, Muslims, trans people and people of colour, the toxic poverty narrative has taken on renewed potency, according to Dolan. The rhetoric has become less dog whistle, more foghorn, she contends. A full-frontal attack.

"I think that especially in the last two years – since the election of 2016 – we have really seen an open war on poor people and people of colour ... this cultural demonization," says Dolan.

"The real attack on welfare programs, on safety net programs, the imposition of challenges and obstacles to just receiving foodstamps or meals on wheels for elderly people, or making fun of people with disabilities.[80] This has been in our living rooms and on our streets. So people can't deny it any more. The safety net is shredded both as a means of social control; to keep people from exercising their political rights, and keeping people down. And people are lulled into submission and don't understand the mechanisms that are happening [and] believe this false narrative about character flaws or being the fault of black and brown people and immigrants."

A very special relationship: why Britain and America excel at the shame game

Britain and America have long had what politicians like to call 'the special relationship', with Britain widely seen (and mocked within its own shores) as the too-eager-to-please junior partner on the global stage.[81] But the relationship, as has been illustrated already, with the subject of 'welfare' is about more than diplomacy and political posturing. The appeal of a narrative that frames the poor as feckless by the cultures of both countries is also special. Blaming and shaming the poor is not a pastime unique to either country but the way they do it, why they do it, and how they've turned it into an art form is very much an Anglo-American pursuit.

The political economist and austerity expert Mark Blyth[82] argues that when it comes to Britain and America, the framing of poverty sets them apart from other wealthy nations. An obsession with 'individual agency' and so-called 'personal responsibility' in British and American political culture underpins both the conceptualisation of the poverty narrative and the ways it is deployed, he says. Blyth (who self-identifies as a 'welfare kid') grew up in relative poverty in Scotland and is now a professor at Brown, one of America's most prestigious Ivy League universities. Blyth offers an analysis of how the ideology of so-called 'personal responsibility' and the 'bootstrap' mythology so beloved in America's culture of rugged individualism in particular plays so effectively at shielding the wealthy while blaming the poor. He told Project Twist-It:[83] "Because of [the centrality of individual agency] the government doesn't owe you a living; nobody owes you a living. It's your fault and if you can't bootstrap yourself – look at him, he can bootstrap himself!"

The degree to which poverty is framed as such in the US and UK is formidably unique, Blyth argues. "That narrative has always been present in a way that is simply not there in continental Europe and Scandinavia. So there is rich and fertile ground to work on." He adds: "There is a way in which you can have these narratives based on the fact that the poor are invisible, are geographically isolated, are socially isolated. You can objectify them almost as a kind of generalised moral miasma. So that is the touchstone. Anyone can touch on to that and say, 'oh, we are not that,' and that's why it becomes an incredibly resilient weapon in politics."

The poverty narrative, and the shame game it manufactures, is propelled (much as inequality is) by *where* real power and influence is exercised and *how* the poverty narrative is deployed to blame the poorest while insulating the better off. This is how Danny Dorling explained it when interviewed for Project Twist-It: the narrative "stands on a code. If you have problems then they are your own fault. If you just worked hard enough, if you tried hard enough, if you studied hard enough at school you could be really well off. Everybody could be rich if they just worked hard enough! That is the philosophy." But, as he adds: "You can't all be rich because part of being rich is that you can afford to make other people do things like clean your house."

The connection between the US and the UK when it comes to portraying poor people as some kind of societal parasite is, as Dorling points out, a strong one with an obdurate heritage.

"It is often said that the US and the UK have a special relationship and, in a way, sadly, they do. But it's over a particular set of philosophies which came to the fore under Ronald Reagan and Margaret Thatcher and these were philosophies that the state should be made as small as possible, that people should look after their own money, that we shouldn't do things collectively. There is only you and your family and there is no such thing as society. Both the US and the UK had movements that propagated these ideas, which is why they are so different from almost every affluent country in the world, where people still believe in the collective good and you do things together and that there is something bigger than just you and your family."

The unique interplay between politics and wealth – and in particular with the super-rich in Britain and America, Dorling argues – has been central to the normalisation of inequality, extreme poverty and the poverty narrative.

> "Unlike most rich countries in the world, the narrative in the United States and the United Kingdom has been so dominant and so successful because a set of people have really driven it forward in a way that they haven't in other affluent countries. There are a series of media outlets that are owned by people who are very rich; a series of newspapers owned by people who are very rich and often don't pay tax. And people with this kind of wealth buy and control a lot of the media because they want to spread this message."[84]

He goes on:

> "The UK and the US have think tanks funded by extremely rich individuals whose entire purpose is to spread the message that everything is up to you and if things don't go well it is your own fault. Other countries don't have the same kind of concentration of money being put into propaganda[85] to tell the population that they should believe this. It is a very, very American, very British thing that has happened in the 80s, 90s and 2000s."

But the purpose of these studies isn't to inform good policymaking. They feed a narrative that the poor are lazy and undeserving...
Joshua Holland, writing for the Bill Moyers website

The entrenchment of the toxic poverty narrative in the UK and the US was helped along by a constellation of think tanks.[86] Through reports and media appearances these have ensured that the dominant narrative about the poor is regularly catapulted into the political arena and media mainstream to shore up policies that both create poverty and harm the already poor.

Many reports end up reinforcing the poverty narrative. In 2013, for example, an article on the Bill Moyers website by Joshua Holland about a Cato Institute report purporting to 'show poor families living high on the hog on public benefits'[87] illustrates the deftness with which stereotypes are reinforced and spread. Holland wrote:

> But the purpose of these studies isn't to inform good policymaking. They feed a narrative that the poor are lazy and undeserving, and provide wonky cover for further weakening our social safety net. When studies like this one are picked up by the conservative media, all of the authors' caveats tend to be stripped away, and they become straightforward claims that poor families sit back enjoying a good life, forcing overburdened tax-payers to pick up the tab.

In Britain, think tanks that reinforce the narrative abound (many of which have direct connections with elected Conservative politicians[88]) and also produce research and field spokespeople to appear on mainstream news such as on the BBC (despite their funding being opaque and their place on the political spectrum not explicitly made clear to viewers).[89] Tom Slater at the University of Edinburgh, for example, argues how one think tank – the Centre for Social Justice – established in 2004 by Iain Duncan Smith, whose tenure as the top welfare minister in Britain gave him carte blanche to unleash the very worst of the welfare upheaval under austerity, was pivotal in framing the welfare state as a source of societal ills. Duncan Smith was an enthusiastic proponent of using his political platform to propagate the idea that the country had a 'growing dependency culture' which could only be solved by 'welfare reform'. However, as Slater showed, his 'vision' was intricately linked to and propelled into the public consciousness via his think tank. Slater wrote in a 2012 paper 'The Myth of Broken Britain: Welfare Reform and the Production of Ignorance':[90]

I illustrate how emotive terms, phrases and concepts have been strategically deployed by a conservative think tank (the *Centre for Social Justice*) to manufacture doubt with respect to the structural causes of unemployment and poverty, and to give the impression that 'welfare' is a lifestyle choice made by dysfunctional families despite the fact that considerable social scientific evidence shatters that impression.[91]

The power of the poverty narrative is that it drowns out factual, rational discussion about the real, structural causes of poverty. As Stephen Pimpare writes: 'Propaganda, stereotypes, and myth govern our thinking about poverty and poor relief much more than the facts do.'[92] Only by acknowledging and documenting this, can we forge an alternative message – one as strong as the current dominant narrative and one that begins from a basic fact: to fight the drivers of poverty it is incumbent that we fight on every available front. First, though, let's examine how the narrative works in practice.

4

Lights, camera, vilification: the narrative in action

"There was a time when our nation fought a War on Poverty; now, it seems, we are waging a war on the poor."
Institute for Policy Studies, 'The Souls of Poor Folk' report, 'auditing' 50 years of poverty in America[1]

"Your society's broken, so who should we blame? Should we blame the rich, powerful people who caused it? No, let's blame the people with no power and no money and these immigrants who don't even have the vote – yeah, it must be their fucking fault."
Iain Banks, novelist, 2013[2]

In 2015, the American satirist Stephen Colbert had a segment[3] in his TV show, *The Colbert Report*, in response to a 'study' from the US-based right-wing think tank, The Heritage Foundation.[4] It was a master class in exposing and simultaneously skewering the common narrative such think tanks propagate and which America's poorest must contend with day in, day out: that they are a throng of grubby layabouts living it large off the state in a house full of luxury goods.

Even without the comic visual devices, the script stands up as a lesson in how the ideological emperor behind the stereotypes of poorer people has no clothes. It went like this:

Colbert:

Jesus said the poor would always be with us. Well, it turns out Jesus does not know everything.

For more, Fox News's Stu Varney makes words come out of his mouth.

Varney:

When you picture poverty, you picture this: [Cut to video of people in a soup kitchen].

But what if I told you it really looks like – this: [Cut to a visual of a line of flat screen televisions].

A new report shows poor families in the United States are not what they used to be.

I'm just gonna give our viewers a quick run through of what items poor families in America have.

• 99 per cent of them have a refrigerator;

• 81 per cent have a microwave.

Colbert:

A refrigerator *and a microwave*? They can preserve *and* heat food?! Ooh La La!

I guess the poor are too good for mould and trichinosis.

It's all here folks, in the conservative think tank, the Heritage Foundation's new report, 'Air conditioning, cable TV, and an Xbox: What is Poverty in the United States Today?'

And if you watch closely in Stu Varney's report just then, you saw that, evidently, poverty is the plasma flat screen aisle at Best Buy.

And you will not believe some of the things poor people have in their homes! Luxuries like ceiling fans, DVD players, answering machines, and coffee makers. I don't have those things!

I have central air, a Blu Ray player, voice mail and I go to Starbucks every day. Must be nice.

And, $10 coffee makers aren't the only luxuries these 'poors' can afford. Stu...

Varney:

I seem to remember being told in the last few years that something like 12 per cent of the children in America go to bed hungry at night. [To guest] You're saying that's flat out not accurate?

Guest:

That's an absolute lie. It's maybe 2 per cent of children at some point in the year would go to bed hungry.

Colbert:

Two per cent hungry. That's the perfect amount! There's about 150 of us in this room. If three of us were hungry children I think we'd feel pretty good about that. I mean, this report proves that poor people are just not living down to our expectations.

If you still have the strength to brush the flies off your eyeballs you're not really poor....

These 'Great Society'[5] anti-poverty programmes were like a dam that we built to hold back the river of poverty. And it worked!

So, let's tear down the dam. I'm sure the river will stay put. But, if not, and the poor start drowning again, we'll throw them a life preserver. Or, a refrigerator. Poor people seem to love those things!

Propaganda, stereotypes, and myth govern our thinking about poverty and poor relief much more than the facts do.
Stephen Pimpare, *A People's History of Poverty in America*, p 12

There are so many instances of poorer people being shamed and blamed and vilified, judged and dismissed and demeaned, and bombarded by outrage at their very existence, that they could easily warrant their own dedicated encyclopaedia.

So, let's consider how the shame game has been deployed by the purveyors of the poverty narrative.

Who are the players of this shame game? What do they do? And, how they do it?

Playing politics: the institutionalisation of the toxic narrative under austerity

In March 2019 a welfare advice worker in the UK published a document handed over by a client who had given permission for it to be circulated.[6] It had originally been included among legal papers in a tribunal case where the client, a disabled woman, was challenging the government's efforts to deprive her of her disability benefits – Personal Independence Payment[7] (PIP). Her assessor had referred to her as 'a lying bitch'. When uploaded onto the website of the human rights group, Rightsnet,[8] the comment alongside it from the advice worker concluded that the inclusion of such an insulting and dismissive epithet was a clear illustration of what had become 'a canteen culture of contempt' among those working at the Department for Work and Pensions (DWP) who were making decisions on benefits eligibility and appeals.

The publicity generated by the exposure of the document would eventually lead to a government apology, but this vivid sample of the sort of casual castigation of people fighting for their *right* to government support were having to confront was formidable. And, it capped years of campaigning by disability rights advocates,[9] in particular highlighting the government's harmful policies.

The assessment by the advice worker of the DWP's attitude and behaviour towards benefits claimants as a 'culture of contempt' was far from an aberration. By mid-2019, austerity – the welfare reforms it ushered in, the benefits freezes and cuts it rolled out, along with the unremitting framing of people in genuine need as scroungers and benefits fraudsters – had meant the poorest and disabled people had been rhetorically and literally bullied, brutalised for the best part of a decade. Various arms of government and agencies charged with enforcing cuts and welfare changes were culpable in repeated attempts to cut or remove benefits and sanction recipients for often minor (or no) infractions of arbitrary rules. Think of the chronically ill person who is five minutes late for an appointment at the Jobcentre, is sanctioned, and then left with zero money to live off for weeks or even months as a result. Or consider the person in hospital and unable to attend the obligatory 'work capability assessment' appointment but being told that's not a good enough reason for lack of attendance. Or the mother transferred onto Universal Credit who is caught up in the new system's delays, meaning she is left with no money to feed her kids.

> **"I could only make it to the kitchen to make food once a day. I had no muscles on the back of my leg, which meant I couldn't stand up at all and had to lean or sit down all the time, but they were telling me I was fit for work."**
> Stephen Smith, claimant denied benefits despite having multiple, debilitating illnesses, talking to *The Liverpool Echo*

The number of such examples in a system set up to keep people poor and to throw as many obstacles in the way as possible to prevent approving benefits support is both staggering and disturbing.[10] Just some examples include:

- Chronically ill and disabled people being left without crucial benefits due to misleading letters sent by the DWP to GPs saying they no longer needed to supply medical evidence.[11]
- The case of a man who died after of being declared fit for work and spent the last 18 months of his life fighting the judgement only for his family to be informed he'd won the appeal seven months after his death.[12]

The Independent newspaper highlighted the rate of suicides and attempted suicides that were connected to reforms including fitness for work tests,[13] and reported in January 2019 that more than 17,000 disabled people had died while waiting for decisions on PIP.[14] In fact, such was the extent of the problems associated with tougher eligibility criteria and other reforms to the benefits system in the wake of austerity in the UK that the film-maker Ken Loach immortalised some of the inhumanity and mercilessness of the system in his blisteringly moving 2016 film, *I, Daniel Blake*.[15] And, in 2019 with his film about the 'gig economy' *Sorry We Missed You*,[16] he showed how a precarious economy makes people even more susceptible to insecurity and penury. In the spring of 2019 came the death of one man whose appalling treatment by the benefits system made national news. Stephen Smith,[17] a person with multiple debilitating illnesses, including chronic obstructive pulmonary disease, made headlines when pictures published in the media showed him emaciated, in hospital with pneumonia and barely able to walk – yet this was a man who had recently been deemed fit to work.[18]

Stephen had failed the government's 'work capability assessment' test in 2017, had his Employment Support Allowance (ESA: a benefit established for people unable to work at a given point)[19] withdrawn and was told, as the system dictated, to report to the Jobcentre regularly to 'prove' he was looking for work. This was despite two doctors confirming that his illnesses were genuinely debilitating. One doctor's note read: 'It is my opinion that Mr Smith could not walk 20 metres without pain or exhaustion.' Stephen himself, whose case had first been highlighted by a local newspaper, *The Liverpool Echo*,[20] had said of his circumstances: "I could only make it to the kitchen to make food once a day. I had no muscles on the back of my leg, which meant I couldn't stand up at all and had to lean or sit down all the time, but they were telling me I was fit for work." Aged 64, Stephen died two years after the government told him he was fit for work. He was one of thousands over the decade who died – confirmed by the government's own figures – not long after being declared 'fit for work'.[21] Even as this book was about to go to press, another death flashed across my social media feeds. This time, a man died while waiting in the queue at a Jobcentre in Wales. He had been declared fit for work earlier in the year.[22]

Among the numerous examples of abysmal behaviour by those tasked with administering and enforcing the harsher benefits and cuts from 2010 were those revealed by a Jobcentre worker who contacted me to expose the degrading and dehumanising practices that she witnessed and was asked to carry out.[23] Angela Neville was a special adviser at a Jobcentre branch in Essex, England. She told me of an instance where she was asked by one boss to call a man in hospital and tell him he needed to attend or risked being sanctioned. She refused. Angela told me how staff, frequently reduced to tears, were being put under extraordinary pressure to haul people in for assessments or sanction them to meet unjustifiable targets leaving both clients and workers in distress. The system, Angela said, was one where staff were rewarded when they sanctioned someone and given "brownie points for cruelty". She decided to write a play about it to shine a light on the ruthlessness of the system.

One benefits advice worker in another part of the country who I had spoken with a couple of years earlier recalled to me how the indefensible brutality of the work capability assessment system was especially agonising for people with mental health issues, many of whom had developed problems as a direct result of the stress induced by the process itself in a kind of terrible feedback loop.[24]

She told me:

> **"**I've actually seen one case in person, and it matched identically another person on a television programme where the suicidal client was asked seriously as part of the medical [assessment]:
>
> **Assessor:** 'Are you suicidal?'
> **Claimant:** 'Yes.'
> **Assessor:** 'Well then, why haven't you achieved it yet?'**"**

A hostile environment

The context in which these sorts of vile behaviours proliferated[25] was one of savage and utterly unnecessary austerity.[26] But savage, deliberate, austerity needs a narrative precisely because it inflicts so much avoidable harm very quickly, some of which will eventually become visible in stories like that of Stephen Smith. As Philip Alston observed, if politicians on the right in the US had taken note of the callous magnitude of what the UK government in the hands of the Conservatives (for a short spell in coalition with the smaller Liberal Democrat Party) had been up to since 2010 and had framed their efforts to undermine policies to alleviate poverty and get rid of the Affordable Care

Act in similar terms, they would have unravelled even more of the US safety net.

The narrative deployed in Britain to justify austerity is inseparable from the poverty narrative. The austerity narrative was an evolution, a brand-new bastard of the poverty version. It was a carefully constructed, weaponised manifestation of an understanding of poverty and poorer people that rested on a principle of 'divide and conquer', turning, as author Iain Banks so astutely observed before his death,[27] ordinary citizens against one another. Who has time to blame bankers, regulators, policy makers and complex financial instruments for an economic collapse when you can point the finger at the poor and immigrants and roll out austerity on the back of it so easily?

Just like the wider narrative around poverty, the austerity narrative was deftly steered by Conservative politicians and the media. Austerity, in effect, signalled that it was open season for any opportunistic politician or pundit with a soundbite to peddle to blame and shame the poorest – and especially people without work – rendering them outcasts in their own society. Unemployed people were the ultimate threat, portrayed and treated as if they constituted a malignant disease that had to be cut out lest their contagion spread to the 'hard-working' population.[28]

The New Economics Foundation summed up succinctly how this narrative was constructed and deployed back in August 2013:[29]

> Well-framed, well-crafted and often repeated, the austerity story is the dominant political narrative in Britain today.... an economic narrative that is the textbook definition of a powerful political story. They have developed a clear plot, with heroes and villains, and use simple, emotional language to make their point clear. Repeated with remarkable discipline over several years, their austerity story has gained real traction with the British public.

And, as Zoe Williams wrote in *The Guardian* in 2018,[30] so powerful was the austerity narrative, so deep went its claws, that even in the face of overwhelming evidence that austerity's so-called medicine was not curing the illness of a troubled economy, people clung to it regardless. The appeal of '… images, metaphors, certainties, and black holes' in logic was clear from research, she explained.

Williams wrote:

> Even once it was plainly, across the country, having devastating impacts on people's lived experience … the notion itself – that we all had to tighten our belts and that was the responsible thing to do – was curiously buoyant.

Instances of politicians using austerity to justify cuts and welfare upheaval by making economically illiterate claims about reducing the national debt as equivalent to managing a household budget[31] (a ludicrous yet effective simplistically framed claim) created a climate in which a sticky web of barriers to and mistreatment of people claiming benefits, including a plethora affecting people with disabilities, could flourish.[32]

Certain mantras became very familiar in Britain after 2010. Some of these might fall into the dog-whistle category and there may be an ebb and flow in the velocity, but on the whole, when austerity was being sold to the British electorate – especially in the earlier years – the language, rhetoric and framing were unvarnished. Disinformation and exaggeration, often wrapped in simplistic metaphors, were regularly deployed.

To listen to some politicians (those most guilty of the toxic rhetoric, like former Prime Minister David Cameron, tended to be independently wealthy) and read some newspaper articles you'd be forgiven for thinking that Britain was overrun by a scourge of gigantic 'troubled' families[33] who were the dangerous zombie vanguard of an out-of-control 'intergenerational' poverty and welfare 'dependency' epidemic.[34] Equally, an alien visitor might expect to find the place held hostage by a horde of predatory benefits cheats bleeding the economy dry and taking advantage of 'hard-working families'. None of this was borne out by the facts – none.

"You can pump more cash into chaotic homes, but if the parents are still neglectful, the kids are still playing truant, they're going to stay poor..."
Former UK Prime Minister, David Cameron

Some notable specimens in the narrative shame game after 2010 included:

- **The former UK Conservative Prime Minister, David Cameron**, who delighted in painting himself as a champion of 'compassionate conservatism' yet oversaw the worst of the austerity cuts, was an enthusiastic purveyor of the austerity narrative. He was especially adept at light metaphors. Take this typical example (my italics):

  > **"**The truth is we can't throw money at the problems and *paper over the cracks*. You can give a drug addict more money in benefits, but that is unlikely to help them out of poverty, indeed it could perpetuate their addiction. You can *pump more cash* into chaotic homes, but *if the parents are still neglectful, the kids are still playing truant*, they're going to stay poor in the most important senses of the word. So this government is challenging the old narrow view that the key to beating poverty is simply more redistribution.**"**[35]

Cameron also loved to talk about "tough choices" and peddling the idea that helping people out of poverty through work was a primary goal, while failing to point out that millions of people receiving help from the state, for example tax credits,[36] needed them to top up substandard, stagnating wages. He was also especially enamoured of the idea that to be poor and on benefits was "a lifestyle choice". A typical example is:

"… we do want to make clear that welfare is there to help people who work hard, it shouldn't be there as a sort of life choice."[37]

- **Former Chancellor of the Exchequer, George Osborne** (and later editor of the London *Evening Standard* newspaper) consolidated the messaging that would support his unprecedented and drastic cuts by the Treasury to public services with a speech at the 2012 Conservative Party conference. Drawing on the poverty narrative's notion of a 'benefits culture' and playing on the mantra of deserving 'hard-working families', he told delegates: "Where is the fairness, we ask, for the shift-worker, leaving home in the dark hours of the early morning, who looks up at the closed blinds of their next-door neighbour sleeping off a life on benefits?" It was a clear case of villains and heroes that appealed to the sense of justice most people might respond to. And yet, Osborne conveniently fails to even consider that the person whose curtains are drawn might themselves have just returned from a tough nightshift and be enjoying a well-earned rest from their low-paid job, or might have to get up later to work or care for family. It didn't matter. The picture had been painted with diabolical effectiveness.

  Osborne's 'pièce de résistance', however, came when he brazenly attempted to link the deaths of six children in a house fire as a result of arson to supposed deficiencies with the Welfare State. On national television news he took the extreme example of a man and his wife found guilty of a heinous crime to extrapolate that this was somehow down to the benefits system. He told the interviewer: "I think there is a question for government and society about the welfare state and the taxpayers who subsidise lifestyles like this and that debate needs to be had." Needless to say, Cameron defended Osborne.[38]

- **Former Secretary of State for Work and Pensions, Iain Duncan Smith – known in Britain as IDS –** (a one-time leader of the Conservative Party who also founded the Centre for Social Justice think tank), was a master at deploying the austerity narrative in defence of his reforms.[39] IDS loved to talk about entrenched "worklessness" (including brazenly misusing benefits statistics[40]) and announced how he was going to sort out those people "parked" on incapacity benefits for decades with no sign of moving off them.[41]

  As frontline welfare rights officer Nick Dilworth based in Plymouth on England's south coast told me: "I think there is a need to shame Duncan Smith. He is running amok."[42]

- In 2013 a one-time single mum on benefits lambasted the **then welfare minister Lord Freud** for pushing the myth of laziness among the poorest. Freud, a wealthy former investment banker, had argued that people on benefits would take more risks if they really wanted to lift themselves out of welfare dependency:[43]

  > **"**… people who are poor should be prepared to take the biggest risks – they've got the least to lose.**"**

  The former single mum, who responded that the minister was guilty of "a profound disconnect"[44] from the reality of the hardship faced by people "struggling to keep their heads above water", was none other than the *Harry Potter* creator, J.K. Rowling who, as president of Gingerbread,[45] a charity for single parents in the UK, and someone who had relied on benefits herself at one point, was proof positive that if a wealthy person reinforces myths, it is a choice.

- Or how about **Michael Gove** who, when **Education Secretary**, blamed poor people for having to go to foodbanks. In Parliament he told other MPs that families turn to food parcels because of a failure to "manage their finances". He said: "I had the opportunity to visit a foodbank in my constituency on Friday. I appreciate that there are families who face considerable pressures. Those pressures are often the result of decisions that they have taken which mean they are not best able to manage their finances."[46]

But let's not forget: the Labour Party, the 'Official Opposition' in the British political system since 2010, were far from immune to reinforcing stereotypes around skivers and strivers. When the Labour Party should have been at the forefront of combatting the demonisation of the poor and unemployed, they were at times complicit in it. Take this from the **then shadow Work and Pensions Secretary, Liam Byrne**, in an interview with the *New Statesman* magazine in 2012: "It's not Britain's shirkers who are having to pay the cost of failure, it's Britain's strivers. The Tories are screwing Britain's strivers."[47] It should also be noted that the seeds for many of the welfare 'reforms' pushed through under the Coalition and Conservative governments were harsher versions of changes the Labour Party introduced while in government between 1997 and 2010, including sanctions that in a later incarnation would be one of the major sources of distress for people claiming benefits.[48]

In his book, *You are not Human: How Words Kill*, former New Labour speechwriter Simon Lancaster provided a window into the ubiquity of denigrating language even within government.[49] In a chapter titled 'Scum', he wrote:

> ... one of the things that struck me during my time in Whitehall was how pejorative the everyday language was in talking about people from poorer backgrounds. This was a Labour government, but much of the talk from the top concerned people living on 'sink estates' going to 'bog-standard' schools, or speaking about bad schools as 'dumping grounds'. And this was not language that was used in private, but very openly. Such terms came up regularly in conversation and usually, it had to be said, by people who had probably never been anywhere near a council estate in their whole lives. The message was clear. Low-life. The dregs. The underclass.

> I found that working-class people were openly
> described using dehumanising metaphors in a way
> that would never have occurred had they been black
> or gay or Jewish. It seemed like a curious blind-spot.

While, under the leadership of Jeremy Corbyn, Labour adopted a notably more critical stance on austerity and all that it entailed, including the toxic rhetoric,[50] there is no getting away from the fact that by not taking the initiative immediately in 2010 when the austerity narrative adopted by the Conservative/Liberal Democrat coalition was injected into the national consciousness, the party missed a critical opportunity to frame the arguments in a way that did not blame the poorest and most vulnerable for a financial cataclysm brought on by bankers. Instead, like rabbits in the headlights, they appeared to panic in the face of the Conservative onslaught, even accepting some of their distorted logic that the previous Labour government was somehow responsible for the global financial crisis.[51] This left the party on the back foot and robbed anti-austerity and anti-poverty campaigners of a crucial potential ally to challenge the narrative and nip its worst excesses in the bud from the get-go.

Partners in crime: the media, culture and the narrative

The right-leaning press in Britain, but especially the infamous tabloids and 'mid-market' *Daily Mail* and *The Express* (the British equivalent of Fox and conservative talk show hosts), have long had a beef with poorer people their editors and owners (like their political counterparts) look upon with disdain, often bleeding news with opinion, and demonstrating a predilection for disparaging certain groups at any opportunity. As we've already seen, regular contestants for society's greatest leeches and perfect tabloid fodder – as J.K. Rowling recognised only too well – were single mothers. But so too (as is also the case in the US) were welfare recipients.

In the eyes of the British press, to be poor or on benefits was basically tantamount to being little more than low-life.

One analysis, which examined a breadth of research in the field, reported that media coverage does little to enhance our understanding of poverty while demonising poorer people.[52] The authors wrote:

> A particularly pervasive trend in the literature suggests stereotyping of the poor in the news media. A number of studies have reported stereotypical media descriptions of the poor as criminals, alcoholics, and drug addicts ... sexually irresponsible, avoiding work, and being lazy ... and lacking in socially desirable qualities ... The media has demonised poor single mothers in particular, who are depicted as immoral, neglectful and responsible for their own plight...

Ministers in the government in 2010 had barely opened the doors to their offices to concoct their austerity plans when *The Sun* (owner one Rupert Murdoch, global billionaire political string-puller extraordinaire) launched a particularly unedifying campaign named 'Beat the Cheats' to address a supposed 'out-of-control hand-outs culture'.[53] The paper's penchant for running stories 'uncovering' the 'faking' of a disability (all in the good cause of undermining incapacity benefits in general, which benefit hundreds of thousands – the vast majority of whom are non-fakers) was ratcheted up as austerity took hold. Needless to say, disability activists and organisations routinely (and correctly) pointed out that there was an increase in the reporting of hate crimes against people with disabilities.[54]

In the aftermath of 2010 and as austerity was rolled out, the tabloids reported with undisguised glee every government manoeuvre, policy or statement that fed the negative narrative about people who were struggling to get by in an ever more unequal society.

Typical stories in the oeuvre:

> *"The priority is to get Britain back to gainful employment, the 'millions of habitual welfare claimants' who must be taken off the 'intravenous drip of tax payer support and made to earn their keep'."*
> **Daily Express**, September 2009[55]

> *"The only way is easy street: How Essex town of Brentwood is skiving capital of Britain"*
> **Daily Mail**, 2012[56]

> *"Jobless man who used a foodbank after blowing his benefits in a casino blames the government for giving him a 'ridiculous' amount of money in one go."*
> **Daily Mail**, 2015[57]

> *"Benefits cheat 'who couldn't dress herself' is seen ice skating and horse riding."*
> **Daily Mirror**, 2019[58]

And on and on and on...

As Robert Walker puts it when examining press coverage of poverty in his book *The Shame of Poverty*, the trend towards people with disabilities being a regular target for press ire was a relatively recent phenomenon:

> Whereas historically people who are sick or living with disabilities have attracted less opprobrium, this is no longer the case and government activation policies now oblige recipients of incapacity benefits to engage in employment-oriented activities.[59]

Since 2010 these bastions of British culture have unleashed some of their finest, poor-pummelling work. What *The Guardian*'s social policy editor Patrick Butler called 'nasty, gratuitous, and casually vicious' articles. And, as Walker points out, the tabloids cemented their enthusiastic propensity for stoking fear among the middle classes of welfare claimants as somehow a moral threat and a danger to the social order with their criminality, child neglect, antisocial behaviour and binge-drinking, drug-abusing ways. '*The Sun* encapsulated these concerns in the phrase "broken Britain", a motif the Conservative Party subsequently took up and used in the 2010 General Election campaign, engendering the full endorsement of *The Sun* for its policies.'[60] The 'dominant media frames reinforce the negative images of poverty' held by the wider public, according to focus group research, Walker argues in his book. 'Moreover,' he contends, in relation to poverty, it is 'not only attributable to individual lack of effort, the very presence of poverty is seen to hold back economic growth and thereby the prosperity of those buying newspapers'.

The rise and rise of 'poverty porn'

While clearly the tabloids and politicians feeding the narrative beast have been instrumental in the framing of poverty and the poor they are far from in a vacuum. The icing on the toxic cake is supplemented by others. The broader cultural stew of negative imagery and portrayals of the poorest – entrenched over years – has played its part and, during austerity, became even more potent.[61] As with shows like *Jerry Springer* in the US, which derived huge ratings from set-piece scraps (sometimes physical) between various representatives of the 'underclass', 'white trash' and other supposed societal miscreants, its nearest equivalent in Britain, *The Jeremy Kyle Show*[62] (and before that, *Trisha*[63]), provided a steady diet of 'undeserving' specimens from the lower orders in the same vein. As with anything of this nature, it played a large role in granting permission for everyone else to mock, laugh at and denigrate people – many of whom (if you watch even a couple of episodes) are in fact vulnerable and ripe for exploitation.[64]

One former employee on *Trisha* would write in 2019, reflecting on the genre, that in her experience people working on the show were trained to use 'master manipulator' tactics to rile people up after having actively sought out the vast majority of 'guests' from deprived areas and because of their clear vulnerabilities.[65] A judge in 2007 went so far as to describe *The Jeremy Kyle Show*, which was the highest ratings mid-morning programme on ITV, as "human bear-baiting".[66] And, in May 2019, the show came a cropper after a 63-year-old guest died from suicide a week after filming, sparking an enormous public outcry.[67] ITV, the programme's broadcaster, abruptly suspended filming and the broadcasting of previous episodes.[68]

It was impossible during the austerity years to be unaware of one of the most disquieting and distinguishing developments in poor-shaming by popular culture on television[69] – and how this opened the floodgates to nasty social media hashtags igniting a chain of threads fulminating against people on benefits. Under the guise of 'documentary' or as depicting 'real lives', TV shows such as Channel 4's *Benefits Street*[70] (first broadcast in 2014) fortified the narrative of people in receipt of benefits as feckless spongers. This demonisation was a natural extension of, and augmented, a cultural moment from the early part of the noughties when the pejorative term 'Chav' (an acronym widely understood to mean 'Council Housed and Violent' or 'Council Housed-Associated Vermin')[71] came to permeate the culture as a proxy for being working class, poor and living in social housing.[72] So significant has been the development of the genre that researchers have named it 'Factual Welfare Television' (FWT),[73] while the term 'poverty porn'[74] to refer to it entered into common parlance in part as a result of the scale of publicity the show and others like it such as *On Benefits and Proud* (2013) attracted.

Benefits Street gave cover to the politicians of the day who enacted the biggest programme of welfare reform in decades, in order to clamp down on 'perceived' abuses.
Abigail Scott Paul, Joseph Rowntree Foundation

Audiences for these shows give an indication of their popularity and reach – the first series of *Benefits Street* drew 5.1 million views, more than Channel 4 had garnered for several years. Critics lambasted *Benefits Street*[75] (other shows in the same vein such as *My Big Benefits Family*[76] and *Skint Britain: Friends without Benefits* triggered criticism also) for calculatingly selecting footage that skewed the participants' behaviour – all from one street in Britain's second largest city, Birmingham – to show them in the worst possible light, and fed into the toxic myths and stereotypes of people 'on welfare'. Hundreds of complaints were received by the regulator, Ofcom, and a fractious public debate ensued around the degree to which *Benefits Street* was wilfully demonising people.

Writing about poverty porn for Project Twist-It in 2019, Abigail Scott Paul of the Joseph Rowntree Foundation, who had been analysing the trend throughout the austerity years, pointed out[77] that, despite recent, more encouraging depictions of people in poverty and their communities such as the BBC's *The Mighty Redcar*,[78] the impact of *Benefits Street* and its ilk was still being felt. And, despite the producers of the more recent example of the genre, *Skint Britain*, claiming their purpose was to juxtapose 'Westminster rhetoric with the reality of poverty', it too sparked a cavalcade of hateful reactions towards the people in the programme. One potent example of the early and incendiary reactions to the genre emerged during the run up to the UK December 2019 General Election. A prospective Conservative Party candidate was exposed as having posted on Facebook that people on the show should be 'put down'. The prospective candidate apologised once the comments went public, saying they were 'off the cuff'. But here's the rub: it is precisely the fact that such judgements are made public off the cuff that illustrates how cavalier the culture is with the reputations and image of poorer people.[79]

Scott Paul wrote:

> … members of the public continue to cite [*Benefits Street*] as evidence of a widespread culture of welfare dependency in the UK. Wilfully or not, it fuelled resentment towards those on benefits and endorsed support for a tightening of the system, because it triggered a deep-seated belief that some people try and some people don't. It made this the only possible explanation of poverty. *Benefits Street* gave cover to the politicians of the day who enacted the biggest programme of welfare reform in decades, in order to clamp down on 'perceived' abuses. The then Work

and Pensions Secretary Iain Duncan Smith, quoted the public's response to the show as evidence of support for his welfare reform package that saw cuts of £18bn.[80]

Regarding the response to *Skint Britain* in particular on social media and the enduring lure of poverty porn, Scott Paul had this to say:

> For many viewers, they defaulted to blaming and shaming those they saw on screen for their decisions and choices. Rather than build a better understanding of the flaws in the system that are pushing people under, it has only served to entrench a stereotyped view of benefit claimants, a perception generated by *Benefits Street* five years earlier.

Indeed, on Twitter, as Scott Paul and others pointed out, social media responses on the #SkintBritain hashtag offered a dismal window into the power of the poverty narrative, toxically played out in real time.

Replying to the geyser of hate-filled responses, one Twitter user, Garrie Coleman, responded with about as good an encapsulation as you can get. Coleman wrote:

> Scrolling through the #skintbritain tag it's clear that demonization of welfare claimants by govt after govt and newspaper after newspaper has been a resounding success. Pig-ignorance has prevailed where this is concerned.[81]

What is clear is that this climate of vilification has percolated through society. Its ripple effects run far and deep. People do bad things to each other. Of course they do. They say bad things about each other. However, when the denigration of the poorest is commonplace – where it is in fact orchestrated or encouraged by those in authority and with power – that is when we see many of the everyday cruelties that most of us would regard as inhumane and shocking in an advanced, wealthy nation. For example, homeless people being abused or attacked, and spikes outside building entrances or other 'defensive design' and 'hostile architecture'[82] ploys being introduced in public spaces, as they have been in Britain in recent years to deny shelter and rest to people who are destitute. Or 'poor doors' – one of the numerous egregious manifestations of inequality and discrimination in the housing market in Britain and America where residents in new developments who didn't pay top dollar are relegated to 'a financial apartheid' – a shaming entrance all their own lest they rub shoulders with their betters.[83]

In one incident in London in 2019 a private developer was eventually forced to cave in to public pressure – a welcome sign that pushback can work – after it emerged that the playground in one of their complexes was segregating the children of less well-off tenants from those whose parents had paid more for their apartments.[84] All of this gives a sense of the scale of the task at hand to challenge a culture in which such behaviour occurs.

State of play: the challenge at hand

As austerity and welfare upheaval approached a ten-year anniversary in 2019 there was a slight dampening down of the harshest political rhetoric (though certainly not in terms of the actions it had shored up).[85] And, going by the success of programmes like *The Mighty Redcar* and Sean McAllister's masterful film, *A Northern Soul*[86] in 2018 – both of which dealt with issues of poverty and insecurity with sensitivity and empathy, showing how the system is stacked against people who are struggling – lessons appear to have been learned by some television commissioners. These developments came on the back of concerted challenges to years of toxic rhetoric, and the policies enforced on the back of them, from a number of individuals and grassroots activists whose campaigning came of age during the worst of austerity. These included for instance Jack Monroe,[87] a single parent who shot to prominence writing about the interminable, everyday strain of keeping hunger at bay for Jack's family and arguably punctured some of the narrative's power with a dose of Jack's own, authentically dispensed, medicine.

That said, the Conservative government's policies continued to be called into question as, for example, homelessness and foodbank use surged and millions of people struggled to make ends meet.[88] This was happening despite Prime Minister Theresa May's pledges to focus on what she called "everyday injustices".[89] It was also occurring against the backdrop of the 'Windrush' controversy which emerged in the wake of the 'hostile environment' around immigration at the Home Office during May's tenure there as Home Secretary.[90] And, May's attempts to position her government as one focused on a 'shared society' was hardly something likely to resonate with people dealing with the everyday grind of poverty or difficulties navigating the benefits system or finding a decent, affordable home.[91]

There were also problems with addressing inequality and mobility, not least when the entire board of the Social Mobility Commission resigned en masse on May's watch because of a lack of progress.[92] While there may have been some sentiment to tackle 'burning injustices' like poverty and inequality, the steady stream of statistics on the number of people, including many in working families, who were on the breadline painted a very different picture of the reality on the ground and of the impact of government policy.[93] And, as *The Times* reported, there was resistance from within the Conservative Party to May's pivot towards a focus on social justice issues and the noticeable shift in the rhetoric she was using.[94]

Within months of May standing down as Prime Minister and being succeeded by Boris Johnson (a contemporary of Cameron's at Eton, and a fellow member of the 'Bullingdon Club' at Oxford), a video of his so-called 'guru'/advisor Dominic Cummings emerged where he told an audience at an event that he knew lots of Conservative MPs and they "largely do not care about these poorer people" and "they don't care about the NHS".[95]

5

The games we play: weaponising the narrative

"I was so embarrassed. It's really weird being denied food in front of everyone. They all talk about you."
A 'lunch-shamed' seventh grader in Pennsylvania, 2017

"Make no mistake. Slashing Medicaid, Medicare, nutrition assistance, affordable housing, disability benefits and other programs that help families afford the basics isn't 'welfare reform' any more than giving huge tax cuts to billionaires and wealthy corporations is 'tax reform'."
Rebecca Vallas, Center for American Progress, 2018

It's party time: fuelling the poverty narrative after the crash

In May 2017 I wrote one of my regular 'Lesson from America' columns[1] for *The Guardian* about a practice taking place in many US schools that on first encounter struck me as so awful as to be unbelievable. 'Lunch shaming' – where youngsters who can't afford to pay for school meals are shunned publicly, and often in front of their peers – was occurring in numerous places across the country.[2] When working on my column I look out for trends related to poverty, and in 2017 instances of children being humiliated in this way were being shared more and more. *The*

New York Times told the story[3] of one child from Pennsylvania on her first day in seventh grade who qualified for free school lunch but, due to a paperwork mix-up leading to an outstanding bill, watched as her tray of food was thrown in the garbage while she stood in line in the cafeteria. "I was so embarrassed," the girl told the *Times*. "It's really weird being denied food in front of everyone. They all talk about you."

The New York Times article recounted other, similar instances:

> A Pennsylvania cafeteria worker posted on Facebook that she had quit after being forced to take lunch from a child with an unpaid bill. In Alabama, a child was stamped on the arm with: 'I Need Lunch Money'. On one day, a Utah elementary school threw away the lunches of about 40 students with unpaid food bills.

As someone who qualified for free cafeteria meals my entire school career, I know that even when a child goes to school in a disadvantaged area with other kids who qualify, there is still a stigma attached to *needing* your food to be paid for by a source other than your parents – especially as a teenager when social status becomes almost all-consuming. You know you are a 'free school meals kid' – and you tend to wish you weren't. At my secondary school, which I attended from age 11 to 18, you could spot the free school dinner crowd from the yellow laminated passes we carried to get into the cafeteria. Our headshot pictures were in the middle of three possible squares. Kids whose families *could* pay (a minority in our school) had a picture in the left-hand box. It was an administratively logical system – there were almost two and a half thousand girls in the school and it would have been chaos if we weren't categorised in some way – but we still *felt* it as a label. Nevertheless, the idea that if I had forgotten my pass on any given day and couldn't prove that my meal had been paid for I would have a stamp put on my hand or I would have to watch as the food meant for me was thrown away in front of me is unthinkable.

Set aside for a moment that for many youngsters who need free school meals it's often the only nutritious food they will receive in a day, the shame alone would have been unbearable. I might also have wondered what the hell the point was of denying food in such a public and punitive manner. Isn't it inferred that by qualifying for free meals or a subsidy that the child is in real need? Who exactly does it serve to have them go hungry? Who does it serve to throw good food away?

An article on the American Bar Association website defines lunch shaming this way:[4]

> Broadly speaking, 'lunch shaming' refers to the overt identification and stigmatization of any student who does not have money to buy a school meal. While the US Department of Agriculture (USDA) narrowly applies this overt identification to students who are eligible for free or reduced lunch, in practice legal lunch shaming occurs against students whose family income exceeds free or reduced lunch eligibility thresholds. The purpose of lunch shaming is to embarrass a student and parent(s) so that a school lunch debt is paid quickly, in turn reducing a school's financial burden.

A number of school districts and individual states have taken action against lunch shaming (New Mexico passed a law to ban it, for example).[5] And, in 2019 one sign of action at a national level came when Democratic Representative Ilhan Omar introduced a Bill to the House to stop lunch shaming.[6] Despite these moves, two years after I first wrote about lunch shaming, yet more reports emerged. In November 2019 a Minnesota school district hit the headlines and apologised when video footage showed that kids with canteen debts of more than $15 had their hot meals thrown out.[7]

That children who could not afford to eat in the school cafeteria – and who had no control over those circumstances – were routinely being shamed was, I thought, a powerful reflection of a wider culture where for a significant proportion of people it was deemed permissible, if not encouraged, to participate in a bamboozling variety of tactics for putting poorer people, including young people, down. For years in the US with its harsh conditionality for welfare recipients, those in need of help have been exposed to shaming by the systems they are required to navigate to stand even a chance of qualifying for assistance.

In the America of lunch shaming, circa 2017, poor shaming was on steroids – and it was no accident. Almost a decade earlier in November 2008, for a certain slice of the US population the absolutely unthinkable had happened – and it wasn't the financial crisis. It was the election of the nation's first black president, Barack Obama, and the possibility that yes – you've guessed it – some poor folk might actually get some help if a black former community organiser had some real power. Having walked into the Oval Office in January 2009 following the greatest financial calamity since the 1929 Great Depression almost a century earlier and grasping (albeit with limitations,[8] but, unlike the Coalition government in Britain, opting not to embark on a full-frontal savage cuts programme) that a government economic stimulus[9] was necessary to give recovery a fighting chance, Obama was quickly met with an impassioned wall of resistance. Writing in *The American Prospect* in September 2008, prior to Obama's election victory, William Spriggs, then chair of the Department of Economics at Howard University, had this to say:

> America faces an economic challenge today that is greater than any it has faced since the Great Depression. At that time, Franklin Roosevelt corrected the faults in the economy and created the Social Security Act to build lifeboats for Americans drowned by the failure of the marketplace. He had to create that out of whole cloth. Today, Americans have endured a withering 30-year-old campaign against the nation's safety net, convinced that we could all go it alone.[10]

The post-crash environment in the US – where the poorest and people on low incomes took the greatest financial hit (and in which the seeds of the populist rebellion that led to the Trump presidency, which were incubated during the previous few decades, took root and sprouted)[11] – was expertly exploited by certain quarters in the political arena, along with their kindred pundits in talk radio and Fox News.[12]

The 'Tea Party'[13] movement, a 21st-century exemplar of just how profoundly virulent America's version of the poverty narrative is and how intricately interwoven it is within parts of the wider culture, emerged in the wake of the 2008 presidential victory and the global financial meltdown, on a mission to dismantle 'big government' and, as part of it, programmes that might help those in need. It was a contemporary embodiment of conservative discontent,[14] populism and libertarianism, with antecedents throughout American history[15] that harked back to a perceived 'golden era' of American rugged individualism, and one which would, for a time, represent a formidable force in the political landscape.[16] As the movement took shape and then gathered momentum in the wake of Obama's election – and especially in response to the stimulus Bill[17] – and as it triggered an upset in the 2010 mid-term elections which saw Democrats face one of their biggest defeats in 70 years[18] – it went hell for leather in the ensuing years after its designated targets:[19]

- Government (too big by far)
- The deficit and national debt (ditto)
- Taxes (too high by far)
- Healthcare reform (an abomination)
- Welfare spending (a blight on American democracy, freedoms and liberty).

As this article from 2010 by the founder of the Dallas Tea Party, Phillip Dennis, explained on CNN,[20] the mission (while evolving) was explicit and powerful:

> The Tea Party groups viewed the stimulus bill as the crowning moment of decades of irresponsible government fiscal behavior. The federal government is addicted to spending, and the consequences are now staring us in the face. The Tea Party's goal from inception has been to replace big-spending politicians from both political parties with common-sense, fiscally responsible leaders...

And:

> We have gone from a nation of self-sufficient producers to a nation divided between overburdened taxpaying producers and some nonproducers who exist on welfare from cradle to grave ... fraud and welfare waste must be eliminated. Welfare and unemployment benefits must be drastically cut. Welfare, health and education services for illegal immigrants must be eliminated.

The fervour of a movement determined to shrink government and root out so-called 'dependency'[21] and which put people like Sarah Palin on the national stage, with a shot at being Vice President,[22] turbo-charged the toxic poverty narrative as a political stick to beat Obama and progressives with and in the process injected fresh steam into the anti-welfare contingents around the country. Flourishing alongside and being awarded policy credence within the Republican Party by Paul Ryan's efforts in his 2008 'Roadmap for America's Future' and later attempts to 'reform' welfare,[23] the pillars of the poverty narrative were buttressed further.

Who can forget Ryan's poetic tendencies on the issue when he declared that the safety net was like: "a hammock that lulls able-bodied people into complacency and dependence"?[24]

Public assistance recipients actually use illegal drugs at lower rates than their more well-to-do counterparts. But hey, no better way to stigmatize people who turn to assistance than to make them all out to be 'addicts'.
Rebecca Vallas, Center for American Progress

Among the many multi-pronged attacks waged by conservatives, one that stood out (although it really is hard to choose) for the sheer vehemence with which it was pursued was the conflating of drug addiction, poverty and welfare.[25] That a link was being made between addiction and welfare wasn't new. However, the Tea Party era ushered in ever-more vigorous attempts in various states at various times to require welfare applicants to 'pee in a cup' before standing a chance of government assistance. Proving 'personal responsibility' by being drug-free to get your benefits was a repeated rhetorical tool. The push included moves to require applicants for cash assistance or unemployment benefits to be drug tested and, if found positive, denied access to assistance programmes, for example. It was a key plank of the Tea Party endeavour to transform the fallout from the financial crisis into a narrative of their choosing and it seeped through to senior ranks of the Republican Party.[26] (The idea was still being pushed after Trump was elected.[27])

Mitt Romney, who under Trump came to be regarded as one of the few Republicans in the Senate willing to occasionally utter a criticism against him, while on a campaign stop during his 2012 presidential bid, endorsed one of Georgia's not so moderate efforts to require people applying for cash assistance to be tested. Romney said: "It's a great idea. People who are receiving welfare benefits, government benefits, we should make sure they are not using the money for drugs."

As Rebecca Vallas at the Center for American Progress would later point out, the aim of pursuing drug testing for claimants intersects with other core objectives on the right of the GOP. It has a dual benefit for its pedlars in that it stigmatises (poor) drug users and (poor) non-drug users simultaneously. The push that came for drug testing of benefits applicants in the aftermath of the Great Recession would serve as extra fuel to the fire of the anti-poor narrative under Trump, including Paul Ryan's (Mitt Romney's running mate back in 2012) mission[28] to upend welfare while Speaker of the House of Representatives. Writing in January 2018[29] in reference to the GOP's rationalisation of cutting welfare to tackle the deficit and where the ongoing obsession with drug testing fits in, Vallas reflected:

> They know their best chance at cutting popular programs is to convince the public — and their counterparts across the aisle — that cuts are 'unavoidable' in the name of deficit reduction. Meanwhile, in a time-honored linguistic sleight of hand, they're trying to smear everything from

Medicaid to nutrition assistance to affordable housing programs as 'welfare' in need of 'reform'.

Make no mistake: Slashing Medicaid, Medicare, nutrition assistance, affordable housing, disability benefits and other programs that help families afford the basics isn't 'welfare reform' any more than giving huge tax cuts to billionaires and wealthy corporations is 'tax reform'.

Rather, it's part of a carefully calculated strategy to reinforce myths about who these programs help, complete with a trusty racist dog-whistle. Ditto the GOP's obsession with drug testing. (Spoiler: Public assistance recipients actually use illegal drugs at lower rates than their more well-to-do counterparts.) But hey, no better way to stigmatize people who turn to assistance than to make them all out to be 'addicts'.

The story being crafted and repeated by Tea Partiers made huge political waves, even when some key progressive messages were getting through. Perhaps most notably from the Occupy Movement, which managed to profoundly puncture the national consciousness with its eminently digestible, comprehensible and compelling catchphrase to frame inequality in a way people could easily understand – 'We are the 99 per cent'.[30] However, it couldn't drown out the potency of the Tea Party's harnessing of an already deeply ingrained anti-poor narrative.

In a quintessentially American fashion, their passion for slashing government spending (backed by numerous conservative economists, think tanks and pundits) cemented the undermining of welfare and healthcare. With its perpetual moralising – including by Tea Party politicians as they took power and gained a national platform – it mirrored in many ways the rhetoric and substance of the austerity engineers in Britain. Also, as with Britain, there are plentiful instances of the shame game in action. We'll divide these into: 'Post-crash, pre-Trump' and 'Trump Time'.

Post-crash, pre-Trump

You don't have to look far for articles or interviews in the early years after the financial crash that employed the poverty narrative's blame and shame game – frequently through the prism of 'dependency' or 'entitlement', a framing that had proven impervious to evidence-based critiques – and which in turn led to that narrative's reinvigoration. Why, you might ask, weren't the rich, who stood to gain spectacularly from tax cuts, labelled 'entitled'?

Perhaps because:

- Poor people aren't politicians.
- Poor people don't fund politicians and lobbyists.
- Poor people don't own the media.

Political goals went hand in hand with a right-wing media environment that was battering the poorest. As with the UK, attacks on welfare 'dependency' were a surrogate for vilification of people who needed some help from the government to get by. The specific mantra-esque framing and repetition of central talking points by politicians and pundits revolving around the core narrative supposition of 'poor = lazy' and existing under an umbrella of an energised Tea Party with rousing conservative voices, made it especially intoxicating. There were numerous examples of the narrative being used.

Take this example from the genre from CNN's *5 Things Newsletter*. With the headline 'Why the US has a culture of dependency',[31] an opinion piece from 2012 (accompanied by a picture of a young man with a mullet haircut) hits many of the primary talking points for a typical anti-welfare article (in this case opinion piece) of the time. In line with the dominant framing, it evokes a mythical bygone era of frontier-spirited individualism as a stark contrast to the indolent hordes of Americans who were supposedly living off the government at the beginning of the 21st century.

Referencing the Heritage Foundation's annual spectacularly named 'Index of Dependence on Government' report 2012,[32] the article read: 'For most of American history, the average farmer, shop owner or entrepreneur could live entirely without getting anything from the federal government except mail service.'

Omitting, as is often the case in this narrative formulation, any acknowledgement of the federal government's somewhat significant role in many everyday functions applicable to people's lives from education to investing in research and development to law enforcement, justice, and civil construction, the report went on:

> [The Heritage Foundation] reports that in 2010, 67.3 million Americans received either Temporary Assistance for Needy Families, Social Security, support for higher education, or other assistance once considered to be the responsibility of individuals, families, neighbourhoods, churches and other civil society institutions....

'These people aren't necessarily dependent on government,' it continues, arguing for 'work requirements' as a way to wean people off welfare:

> ...many could live (even live well) without their social security check, Pell grant or crop subsidy .... Under a culture of dependency, poverty becomes a trap and recipients get stuck. Long-term welfare recipients lost work habits and job skills ....

There are so many holes in the argument it's practically a colander – that Social Security is an earned benefit after a lifetime of contributions, for example, is never mentioned, nor that millions of people on low wages apply for assistance to top these up or when in between jobs (or, in the case of the Great Recession, when bankers almost blew up the system and threw them into destitution), to say nothing of the dissonance of arguing that while on the one hand poverty is 'a trap', apparently the people going to government with their begging bowls could actually 'live well' without the government's help, suggesting they are not trapped by poverty at all.

Other typical article headlines included:

'The tragedy of the dependency culture'
National Review, November 2013[33]

'The entitlement culture is making us a welfare nation'
Bill O'Reilly, 2013[34]

'President Obama admits welfare encourages dependency'
The Daily Signal, 2010[35]

'Number of "able-bodied" adults on foodstamps doubled after stimulus change'
Fox News, 2012[36]

'Why welfare, minimum wage make it harder for poor Americans to succeed'
Fox News, October 2014[37]

And on and on and on...

... the issue of welfare is the issue of dependency. It is different from poverty.
Democrat, Daniel Patrick Moynihan (1970s)

As Paul Michael Garrett writes in his book, *Welfare Words,*[38] 'In recent years for example the "Tea Partiers have been obsessed with demonising the unemployed and the uninsured as undeserving and sucking at the teat of government".' True to well-worn divide-and-rule tactics, Garrett adds: 'Here, a key rhetorical distinction has been made between the productive "makers" (the employed) and the indolent, freeloading "takers" (the unemployed having recourse to welfare).' And, as Garrett also recognises, this positioning is not the sole domain of Tea Partiers or those on the right of American politics. He points for example to Democrat Daniel Patrick Moynihan[39] 'unequivocally' asserting in the 1970s:

> ... the issue of welfare is the issue of dependency. It is different from poverty. To be poor is an objective condition; to be dependent, a subjective one as well... Being poor is often associated with considerable personal qualities; being dependent is rarely so.

"There are 47 per cent of the people who will vote for the President no matter what. All right, there are 47 per cent who are with him, who are dependent upon government, who believe that they are victims, who believe the government has a responsibility to care for them, who believe that they are entitled to health care, to food, to housing, to you-name-it."
Former Republican presidential candidate, Mitt Romney, 2012

Perhaps because it was widely regarded as a decisive nail in the coffin of his presidential bid,[40] Mitt Romney's comments to attendees at a private function for wealthy donors to his campaign in 2012 have special resonance for how the poverty shame game is played out within the very sinew of mainstream politics. The regular barrage of poverty narrative reinforcing from the likes of Fox News, while profoundly problematic, could nevertheless have been dismissed as extreme, marginal hyperbole, but when in a meeting an establishment Republican makes such a controversial statement the toxicity of the poverty narrative is laid bare.

Somehow during his speech Romney managed to encapsulate the poverty narrative's potency in one fateful statistic of his own choosing/conjuring. In the early part of 2012 he asserted that 47 per cent of the country was dependent on welfare[41] and that he wouldn't be able to convince "those people" to take responsibility for themselves. As *The Washington Post* put it: '... the leaked video shows him dismissing President Obama's supporters as people who take no responsibility for their livelihoods and who think they are entitled to government handouts'.

David Corn's *Mother Jones* article documented Romney's reply to a donor questioning how he could triumph in the November election:

> "There are 47 per cent of the people who will vote for the President no matter what. All right, there are 47 per cent who are with him, who are dependent upon government, who believe that they are victims, who believe the government has a responsibility to care for them, who believe that they are entitled to health care, to food, to housing, to you-name-it. That that's an entitlement. And the government should give it to them. And they will vote for this president no matter what... These are people who pay no income tax. [M]y job is not to worry about those people. I'll never convince them they should take personal responsibility and care for their lives."

Obama could count on the votes of almost half the US adult population apparently because they were scroungers. Of course, what Romney failed to mention is the reason why so many Americans don't pay federal income tax: they don't earn enough. Shouldn't the appallingly low wages of millions of workers be the issue? Shouldn't the issue be the national embarrassment that these people aren't protected by a decent, liveable federal minimum wage – something that would actually benefit families and the economy?[42] Shouldn't it be – if we're really going to talk about fairness and what is the right thing to do rather than partisan tropes – that, instead of ploughing cash into the pockets of the rich in the form of tax breaks, that money is directed towards the least well off so that perhaps they wouldn't have to rely on foodstamps while working?

The statement was met with an almost immediate backlash from progressives. Yet, when Romney tried to walk back his comments, saying he meant there was a safety net in place for the 47 per cent and that if it was flawed he would try to fix it, a reliable purveyor of the poverty narrative on the right, Rush

Limbaugh, responded "The safety net is one of the biggest cultural problems we've got."[43]

"So the Democrat Party and Obama are making it official. We're going after life's losers, and we're going to empower them..."
Rush Limbaugh, 2012

True to form in the Tea Party era, Limbaugh did what talk show hosts on the right do and invested his time and energy in propagating the various stereotypes that are the lifeblood of the poverty narrative and its devotees by attacking the poor and hungry,[44] for example, opposing measures to provide meals for hungry children during the summer months.

And, when a *New York Times* article mentioned how Democrats '... were wooing voters – especially minority voters – who depended on safety net programmes, in particular those on foodstamps', Limbaugh was quick off the mark: 'So the Democrat Party and Obama are making it official. We're going after life's losers, and we're going to empower them... This is what the Democrat Party's been doing for years, they're admitting it now.... They are saying they're not interested in voters who work.'

Shaming in 'Trump Time'

Going after what he defines as life's 'losers' is arguably one of Trump's defining preoccupations – marginalising a whole host of different societal groups from immigrants to disabled people to the LGBTQ community – so it's not surprising that poorer people in need of the safety net are choice targets. This targeting stands on the shoulders of a long line of conservative smearing of the poorest.

"Millions of able-bodied working-age adults continue to collect food-stamps without working, or even looking for work. Our goal is to move these Americans from dependence to independence, and into a good-paying job and rewarding career."
Donald Trump, 2017

As this book has already illustrated, social programmes and other assistance, including the Affordable Care Act and foodstamps, were under almost constant bombardment from the White House literally and rhetorically, in the halls of Congress – and far beyond. This included attacks from Trump himself.[45]

Take this from a typical 'speech', in 2017 while calling for welfare reform:

> **"People are taking advantage of the system."**

Welfare was becoming:

> **"**... a very, very big subject, and people are taking advantage of the system.**"**

And later the same year as Trump attempted to justify proposals for enhanced work requirements:

> **"Millions of able-bodied working-age adults continue to collect food-stamps without working, or even looking for work. Our goal is to move these Americans from dependence to independence, and into a good-paying job and rewarding career."**

Or this more typical linguistic muddle-fest from November 2017:

> "But welfare reform, I see it, and I've talked to people I know that work three jobs and they live next door to somebody who doesn't work at all. I know the person who is not working at all and has no intention of working at all is making more money and doing better than the person that's working his and her ass off. And it's not going to happen. Not going to happen."

Trump may not possess the rhetorical verve or precision of some other anti-poor proponents, but he is crudely repetitive and that takes his messages a long way.

If Trump and his enablers from the outset had shrewdly framed the President as the champion of the group that came to be euphemistically known as 'the left behind', or the average working citizen,[46] it certainly didn't stop them, their financial/think tank backers and their pundit counterparts from habitually blaming and shaming in a dizzying confection of ways, the people who need help most. The disregard for anything resembling a moderately progressive idea reached legendary proportions with extraordinary speed in the Trump era. So toxic was the entire political discourse and the policy proposals[47] they supported post-2016, including punitive work requirements, that it constituted a blizzard of often-repeated, dangerous, Grade A garbage.

With a little help from our 'friends'

As with the steadfast dog whistles from Reagan to Clinton and beyond, much of the media, as Sarah Jaffe argued in her January 2018 *New Republic* article, 'How the Media is Abetting the GOP's War on "Welfare",'[48] were complicit (either consciously or unconsciously) in reinforcing the narrative framing around poverty and welfare. By unquestioningly repeating the framing used by Paul Ryan et al during the latter days of his mission to 'reform' (that is, shred) the welfare safety net after Trump was elected, readers, viewers and listeners were frequently left with the impression that such 'reforms' and 'revamps' – as articles tended to report – were benign, or reflected legitimate attempts by policymakers to 'fix' welfare (as defined by Republicans). And – as Jaffe rightly points out – we know that it's rare for readers to reach the end, where the context tends to live, of online articles with such headlines as:

> *"After Push on Taxes, Republicans line up*
> *for Welfare Revamp"*
> **Wall Street Journal, December 2017**[49]

Jaffe writes:

> The problem with using 'welfare' as shorthand [for a range of programmes from Medicaid to Temporary Assistance for Needy Families] is that it slips into the way we talk about and understand the issue. Republicans, in fact, are counting on it since it amounts to a concession to how they are framing their arguments.

Writing about how safety net programmes were being targeted for cuts, she continues: 'In that context, uncritically repeating their "welfare reform" framing is beyond lazy. It's actively taking a side, aiding those who want to slash the safety net that is already in tatters....'

The 'drip, drip' of media messages that normalise the coded rhetoric are problematic enough. But, as the writer Sarah Smarsh pointed out in a piece published the month before Trump's election,[50] this sits alongside outright attacks and misrepresentations of poor and working-class Americans as well as people of colour. National media outlets 'comprised largely of middle- and upper-class liberals' who tended to depict poorer people, including white poor people, as a 'problem', embellishing and solidifying stereotypes. These media-indulged stereotypes exist along a spectrum that ranges from contempt to pity, both of which, Smarsh astutely argues, contribute to a culture of blaming and shaming. In the context of Trump's grossly divisive tactics spanning class, gender, race, religion, disability and identity, her analysis is all the more resonant.

Smarsh writes of the depiction of the white working class:

> One-dimensional stereotypes fester where journalism fails to tread. The last time I saw my native class receive such substantial focus … was over 20 years ago – not in the news but on the television show, *Roseanne*, the fictional storylines of which remain more accurate than the musings of comfortable commentators in New York studios.

In terms of distorting news coverage, she adds: 'In lieu of such coverage, media makers cast the white working class as a monolith and imply an old, treacherous story convenient to capitalism: that the poor are dangerous idiots.' Election commentary pivoted on 'notions' of 'poor whiteness and poor character' being 'routinely conflated', Smarsh concludes.

Beyond the missteps of the mainstream there was always, like an infuriating toxic uncle at Christmas dinner who just won't shut the hell up, the likes of Fox News (and in the early days of Trump, Breitbart News) to make sure that their viewers – evermore polarised under Trump from the wider populace – were fed a steady stream of vitriol that caricatured the poor. Think of the 'special investigation' Fox launched into SNAP before Trump was in the White House, where a self-proclaimed shiftless surfer 'moocher' was the new 'face' of foodstamps during what was apparently, according to the headline, a 'foodstamps binge'.[51] As Salon reported: 'That slipshod piece of journalism ended up playing a factor in efforts by congressional Republicans to cut funding for the program.'[52]

And other typical headlines:

'Marco Rubio: Tax code shouldn't encourage welfare
over work'
Fox News Insider, November 2017[53]

'Time is just right for moving more Americans from
Welfare to work'
Fox News, March 2019[54]

'Hope for those trapped in welfare dependency –
thanks to Trump'
**Newt Gingrich and Mary Mayhew, Fox News,
May 2018**[55]

'It's time to overhaul welfare the right way – here's how'
Fox News, May 2018[56]

**"You take somebody with the wrong mindset, you can give
them everything in the world [and] they'll work their way back
down to the bottom."**
Ben Carson, when Secretary for Housing and Urban
Development

Of course when it comes to the instances of how the poverty
shame game played out in full public view – almost as spectacle
– the news media were hardly alone. Paul Ryan's political project
to 'reform welfare' – with his dog whistles about getting people
"from welfare into work"[57] – was one way of doing it, but others
offered a window to the deep-seated attitudes of the wealthy
and the people obsessed with money.

Take Trump's millionaire cabinet.[58] Whether making formal announcements or just going about the business of being rich, there are plenty of examples to choose from. Here are just some of the delights unleashed:

- According to the self-styled model for the 'pulling yourself up by your bootstraps' narrative, as he rose from modest beginnings to acclaimed neurosurgeon and one-time presidential hopeful, **Ben Carson** while **Secretary of Housing and Urban Development (HUD)** voiced his opinion that that poverty "to a large extent is also a state of mind".[59] This at a time when his department was about to inflict a savage cut to its budget aimed at helping low-income families. If a person had "the right mindset", he mused, then even if they had everything taken away from them "they'll pull themselves up". Conversely, he added: "You take somebody with the wrong mindset, you can give them everything in the world (and) they'll work their way back down to the bottom."

- In May 2017, **the then director of the Office of Management and Budget, Mick Mulvaney** – while presenting the administration's budget proposal to slash hundreds of billions of dollars from safety net programmes over ten years – provided his particular nuggets of wisdom about how the poor can sort themselves out. He asserted: "If you're on foodstamps and you're able-bodied, we need you to go to work. If you're on disability insurance and you're not supposed to be – if you're not truly disabled, we need you to go back to work."[60] Pulling the old reliable tactic of divide and rule of the 'deserving' and 'underserving' out of his hat, he added: "What we've done is not to try and remove the safety net for folks who need it, but to try and figure out if there's folks who don't need it that need to be back in the workforce."

- **Sonny Purdue**, while **Agriculture Secretary**, insisted just before Christmas 2018 that taking away foodstamps was all about restoring dignity. He suggested that withholding foodstamps if a claimant can't find a job was doing them a favour. "This has become a way of life for some people," he said during a Fox News segment, "...this is to help facilitate them back to the dignity of work."[61] Purdue had also in 2018 proclaimed: "Long term dependency has never been part of the American dream."[62]

- Multi-millionaire **Wilbur Ross** as **Secretary of Commerce** in 2019 found himself in an interesting situation[63] on the slopes of Davos, of all places, where the uber-rich like to go and wax lyrical about their take on global issues, including poverty. When federal workers caught up in Trump's imposed 'furlough' were patently in financial difficulty and many were turning to foodbanks in the absence of their paychecks, Ross declared that he didn't understand why they had to do so. "I don't really quite understand why," he told interviewers, even as the media back in the US were documenting exactly why the lack of a single paycheck could push a worker and their family into desperate need. Federal workers should take out loans, according to the multi-millionaire. Needless to say, the criticisms came thick and fast. The most memorable came from Nancy Pelosi with her quip referencing Marie Antoinette: "Is this the 'let them eat cake' kind of attitude? Or 'call your father' money?"

Chuck Schumer, minority leader in the Senate, called Ross's comments 'unreal' on Twitter:

> Wilbur Ross is @realDonaldTrump's Secretary of Commerce.
>
> Wilbur Ross is a billionaire.
>
> And this billionaire Wilbur Ross saying he doesn't understand why federal workers not getting paid during the #TrumpShutdown don't just take out loans to *feed their families*
>
> Unreal

The horrible part is of course that the sentiment was in fact all too real. For the poorest, used to being blamed and shamed, Ross's public statements – or indeed those of Trump's other super-rich acolytes – would come as no shock at all. So many of the people I've interviewed over the years about poverty and inequality, including people affected directly by poverty, say it is vital that the rising inequalities in our societies are highlighted and challenged. They have told me time and again that it needs to be more widely understood that when poverty rises and when children go hungry, in the long run it affects our entire society – but also that we have it within our power to prevent this. Many have argued that we must really begin to listen to people with lived experience, and to try to understand how poverty not only denies individuals and families vital resources, but that being blamed for it erodes self-respect and our collective capacity to fight for policies that can make life so much better. And, as I've learned more and more, ending the shaming of poorer people is crucial to improving people's lives.

6

Shame on you: making the toxic narrative stick

"I think shame is used as a tool against people who grow up with no money."
Jameela Jamil, actor and activist, talking to Project Twist-It

"Poverty kills the dreams and cages the dreamers."
Participant in ATD Fourth World research, England[1]

Shame: the weapon of choice

In early 2019 I sat down to talk with a young woman for Project Twist-It who, like me, spent much of her childhood in the UK in poverty and who relied, as my family did, on various forms of government benefits to get by. Now in her early 30s with a successful career and living in the US, the experience of being poor, and the shame, fear and ridicule it brought with it, endures. She told me:

"I grew up with no money and I was raised by a single mother. Growing up poor just instils in you a feeling sometimes of hopelessness. Because it feels like the system is stacked against you. Children absorb everything. Even if they don't understand it, they are ingesting it. All I can say is that it's like a constant

173

feeling of fear, like a low boil of fear with moments of extreme fear. I moved 13 times before I was 12 years old because we would run out of money and be unable to pay the rent and bailiffs would come to our house, which is a very scary situation.

Being seen as some sort of lowly liar or being lazy because you have to accept money from the state is common. We don't take into account people's actual situations. Politicians, especially in the last ten years, use more words that allude to people who are on benefits or people who need help from the system … as lazy dependants. As vampires just sucking the blood out of the economy. And their wording is condescending and patronising. They are dismissive. [They] couldn't even imagine a day in most of these people's shoes. They don't think of the context. **"**

The young woman is the actor, activist and star of the NBC hit comedy *The Good Place*,[2] Jameela Jamil.[3] When we met, Jameela, as someone who spent so much of her youth in poverty, wanted to tell her story and help put a spotlight on the truth of being poor – including the role that shaming plays in upholding a narrative of 'undeservedness'. The shaming of poorer people by politicians and the press was too often missing from the conversation on poverty, she said, despite it being such a powerful cultural weapon.

In common with others who contributed to Project Twist-It, Jameela articulated the gruelling, exhausting and stressful existence that is the everyday reality for people caught in the currents of poverty, but she also wanted to talk about what it *feels* like to be on the receiving end of a narrative that is used to dehumanise, malign and shame people when they need help the most. She was interested in the role poverty shaming played in sustaining and embedding poverty, and how this 'story' percolates throughout society, shaping our outlook and attitudes. And, as someone interested in how shame more generally is deployed against specific groups in society, for example the body shaming of women, of which Jameela has been a fearless critic, she argues that it is vital to openly acknowledge how, why and where poverty shaming is applied – and to challenge it head-on.

Jameela said:

> "I think shame is used as a tool against people who grow up with no money. The narrative that's written in the media around poor people is really where you see the discrimination take place. The case studies that they choose to show us of people who are poor are always so extreme. In order to twist the narrative around all poor people, they'll find a picture of one young man smoking weed in a council flat and they'll use that image as the poster child for all poor people. I think there's a deliberate twisting of the story of poor people in order for the media to help the government justify not helping them: to make it seem like they don't want to help themselves.
>
> To be treated like a burden when you're suffering is not helpful. Nobody has ever benefited from being shamed. It only holds you back. No one wants to go and pick up a minimum wage check. Nobody would choose that for themselves."

Even as someone who has managed to circumvent the odds that were stacked against her (on top of the hardship of having no money as a child and teenager Jameela also faced life-threatening health issues), the memory of being in a family struggling to get by, living in fear of eviction, and of being looked down upon for it, sits heavily. "It's definitely an emotional journey to grow up with less money than other kids," Jameela explained. "It affects your entire mind and body health. And that definitely plays into what you end up doing with your life and ... opportunity."

Making sense of shame

When he published his groundbreaking essay, 'Poor, relatively speaking', the Nobel Laureate Amartya Sen brought to widespread attention the connection between poverty and shame that had been long neglected in the conceptualisation of poverty.[4] Sen, who had a long-standing interest in poverty, including his work on famine, helped steer a conversation on the subject into unfamiliar terrain when he placed shame at the core of what it means to be poor. Other thinkers had theorised on the relationship between poverty and shame before (notably the 19th-century British philosopher and economist Adam Smith[5] when he wrote *The Theory of Moral Sentiments*, and on whose work Sen draws in his essay) but Sen cleared the path for a fresh understanding of poverty that, while in line with a number of other approaches in stressing the non-monetary or material aspects of poverty such as access to education, also addressed the psycho-social experience of poverty, and in Sen's case, feeling shame and being shamed. He writes: 'The ability to go about without shame is at the irreducible absolutist core in the idea of poverty.'[6]

Understanding shame, as Sen realised, is essential to understanding poverty. As Jameela identified, the most powerful in society use shaming with expert skill to discriminate, bully and stigmatise – to 'brand' individuals or groups and even kids as morally deplorable and in need of punishment. The author of *Pauperland: Poverty and the Poor in Britain*,[7] historian Jeremy Seabrook, puts it this way: 'Shame is the most persistent attribute of contemporary poverty.'[8]

When considering the public shaming of children in the US for not having enough to pay for meals in the school cafeteria, or youngsters in Britain missing school because they can't afford sanitary products it would be difficult to deny the connection between shame and poverty.

Seabrook argues that as the collective action and solidarity engendered by early labour movements in Britain, with ideas of the poorest as 'proud, dignified, stoical', gave way to an era of neoliberalism, shame became all the more important as a defining feature of the age. '[The poorest] have showed solidarity, even defiance, facing the condition of being poor. Why should shame be the particular inflection of poverty in this enlightened age?', he ponders. The same could be said for the US.

A considerable body of research, including by Tracy Shildrick et al in the UK and Stephen Pimpare et al in the US,[9] shows that in a culture where shaming the poor has become common practice, a sizeable proportion of wider society – as well as many of those most affected by poverty – believe that the poor alone are to blame. '[Poorer people] have become aware of their own [perceived] bad conduct or faulty actions,' Seabrook writes.

> And this is precisely what the government intends people to experience, since punitive policies enhance a sense of guilt. It seems the poor have internalised the assessment of – who? Their betters, the rich, legislators, moralists? How has this ideological fiction passed into everyday acceptance?[10]

As the Illinois-based community activist Sheilah Garland-Olaniran summed it up when we met in the spring of 2018: "You are shamed and isolated. It is a learned response."

So why is shame such an effective weapon in the arsenal of those who wield the toxic poverty narrative?

The Merriam Webster dictionary definition of shame breaks down like this:[11]

NOUN: Shame
1 a :a painful emotion caused by consciousness of guilt, shortcoming or impropriety;
    b :the susceptibility to such an emotion;
2 :a condition of humiliating disgrace or disrepute – ignominy;
3 a :something that brings censure or reproach. *Also* – something to be regretted – pity;
    b : a cause of feeling shame.

VERB: Shame
1 : to bring shame to: disgrace;
2 : to be put to shame by outdoing;
3 : to cause to feel shame;
4 : to force by causing to feel guilty.

That we as humans experience shame – what psychologists determine to be a 'self-conscious and moral emotion as opposed to so-called basic emotions such as anger or fear'[12] – is significant. Shame has a profound role to play in sustaining the toxic narrative and feeding the power imbalance between those at the bottom of society and those at the top. It ensures there is a failure to tackle either the misconceptions fed by the narrative, or the poverty it promotes. Shame has 'the status of a premier social emotion' in sociology, as Robert Walker[13] points out in his book. It has an enduring and profound role in human history as a mechanism for encouraging conformity and harmony in societies by acting to prevent serious deviation from the norms that stitch a culture together. In historical terms, when groups of humans were generally small or tribal, the survival of the community may have been at stake if errant behaviour was tolerated. As societies grew in size and complexity, the nature and deployment of shaming altered too. As Walker puts it, shame has a function that ranges from being a 'glue that holds social relationships and societies together' to being a force that can 'blow them apart'. Yet, as he has also pointed out, when it comes to poverty the concept of shame, despite playing such a pivotal role in the experience of being poor, has tended to hover on the margins of analysis.

This is not surprising perhaps when the terms of discourse have tended to be set by the socially mobile, the connected, the powerful and the non-poor. It is a vital tool for preventing redistribution of wealth from the richest to the poorest.

As the dictionary definition suggests, being shamed and feeling shame is painful and visceral. It brings with it guilt that can sometimes not be fully articulated or may be wholly unjustified. It is a humiliation, sometimes public, sometimes private. It is something to be regretted because it is in a constant battle with our search for dignity, respect and self-worth. The act of shaming can bring with it a sense of disgrace and lack of value or belonging in the eyes of society for people within groups deemed to deviate from 'the norm'. While working on Project Twist-It I found that interviewees in both the US and the UK, just like Jameela, understood that the role of shame was a profound one.

In one report published by the international anti-poverty organisation ATD Fourth World,[14] outlining research which had people with lived experience of poverty working alongside researchers, six dimensions of poverty were identified. These were:

- Disempowering systems and structures
- Financial insecurity, financial exclusion and debt
- Damaged health and wellbeing
- Lack of control over choices
- Unrecognised struggles, skills and contributions
- Stigma, blame and judgement.

Under the latter dimension, participants identified the power that negative stereotypes wielded and how the judgements of others were often internalised. People with lived experience reported that "being in poverty makes you feel ashamed; you are made to feel worthless because people are judged by their bank balances"; and that they are "conditioned to suffer in silence and not ask for help – to just get up, shut up ...". As one participant succinctly put it: "Being in poverty makes you feel ashamed."

In his 2015 book, *So You've Been Publicly Shamed*,[15] Jon Ronson nimbly illustrated that in our super-connected, often alarmingly judgemental online culture in particular shaming has morphed in such a way that it can go viral in the blink of an eye and demolish a person's reputation before they've had time to compute that it's even happening, never mind defend themselves. 'And then one day it hit me,' Ronson writes.

> Something of real consequence was happening. We were at the start of a great renaissance of public shaming.... When we deployed shame we were utilising an immensely powerful tool. It was coercive, borderless, and increasing in speed and influence.

Poverty-induced shame is at once complex and elementary. It may differ in manifestation and extent between cultures, groups, or individuals and across time. Or it may, as Walker et al's landmark global research initiative found,[16] share extensive commonalities across cultures and continents. On a personal level it may be that we feel poverty-related shame to varying degrees at different points in our lives. For instance, if a new crop of politicians and pundits suddenly decides to justify policies by ratcheting up anti-welfare rhetoric, then there's a fair chance if you're struggling to get by you will feel greater shame than during more benign political times. It may be that as individuals there are occasions when (as I have done) we deny being poor full stop to shield ourselves from judgement and ridicule. If we do admit to being in poverty, we might feel deeply the shaming levelled at us, which can in turn have a long-standing negative impact on our self-worth. Alternatively, we might deny feeling shame because to do so is to admit you have failed, by society's standards.

In Britain and America, the fact that the wider culture and benefits systems are wedded for the most part to a construction of poverty that rests on an assumption that individual failure produces poverty[17] makes it especially fertile ground for shaming.[18] This is something that came across loud and clear in interviews for Project Twist-It – including among young people.

How poverty shaming leaves its mark

Charlotte Bilo of the International Policy Centre for Inclusive Growth wrote a blog in 2017[19] that outlined some of the multiple and interlinked factors at play when it comes to shame, poverty and policy.

Bilo writes in her blog:

> When it comes to poverty, shame can take many forms. For instance, being unable to meet one's own necessities is often accompanied by a feeling of shame, even more so when it comes to the needs of one's own children. Shame is also experienced when one is unable to do what is customary in society, such as the celebration of religious or traditional festivities. Unemployment is another dimension that

is closely related to poverty-induced shame as being unemployed often evokes a feeling of uselessness. Having to accept alms or special treatment can further exacerbate the feeling of shame as well as encounters with those administering welfare or social protection programmes. Poverty-induced shame can have several negative consequences, including low self-esteem and withdrawal from society, often perpetuating the vicious cycle of poverty even more.

She continues:

> From a policy perspective, it is important to note that anti-poverty policies can heighten or lessen the level of shame. Policies, including social protection policies such as cash transfer programmes, are an important instrument for poverty reduction and help to make households more resilient against a variety of shocks. Yet, the design of these policies and how they are presented in public can easily increase the feeling of shame.

The shame and stigma associated with being poor, or on a very low income, or on benefits, is painful and circular. People are shamed by others (external shaming) and often this translates to being ashamed of your position (internalising the shame). This may in turn lead to acceptance of an inferior status or distancing oneself from others in the same difficult circumstances in order not to see yourself as 'like them'. As Walker et al's research on poverty and shame has documented,[20] when it comes to the UK, even people at whom the pejorative slurs are directed can look for another group, a scapegoat, to deflect their own discomfort.

The British academic Ruth Patrick sums up this process in her research looking at poverty stigma against a backdrop of derogatory rhetoric aimed at people in receipt of certain welfare benefits in the UK.[21]

> What is important is that stigmatisation, and what Chase and Walker (2013)[22] term the 'co-construction

of shame', are processes that have both internal and external constituents: individuals feel and take on a shamed and stigmatised identity, just as they also respond to and sense external forces of stigmatisation and exclusion.

" ... when we see other people perform actions, we are more likely to attribute their actions to their characteristics – so who they are as people – whereas when we perform an action, we are more likely to attribute it to our situation and or circumstances."
Dr Adi Jaffe, talking to Project Twist-It

Dr Adi Jaffe is a US-based expert on shame, addiction and mental health. When interviewed for Project Twist-It, he suggested that part of reason we are so receptive to the negative messages and condemnation of people who are struggling financially, why high levels of public opprobrium are commonplace, and why we don't necessarily challenge the stigma that results, could be linked to the 'Fundamental Attribution Error'. Jaffe said:

> "The fundamental attribution error tells us that when we see other people perform actions, we are more likely to attribute their actions to their characteristics – so who they are as people – whereas when we perform an action, we are more likely to attribute it to our situation and or circumstances."

"Let's take that into this discussion about poor people and stigmatisation," Jaffe adds.

> "We see other people as losing money and losing their homes as 'there's something wrong with them'. If we suffer financial setback, we talk about the unfair loans that we took on, the recession and job loss and maybe our parents dying and having to take care of them at great financial cost to us, which ended up exacerbating our financial decline. The same exact situation – two people losing their homes because

they are poor – but one of them is fully attributed to characteristics of the person.**"**

As Robert Walker says: 'Firstly, poverty is inherently political because it poses a threat to the status quo. Secondly, because poverty is often taken to be the result of individual failure, a powerful social construction, it is replete with possibilities for shaming.'[23]

The act of poverty shaming forces upon many of us a self-reproach that is manufactured and unjustified. And, even when we know that shaming is wrong, it is powerful enough to stop us – it stopped me for a time – from talking openly about our experiences of impoverishment and the injustices of the system. This impedes our capacity for challenging bad policy. It takes away by stealth our motivation to challenge the powerful.

Mind the gap: public attitudes towards the poor

In 2018 Dr Rodolfo Leyva in the Department of Media Communications at the London School of Economics published a paper in the journal *Media Psychology*.[24] In it, he reported the results of an experiment he completed in the UK into the impact of materialistic media on attitudes towards poorer people. The conclusion? People who are regularly exposed to shows that glamorise wealth, luxury and fame such as *The Apprentice* or *Keeping up with the Kardashians* are potentially much more likely to hold 'stronger materialistic and anti-welfare attitudes than lighter consumers of these shows'.

If there is more emphasis on materialism as a way to be happy, this makes us more inclined to be selfish and anti-social, and therefore unsympathetic to people less fortunate.
Dr Rodolfo Leyva, Department of Media Communications, London School of Economics

The relentless promulgation of 'cultural representations and endorsements of materialism', according to Dr Leyva, '… are particularly endemic' in richer countries. When participants in his study were asked about their media consumption after having taken part in an experiment which exposed the 'treatment' group to images of celebrities and luxury products as well as to newspaper headlines of rags-to-riches stories (the control group were shown neutral stimuli), the results were striking. They showed a 'significant treatment effect' of even momentary exposure to materialistic media 'on both anti-welfare attitudes and support for anti-welfare policies'. Dr Leyva sums up the implications this way:

> Humans are inherently materialistic but also very social and communal. The way this is expressed depends on our culture. If there is more emphasis on materialism as a way to be happy, this makes us more inclined to be selfish and anti-social, and therefore unsympathetic to people less fortunate ... This study can contribute to explanations for why the UK public's support for welfare to aid the impoverished and unemployed has been decreasing during a time of rapidly growing wealth disparities, living costs and rates of precarious and under-employment.

Leyva's experiment was relatively small (487 British adults responded) but, as he pointed out when the report was published, it's part of a wider tapestry of research on attitudes towards poverty and poorer people – especially about those who are unemployed or who receive benefits – and by extension, attitudes towards wealth and the wealthy.

For the dominant poverty narrative to hold, it has to be accepted by the public. So, what do we know? The available research on attitudes to poverty, poorer people and welfare in Britain and America is very much in line with the assessments and observations of the people I've interviewed and who contributed to Project Twist-It. It's not just that politicians and pundits peddle the narrative and use it to defend indefensible policies like austerity and to protect the powerful and the rich. That is bad enough. It's that your relatives, friends, neighbours and wider society buy into the propaganda. That they can harbour thoughts and beliefs about you and your predicament that are prejudiced, and that they might help propagate depictions of lower income people as 'lesser', which then helps shape and amplify the stigma and shame you feel on a very personal level. It's that they can't see that this most toxic of stories is used to keep people like you poor.

As the American writer Sarah Smarsh told Project Twist-It:

> "Growing up among a group that in the US are diminished with the slurs 'white trash' or 'rednecks' made me keenly aware of how language and narratives are harnessed to preserve unjust power structures. I am for stories that break us free from the confines of reductive, often destructive labels, and get closer to the truth."

The tendency to attribute blame to individual, rather than structural, causes is a thread that runs through much of academic findings and popular surveys on the topic of why people are poor – or not. Research suggests that the concept of the deserving and undeserving poor person is ingrained. Attitudes are not set in stone of course. They alter over time, differ between social and political groupings and generationally. However, the research in general indicates that enough people align with the dominant narrative around poverty to render it distinctly problematic.

The existing research offers some valuable insights. When it comes to studying public attitudes towards the poor – and examining who or what causes poverty – research shows that people on the left of the political spectrum are, as you'd expect, more likely to agree with structural explanations for poverty and collective responses to the problem, while those who are right-leaning tend to favour the individual-as-lazy/pull-yourself-up-by-your-bootstraps conceptualisation. Even with a sizeable portion of the population absorbing the actual facts and scale of poverty and grasping the structural nature of it despite the toxic narrative, it remains the case that a significant proportion of people buy into the powerful poverty narrative Kool-Aid in both the US and the UK.

Attitudes – what we believe (and what we *say* we believe) – about the poorest in society are a crucial element of the poverty narrative picture. They are an important barometer for gauging not just what the relationship is between the dominant narrative around poverty and people's views, but also what prompts people to accept or reject the narrative, how deeply the narrative is entrenched and among whom, and how engagement with the narrative fluctuates over time and between different groups.

As a focus for researchers and scholars, understanding these patterns acquired a greater sense of urgency as the impact of poverty and rampant inequality hit national agendas in both Britain and America. Interrogating public attitudes around poverty is necessary not least because what the public believes, backs, or tolerates, has a role to play in policymaking. They either will or won't elect politicians who, when it suits them, weaponise the poverty narrative to justify cutting social programmes for the neediest while indulging in 'corporate welfare'[25] such as tax relief for corporations.

It was a welcome change when, as the race to unseat Trump heated up in 2019, there was a notable shift among some Democratic Party presidential contenders towards pushing for more ambitious progressive policies, including tackling inequality and low wages,[26] but on the whole politicians on the right (and all too frequently among those left-of-centre when in power) in recent years have generally tended to shy away from more radical actions that would significantly reduce inequality or poverty. If anything – as demonstrated by austerity in Britain and tax cuts for the rich in the US, which reinforced an already vast inequality problem of supercharged wealth concentration and dynastic wealth transference to a handful of super-rich families[27] – they've mostly done the opposite – and deployed the narrative to assist them on their way.[28]

It's not the case that politicians necessarily take their lead from voters, of course. (If they did, Britain would still have the death penalty and America would have much stricter gun laws – and the rich would pay more tax.) Some survey results have suggested, for example, that despite the poverty narrative being pushed hard, it is vulnerable to public opinion that wants much more to be done to address poverty and inequality.[29]

Most people in the UK and the US say when surveyed that they are concerned about inequality, poverty and the gaps between rich and poor, but the implementation of substantive or widespread progressive policies to address them has been notable by its absence.[30] In one 2011 poll, 60 per cent of Americans agreed that the government should do more to reduce the gap between the rich and the poor.[31] A Pew Research Center study in 2018 concluded that the majority – around six in ten Americans – believe the economic system unfairly benefits powerful interests (this attitude is heavily skewed towards Democrats and Democratic-leaning voters, with more of this group – 84 per cent – feeling this way in 2018 versus 76 per cent in 2016).[32] More generally, opinion surveys indicate that Americans want to live in a more equitable society, with widespread support for a stronger safety net, and that they tend to support policies such as increasing the minimum wage and taxing the better off.[33]

In Britain, according to a 2018 Nat Cen British Social Attitudes Survey,[34] 71 per cent of people feel the minimum wage should be increased, while 70 per cent say the government should top up the wages of lone parents struggling to make ends meet. On the face of it, none of this suggests an electorate that blames the poor, but rather one that identifies people as needing help. And yet, governments are elected that implement policies that harm the poorest while, crucially, other research findings suggest that the idea of a poor person as the architect of his or her misfortune runs deep.

Studies illustrate how prevailing attitudes to poverty have clear fault lines along race, political leanings and economic status. In the US, 2018 Pew Research describes how partisan divisions in attitudes towards poorer people have become more inveterate. For example, the research found:

- The share of **Republicans** who attribute wealth more to hard work shot up from **54%** in 2016 to **71%** in 2018.
- **Democrats** shifted by **7%** in the opposite direction.

When it comes to income, the wealthier a household is, the more likely people are to attribute wealth to personal effort.[35] The research found:

- Those with annual family incomes of $75,000 or more are more likely than those with incomes of less than $30,000

(49% versus 36%) to say being wealthy is more attributable to hard work than to a person's advantages.

- Those with lower incomes are more likely than those with higher incomes to say a person is poor more because of circumstances beyond their control than because of a lack of effort.

In terms of associating poverty with laziness Pew's findings were that:

- Just over half of American adults overall (52%) see poverty as linked to circumstances beyond the individual's control but a third (31%) put it down to 'lack of effort'.
- Republicans and right-leaning people are far more likely to associate poverty with laziness, with almost half (48%) saying people are poor more as a result of lack of individual effort.

Other research has identified that some attitudes towards the poor have been largely consistent for decades. For example, a 2016 poll conducted by the *Los Angeles Times* with think tank the American Enterprise Institute, which updated a similar piece of work from three decades earlier,[36] concluded that despite significant social change, attitudes were relatively constant over time. Writing about the results in the *Los Angeles Times* in August 2016, David Lauter explained:

> [The poll] illustrates how attitudes about poverty have remained largely consistent over time despite dramatic economic and social change.

As with other research, Lauter notes, of those who self-identify as conservative: 'Roughly a third … say that the poor do not work very hard, a view at odds with big majorities of moderates and liberals.'
He added that:

> … criticism of the poor – a belief that there are 'plenty of jobs available for poor people,' that government programs breed dependency and that most poor

people would 'prefer to stay on welfare' – is especially common among the blue-collar, white Americans who have given the strongest support to Donald Trump.

Among the poll's findings were a sizeable minority are inclined to believe that people on welfare benefits want to stay on them.

Do you think that most poor people who receive welfare benefits prefer to stay on welfare or would rather earn their own living?

Prefer to stay on welfare:

• White with no college degree: 44 per cent
• White with a college degree: 25 per cent
• Total non-white: 35 per cent

Lauter wrote:

> Blue-collar whites were much more likely than non-whites to view the poor as a class set apart from the rest of society – trapped in poverty as a more or less permanent condition. Minority Americans, particularly blacks, tended to say that 'for most poor people, poverty is a temporary condition'.

In addition, the research found that most Americans do not believe it is the role of government to bear the main burden of taking care of the poor: just one in five believed the onus was on government.

On the effectiveness of government anti-poverty programmes, a sizeable minority believe they don't work (although this can be for different reasons).[37] For example, in answer to the question:

What impact have anti-poverty government efforts had?

Respondents who say they have had a big impact:

• People below the poverty line: 8 per cent

- People above the poverty line: 5 per cent
- All respondents: 5 per cent

In the UK, research by the Joseph Rowntree Foundation[38] showed how support for the benefits system had fallen dramatically since the early 1990s. After a decade of listening to the Thatcherite rhetoric justifying demolishing the welfare state and declaring 'personal responsibility' to be the lens through which we judge each other, the narrative was doing its toxic job. While some groups, such as pensioners and disabled people, were still regarded as worthy up to a point, the shift in attitudes towards the negative in regard to welfare generally was 'dramatic', the research suggested. It concluded: 'People have become less likely to support greater spending on welfare, and more likely to believe that the system produces the wrong results.'[39]

And, the same 2017 Nat Cen British Social Attitudes survey[40] that reported the welcome news that nearly two thirds of people would like government to increase the minimum wage, also reported a less positive result: that 43 per cent agreed with statements that generous welfare benefits created 'dependency'.[41]

Writing in *The Guardian* in September 2018, Simon Tilford, chief economist at the Institute for Global Change,[42] wondered why, when the Nat Cen research showed two thirds of Brits wanting the government to do more to reduce the gap between rich and poor, only 15 per cent 'agree strongly that ordinary people do not get their fair share of the national wealth – despite wealth inequality being twice as high as that of income'. He pointed out too, for example, how almost three fifths of British voters think that inheritance taxes, which impact only a few well-off citizens, are unfair.

A month after Tilford's article, the newspaper also reported that an increasing number of Britons think empathy is on the wane.[43] A YouGov survey commissioned by the Scout movement found that 51 per cent of British adults said they thought there was less empathy towards others, making it harder to put yourself in someone else's shoes. Bear Grylls, the explorer, TV presenter and chief scout, concluded there was a risk of 'more division in our communities' if this was not addressed. The chief executive of Ipsos Mori said studies suggested 'we have become a society less empathetic to the work-age poor'.[44]

A matter of disrepute

For those of us with experience of being poor in Britain and America the conclusion that shaming is intimately intertwined with poverty is, quite frankly, an observable, everyday fact. So too is the understanding that a large chunk of the public think badly of poorer people.

To feel shame, to be shamed, and being subjected to toxic attitudes are part and parcel of being poor.

Robert Walker points out in his book, *The Shame of Poverty*, that shame can only become part of a broader discussion and understanding of poverty 'when the voices of people with direct experience of poverty are heard'. In other words, we can only really construct a meaningful and truthful story of poverty and the power structures that produce and sustain it when the people on the receiving end of poverty shaming are directly involved in the construction of that story. Without this, a more rounded grasp of the mechanisms at play is missing and so too are perhaps the most effective means of overturning the dominant narrative and the terrible policies that shaming fortifies.

III
Flipping the script: challenging the narrative war on the poor

"You never know where a person has come from until you walk a mile in their shoes. You don't know what that person's story is."
June Cigar, former homeless person and social justice campaigner, Skid Row, Los Angeles

"Poverty takes something from your soul on a daily, day-to-day basis."
Linda Tirado, author of *Hand to Mouth*, talking to Project Twist-It

The great escape

My dad had been showing me how to knot my new school tie all week. By the time it came to putting it and the rest of my uniform on – brown pleated skirt, jumper with two yellow stripes on the cuffs, white shirt, beige socks and brown blazer – for the first day of secondary school, he'd had enough of my efforts and given up, but I eventually had it down.

Somehow, the family had mustered enough money to make sure I had a 'proper' wool blazer and not the thin polyester kind that the government grant for poorer families covered. "This is a good one. It will make sure you're warm in the winter," the woman in the shop had told me as she took the government voucher and cash from me.

That I was putting on a brown uniform, and not a maroon one, was significant. This single fact weighed on me more than the guilt of where the money had come from to fund the better blazer. You see, a few months earlier I'd unexpectedly failed my 11+,[1] the exam that determined which kids in Northern Ireland would go to the 'grammar' school (where the focus was on academic achievement) or the alternative (usually a school where poorer youngsters ended up and which saw most pupils leave at 16 with no chance of further education, never mind university).

The day the 11+ results came in my legs felt hollow, my stomach tumbled. In a single announcement all of my dreams seemed to die.

I. Had. Failed.

My aspiration of one day going to university had been stolen by an arbitrary exam that assumed you could decide the entire future of an 11-year-old on the basis of a couple of test papers, no matter what circumstances that child lived in when she had to sit those papers.

For months the whole class had been doing practice exams. The idea was that if we did enough 'mock' tests we'd be ready when the big day came. What I didn't grasp was that it didn't matter that my scores in the mock tests had always been extremely high – way above the pass rate. What mattered was how I performed on the day. And I didn't. The exam didn't care that I was exhausted because of unforeseen stresses at home and no sleep. It meant nothing that circumstances far beyond my 11-year-old control rendered all my hard work useless on the day.

As I stood in the principal's office on the morning the results were read out, throat dry and tear ducts swollen, the head teacher opened her desk drawer and took out a small rectangular package. "For you," she said, putting her hand on my shoulder.

"Me? Why?"

My class teacher, Frances Egan, had come in and was standing behind me.

"But I failed," I told them, heartbroken and believing I had let them as well as myself down.

They watched in silence as I opened my gift – a beautiful fountain pen. They explained that not getting into the grammar school wasn't the end of everything. The school I was going to would take care of me, they reassured. At St Louise's Comprehensive College I could excel.[2] No, it wasn't a grammar school. It was a comprehensive – uncommon in Northern Ireland[3] – but they had a philosophy that would back me all the way. They did not label kids who didn't pass the 11+ as failures.

When the first day of school came and my friends and I walked the half mile to the bus stop we were among a sea of brown. On the other side of the road, waves of maroon headed for St Dominic's. We all understood – felt – the difference. No one needed to say it out loud. We were second-rate in the eyes of the system; failures on the road, if we were lucky, to factory or shop work. The girls in the maroon uniforms had 'potential'. They were on the road to better things. They were expected to go to university.

The assembly hall at St Louise's was packed with raucous 11-year-olds. The room was huge compared to our little primary school. After being allocated classes – 12 groups of 30+ pupils in a school with almost 2,500 girls attending – a hush fell over the room. We heard the approaching march-like strut of Sister Genevieve[4] as she strode up the aisle, a feminist nun with a mission.

In a few short sentences she gave us permission to believe we could defy expectations.

On so many occasions I lost count, we were told by Sister Genevieve (or 'Gen', as she was referred to by pupils when out of earshot) that we were as good as anyone else. Our circumstances would not be permitted to hold us back or to define who we were. We did not have to listen when people tried to put us down or dismiss us. We would take ourselves seriously and we would go out into the world with our heads held high. We would not accept prejudice or discrimination as immoveable fact. The enemy, poverty, would not stand in our way. Seven years later, at age 18, I began my first year at Cambridge University – one of the (still) negligible[5] number of young people from poor backgrounds who do so.

7

Feeling it: the truth about living in poverty

"Poverty consists in feeling poor."
Ralph Waldo Emerson

"There is a general ignorance about the lives led by poor Americans, an ignorance, whether real or feigned, that shapes public discourse about poverty and welfare, and policy itself."
Stephen Pimpare, *A People's History of Poverty in America*, **p 5**

Telling it like it is: the people on the poverty frontline

When I first began to speak to people for Project Twist-It, a central part of what drove me was to gather and provide a place for the voices and insights of people with lived experience of poverty. What could they tell me about the reality of life when it is defined by financial insecurity? What would they tell all of us if they had a platform to talk about poverty? What would they say about the imbalance and inequality within our societies that kept people poor? How would they challenge the toxic poverty narrative? It turns out – they had a hell of a lot to say.

One of the first people to become involved with the project was the young documentary-maker Billie J.D. Porter, who grew up in poverty in London. Billie, an outspoken critic of the way poorer people are depicted and treated, wrote a blog for the website.[1]

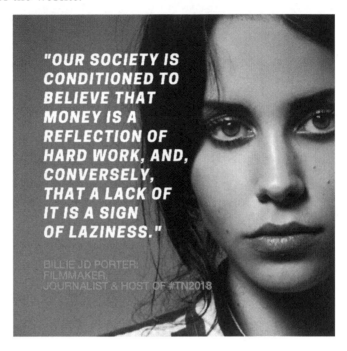

"OUR SOCIETY IS CONDITIONED TO BELIEVE THAT MONEY IS A REFLECTION OF HARD WORK, AND, CONVERSELY, THAT A LACK OF IT IS A SIGN OF LAZINESS."

BILLIE JD PORTER:
FILMMAKER,
JOURNALIST & HOST OF #TN2018

These are some of Billie's thoughts and observations:

> There's such an overwhelming sense of guilt and shame when it comes to financial struggle. I was conflicted about how open to be in this post, because part of me almost feels disloyal by speaking about the difficulties my parents have faced over the years. It's not nice to think about the period not long ago when my father was begging on the street, or that my mum has to do a part-time cleaning job while having a lung disease and nearing retirement age. My decision to be private about this stuff, even to some of my close friends, has been nothing to do with vanity or pride, but more how twisted the public perception is of people who find themselves in similar, or worse, positions to those my parents have been in.

Billie continues:

> Our society is conditioned to believe that money is
> a reflection of hard work, and, conversely, that a lack
> of it is a sign of laziness. 'Poor' was the label we were
> all desperate to avoid at my school, even though most
> of us came from low-income families, or households
> with unemployment. I was perpetually anxious about
> being judged for things that seem so trivial now; using
> own brand supermarket goods in Food Tech class, or
> being on the free school meals programme. Poverty
> isn't simple. It never has been. Poverty is intersectional.
> Poverty can be short-term, long-term, and about more
> than just the money in your bank account.

**"Poverty is the experience of being unable to control the
economic circumstances around you. What you're actually
talking about is never having the security of knowing the
world is a benign place. People go: 'oh, poor people make stupid
decisions' and it's, well, shut up. Rich people make incredibly
stupid decisions all the time."**
Mark Brown, writer and mental health campaigner[2]

Around the same time, I met with campaigner and writer Mark
Brown. As someone who has been on the margins of or in
poverty in today's low-wage,[3] precarious economy,[4] Mark spoke
about the everyday setbacks and anxieties of being trapped by
poverty, how these feed off each other, and how, bearing in mind
what those in poverty know about it, the ways in which the
dominant story we are told about the poor is not only patently
untruthful, but disingenuous and harmful.

"We talk about poverty as if it's almost a health condition: you
acquire poverty and you become a 'poverty-type' person and it
does all these things to you and then you're kind of imperilled
by it," Mark explains. "But it's not. Poverty is the experience of
being unable to control the economic circumstances around you.
What you're actually talking about is never having the security
of knowing the world is a benign place."

"The thing about being poor is kind of the horizon gets closer and closer to your face. And people go, 'oh, poor people make stupid decisions' and it's, well, shut up. Rich people make incredibly stupid decisions all the time but if it comes to it and you have £1 in your pocket, you could put it in your [financial investment] or you could buy some chips. It's like, Fuck off."

When it comes to why poorer people are ritually demonised by politicians and the media and the impact of this, Mark had this to say:

"When you politicise and you weaponise notions of poverty, you are never speaking to people in poverty. You are never addressing people who are poor because you assume A: they're not listening, B: they don't vote, C: they're stupid, D: they're a bit smelly."

In this, Mark was echoing what a number of Project Twist-It interviewees observed about the daily grind of poverty in America, and how the system works against reducing poverty. I met Sylvia Hernandez, a young mother who had lived on Skid Row for a time in Downtown Los Angeles. As a person with lived experience of poverty who has committed herself to exposing the injustice of it whenever possible, she told me: "It is a social, cultural, political system that keeps blaming the person... It's just the people doesn't have any support system. You never have nothing stable, you never have anything consistent."

"You have to choose to be blind to walk over the homeless guy on your way to work."
Gloria Downey, US army veteran

In the US, where Project Twist-It spoke with a number of army veterans with experience of poverty, a theme that came up time and again was how just one life-changing event could render someone destitute and yet the individual was blamed. The broader factors behind their misfortune were ignored. Gloria

Downey, who was left disabled and impoverished after military service, was one of these people.

Gloria, who also knew poverty as a child, told Project Twist-It:[5]

> "I remember my mom working three jobs at Christmas so I would have presents and I just remember being there alone at night and wanting to know why my mother wasn't there with me."

As an adult after doing military service in the Middle East, she adds:

> "I completely fell apart. I couldn't work. I think a lot of it was American wilful blindness, like the same kind that causes poverty and every other injustice in our society. You have to choose to be blind to walk over the homeless guy on your way to work, when you're the reason he's homeless because you need to live in your $7,000 apartment. The problem with most of this is that people are comfortable. As long as they are comfortable in their own privileges and they can find a way to justify ignoring you and thinking they deserve what they have over you, then they can continue to allow it."

Gloria continues:

> "I think it's important for people with privilege who think they are otherwise good people to find a reason to blame poor people so that they don't have [to face] their own guilt or give anything up."

Sometimes when I've interviewed people with experience of poverty, they have told me of times when, because they've reached a point of true desperation, they have been forced to push aside the humiliation they feel about being unable to make ends meet and resort to behaviours they never thought possible and are ashamed to talk to others about. The sort of desperate behaviours that the poor often end up criminalised for – like shoplifting.

Desperation – and the degree to which so many people are forced to do things they would never have dreamt of doing – was something that came up time and again among Project Twist-It contributors and interviewees. Sylvia Hernandez was a hairdresser from California when I met her and originally from Mexico. She had run the gamut of impoverishment, including living in sub-standard, cramped housing and homelessness while trying to take care of her young family. At times, as she did her best to raise her family, Sylvia felt she had no choice but to take drastic – yet necessary action. While working various low-paid jobs in the wake of the Great Recession, Sylvia sometimes found herself with just $15 – after rent. That $15 was all she had to last for two weeks and with it she was supposed to feed her three young children. In dire need, and despite feeling ashamed, Sylvia told me how she swallowed her pride and went to apply for foodstamps. She was accused of "making a scene" in the office when told she didn't qualify. Eventually "they gave it to me for a month, that's it," but it was a sticking plaster.

When the foodstamps ran out Sylvia had so little food in the cupboard she went to a neighbour who was also struggling and asked to borrow some basic provisions. "I was struggling, you know. And one day I didn't have milk and tortillas, you know? And the kids needed milk for the cereal so I went to a neighbour." Her neighbour came round later with two bags of food and an idea. "If you're willing to come tomorrow at 5am across the street to a big [grocery] store I'll take you to the trash can and get all the good stuff that they throw away," Sylvia's neighbour told her. "I said ok. I [lived] like that for two years. Everything was clean, everything was packaged." Eventually, a manager put a lock on the dumpster where Sylvia and her neighbour were foraging for discarded food. "He was mean ... they locked it and we couldn't go no more."

Much of what Sylvia, Jameela, Billie, Gloria and Mark said about the lived experience of poverty, be it as a child or adult, centres on the reality that being poor, as much of the most recent research in the area stresses, is about far more than the fact of material deprivation. As hard and as widespread as this financial penury is, poverty is also intrinsically about *how* that lack of resources and the way we are viewed and portrayed in wider society impacts on every aspect of life; how it affects capacity, autonomy, decision-making, anxiety, our health, our self-belief and so much more. It deprives poorer people of self-respect and of power.

Stigma, shame, discrimination and how the wider society views people in poverty produces layers of pain and struggle.

As Mark Brown told me, by being kept at a distance and "othered", the potential to understand and empathise with a poorer person's experience is curtailed. The possibility of buying into the dominant narrative increases and this in turn reduces the chances of building alliances across social classes to fight the primary problem – that poverty exists at all. Without authentic voices loudly, repeatedly and collectively challenging prejudice, stigma and structural inequalities, alternatives are drowned out. Even within political parties purporting to be progressive the direct input and voices of those most affected are all too often absent or convenient tokenistic political tools. How many times have you seen a poorer person or a group of poorer people on television news speaking their truth or calling into question the decisions, policies or depictions of poverty that affect them?

It is, quite simply, a no-brainer that shame and blame are inseparable from the experience of being poor and from entrenching poverty, yet these, as with the people most impacted, are rarely part of the wider conversation.

Poverty is as poverty does

Surely, a curious person might wonder, for the notion of the poor as a mass of shiftless, idle scroungers to be so rampant, it must spring from at least a partially reasoned assessment of life as it has been lived by most people on the breadline? Well, no. Are there poorer people who 'play the system' and defraud benefits and welfare for their own gain? Yes. But the numbers are miniscule and they pale in comparison to say, tax evasion.[6] There is zero evidence[7] of benefits fraud reaching anywhere remotely near the levels the public perceive it to be.[8] Nor is fraud anywhere close to the rates that politicians and pundits allude to in order to demonise benefits recipients. Are there poorer people who don't work hard or have given up? Yes. But again, proving it's any more or less prevalent than in any other social group is another thing altogether. And, frankly who could blame someone slogging away at a thankless low-paid, insecure job for giving up now and then?

The worst task I was ever given in a job was while working in a fast-food restaurant. I was made to scrub the tiles outside the entrance (about five square feet and filthy) with a toothbrush. I'd already been moving containers of fat in the kitchen (as dangerous as it sounds) but at least it wasn't in public view. When I finished scrubbing the tiles out front as people walked past me to get their burgers, I went inside and handed in my notice. The tiles were the last in a long line of daily humiliations. But I was lucky, I was a student at the time and the government had given me a maintenance grant because I was from a poor family, so while I needed the cash, I wouldn't starve if I had to walk away. Plus, as with many people, this was only one of my two part-time jobs. And, this wasn't me trying to feed a family while I was being humiliated by colleagues.

The thing is, poorer people are human beings, and all groups and classes of human beings include some individuals who display any number of questionable attributes and behaviours. (I've met plenty as I've made my way around various tiers of the social structure.) There are cheats, liars and layabouts in every class of people, at every strata of society – however these may be defined. It is nevertheless an entirely sound argument to suggest that indolence and an eagerness to live off 'hand-outs' is *in fact* a widely identifiable feature of the well off and the 'super-rich'. Not least among the 'New Gilded Age' aristocracy of the dynastic variety so well documented by Chuck Collins and Josh Hoxie at the Institute for Policy Studies[9] – a cluster of folk brought up to believe in an innate superiority who live off inherited wealth they believe they are entitled to while hoarding ever more of it for themselves and a tiny group of families.

I was grateful for programs that fed my family, but I'd also carry back home a bag of shame, each time mentally wrestling with what the cashier thought of me…
Stephanie Land, in *Maid: Hard Work, Low Pay, and a Mother's Will to Survive*

In his book, *A People's History of Poverty in America*,[10] academic and poverty expert Stephen Pimpare quotes a welfare recipient from the 1970s reflecting on the twisted nature of how myths around poverty and government assistance obscure the real issue of power and wealth. What this person says is about as compelling a summation of the dissonance and misdirection engendered by the poverty narrative as you're likely to find:

> Myths are needed to justify the welfare system, a system that cheats the very people it is supposed to help. Myths are needed to discourage eligible, low-paid workers from applying for aid. Myths are needed to divert taxpayer frustrations away from the country's big welfare recipients – the rich and the military – and onto the defenceless, powerless, poor. In short, myths are needed to hide the real welfare crisis.

Is idleness and an eagerness to live off 'hand-outs' a generic characteristic of people who are poor or struggling to keep their financial heads above the poverty line? No. It is not. Rather, the generic characteristic that most applies is more likely to be just how bloody hard it is to be poor and how difficult it is to escape from it. Stephanie Land, in her 2019 book *Maid: Hard Work, Low Pay, and a Mother's Will to Survive*,[11] outlines with harrowing precision the routine struggles of poverty in the US, including how commonplace the obstacles to getting help from the benefits system are. Throughout her book she also illustrates the general and ritual shaming involved in accessing or using assistance, be it foodstamps or help with housing. The system as configured – and the culture that permits it – is set up, Land observes, to judge and to inflict humiliation:

I was grateful for programs that fed my family, but I'd also carry back home a bag of shame, each time mentally wrestling with what the cashier thought of me, a woman with an infant in a sling, purchasing food on public assistance. All they saw were the foodstamps, the large WIC paper coupons that bought us eggs, cheese, milk, and peanut butter. What they didn't see was the balance.... I had to stretch it to the end of each month until the balance was re-upped after the beginning of the month. They didn't see me eating peanut butter sandwiches and hard-boiled eggs, rationing my morning cup of coffee to make it stretch. Though I didn't know it then, the government had worked that year to change the stigma surrounding the 29 million people who used foodstamps by giving it a new name: the Supplemental Nutrition Assistance Program (SNAP). But whether you called it SNAP or foodstamps, the assumption that the poor stole hardworking Americans' tax money to buy junk food was unchanged.

Poverty sucks

We know from the research[12] that poverty is, to put it bluntly, really, really bad for us – on multiple levels. Apart from the daily grind of hardship and the cumulative effect of this over time, far too often being poor deprives people of the opportunity to improve their situation or to reach their potential. Poverty entraps. If you are someone who has lived in poverty at any point you will know this already. If you are someone who hasn't experienced poverty but has spent even a modicum of effort trying to understand the structural causes and reality of it, this won't necessarily be news to you. But, just in case you don't fall into these categories, here are just a few indicators of what you're likely to face as *par for the course* if on the breadline and which can gravely impact on the lives of adults and children alike.

If you are poor or on a very low income, chances are:

- You live, as I did for much of my childhood, in unfit or temporary housing[13] that damages your health.[14]
- You are forced, as Jameela's family was, to move repeatedly just to have an unfit roof over your head, or you have experienced homelessness.[15]
- Your home is in a run-down area with fewer public amenities, or worse, near toxic or other waste[16] that causes life-threatening health conditions,[17] or you are exposed to higher levels of other pollutants and the effects of climate change events that affect your health and habitat.[18]
- When you have a job/s it's likely to be minimum-wage (or worse), with no secure contract of employment or guaranteed hours, which makes it impossible to plan ahead for a week (never mind longer term) and brings incredible stress; and you are no stranger to spending hours hopping on and off public transport just to get to your badly paid, exhausting, frequently humiliating work.[19]
- You have low status at work and your employer makes sure you know it; and you are highly likely to be denied wages and protections you are legally entitled to, making your poverty worse.[20]
- You regularly need to borrow cash (from neighbours, family, pay-day lenders, loan sharks, pawn shops) just to stay afloat from one day to the next and then drown under exorbitant interest payments and relentless cycles of debt.[21]
- You need to supplement your low income with state help, even though you'd rather not, because just one minor, temporary change in your circumstances, or one unforeseen bill, can render you destitute.[22]
- When you apply for help from government in the form of benefits or other assistance you will be made to jump through impossible hoops, fill in impenetrable and incomprehensible forms, be made to feel like you are begging for 'hand-outs' yet also supposedly behaving as if you are 'entitled', and – in many instances – are then denied the help you were asking for and have gone through all of the above degrading experiences to try to get.[23]

- When in contact with authorities, be it the benefits system, school system or justice system, you will know the feeling of being judged and having your behaviour and choices overly scrutinised and criticised and, if you are a person of colour, go ahead and multiply these feelings because your experiences will likely be a hell of a lot worse than for others.

This is far from the whole story. These are just some of the ways in which being poor, dealing with the multitude of consequences arising from poverty and being made to feel worthless intersect. The full experience is much more troubling. For example, poverty is one of the most significant social determinants of physical health and mental well-being, as well as of a host of convergent negative outcomes such as low educational attainment and increased likelihood of incarceration. All of these impact our quality of life and our potential to grasp opportunities for work and for a better, less stressful life in general. To be denied access to opportunity and a decent standard of living due to lack of resources is only one piece of the jigsaw. The others, including access to networks, social capital and the respect and dignity that accompany these, constitute an additional layer of barriers for poorer people. And, when you are 'othered', when you are repeatedly attacked for your impoverishment and stripped of your self-respect, this too affects your life chances and how you see yourself.

People who develop a mental disorder may not be able to work because of their illness. Others, because of discrimination, may be systematically denied work opportunities or may lose their existing job. Lack of employment drives people deeper into poverty.
World Health Organization

On the most fundamentally basic of levels – survival – poverty matters. It is a major factor in high rates of infant and maternal mortality and for lower life expectancy.[24]

The US fares especially badly on infant and maternal mortality. Infants in the US are less likely to reach one year of age than in other rich nations, according to the OECD. While infant mortality rates have fallen overall in the last half century, America has failed to keep pace with its wealthy counterparts. Babies in the US were three times more likely than in 19 equivalent rich countries to die from extreme immaturity, according to the research. The lead author, Ashish Thakra, concluded that higher relative rates of poverty and a weak social safety net were important factors. The study concluded that a lack of preventative care also played a part. He said: "We spend more on healthcare that's taking care of children that are already sick. But we spend far less money on welfare programs to keep children from becoming sick, and on keeping them safe from injuries."

We know too that childhood poverty is linked[25] to higher rates of behavioural and emotional difficulties, depression and anxiety disorders, and to higher rates of mental health disorders in adulthood. Meanwhile, for adults who are poor there are well-documented links with depression, anxiety and suicide. The World Health Organization (WHO) MIND Project reports that common mental health disorders are twice as frequent among the poorest than the richest.[26] And, as the WHO also points out, the evidence indicates that links between poverty and mental health are cyclical. Plus (and of course this refutes the poor person as lazy trope) mental health problems can be a cause of poverty.

'Poverty increases the risk of mental disorders and having a mental disorder increases the likelihood of descending into poverty,' the WHO explains. And, in reference to one of the major systemic causes of poverty (and frequently homelessness) it adds:

> People who develop a mental disorder may not be able to work because of their illness. Others, because of discrimination, may be systematically denied work opportunities or may lose their existing job. Lack of employment drives people deeper into poverty.

In addition, as the fallout of austerity in the UK showed us all too clearly, when the poorest and most vulnerable among us are deliberately made poorer, when vital social programmes and benefits are slashed, when the conditions of applying and getting state help become ever more barbarous and unbearable, and when they are repeatedly vilified, the outcomes – including a rise in mental health problems and suicides related to the process of welfare 'reform' – can be catastrophic.[27]

More than the state of being 'in poverty', however, as Richard Wilkinson and Kate Pickett so deftly argue in their groundbreaking books *The Spirit Level*[28] and, more recently, *The Inner Level*,[29] the level and manifestation of inequality within societies has a major role to play in our likelihood of suffering from a phalanx of health and social problems. It also seriously impacts on our conception of self-worth, fuelling 'status anxiety' among other problems, including for the poorest. In America and Britain, with their very high levels of inequality, to be poor therefore brings with it a multitude of additional challenges.

As Jameela and Billie highlighted, the non-material impact of poverty specifically that manifests as stigma and shame is corrosive and debilitating – especially for children. Studies show for instance that for children from low-income backgrounds, the stigmatising stereotypes associated with poverty amplify material hardships.[30] Reflecting what both Jameela and Billie had to say, what researchers have called 'hidden injuries' are endured by children and young people as a result of exposure to negative attitudes, rhetoric and behaviour related to perceived lower status.

Experiences of both shame and humiliation are endemic in poverty, due to the low status assigned to people on low incomes, and rhetoric that blames poor people for their own need.
Psychologists for Social Change

In a presentation in 2017,[31] drawing on her long-standing work and research on economic justice as well as that of others including the Pew Research Center, the psychologist Professor Heather Bullock at the University of California Santa Cruz[32] offers a prescient distillation of the broader damage done to children by poverty stigma and the cultural backdrop that enables it. Entitled 'The Hidden Injuries of Childhood Poverty:

the impact of class stigma, stereotypes and bias', Bullock's presentation offered these key insights, which I summarise here.

On the wider culture:

- First of all, the concept of 'individualism' in US culture is deeply embedded compared with most European countries – with the UK a notable exception running a close second to the US. For example, the percentage of people surveyed by Pew Research who *disagreed* that success in life is pretty much determined by forces outside our control was found to be 57 per cent in the US and 55 per cent in the UK. In Germany by contrast, the percentage was just 31. When it comes to believing in the importance of hard work to get ahead in life, the percentage of Americans who said it was very important was 73 per cent with – again – the UK in second place with 60 per cent. This compared with 21 per cent for Greece, 25 per cent for France and 50 per cent for Germany.
- Faith in 'meritocracy' is also more evident in America and Britain, with 70 per cent of Americans believing most people succeed because they've worked hard and the proportion of those in the UK agreeing standing at 57 per cent. Again, the two countries top the table internationally.

On poverty and children:

- Children are aware of poverty and social class at an early age.
- Low-income children are aware of negative beliefs about themselves and their families.
- Research shows that low-income children aged 5–12 perceived societal messages as disparaging the poor and experienced difficulty in having positive views of themselves.
- Studies reveal that elementary school-age children rated the poor as having fewer positive attributes such as being hard-working and honest, and as having more negative characteristics, for example, being lazy, dirty and rude. Interestingly, lower-income children – in an example of internalising the stigma – had less positive attitudes towards the poor than did middle-income children.

- The potential effects on low-income children's well-being include:
  - internalised classism: lower self-esteem, depression, anxiety, distancing from lower-income groups;
  - stereotype threats: compromised academic performance;
  - social exclusion and discrimination: both in interpersonal and institutional contexts.

Reinforcing other research in the field, Bullock also drew links between how people felt about the poor and support for safety net programmes. For example, support for individualistic attributions for poverty tended to lead to support for restrictive welfare policies while support for structural attributions tended to link to favouring progressive welfare policies.

The organisation Psychologists for Social Change/Psychologists Against Austerity (PAA) in the UK highlighted the links between poverty and mental well-being as austerity began hitting the UK hard after 2010.[33] One aspect they were interested in was how poverty, shame and humiliation were interconnected and how the turbocharged, belittling hostile environment of austerity amplified this.[34]

They wrote:

> Experiences of both shame and humiliation are endemic in poverty, due to the low status assigned to people on low incomes, and rhetoric that blames poor people for their own need. Both shame and humiliation are social emotions. Humiliation arises when people are made to feel that they are lesser in status or worth, while shame occurs when people are made to feel that they have violated a social or moral standard. These feelings have been compounded by the punitive benefits rhetoric used to drive through austerity policies, which has promoted the idea that those who use welfare benefits are worth less ('shirkers') than those who work ('strivers').

We live in a very capitalist society and needing help is weak. We need to realise that benefits aren't weak. Help isn't weak.
Young person, Kent, England, 2018

In my experience, those affected can be acutely alert to the harmful rituals of poverty-induced shame. As part of Project Twist-It we spoke with numerous young people about how they perceived the way poorer people and people on benefits – including kids – were portrayed in wider culture and how they were depicted by politicians.

While being interviewed for a short film in Britain in 2018 a group of teenagers with experience of poverty and whose families relied on government assistance like free school meals, some of whom were carers for sick or disabled parents, articulated why talking about being poor can be so difficult in the face of a relentless negative narrative. In a hyper-consumer culture saturated by social media, they told us, the constant judgement that comes with not having the same "stuff" as other kids and being "looked down on" made it hard to even bring the issue up. In large and small ways, every day, these young people, who lived by the way in one of the wealthiest regions of England but where there are still large pockets of poverty,[35] were reminded that they were 'different' and that they and their families were perceived negatively for needing help. As a result, they explained, young people from poorer backgrounds tend to take the path of least resistance by staying silent to avoid shame and bullying.

"It's not something we ever talk about," one young girl explains when asked. Another, who cares for both parents, recalled a rare lesson in school where the topic of poverty came up. "It was really awkward for me. Everybody was talking about it and I was just sitting there. What do I say without being judged? A lot of people were saying people [on benefits], 'well, they're stupid and these are people who just don't work, [they] just need to get a job', and that kind of hit me; my parents aren't actually able to [work]." Another young person added: "We live in a very capitalist society and needing help is weak. We need to realise that benefits aren't weak. Help isn't weak."

A different group of older teenagers – this time in Wigan, a city in the north of England – focused on the ways in which poorer people are depicted in the media and on television – especially by what has come to be known as 'poverty porn', where highly controversial reality TV programmes such as *Benefits Street* reinforce the stereotypes of poorer people as entitled layabouts on sofas watching flat-screen TVs all day. In the view of these teenagers, to be poor or on benefits means being blamed and ridiculed by TV programmes that distort, not reflect, reality. "You see, in media it's just negative all the time," one young woman observed. "A lot of TV shows see poor people as these uneducated, you know, junkies that just don't give a damn about life and want to be in that position. It feels like a choice rather than circumstances."

Agreeing with her, one young man added: "They might depict people that are poor as being quite bad; it's all to do with crime and stuff like that." On how these depictions impact on real life another added: "Is bias a factor of poverty? Definitely. Because it affects your ability to get a job and correct your financial situation."

Referring to the way poor people are portrayed versus the rich, one young person reflected: "As a society we give praise to the rich man. We give praise to those who are in a better economic position, we sort of idolise them."

A cognitive load

One significant recent strand of research – and one that blows a gaping hole in the narrative's assertion that poorer people are lazy, incapable, and just make bad choices – explores the cognitive 'load'[36] impact of poverty. Looking at the burden placed by poverty and on people's mental resources, researchers point to how the toll of struggling financially on low or no incomes makes it harder for people who are poor to act in ways that better-off people with far fewer relentless difficulties and much greater resources generally are able to. For example, in their paper, 'Poverty Impedes Cognitive Function',[37] Professor Anandi Mani et al, of Warwick University, write that the poor 'are less capable not because of inherent traits, but because the very context of poverty imposes load and impedes cognitive capacity'.

The researchers concluded:

It appears that poverty itself reduces cognitive capacity. We suggest that this is because poverty-related concerns consume mental resources, leaving less for other tasks.

Scarcity is more than just the displeasure of having very little. It changes how we think. It imposes itself on our minds.
Sendhil Mullainathan, Harvard economist and Eldar Shafir, Princeton psychologist[38]

In a similar vein, in their book *Scarcity: Why having too little means so much,*[39] Harvard economist Sendhil Mullainathan and Princeton psychologist Eldar Shafir argue that mentally taxing circumstances can affect cognitive functioning. At its core, having to confront scarcity – including the material scarcity of poverty – is so absorbing that the people impacted direct their mental energy towards it. If you can't make next week's rent and you and your kids are facing being put out on the street, it turns out that the research shows this will consume your mental energy to the point where other things simply fall down the priority list, making it harder to engage with even essential daily tasks, never mind any one of the multiple challenges thrown at a poorer person that takes them by surprise. And, crucially, from a poverty policy standpoint, and as has been pointed out time and again by research, anti-poverty organisations and people with lived experience of poverty, punitive benefits systems such as the ones currently in operation in the US and the UK that put an additional burden on the poorest by overloading them with 'conditions' and labyrinthine forms to prove eligibility – and then hit people with sanctions if they can't comply – compound the stresses that exacerbate cognitive load.

We just don't have the 'mental bandwidth', this research suggests, to deal with these sorts of pressures in a productive manner if we are poor. 'Scarcity is more than just the displeasure of having very little. It changes how we think. It imposes itself on our minds.'[40]

In Britain and America there is no shortage of people in poverty or on government benefits for whom these stressors and 'cognitive loads' constitute everyday reality and who, on top of the financial hardship, must contend with being blamed for the difficulties that their impoverishment produces and compounds. There are, as Chapters 1 and 2 of this book have already laid out, literally tens of millions of these people. When we met in London in 2018, Mark Brown had this to say on the relentlessness of poverty:[41]

> "[The thing] about having no money at all, is it's kind of a cumulative effect. If you've never been poor you can imagine what it's like to have three or four days at the end of the month before your paycheck arrives and that's like a great laugh and you keep calm and you carry on and you eat dried pasta and all that sort of stuff. [But] it's kind of the cumulative effect. It's the way that … being poor, not having access to resources, not having access to change your situation; it's the way that kind of mounts up on you. The straw that broke the camel's back is obviously a terrible cliché, but it feels like the longer you're poor, the more you're carrying. It's like not being able to fix a car. You get a little rattle, you get a little knock, but if you can't fix it for five years, the wheel falls off and then you're in a ditch somewhere. It's kind of that thing."

"The problem isn't that people are lazy, the problem is that wages aren't high enough."
Linda Tirado, author of *Hand to Mouth: Living in Bootstrap America*

The author Linda Tirado, whose groundbreaking book, *Hand to Mouth: Living in Bootstrap America*,[42] rocketed into the US public's consciousness in 2014 (*The Guardian* called it a 'howl of protest about the plight of the poor'[43]), encapsulates what so many people with experience of the grind of poverty say and how this absolutely lines up with the research. Linda, whose spirit-sapping, thankless, low-paid work in restaurants and bars in low-wage America gave her first-hand experience of the gruelling wretchedness of everyday poverty (even while earning), is a much-needed contributor to any discussion about how this limits every conceivable horizon. Her extraordinary book presents a searing analysis of how the misery of scraping by on next to nothing is intensified by the overwhelming exhaustion and miserable daily slog of being poor. On top of the financial challenges of poverty the impact of the wider narrative about poorer people bleeds through the text as it illustrates from a personal perspective how the misconceptions that narrative propagates reinforces a society-wide failure to grasp the hideous reality of poverty and what it does to those caught up in it.

The narrative, as Linda put it to me, is "bullshit". And, as she argues powerfully, it is dangerous bullshit that serves to keep the poor in poverty while, as Gloria Downey also highlights, allowing the better-off to believe it's not the system's fault, but rather that it's all down to individual endeavour.

Linda got a book deal – to her total shock and surprise – shortly after an online commentary she wrote refuting the toxic idea that poorer people made bad life choices and should just work harder went viral. When we met in Chicago in the early spring of 2018[44] she talked to me about the misguided and enduring adage in American culture that if you had a job and worked hard enough then you could have as much of a chance of attaining the 'American Dream' as anyone. That Americans cling to this idealised notion of individualism and success is so counter to reality that Linda's incredulity is the only truly viable, rational response.

> **"**There's no amount of work you can do to become not poor. The problem isn't that people are lazy, the problem is that wages aren't high enough … And so you get these things where people are like, 'oh, if you just work a little harder….' Ok, look, meritocracy is a bullshit word we made up. The fact that we've taken meritocracy and pulling yourself up by your bootstraps and turned them into some kind of life advice for the poor, it goes beyond idiocy… It doesn't make any sense. The thing is that we've bought into this American Dream, made it unattainable, and then continued to tell people to dream that.**"**

Of what it actually *felt* like to be poor when she was barely keeping her family's head above water, Linda added: "There's two words that applied to my life and they were the perfect descriptor in their totality. One is exhausted and the other is hopeless." Referencing the research on the mental strain of poverty she added:

> "They've just come out with a study – and people are hailing it as a landmark new discovery – that it turns out poor people have a lot of shit on their minds and the cognitive load of poverty actually does impact your brain and the way you can function. You could have asked any poor person for the last 50 damn years and they would have told you that the cognitive load, the cognitive stress, the emotional stress of poverty takes something out of your soul on a daily, day-to-day basis."

"We live in a structure where the fortunate become more fortunate because they are fortunate."
Kat Woods, writer and director

Echoing Linda's main themes the Northern Irish playwright Kat Woods, who writes plays about the experiences of people like herself who grew up in families that needed government assistance, talked to Project Twist-It about the insidious nature of the poverty narrative. Kat wanted to highlight how, when you are told often enough that you are 'less than' or 'not good enough' to dream big, this, on top of other barriers, can contribute to hindering people from poorer backgrounds from reaching their full potential. It's not that poorer people lack aspiration – it's that the possibility of acting on them is curtailed from the get-go. In her own experience, it took encouragement from someone outside her own background to help her believe that she could be a playwright. "I just assumed that the arts weren't for me." Kat says:

> "I think that there's sociological terminology that we can bring in here, like playing to the self-fulfilling

prophecy. If you're told that you're useless, if you're told you're lazy, if you're told these things so often, you will solely think of yourself as being those things and never want to reach for any better. I think that I really struggle with the fact that we are constantly told that if you work hard you will achieve – work hard you'll achieve, work hard you'll achieve – but unfortunately we don't live in a meritocracy. We live in a structure where the fortunate become more fortunate because they are fortunate. **"**

Kat, who grew up on a council estate in Northern Ireland, describes her situation throughout her life as 'benefits class' (she still works mainly minimum-wage jobs to pay the rent while working on her art), a distinction she believes is vital to make as it tends to be people who are unemployed or rely on government assistance at whom the lion's share of negative rhetoric and stereotyping is directed. She adds:

> **"**I think that if the banking community was spoken of in the same light as the benefit claimant we would have a totally different economic structure. [It's] the blame game. The lower classes are always blamed for everything in society because we're seen as the layabouts, the lazy, the good-for-nothings. Whereas the highest paid demographic … don't get punished. If you or I were to steal an apple from a shop, we would get punished. Whereas the bankers and the people that caused the austerity – as it was labelled – they get away scot-free. And it's just so sad. It just makes my heart bleed slightly that that's how justice is, that's how justice is seen. **"**

"My greatest hope now is to use that good fortune to keep on resisting, to persist against the idea that poverty is shameful, that it is an individual fault and not structurally created."
Kerry Hudson, novelist and memoirist

The British novelist and author of *Lowborn*,[45] a memoir of growing up in some of the UK's poorest towns, Kerry Hudson thinks a lot about poverty, about what it does to a person and about the shame and stigma attached to it. Growing up poor in various less well-off parts of Britain understanding that the wider culture had low expectations for someone from her background was a struggle, she says. Another contributor to the many stories collated by Project Twist-It, Kerry believes that stories – our stories – have the power to bring about change:

> "I grew up believing (because I was so frequently told) that what I had to say meant nothing ... that I would somehow have got to a position where I might have a platform to talk about things that matter to me seems miraculous. My greatest hope now is to use that good fortune to keep on resisting, to persist against the idea that poverty is shameful, that it is an individual fault and not structurally created. I hope girls like me will read my work and know they are capable of so much more than they're told they are."

She adds:

> "There are many, many ways this narrative is perpetuated, and I think we all have a role in interrogating those lazy stereotypes ... and using that to dismantle those inequalities where we can."

It turns out Kerry is far from alone. It turns out that – right now as I write this in 2019 – there is a genuine and invigorating momentum building for change. It turns out that an awful lot of hard work you've most likely never even heard of is in motion – by writers, musicians, academics, activists, artists, institutions and individuals – determined to take down the toxic narrative.

The shame game that tells millions of people caught in poverty's clutches that it is their fault is not a given.

8

Changing times: fighting poverty, not the poor

"We have a saying that movements begin with the telling of untold stories. These untold stories change people's understanding."
Rev Dr Liz Theoharis, Co-Chair, Poor People's Campaign, talking to Project Twist-It

"It's through listening to each other's stories, through exploring each other's perspectives that we will learn to transcend the fixed idea of ourselves and come together."
Shona McCarthy, Chief Executive, Edinburgh Festival Fringe[1]

Speaking up and speaking out: making ourselves heard

With all that we now know about the potency and impact of the poverty narrative, the challenge we face boils down to this: can we come to a collective understanding of the role played by this 'story', by this powerful poverty 'narrative' that is strategically framed and weaponised ad nauseam, in shaping our perceptions and, importantly, in keeping people poor and marginalised? And crucially, if we accept that this narrative has a fundamental and negative role in our societies, what can we do to change it? Can we end the shame game? Can we overthrow the labels, stereotypes and stigma? What can we do to tell a different story *that can then be used* to help fight for policies that protect the poor and give people a fighting chance, rather than cement and promote the privileges of the rich?

Can we tell a *different* story?

The answer, it turns out, is that awareness of the narrative, how it frames the poor, and how it contributes to entrenching poverty and social injustice, is growing. A different story *is already* beginning to take shape. Telling a different story – reworking how we communicate about poverty and inequality – is by necessity part and parcel of the political landscape. The dominant poverty narrative is pervasive because it penetrates the entire culture from politics and media to television and beyond.

However, the emergence of a different story to counter this toxic, destructive narrative is happening on a number of fronts.

In the first instance, alternative, sensitive and humane portrayals of poverty are breaking through as people find platforms, including books and social media, to tell their own stories and, by doing so, challenge cultural norms about what it is to be poor. These alternative stories are countering the myths we have been spoon-fed for so long, are emerging from multiple sources and are creating a sense that it is possible – indeed, essential – to discuss the horrors and tragedies of poverty but to do so without pitying, labelling or disparaging those affected and without pandering to 'misery memoir' tropes. A shift in thinking and action is evident in a growing body of books and writings – many from artists, including musicians, film-makers and writers with first-hand experience of poverty. These are helping to shake up our thinking and to carve a new understanding.

Rapper, Darren 'Loki' McGarvey in Britain, with his Orwell Award-winning book *Poverty Safari*,[2] which takes readers on a journey through his life but also the many complex and confounding aspects of grappling with financial hardship and the systems that surround it, is among this new breed of artists. McGarvey, a straight-talking Scotsman who has also taken his stories and thoughts on poverty and inequality to the stage, to newspaper commentary and media interviews, offers a master class in how to puncture misconceptions about the poor across the wider culture with unignorable wit, candidness and rage.

And there are others making headway in the same space. There are documentary films like Sean McAllister's *A Northern Soul*, and *Fighting Shame* (2019),[3] a film where five women from the city of Leeds in England living in poverty tell their own stories – in their own words – about life on the breadline. There's the anthology of British working-class writers edited by novelist Kit de Waal, *Common People*,[4] for example, and the bestselling memoir, *Lowborn: Growing Up, Getting Away, and Returning to Britain's Poorest Towns*[5] by Kerry Hudson reflecting on childhood impoverishment. Meanwhile in 2019, writer and spoken-word artist Cash Carraway's searing book, *Skint Estate: A Memoir of Poverty, Motherhood and Survival*,[6] recounted with the rawest of honesty and gut-wrenching prose, life as a single mother on the breadline in 21st-century Britain, taking to task those who undermine poorer, working-class women.

Carraway writes in *Skint Estate* of what the consequences might be of daring to speak up: 'I'll be ridiculed to the point where I'll never be able to work again, right? What if all this ruins my life? What if I've revealed too much and I become a figure of national mockery and end up like all the poverty porn stars who rose and quickly fell before me?'

Even when she was met with outright hostility (especially on social media) for speaking her mind and telling the truth, Carraway was somehow able to push back at disparagement with uncompromising dignity. She wrote this on Twitter:

> This time last year my daughter & I relied on foodbanks & holiday schemes on the estate where she would sneak food into her pockets for later. You feel humiliated, failure, like your child is the only one – but it's 4.1 million.

In the US there has been Linda Tirado's writing, which cuts through poverty stereotypes in America like a chainsaw cuts through wood,[7] and Matthew Desmond's Pulitzer Prize-winning book *Evicted: Poverty and Profit in the American City*,[8] which tells the story of eight families on the edge in Milwaukee, exposing the fragility of a housing market gone drastically wrong and the personal price paid for raging inequality. There is also Stephanie

Land's very personal story, *Maid: Hard Work, Low Pay and a Mother's Will to Survive*[9] (which made it to Barack Obama's recommended summer reading list in 2019). And there's Sarah Smarsh, who writes explicitly in her journalism and in her 2018 book, *Heartland: A Memoir of Working Hard and Being Broke in the Richest Country on Earth*, about her own story of life in working-class communities in America's Midwest that directly counters the dominant narrative core assumptions.[10]

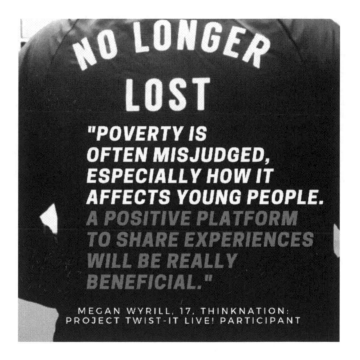

It is early days, and there isn't necessarily a consensus as to what will work to shift such deep-rooted perceptions or to counter the arguments of those who propagate them, but there can be little doubt that a genuine *conversation* about how to alter the way poverty — and people living in it — is portrayed is under way. While it may not constitute anything that could be defined as a 'movement' (yet), fresh efforts in Britain and America to bring the shame game to an end by experimenting with new strategies for changing the minds of people who might buy into the dominant narrative, including pushing *our own* stories into the public domain, are nevertheless coming to the fore.

In the autumn of 2019 the Bill & Melinda Gates Foundation even took up the mantle of fighting the poverty narrative specifically when it launched a call for new and innovative ideas that would contribute to 'to the long-term work of correcting mistaken assumptions and improving understanding of poverty through the actual stories of those that experience poverty'. The Voices for Economic Opportunity programme was offering $100,000 to the winning projects.

The Foundation said: 'We seek proposals for creative, scalable, strategic new ways to generate awareness of the structural and historic barriers to economic mobility; to communicate that poverty is not just something that happens to other people and everyone is deserving of the chance to move out of it; and to change the predominant misconceptions about poverty in a way that creates the conditions for effective programs and policies to be adopted by the public and private sectors.'[11]

Over the course of two years working on Project Twist-It[12] I found a deep-felt and burgeoning desire to put the emperor's clothes back on and bring an end to the entire, sorry poverty narrative charade. This desire was evident across the political, cultural and social space among researchers, activists, advocates and artists of all hues. When I began reaching out to people to be interviewed or to contribute to PTI, not once did someone demur. In fact, I was told time and again – including by young people – that an initiative that acted as a hub and as a springboard for people's stories and ideas about challenging the narrative was both necessary and timely.

As one young person who participated in a live event held by the project in Kent, England, put it: "Poverty is often misjudged, especially how it affects young people. A positive platform to share experiences and messages will be really beneficial."

Project Twist-It was still in its infancy when I began writing this book but as it became more established and networks began to form on social media and in the real world, individuals and groups ranging from local to national, from different ethnicities and backgrounds and ages, began asking to be part of it – and were finding and connecting with each other beyond the project itself.

Working on PTI prior to the publication of this book, I encountered individuals eager to contribute to shaping a new discourse – who recognised that even with the best intentions, efforts to date to upend the denigration of poorer people had failed. Their stories, their insights and their determination to be part of a change convinced me of the centrality of disseminating personal, individual experiences as part of any effort to combat predominant misconceptions. They showed me how the exclusion of the voices of people with lived experience has come at a price: that it inhibits our understanding of what it is to be poor or struggling to get by, and hampers the development of empathy towards those in difficulty among a substantial slice of the population. It removes the human being from the centre of the story – it dehumanises. Sometimes this silencing of people with lived experience occurs because poorer people are simply not consulted by those who are fighting to reduce or end poverty, or by anyone else for that matter. Sometimes we silence ourselves.

We are not alone

Asking people to speak publicly about anything that is stigmatised by wider society is never easy. As a journalist who has worked on numerous topics that fall into this category, including mental health,[13] I've learned what a huge factor stigma is in people's perceptions of themselves and others – and in their capacity to speak out. When it comes to poverty, the prevalence of the dominant narrative and the fear it induces of being publicly vilified, as Cash Carraway so elegantly expressed it, constitutes a forbidding backdrop.

When poor and low-income people are, out of necessity, consumed by merely trying to survive the poverty trap, it would be entirely understandable if telling their story and speaking out was just another thing to add to an already exhausting existence and so isn't even considered. Plus, when being so cavalierly and repeatedly belittled in public for the very fact of being poor, who could blame a person for never putting their head above the parapet to speak about their reality? Why would you speak out as an individual when, rather than being treated with respect, you are subsequently treated with disdain, or pity? Why agree to tell your story when if you're talking to a journalist or a television producer they might produce a sensationalised portrayal that labels you a 'scrounger' or a 'shirker' or a 'benefits cheat'?[14] Why would you speak publicly when you are almost certain to be judged and castigated by the media or politicians telling you to pull yourself up by your bootstraps and stop living off 'hard-working' taxpayers' money and to cease making 'bad life choices' and then making excuses for them?[15]

Why would you put yourself in the firing line of a narrative so toxic and so potent? And yet, people do. And they are doing so in all kinds of ways. So, what happens when you ask someone who is poor, or has lived in poverty at some point, to talk about it? In my experience it tends to go one of five ways:

1. The person doesn't want to talk about their poverty in case it comes to define them or is the primary prism through which they are seen by other people.
2. The person doesn't want to talk about their poverty because they don't want to/can't admit to themselves or anyone else that they actually classify as poor.
3. The person doesn't want to talk about their poverty because they don't want to/can't admit to themselves or anyone else that they actually classify as poor ... and they react to enquiries by distancing themselves from fellow poorer people – sometimes even ridiculing or criticising other people in the same situation as them as 'lazy', 'irresponsible', or 'scrounging', to reinforce the point.[16]
4. The person doesn't want to talk about their poverty (on the record at least) due to feeling ashamed or embarrassed about being poor *or* (whether they feel ashamed personally or not) they're concerned about being judged or shamed and stigmatised by others if they speak publicly.
5. The person is willing to talk about their poverty – may even be eager to talk about it – so that their voice – their story – is heard and thereby the real, lived experience of being poor might be better understood.

"I am not speaking about the poor. I am the poor."
Claudia Cruz, a supporter of the Poor People's Campaign speaking
in Washington DC in the spring of 2018

It is this latter group that I have been encountering with ever greater frequency. The people in this group tend to be driven by a hope that adding their voices might, in some small way, contribute to a shift in wider attitudes around poverty away from the negative. Many people, and especially young people, talk about wanting to discard labels and to play a part in promoting practical outcomes – they want to be catalysts for change by helping to advocate for the reform of policies that hinder or harm poorer people. People like Mark Brown, Christine Riccione, Sylvia Hernandez, Billie J.D. Porter and Jameela Jamil.

Among people with first-hand experience of poverty or who were subsisting on poverty wages, working on PTI, I found a voracious appetite for speaking up and using personal stories as a conduit to do so. The same applied to people like myself who experienced poverty in our childhoods and were fortunate enough to escape it. And, through Project Twist-It, I heard arguments for why constructing and deploying a *new narrative* as a foundation for changing people's lives must first and foremost involve people telling their own stories, in their own voice.

By putting these stories in context and by accepting their validity in a wider conversation, there is a possibility that, piece by piece, a tapestry with a more accurate and rounded picture of those caught in poverty's clutches might emerge and contribute not only to the shifting of the poverty narrative – but to upending it.

I learned that the message – and the messenger – matter. *Stories matter.*

As co-chair of the Poor People's Campaign Reverend Liz Theoharis told me:

> **"**Telling those stories really matters. I talk about the plight, the fight and the insight of poor people and of these struggles. And so I think that those stories are really important.**"**

And, as Claudia Cruz, a woman who stood up to speak at the launch of the Poor People's Campaign, said when explaining why she was telling her own story: "I am not speaking about the poor. I am the poor."

I should point out that I am personally guilty of not speaking up, of not telling my story, of not taking my experience and using it to help people better understand what living in poverty is really like. When I finally made it to university and then into full-time employment in my early 20s I chose not to talk much about my background except to my closest friends. I would say my piece on women's rights and any number of other issues (no one ever accused me of not having an opinion) but, as a young person left scarred by poverty, I resisted revisiting the topic until well into my 20s. I know why I did it. I didn't want to be labelled. I didn't want to be judged only through that prism. I certainly didn't want to be pitied. Plus I really wasn't someone who was in any way an activist. But also, I didn't see the point. What could my story possibly teach people about child poverty or deprivation or social 'mobility'? And why would I want to relive and relay what were very painful memories?

Why would I tell people that if it hadn't been for the NHS fixing my teeth for free when I was 14 years old they would be rotten? (I would never have contemplated going to university with rotten teeth.) How do you explain to someone that you had biscuits on your grocery list but no toothpaste? How could they possibly comprehend that my siblings and I were given sweets and cake (a much-relished treat) or that the family rented a television, yet I didn't possess a toothbrush? There are only so many sacrifices you can make before life is completely devoid of joy and while I sorely wish I had been provided with a toothbrush and toothpaste, not having a television as a kid would have made me feel a lot poorer. I just didn't think people would understand this if I attempted to explain it. By my 20s I was more than aware that people who were in poverty having a TV (renting not even owning one) was somehow deemed an unnecessary extravagance and to tell people this would mean to actively invite judgement.

"It's not like your father went here."
Fellow student, Cambridge, on my supposed lack of suitability
to attend the university

Why would I want anyone to know that a family friend who
worked in public toilets stole toilet paper for our family every
week so that we had one less expense? Why would I want to
tell someone that as a young teenager I had the responsibility of
managing the weekly grocery budget for the entire family and
enduring the disdainful glances of the shopkeeper as I scrabbled
around for the exact change in my pocket, or that I didn't have
enough underwear, or that I washed my school uniform, paid
for by the state, by hand in the sink every Saturday night? Or
that I felt like I was begging when I needed a neighbour's help
to get basic items for school or dancing.

Not talking about it didn't mean others were oblivious to
something beneath the surface, however. At Cambridge, one
of my friends nicknamed me 'Old-Mary' in my first term. He
meant it affectionately and only used it in my company, as he
reminded me that I didn't have to carry the weight of the world
on my shoulders. He seemed to sense that invisible burden I
carried. He seemed to discern, without my saying much at all,
the guilt I felt at having 'escaped' and for leaving my younger
brothers and sisters behind. Still, I couldn't tell him the full
truth. It was obvious to anyone who encountered me in the
meticulously class stratified, snobbish environment of Cambridge
University that I was *working class* and that I was in receipt of the
full government grant given at the time to people from lower-
income families. It would have been obvious to anyone that I
was far from extravagant because funds were limited; but poverty,
of course, is different. Poverty is shame-filled.

I had studied politics, history and sociology. I had learned about
political philosophies and ideologies and social theory and class
struggle so I was more than equipped to talk about a whole range
of interlocking aspects of social issues on a relatively informed
level. But the truth is that I was afraid to speak about poverty
on a personal level. Some of my experiences at Cambridge fed
my reticence. Like the time some posh bloke, who was the
latest generation of his family to attend, was drinking up a tree

(yes – up a tree) as a friend and I walked by and began shouting about how come I was even 'allowed' to be there. "It's not like your father went here," he slurred contemptuously. Gobsmacked, it took a while for me to register what was happening and my friend filled the void, telling the arsehole up the tree: "She earned it!"

The few times I had mentioned my background and how I ended up at one of the world's top universities once I'd begun working life, the response I was most likely to get was how my story showed that, indeed, anyone can do it! If they only worked hard enough! It was exhausting having to argue the same points over and over – that, yes, I busted my ass but I didn't do it alone and that I almost didn't follow that trajectory in a thousand small ways because of all the challenges and obstacles I faced every day in my early life, and how the sheer cultural shock of moving from a working-class community rife with poverty to a place of ostentatious privilege was profoundly destabilising.

The other reaction I got, usually from the middle-class people on the left of the political spectrum who I came into contact with professionally and socially, was to regard me as symbolic, as someone whose story countered the stereotypes of people who grew up on council estates or whose families were on benefits or who went to a state school. I was even used once as evidence to claim my employer was not elitist. I recall one instance while working at *The Guardian* when I overheard a colleague nearby inform someone on the phone that, no, the place wasn't just upper middle-class, privately educated people. "Right opposite me is someone who grew up on a council estate and went to a comprehensive," they told the caller. I rolled my eyes and got on with my work.

On another occasion, when I mentioned the type of house I'd lived in up until the age of seven, one colleague declared incredulously that it was impossible. More like the 1930s, he said, never having been poor or encountered such conditions himself. It never occurred to him that I was telling my own story – that what I had to say was truthful and accurate and real.

I didn't stay quiet forever, as you will have guessed. By the time I reached my 30s and was working as a reporter and hoping to get to write about social policy I began, tentatively, to tell people more about my background and my story. Sometimes I wrote about it. What happened surprised me. The more I told, the more (most) people wanted to hear. One night in the pub an editor who had been very supportive of me when I was a nervous rookie who felt out of her depth on the business pages encouraged me to write comment pieces about social issues. My voice was important, unique and necessary, he told me. There weren't enough people 'like' me in the media, so the deck was stacked against us as a result and readers were denied a different perspective on important issues.

Of course I ignored him – at first. But he was right. There were so few people around me in the British media writing from personal experience about poverty that it began to feel like a duty. Yes, it was painful sometimes (it still is) but I did it anyway, and I tilted towards a type of journalism that permitted me to combine both my personal experience and my wider knowledge on poverty and interrelated social issues. Over time, I have only become more convinced of the need to speak up and speak out – to share stories to break through the din of negativity. That said, I am also aware that it is a Big Ask.

Tell me something I don't know: the value of a good story well told

While bringing together people's personal stories for PTI, something that was really striking was the use of the word 'narrative'. Regular references to a poverty narrative was not something I recall encountering even a few years prior when interviewing people as a reporter. As the academic research shows, the public have been aware for some time that 'rhetoric' and 'language' are politically charged (especially when talking about austerity where pejoratives are thrown around like wedding confetti). But, as I travelled around and as I spoke with people, something in the wider cultures of America and Britain, it seemed to me, meant that there was now a heightened awareness that 'narrative' – how stories are constructed and disseminated in relation to poverty – was something worthy of greater examination. In the UK, this felt in part connected to a deeper grasp over time of how austerity had been sold and the ubiquity of poverty porn, while in the US there was a thread stretching back to inequality consciousness-raising in the wake of the financial crisis and to the polarising hyperbole so evident at the dawn of the Trump era and in the explicit mission of the Poor People's Campaign.

What was abundantly clear was that there was a growing realisation among activists and non-activists alike that merely laying bare the problem of poverty, citing shocking statistics, calling out the consequences, and demanding a change in attitudes or policies because it was the right and decent thing to do, wasn't cutting it.

Highlighting shocking poverty statistics or the popular myths surrounding it is important, but it doesn't win over people who have been convinced by the narrative, or gravitate towards believing that the most dominant set of messages and misconceptions equal the truth.

The cognitive scientist George Lakoff argues in his seminal book *Don't Think of an Elephant: Know Your Values and Frame the Debate*,[17] that direct attacks on the framing of a topic (for example with poverty, arguing that poor people *aren't* lazy) can actually have the opposite effect. Lakoff argues that this approach 'activates' that particular framing of the topic and, 'the more it is activated, the stronger it gets'.

Lakoff writes:

> The moral for political discourse is clear: when you argue against someone on the other side using their language and frames [e.g. lazy], you are activating their frames, strengthening their frames in those who hear you, and undermining your own views. For progressives ... [it] means that you should say what you believe using your language, not theirs.

In the course of working on Project Twist-It in the US and the UK I found that the poverty narrative was being challenged on five key fronts:

- By individuals with experience of hardship speaking up and telling their stories

- By young people actively engaging and making their views heard
- By artists and writers using their work as a platform for change
- By grassroots groups coalescing around the issue of narrative and elevating individual voices
- By researchers, academics, media professionals and advocates working assiduously to explore new ways to frame the issue of poverty – and wealth – with the goal of reshaping the wider discourse, including in the media, by politicians, and across the wider culture.

Objectively, overturning such a powerfully entrenched poverty narrative and replacing it with something more truthful that empowers rather than harms may be an uphill struggle, but it is a struggle we can win. We have already seen from attitudinal research that people often hold contradictory beliefs about poorer people or may support an issue when framed in one way but not in another. There are two key aspects to revising how we approach the poverty narrative. **The first**, explored in this chapter and the next, relates – as Reverend Barber from the Poor People's Campaign alluded to in Chapter 2 – to *whose story* is being told, *who* is doing the telling and *how* it is being told. **The second**, which we'll look at in the final chapter, concerns how a coherent, co-ordinated, alternative framing might begin to take shape that provides a countervailing, compelling and robust rebuttal to the dominant narrative – one that actively takes account of the diversity of stories and voices of experience and which emphasises values such as compassion, community, common cause, fairness, strength, resilience, hope and dignity – and which eschews victimhood.

Using our voice

One of the most glaring absences in the discourse has been the voices, ideas and direct input of people with actual, lived experience of poverty. Where such voices have been presented in a way intended to shed light on poverty, in the media for example, they have been frequently wheeled out as 'case studies' to drum home a specific point (for example the damage inflicted by a particular policy) – including by journalists such as myself.

Further, when featured at all, the voices of people with lived experience have tended to be subservient to the views of others including (usually) well-meaning professionals working in the space ranging from social workers to policy makers who speak 'for' people or 'advocate' on their behalf, or whose function it is to highlight the blight of poverty or run anti-poverty programmes. (Something many have critiqued as contributing to a 'poverty industry'[18] or 'poverty pimping', where certain professionals rely on poverty to be in a job.)

As the MacArthur 'Genius' Fellow, former social worker and anti-poverty campaigner Mauricio Lim Miller told me in the US back in 2012,[19] poorer people are neither the 'victims' the left sometimes categorises them as, nor the 'lazy' freeloaders those on the right of the political spectrum tend to portray them as being. This, he argues, makes it all the more important that poorer people's stories and views are driving the conversation for reshaping the discourse on poverty.

"I have been working with low-income families for over 20 years," he told me back then. "These are families who are trying, who want to get out [of poverty], but are stuck."

"By highlighting the contributions of low-income families we can also begin to challenge some of the racist, classist and gender-based prejudice that continues to divide our country."
Mauricio Lim Miller, author, talking to Project Twist-It

I met with Miller again in 2018 in Oakland to interview him for PTI, a year after the publication of his book *The Alternative: Most of What You Believe About Poverty is Wrong*.[20] Brought up by an immigrant single mother, Miller experienced poverty in his own childhood and drew on this when he went on to found the community-led Family Independence Initiative (FII)[21] which directly challenges the enduring tropes of dependency and paternalism embedded in many anti-poverty programmes. The book melds his personal and professional experiences.

"I have gotten involved in anti-poverty work because I came out of a very poor single-mom family," he tells me when we sit down to talk in Oakland.

> **"**My mother was from Mexico with a third-grade education. We came to the US in order to build a better life, thinking that if you worked hard in this country that things would go well. Things did not go well for my sister in particular and my mother. I lost my mother pretty early in my 20s, heavily due to the poverty and the fact that she was not recognised for what she could do, and so instead of pursuing design, which is what I wanted to do, I joined the War on Poverty in the United States and quickly learned that, even though I ran a lot of social service programs, that I wouldn't bring my own family through my own services and that the system was patronising; the system was something that if you had money you would never send your children through it.**"**

For Miller, reflecting on personal experiences of poverty – and where possible using this to reconfigure how others think about it – is crucial if either the narrative, or the system it supports are to change.

He writes in his book:

> Today most *poverty experts* [Miller's italics], of any color, have a very shallow understanding of life in poverty and they promote a view of families like mine as somehow deficient. These experts highlight only the data or stories that backs a deficit view of low-income families. Our helping system for the poor is based on charity, on well-meaning outsiders saving the poor. If, instead, they focused on the strengths of low-income families we would all see they are important contributors to society and as such we should invest in their talents, much as our society invests in the rich.

The 'alternative' proposed in his book's title, Miller explains, recognises the value of investing in talent – both for families and the wider community. "The *alternative* is fairly simple; look for what people are already doing for themselves and others, and then invest in it. Follow rather than 'lead' them."

"We can break cycle of poverty," he argues. "By highlighting the contributions of low-income families we can also begin to challenge some of the racist, classist, and gender-based prejudice that continues to divide our country."

Having moved on from FII, Miller has his sights clearly set on shifting the narrative. "What we need to do is look at [the] information [we have] and start thinking about how the prejudices and the different stereotypes – that I think are much clearer today – how those are influencing our decisions and the view that we have," he told me.

> **"**The views are so deeply embedded in even the good folks about low-income people not having capacity, making bad decisions, being takers from society; those views are so deeply embedded that we as a society who are privileged don't actually stop and try to understand what is really in front of us. Which is really common sense.**"**

In terms of the possibility of change – of successfully challenging the narrative and thereby having poorer people themselves in the driver's seat – Miller says that while the multiple barriers including racism and ingrained prejudice are profoundly difficult, we should look to where once seemingly intransigent attitudes and beliefs have been dramatically altered for a sense of hopefulness and possibility.

> **"**You have seen stuff around gay rights, you have seen stuff around drunk driving, you have seen attitudes around a number of issues change. So, we know that historically attitudes have been changed. I don't know that we know how to deal with classism and racism and everything, but it isn't that it can't happen. So, one

hope is that I know it has happened around attitudes on other issues."

Stories are a powerful way to persuade people.... We become more interested in issues that do not affect us personally, more likely to change our minds and less sceptical – we literally suspend disbelief.
New Economics Foundation report, 2013

The place of storytelling in human society has been extensively researched and documented across a number of fields ranging from anthropology and psychology to cognitive science.[22] The role it plays has been examined across a wide assortment of areas, from child development to political messaging. We know that the telling of stories actively influences our thinking about, empathy towards, and understanding of, those outside of our immediate sphere. When the New Economics Foundation was assessing the power and potency and effectiveness of the narrative constructed around austerity in the UK, for example, its 2013 report, 'Framing the Economy', summarised the significance of stories this way:[23]

> Stories are a powerful way to persuade people. Research suggests our minds process arguments presented in stories differently. We become more interested in issues that do not affect us personally, more likely to change our minds and less sceptical – we literally suspend disbelief.

"Storytelling is one of humanity's oldest methods of possessing information and representing reality and is incredibly important in telling stories of poverty."
Natasha Carthew, poet and novelist, talking to Project Twist-It

Some of the earliest and keenest contributors to PTI were writers, storytellers, artists – many, like Kerry Hudson, with lived experience of impoverishment. All were interested in depictions of social class and of poverty and in the fundamental ways stories have the potential to alter our perspective. Natasha

Carthew, an award-winning British poet and novelist[24] and passionate advocate for fostering and promoting writers from working-class and marginalised backgrounds, explained the role she felt storytelling in literature has to play and why the messenger – not just the message – matters in challenging the toxic narrative that surrounds poorer people.

"Literature should challenge the under-representation, negative stereotyping and discrimination in society. We can trigger a different way of thinking about poverty and increase support for better policies by talking about the issues and telling our own stories. I like to talk about my own background," Natasha says, "raised by a single parent in a council house, no money, no transport, no visible prospects, in order to inspire others to believe we can change our own narrative. We as writers and creators, we need to work together to change the story people hear."

She continues:

> **"**Storytelling is one of humanity's oldest methods of possessing information and representing reality and is incredibly important in telling stories of poverty, especially from a working-class perspective. These kinds of voices are rarely heard, and when they are, we hear them written by people who might not have experienced any kind of marginalisation themselves.**"**

Mahsuda Snaith, another novelist who grew up in public housing in England and whose work is infused with stories that challenge conventional wisdom on the 'type' of people who live there, including racial minorities, told PTI how she wanted her work to help break down stereotypes of people who live on council estates. In her first novel *The Things We Thought We Knew*,[25] for example, Mahsuda manages to depict a world of multi-dimensional characters, who by their existence, demolish clichés. She says: "I grew up on a council estate to a single parent mother who was living on benefits. Two things I noticed growing up. One was I was very aware of being poor and separated from mainstream society and second that there was this overriding image of council estates in the media that were largely based around drugs, gang violence and benefit fraud, [yet, this was] far removed from the reality." When writing *The Things We Thought We Knew*, Mahsuda says, "I wanted to smash the stereotypes… So I didn't write about drugs and gang violence and benefit fraud. I hope that my novel and my story contribute to smashing the negative stereotypes we have about poverty."

The American writer Sarah Smarsh believes journalists and editors have a crucial role in shaping the wider narratives around class and poverty and that the filtering of stories by such gatekeepers requires examination. "I find myself frequently critiquing my own journalism industry for classist narratives or frameworks," she told PTI. Why does she point this out? To provide "a necessary corrective, to make way for the stories I seek to tell, which often challenge stereotypes about the poor".

For Sarah, the place of storytelling in the fight against shaming and blaming, is paramount.

> "Stories create our reality, I think, just as much as reality creates our stories. Narratives from people who have experienced poverty first-hand are crucial. Ownership of an experience often allows one to bear witness to a fuller truth."

Similar observations and themes were put forward by visual artists involved with the project. The British artist Zita Holbourne, who campaigns on minority rights issues and fair employment, argues that art is a vital implement in the anti-poverty, new narrative tool box.

> "I think there is very much a blame culture that is … politicians and political parties and the media [don't look] at the stories behind why people are in dire poverty, why people have to make really difficult choices about what they do in life because they feel stuck or that they have no other choice. It is labelling and demonising. I think we need to ensure that there is a really strong and powerful counter-narrative.

The real-life stories as well as the statistics and the research. I think that using stories and art and other creativity is really important in getting positive messages out – and also to illustrate what is happening to people. I think actually the arts is a really positive and interesting and effective way of bringing people together, because it is something that connects people, that people can relate to wherever you are in the world. [Whatever] your political standard, your background, your heritage you can relate to creativity. A piece of art or a poem or a song, can really capture somebody's mind. I think that this does help to shift perspective. I can see it myself by the sort of feedback I get."

Janet Owen-Driggs[26] is a US-based artist and art history professor. Her students mostly come from low-income backgrounds, many of whom work full-time jobs while at college and have the odds of graduating stacked against them. Her art, her work with young people, and personal experience of financial struggles her family had while she was growing up, have together inspired Janet to be part of trying to push back against the narrative.

"With the help of the UK's National Health Service, public housing, public education, and my parents' fierce-but-loving determination, I escaped the drudge life that was pre-ordained for me by the circumstances of my birth," Janet told PTI.

"The bootstraps narratives that give me credit for my successes and make poverty a matter of individual responsibility are the waters in which we swim. I think narrative is the most important tool that we have as humans. We are storytellers and we need to understand the stories that we live and that we live them because they are being told to us. The narrative of blame and shame is probably the most important narrative for maintaining the status quo, that requires a large number of people to be in poverty in order to support the abundant lifestyles of the rest of us."

"What is to be done?" Janet asks.

> "We need to identify the narratives that underpin structural inequality and consider how they keep us swirling, applauding, and too often, drowning. And we need to tell each other about possible futures. Art has an enormously powerful function to play in imagining possible futures, in dreaming, but it is also the capacity to do it collectively, to imagine collectively."

The elephant(s) in the street: harnessing an individual story

June Cigar has an expression of deep concentration on her face as she diligently selects small fragments of thick glass and broken tiles from a small plastic container. Inspecting each piece carefully, she tests how they look against the naked wood of a picture frame sitting on the portable work table in front of her. A rainbow of colours rest in the box but, just like the bright zip-up sweatshirt she's wearing beneath her apron, the pieces she chooses are as blue and bright as the California sky above her.

June is hard at work on her latest piece of mosaic art, as are the other ten or so artists on the rooftop work space run by the organisation Piece by Piece in downtown Los Angeles.[27] The artists here make and sell mosaic plant pots, coasters, picture frames and other creations. "Hello there," the (then) 61-year-old says with a beaming smile. "Welcome!" June beckons me towards the workspace and makes introductions to others sitting nearby.

"I've made a lot of things for family; for other people. I like to be creative." June is explaining how much the work at Piece by Piece, where she has been since 2015, means to her, how important it is financially, but also its role in helping her to earn a living doing something she loves. Before this June was homeless. "To be able to create something with your own hands and just to look at it?" June says with a beaming smile. "That's a beautiful thing."

"I wanted to fight. I wanted to fight for my rights for housing, and I wanted to fight for my rights as a human being. I want to shift perceptions."
June Cigar, former homeless person and artist, Los Angeles, 2018, talking to Project Twist-It

June and I are meeting to talk about her life and the time she was forced to live on Skid Row – a completely unanticipated turn of events for a self-sufficient, proud woman – and an experience which forged a determination in her to become an advocate for social justice. Like so many people who have fallen on hard times only to find no safety net, once June had made it to a more secure place, she began using her experience to shed light on the factors that thrust people just like her into destitution. "You know, when you've been homeless, you already feel displaced because you are used to sleeping out in such a hellacious environment," she says of the circumstances she found herself in. "When you hit rock bottom, that's it." As a public speaker, June spends much of her time telling her story and, through that, reminding people that to be poor, to be homeless, is to be human. She speaks out, June told me, because she wants to give back – and fight back. She wants to challenge the stereotypes and stigma that surround people who are homeless and living in poverty through the telling of her own story.

June's story is very much of our time. Her story of poverty and homelessness holds up a mirror to our collective, current condition.

June Cigar ended up homeless through no fault of her own when she was being domestically abused. It was a case of 'fight or flight'. Becoming homeless was not a choice June would have made were it not for unbearable circumstances and a lack of alternatives. Homelessness, along with a cancer diagnosis, made her acutely aware not just of how quickly a person's life can radically alter but also how shaming it is to be poor, without a home, and without a sense of control over your own circumstances. "It's a struggle out here, Mary," June told me as we sat in a small, communal space away from the other artists at Piece by Piece. Sometimes, as she spoke, she had tears in her eyes.

"Once you've given up your dignity you have nothing. You are pretty much stripped as a human being. Homelessness will do that to you. And you know what? Homelessness covers every ethnicity, every race, every creed, education. It doesn't matter. Everybody could be one paycheck away from being homeless.**"**

I had arranged to meet June after seeing her give a rousing speech at an Into Action[28] event in downtown LA in January 2018. Her speech was so impressive and her story so captivating that June would be one of the very first people I reached out to as I began my research for Project Twist-It. Into Action, a 'pop-up' social justice festival, had brought artists, writers, performers, activists and members of the community together over the course of a week in a number of downtown warehouse spaces with the goal of galvanising local action and to issue a call for, as its organisers put it, 'empathy, accountability, equality and compassion' in order to counteract broader societal injustices including poverty and racism.

Everywhere you looked during the Into Action week, people from a range of backgrounds were talking about poverty justice, about stigma, about the kinds of stereotypes that made it possible for wider society to ignore the misery of fellow citizens. Through its exhibitions, performances and talks, there was a thread that was challenging the dominant narrative.

In her Sunday morning talk June electrified the 100-plus audience with her story of finding herself homeless and then an activist. She explained how while homeless she was diagnosed with breast cancer and how finding the right kind of help from agencies and voluntary organisations made all the difference to her chances of survival and, eventually, to finding her own home. Looking around the room that morning June's story was clearly resonating. People seemed to be responding to her outlining of the daily struggles homeless people face.

But this was no pity party.

What June told the audience, and *the way* she told it – with humour and grace and positivity for the future – put a human face to the huddles of people barely surviving outside on LA's and America's streets. These were the most unfortunate of the unfortunate but they were not to be dismissed if June had anything to do with it. She was calling time on the attitudes and policies that led to hundreds of thousands of people being relegated to the margins of society, their dignity and humanity diminished because they lack resources.

At Piece by Piece, as she put down her artwork in progress to sit and talk more about her life and her activities June spoke first about her daughter, who graduated not long before from one of the country's premier universities, UC Berkeley, in the northern part of the state. Despite her challenges with poverty and her health, June did her best to inculcate her daughter with a sense of purpose and pride. "I told her not to give up hope, that we may not be financially well off but we have brain power. I also instilled in her that once she got her education that she would break the back of poverty and that she wouldn't be a statistic out there on the street." Her daughter, June says, her eyes shining, is "definitely soaring like an eagle". Emphatically, she adds, "She's not coming back down here with the chickens."

The 'down here' June is referring to is Skid Row.[29]

Skid Row in downtown Los Angeles is synonymous with poverty and destitution. One reason why people like June have congregated around the area over the years, making it the hallmark for homelessness it has become, is that facilities and services have sprung up to help with everything from nutrition to healthcare. Provision of basic necessities and much-needed advice and assistance people would not otherwise have access to and weren't getting from government, are (to a degree) available. June told me that, in a country almost completely devoid of a welfare safety net,[30] it offers a community support system – of sorts.

'Ending up on Skid Row' tends to be a term used euphemistically to mean that a person is at a low point in their life; that they have, as June puts it, hit rock bottom; that they have nothing; that they have failed. In Los Angeles, however, Skid Row is as real a place as can be conjured and is as close a shop window for contemporary poverty as you can get. Thousands of people without permanent homes – of whom June was one for two and a half years – migrate in and out of Skid Row, living cheek by jowl in a space of just 0.4 square miles. Most are on the streets. Some find temporary accommodation. Even for people familiar with the statistics on homelessness in America – over a half million people at last count, 34 per cent of whom were living on the streets or in places 'unfit for human habitation', according to the National Alliance to End Homelessness[31] – or how bad it is in California, a walk around this part of downtown Los Angeles can be especially shocking. Rows and rows of shabby tents and makeshift abodes with bundles of possessions squeezed in, line streets densely packed with vulnerable citizens, many of whom are elderly, sick or disabled, or who are dealing with complex conditions like addictions or mental illness, rendering them susceptible to a multiplicity of abuses. The sense of 'otherness' and desperation, of a place on the fringe, is palpable.

Skid Row is like the capital city of the 'tent cities' so visible in 2019 across America.[32]

The men curled up in the sleeping bags and the women pushing the overflowing shopping carts or talking to invisible interlocutors on the subways could, if the world were just a slightly different place, be our mothers, our brothers, our friends, ourselves.
LA Times Editorial, February 2018

In February 2018, the editorial board of the *Los Angeles Times* in a searing editorial,[33] declared Skid Row to be a 'national disgrace'. Pulling no punches, the article described it as a 'teaming Dickensian Dystopia' reminiscent of Medieval Europe, Calcutta in the 1980s or the sprawling slums of Rio de Janeiro. The editorial did more than bemoan the problem, however – a problem which had 'spilled' throughout the county and which was evident around the country. Rather it offered a blistering denunciation of a society that tolerated attitudes, policies and conditions that led people in their thousands – people like June – to living rough:

> Today, a confluence of factors is driving people onto the streets. The shredding of the safety net in Washington and here in California is one. Today, a

greater and greater proportion of people living on the streets are there because of bad luck or a series of mistakes, or because the economy forgot them – they lost a job or were evicted or fled an abusive marriage just as the housing market was growing increasingly unforgiving.

In the world's richest nation, homelessness on this scale should be shameful and shocking. But most Angelenos are no longer either shocked or shamed. Increasingly, we are uncomfortable, irritated, disgusted, scared or oblivious. Compassion is being replaced by resignation. Yet we all know the truth: the men curled up in the sleeping bags and the women pushing the overflowing shopping carts or talking to invisible interlocutors on the subways could, if the world were just a slightly different place, be our mothers, our brothers, our friends, ourselves. It is imperative that we act now so that we don't wake up in five, 10 or 20 years wondering where we were or what we could possibly have been thinking or why we kept quiet and did nothing as this unconscionable catastrophe took hold.

Street homelessness has become so completely normalised in LA that it's a part of the urban landscape, like parking lots or neon signs. Just a half mile from where I lived at the time I met June, and a stone's throw from the Hollywood Walk of Fame, an underpass below the 101 Freeway was home to (depending on the day) a colony of 8–20 tents, a makeshift encampment of the sort scattered across various parts of the city. Meanwhile in what were recently vacant lots of waste ground, hip new hotels and apartment blocks – part of the area's rapid regeneration[34] – were springing up all around the Hollywood homeless population. Hundreds of luxury apartments were sprouting like beautiful weeds while the people subsisting in tents could only look on. There were so many occasions that I witnessed police moving people who were camped out – even when it was raining – that I gave up counting. And this is only the 'obvious' homelessness.

All across LA country there are thousands of 'hidden' homeless,[35] people living in cars for example.

When I talked with June in the spring of 2018 the state of California was about to become the world's fifth largest economy,[36] knocking the UK into sixth place for a time following its economically self-defeating referendum vote to leave the European Union. California, America's most populous state – hovering just below 40 million in 2018 (10 million more than the next most populated, Texas) and projected to exceed that by 2020 – was widely regarded as a bastion of liberal progressiveness as the Trump era took hold. When there were threats to environmental policies or to the rule of law from Trump's Washington, California was a stalwart of resistance.

But for all of its status as the bright, shiny beacon of hope at the western edge of the country, California is emblematic of a much broader and deeper malaise that sees people like June end up destitute: that extreme wealth and poverty are close neighbours in today's America. As the sociologist David Grusky of Stanford University's Center on Poverty and Inequality pointed out when publishing a study in 2018,[37] 'the land of plenty' also had the largest poverty rate in the country. Some 20 per cent of California's residents live in poverty, according to the Census Bureau's Supplemental Poverty Measure.[38] The stark – and rising – problem of homelessness was only the most visible manifestation of the abject need all around.

Ultimately, Skid Row is a living, breathing testament to the society's normalisation of extreme poverty and destitution and the shame associated with that. The improvised accommodations could give the 'Hooverville'[39] encampments of the Great Depression a run for their money in terms of public displays of human wretchedness. Yet these people weren't in Depression-era photographic images in a museum or a book that we are all supposed to react to with 'oh dear, it must have been terrible back then'. This was the here and now – and it wasn't even in the midst of a recession, never mind a full-scale depression.[40]

"The structures can only be possible because we buy the story."
Tim Molina, the Courage Campaign, talking to Project Twist-It

Tim Molina, (then) the Organising Director with the Courage Campaign,[41] reflected on the situation when being interviewed for Project Twist-It:

> "In California we do have one of the highest minimum wages in the country, but there is still a lot that we are falling short on. We believe in this American Dream, this capitalist-sponsored American Dream, where if you work hard enough you are going to make it, where you have the choice whether to make it or not. And that's complete and utter bullshit. It is complete utter falseness. I think as long as we prioritise financial capital over people and human dignity and rights and prosperity, we'll always have that narrative."

Asked if the dream – the story – could be challenged – if it could be reconstructed, he offered: "The structures can only be possible because we buy the story. I think if we could believe in an American Dream that's fair and that also addresses our biases and breaks down those narratives, hell yeah."

When she spoke with me after the Into Action event, June Cigar got right to the heart of why, despite all the challenges it brings, she has put her head above the parapet to talk about poverty and homelessness.

> "The sad part about it is we live in one of the richest countries in the world. I was born and raised here. I never in my life thought I would be homeless. To me [homelessness is] a social justice issue. It's not [just] a blemish on Los Angeles, but on humanity. It's a human rights issue. It shouldn't have to be that way."

After her cancer was treated and had gone into remission thanks to a women's health clinic, and when she had found help getting a small apartment and work at Piece by Piece, June set herself some goals. "I said, you know what, Mary? If I can overcome this I will have testimony for somebody else." June said she wanted to: "speak truth to power", to be a "voice for the voiceless".

Because "homelessness is no joke, it's very traumatic. I was not going to just be a statistic". She added:

> "I've met all kinds of people [while homeless] and it just opened my mind's eye to realise that the human condition is all the same, you know? The point is that I didn't want to be a statistic. I wanted to fight. I wanted to fight for my rights for housing, and I wanted to fight for my rights as a human being. There is a right and a wrong and we all need each other."

Choking back tears at one point, June said this of why our stories matter: "I feel free when I'm speaking about my life. I want to shift perceptions. You never know where a person has come from until you walk a mile in their shoes. *You don't know what that person's story is.*"

9

Next generation: young people writing their own script

"When you're poor, you don't see yourself as poor, until you realise there are many more people much more privileged than you."
Young apprentice, 16, London

POSSIBLE

"SO MUCH OF THE NARRATIVE SHOWS POVERTY IN A NEGATIVE WAY WITH NO HOPE. WE NEED TO EMPOWER PEOPLE TO MAKE A CHANGE."

CARLY MALING, THINKNATION: PROJECT TWIST-IT LIVE! PARTICIPANT

Lost and confused
Having to find my own way growing up
I was told I was equal to everyone else
But soon realising my upbringing was a little bit messed up
Because of this I have a lot to prove
I've been born into disadvantage
But I'm determined to take what I have
And turn it into an ad-vantage
The only way is up from here
I can only win
I can only succeed
And if I fall down, I'll get up and fight back again
Hard times prepare you for a tough world
I'll get rid of all the labels
The ones society puts on people who grow up on benefits
And the ones that I've given myself in my head
The only way is up
I've got only one life

Extract: by young beatboxer, Luke, Battersea Arts Centre,
London, 2018, original beatbox composition about growing
up with poverty stigma for Project Twist-It

Pushing open the heavy soundproof doors to the auditorium at the Gulbenkian Theatre in Canterbury, England, in December 2018, it took a moment for me to register through the thick darkness that there were people on stage. A rehearsal was under way and a group of young beatboxers from London, the Battersea Arts Centre's Beatbox Academy,[1] were running through a soundcheck for a performance they were to give that evening. Mics were being tapped, levels and lighting checked, and physical positions on stage mapped out.

Like scores of other young teenagers scattered around the theatre building that day, they had given up their Saturday to work together to explore ways to 'smash poverty stigma'.

From 9am, as part of a PTI collaboration with the youth tech organisation ThinkNation,[2] teams of young people had been beavering away with volunteer mentors from across business, technology and the arts in workshops to come up with their own ideas for how to challenge the stigma and shame that comes with being poor – and especially the sort of shaming that impacts on young people from families that might be struggling.

By the end of a long day of creativity and graft, when the youngsters presented or performed their ideas and proposals live on stage to a full audience, there was an embarrassment of riches. One group had made a short film – from scratch – that dealt with isolation and judgement of poorer kids, and through scripted dialogue put to film told a story about the pain this could inflict. Others, young poets from Hull in the North East of the country who were part of a Spoken Word Collective at The Warren,[3] a youth-led community organisation that works with many vulnerable youngsters in the city, performed poems that peeled away the layers from labels and stereotypes associated with poverty.

One of the young poets, Jodie Langford,[4] focused on how categorising young people as dangerous or a threat served to reinforce negative representations about kids from poorer backgrounds and contributed to robbing them of opportunity.

Extract:

Putting hooligans on the screen at seventeen
Brainwashing the public to perceive that youngins' are thieves
Not all fall in to a jail cell over a uni degree
But some can't help being rejected by society
Complain about knife crime, but leave them to dwell in their poverty
You don't leave them much when they have
to provide their own security

Andrew Gooch, another member of the Collective, took on homelessness in his poem, The Riddle:

Extract:

Have the homeless always nestled within plain site?
Have the destitute been forced out of the shadows
and made to come out into the light?
Have their squalors been converted into

homes for families and dependents?
Have their faces been morphed by poverty into
looks of despair without resplendence?

What was remarkable was their acute awareness of the dominant narrative around poverty and of the role that stigma and shame play in our collective understanding of what it means to be poor. They also had a clear grasp of how misleading and harmful the narrative was, and they had a desire to be a part of changing this. For the young people, a number of themes recurred when they described the dominant narrative and how shame and stigma intersected with poverty across the culture. These included:

- The dominance of conspicuous consumption
- The worshipping of wealth and the wealthy
- The proliferation of labels and pejoratives
- The embracing of the 'othering' of marginalised groups
- The role of social media in perpetuating all of the above and in reinforcing stereotypes
- The moral vacuum left by our failures to effectively challenge stigma and the poverty narrative.

A range of priorities they wanted to be a part of tackling emerged. These included:

- Achieving a more accurate, empathetic portrayal of poorer people in the media and culture
- Rejecting labels and stereotypes in favour of empathy and inclusion
- Refusing to accept stigma as a given
- Breaking down barriers and divisions between people in different social groups
- Fostering a sense of community and social responsibility;
- Harnessing stories and lived experience
- Drawing from other movements, such as environmentalists, LGBTQ activism and disability rights campaigners, to highlight what is possible when young people come together
- Fighting poverty and refusing to see it as inevitable.

Most of all, they were passionate and positive about the role that their generation could play in being part of the *solution*.

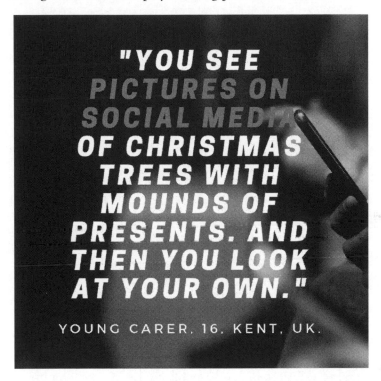

"YOU SEE PICTURES ON SOCIAL MEDIA OF CHRISTMAS TREES WITH MOUNDS OF PRESENTS. AND THEN YOU LOOK AT YOUR OWN."

YOUNG CARER, 16, KENT, UK.

One group at the live event, tasked with the challenge of 'smashing stigma in society', came up with the idea of an 'Alternative Census' whereby rather than asking people to answer questions about income or wealth, they suggested we ask questions about things that are levellers, things we share, like music or nature.[5] After the event, the young people took their idea out into the wider world – they took it upon themselves to launch the census as an antidote to negativity and judgements based on financial well-being and see what came back.

Presenting their idea on stage at the Gulbenkian they had this to say:

    "As a society we have a huge obsession with money and materialism yet there are so many other things that make us up. The same way we are not defined by our race or if we have disabilities, we should not be defined by how much money we have. So, we thought, in order to switch up the poverty stigma, we need to start asking different questions.

Our main idea was that in order to change the narrative of the stigma of poverty in society we need to be changing the conversation. We all have labels. If you think about it, we categorise ourselves and self-segregate. We think, 'he's rich, he's poor, he's cool, he's not'. That's counter-progressive to these ideas that we've been [talking about] of personal experience and human experience."

Through social media, the group concluded:

We are always connected yet we are consumed by our divisions. That's what we're trying to combat: is being able to dismantle this whole idea of stigmatising around poverty and being able to say – we're all the same in certain ways. We just want to smash poverty for everyone.

Lizzie Hodgson, founder of ThinkNation and the organiser of the Canterbury Live Event with PTI, said that working alongside the young people for months on the issue, she'd discerned a genuine commitment to shedding labels and rejecting the poverty narrative. "Young people have empathy. This is hands down the biggest thing I've learned on this project. What we didn't expect was how so many young people felt inspired to the extent they did." On the 'Alternative Census', Lizzie added:

"It puts people's personal experiences and feelings first. It doesn't focus on materialism, money or status. It doesn't look at things that divide people. Instead, it identifies things that connect us. A simple, but hugely powerful concept. And, these young people have taken their concept out into the real world and are building a longer-term way to fight poverty stigma designed and managed by them. That's incredible. "

"PEOPLE ARE REALLY QUICK TO JUDGE OTHERS WHO DON'T HAVE AS MUCH MONEY."

APPRENTICE, 19, LONDON

To the beat of their own drum

A few months before the Canterbury event, when I first met with theatre-maker Conrad Murray and a group of his young beatboxers at the Battersea Arts Centre in London, there was a similar vibe. By the time I arrived at the rehearsal space on a weekday afternoon in the theatre's complex in South London the young people had already been contemplating a 'word provocation' exercise to inspire them to think about the issue of poverty, shame and narrative. After introductions they dispersed into small groups where they composed lyrics and tunes.

What they emerged with – including the poem at the top of this chapter by Luke – were perceptive, thoughtful pieces of work. They put their poetry to their own beatbox rhythm combinations and performed their compositions for each other.

Afterwards, they shared their thought processes on the lyrics. The youngsters raised points that directly, as one put it, could "flip the script" on poverty – that would 'twist' the narrative. Once asked to think and write about misconceptions of poverty, these young people demonstrated a canny insight into how the narrative infiltrates our thinking.

Incorporating their lived experience and the word provocations, they challenged the fatalistic assumption, for example, that to be from a poorer background must mean that you *always* feel materially deprived, or miserable or hopeless. Yes, things were tough, they said, but there was much more to life than a lack of resources. Yet, they argued, this is something rarely talked about. And as for the one-dimensional caricatures of slovenly people who make only bad choices that we hear so much about? Well, they knocked those stereotypes straight out of the water.

For instance, they wrote about how most families made the best they could of straitened circumstances, and that while there are challenges, and opportunities might be harder to come by, to be poor does not necessarily mean to be denied joy or fun. They explored concepts including politics, the media, the structural causes of poverty, stereotypes, shame, employment, dignity, respect, opportunity, and social mobility, with wit and inventiveness.

For example, they wrote and recorded this for a PTI short film:

[Singer]
Poor me
making minimum wage in these streets
I must not be happy
Living the life I lead
Living day to day,
waiting for change
it's always the same
there's just no way that I could
be happy living the life I lead
Cos it's all about the
Money money money money money money
Yeah it's all about the
Money money money money money money

[Rap]
Maybe I should have a think
Just outside the box
Change my life in a blink
If I weren't so lazy I'd be raking it in
But let me tell you
What I really think Oh oh

I think I'm having fun on a budget
Holidays in Margate [?]
Yeah I used to love it
Media got me thinking I could be someone else
But I can't afford the tickets on the top shelf
Uh Beans on toast
A roast at Wetherspoons
Church hall birthdays with the best tunes
Inner city kids breathing in all the fumes
I didn't need it without a silver spoon
Uh, Cinema Saturday pound a pop
I was just a kid I thought it was a lot
So what we do with what we've got
So what we do with what we've got
[Singer]
Poor me making minimum wage in these streets
I must not be happy
Living day to day
I'm waiting to change
there's just no way
I could be happy
Living the life I lead
Cos it's all about the
Money money money money money money
yo yo
[Second male rapper]
What's does it seem that we're
living all the challenges
Poverty, government
you refuse to help them out with it
But the towns filled with the powerless

Scrounging for allowances for hours
But in the end they still got the house and shit
Now I wouldn't class myself a Marxist
But it seems like employers only care for what my past is
Never worked, never kept a job
You know I'm on hard times cos I don't know
what the good times are made of
I'm a criminal by night, criminal by day
Criminals in parliament can't even run the state
I'm criminal even when I'm in the job centre for days
What a fucked up world that we're living in today
It's the silence in our homes that got me on the streets
Marginalised and pushing people into poverty
Hours not at work there's not a lot of me
Know what, there's never enough what I need
[Singer and rap merge]
Poor me, making minimum wage in these streets
I just might be happy
[There's never enough of what I need]
Living day to day I'm waiting for change
There's just no way I could be happy
I'm living the life I lead
It's not all about the
money money money money money money
I might just be happy
Living the life I lead
It's not all about the
money money money money money money

Most of the young people Conrad works with are from neighbouring council estates and low-income backgrounds (he himself grew up nearby and his theatre work takes inspiration from class and related topics). The age range for BBA spans pre-teens to 20-somethings, and many of the youngsters who have been a part of it have performed their work in large venues and even on television. Some kids have been in trouble with the police, or had difficult childhoods, including interactions with the care system. But, Conrad says, beatboxing provides an outlet.

Music and poetry are the process of self-expression but the beating heart is "also getting the young people to talk about their lives so they can open up and explore their own background and stories …" he explains. When it came to producing beatbox work on poverty and perceptions, all the young people raised their game, Conrad says.

> **"**The young people were dealing with perceptions of poverty and people from low economic backgrounds and I thought that the responses were great, they were really creative responses. I think that they learned there are many perspectives about poverty. The media and everyone has one perception, but their own gut perceptions that they don't talk about are real and important.**"**

"POVERTY ISN'T JUST ABOUT A LACK OF POSSESSIONS."

APPRENTICE, 18, LONDON

The youngsters at BBA gathered around to discuss poverty portrayal in between performing their work. One young person,

Nate, reflected, "Most people don't have a choice of becoming poor. It's not a choice. It's not something where it's like, 'oh yeah, today I feel like I'm going to be poor but tomorrow I'm going to be rich.' You know what I'm saying?" Another contemplated how individuals are blamed for difficult circumstances when a lack of opportunity was the real culprit.

> "It's a Catch-22. Some people say it's you're not taking advantage of the life you have, [but] some people there is no advantage to take; it's not their fault. These days you are only two paychecks away. If you lose your job and you can't get another one within two months then you can be homeless, and that's it. And it's not really your fault."

And another, Luke, added, "Like, you can just be born into poverty. The pressure is on them 'cos their parents didn't have nothing." On the poverty porn, another one of the group observed: "Them shows? I think it's just the media promoting [poverty] in a bad way. There are other shows like *The Undateables*,[6] like with special needs and that. And that's demonising as well. It's just like, 'Why do they do this?' I don't know. It's definitely bad."

Similar themes came up time and again with young people in the US and the UK. Throughout 2018 and into 2019, Project Twist-It engaged with children and young adults ranging from film-makers and photographers pursuing creative avenues to tell stories about inequality, poverty and marginalisation, to those dealing with mental health problems or chaotic home lives speaking about it for the first time, and younger children from deprived communities aspiring to write and become storytellers. The more Project Twist-It developed, the more of these younger people – from pre-teens to millennials – I came across. What was especially striking was that they were not necessarily directly connected to one another or to a conventional 'movement'. They may have identified with, say, the environmental movement's boosting of young people's collective voices galvanised by Swedish activist, Greta Thunberg,[7] but they were on virgin territory finding what might be described as a common voice on poverty. Everyone was interested in the power of storytelling to challenge conventional ideas around poverty and poorer people and how this might bring about much bigger societal change.

One of the first people I interviewed for PTI was a young storyteller and homelessness activist, Antonio Rodrigues. This is what he told me when I asked him how significant the poverty narrative was in America, especially for people like June living on the literal margins of society in places like Skid Row.

> **"**I think there's a story problem clearly at the heart of this, which is that generally speaking when people think about Skid Row residents, they think about them as criminals and lazy ... who are drug addicts and drunks. And that's the dominant narrative and that comes from this idea that folks who are in that position, or residents of that community or experiencing homelessness ... did something to deserve it.**"**

Antonio was convinced that alternative stories – from people with experience – were crucial to bringing about meaningful change.

> **"**Having stories that counter that narrative are really important because it's a dangerous idea; it's a dangerous story," he concluded. "It's really dangerous especially when you get one that dehumanises an entire population of people, which is what happens to homeless folks.**"**

"I was just mainly trying to inspire people.**"**
Young film-maker, Wale Shittu. talking about his film, *Council in Me*

In London not long after, I met with young playwright and actor, Kieton Saunders-Browne. Being from a low-income background in a city like London with stark and vast inequalities bumping up against one another (and worsening),[8] and attempting to break into a profession increasingly the purview of the well off,[9] 20-year-old Kieton had set up a production company[10] with friends and was writing his own plays to generate roles. One of these plays was *Socks*,[11] a dystopian story about inequality and severed community.

The play – which took its title from a moment one morning when Kieton realised his socks had holes in them, something mundanely ubiquitous in his life but which he realised wouldn't even cross the mind of a wealthier person – was written to make people "think", as theatre should do, the young actor told me, "not to attack anyone".

"The place is a kind of metaphor of the rich 1 per cent and an exaggeration of how it could be if it carried on that way," he says of the bleak, dystopian backdrop he chose. "The story follows someone that goes into this place where all the top 1 per cent people live, which is basically sectioned off. No one else is allowed in, everywhere else other than those places, which are called wharfs, is basically ruined." Kieton produced the play and used its run in London to raise awareness of the charity Child Poverty Action Group.

The theatre and drama generally is a place where, he believes, stories have the power to generate empathy and to expose people to different world views – something he's keen to do. "I think theatre changes people's minds so much."

Wale Shittu is a young film-maker who grew up on a council estate in the south of England. He told PTI about how, on returning home from university, he wanted to make a short film that encapsulated life on an estate and which countered negative stereotypes about people who live in public housing. Collaborating with friends, the film, *Council in Me*,[12] is a visually arresting antidote to the stigma placed on people that employs music, imagery and poetry to tell a story that punches through clichés. The film was selected for the 2019 London Short Film Festival.

> "I was just mainly trying to inspire people, cos people think [if] you live in a council estate that [your] dreams are limited. I think with the film I was just

trying to portray: 'you can use your experiences you can do something with your life'. "

"I didn't really leave the [estate] until I went to university," he says, referring to how being cut off from the rest of society can sometimes happen with public housing complexes. Shittu's goal was to have people watch the film who might never otherwise encounter someone from an estate. "This is where I'm from, and these are the kinds of hardships in life we have to live through," he says of the story he wished to tell. "And it kind of just educates people: ok, cool, this is what I have to go through in terms of surviving as a working-class citizen."

Nadine Shah, a Mercury Prize-nominated young songwriter and musician from the North East of England, has been working with young people raising awareness of issues including poverty and opportunity. The power of art to counteract negative stereotypes around poverty is something she says she has come to appreciate – especially working with younger people.

> "I do believe that artists, including musicians, we can make a difference. We have this platform. We are so lucky in that we are able to talk to thousands of people and I think it would be a real shame if we didn't use it properly, because part of our job is documenting the times that we live in. "

Another young songwriter and musician, Louisa Roach from the band She Drew The Gun, some of whose work has also been rooted in social justice issues including poverty and homelessness, wrote her song 'Poem' after reading an article about homeless people being moved from parts of London because they 'were an eyesore for tourists'. "['Poem'] touched a lot of people," Roach said of the responses she gets to it. "Homelessness is a bit of an epidemic now. It's part of the system we live in. It requires people to be at the bottom and poor. That works globally [too]. There's always a fall guy."

On the value of building a collective of people and organisations working to challenge the poverty narrative and opening up space for young people to be heard she added: "I wanted to see what PTI was all about. It's interesting to see something quite collaborative and a lot of action going on."

> **"They will just judge a book by its cover without really giving us a chance to open up and speak about certain things."**
> 'Paul', 19, East London, talking to Project Twist-It

Then there were the younger people who spoke to the project about their own personal journeys and challenges. Nineteen-year-old 'Paul' [name changed at his request to protect his anonymity], who after a chaotic start to his life due to poverty and being excluded from school, was talking for the first time for public consumption about his thoughts on stigma and poverty when he recorded an interview with PTI. He wanted to talk about how poverty and the other issues that intersect with it, such as access to education and encounters with the criminal justice system, can hold young people back. Where he grew up was "sort of a poverty place", he explains, where many families like his were reliant on benefits and faced multiple hardships.

> **"**It was very difficult for me as growing up. You have got a harsh life and there's gangs and all sorts of things like that. I didn't want to get into a problem where I had to either pick gang [life] or the education life, because I never really had someone to show me a pathway where you need to do this you need to do that in order to focus on your long term.**"**

Paul's aspiration was to get a plumbing apprenticeship and, when we met, he was working two days a week at the Shoreditch Trust,[13] a grassroots anti-poverty organisation. "I thought, oh, my whole life is going to be coming to an end," he said, after being kicked out of school as a young teen. Paul managed to get a few qualifications and some help putting his life back on track, but he was anxious to explain that while his early life circumstances were not of his choosing, many youngsters facing similar challenges tend to be blamed by wider society rather than understood, and that they are rarely heard or listened to.

He told me he felt, now, that it was "really important" to speak up "because that can actually change our lives". He recalled that he felt the sting of being judged as a teenager in difficult circumstances.

> "People would [think], like, if we never got an opportunity, it's because of our fault. They don't really know what's literally happening behind the scenes ... because they have a different mindset and they would never know actually where we are coming from. That's why we wouldn't really speak and we would keep ourselves to ourselves."

"People actually like to judge a book by its cover nowadays," Paul concludes. "And it's hard. It's literally hard showing someone your actions, showing someone where you are coming from, because they don't really know. They will just judge a book by its cover without really giving us a chance to open up and speak about certain things."

No child left behind

Emblazoned in bold, colourful lettering on a large tarpaulin strewn across an otherwise nondescript two-storey corner building in the heart of Philadelphia are two words: Mighty Writers.[14] To walk inside is to be embraced by a blast of vitality and the joyful, anarchic din of young kids talking excitedly to each other, playing music, clattering pens and pencils and asking seemingly endless questions of the mentors on site. When I'm introduced to the 20 or so pre-teens in the large downstairs open-plan space – they are gathered around tables with poster paper spread out before them on which they are drawing and writing slogans for a Black Lives Matter protest the following day – I'm met with a wall of grins and a collective, sing-song "hell-ooh Ma-reee".

I explain I'll be hanging around to talk to them and to ask questions about the Mighty Writers project and what they do while at the after-school programme and, as I go to set up some equipment, one boy sheepishly asks if I'm a famous writer. I answer, not in the way he's suggesting, and he chuckles knowingly.

The Mighty Writers kids were the youngest group of people I interviewed[15] for Project Twist-It – 11-year-olds mainly – and they would eventually come to form the core of a three-part podcast series made especially for PTI on child literacy and poverty.[16] Mighty Writers was founded by former journalist, Tim Whitaker, in Philadelphia and as of my visit in 2018, there were seven sites around the city, all funded by donations and supported by writers, with a focus on writing and literacy – skills which, sadly, are marginalised in many public schools. Providing after-school and summer programmes for free, Mighty Writers courses are attended predominantly by kids from poor and low-income backgrounds and tend to fill up as fast as they're advertised. Every genre of writing is covered by the classes, with storytelling playing a big part. Many of the young people return year after year.

"You know, one of the biggest fallacies I think that's floating out there is that city parents don't care about their kids' education," Tim told me of the misconceptions he frequently encounters around poorer communities. "They care about their kids' education dramatically. They are often working a lot and dealing with a lot of personal family issues, but as soon as we announce a new location, we are filled up immediately. That, 'up by your bootstraps' narrative is one that we hear a lot and it holds no meaning for me."

Tim explained that for a lot of the children, having a place to go where they can find ways to express themselves and to make sense of the challenges around them, including poverty, was a factor in the programme's attraction. "They have to come every day, it's not a drop-in programme. So, they come every day, over the course of a year they go through every genre of writing," he told me. "It makes a difference immediately. The younger we can get the kids the better." On the topics most talked about in 2018, he says: "I think many of the kids – many of the African-American kids, which is the majority of the kids that we deal with – talk about police violence, talk about racism in general, Donald Trump, talk about the acceptance of bigotry in this country right now. The kids in the Mexican community, immigration or migration."

Self-esteem is a key element of what the youngsters get from Mighty Writers, according to Tim. "These kids' personalities just change, you know. And it's all because they are learning how to express themselves."

"I love this topic so much because a lot of kids are dying every day in gun violence, and the NRA, the government, is not going to do anything about it. So, we can do something about it."
Tyler, 11, Mighty Writers attendee

Sitting with the kids, they talked about what the project has meant to them and of how it is helping shape their ambitions for the future. Despite being so young, many of the kids were firmly focused on not having their background define them. Some had been going to Mighty Writers for a few weeks, others for a number of years. Anaya, 11, talked about why the week's topic – gun violence – was important to her. It was her first day at Mighty Writers.

> "I'm writing about Black Lives Matter because there's a lot of people dying ... teenager kids dying today. And I just want the violence to stop because I want to grow up ... Lots of people care for young kids but there are some people in this world that don't really care.
>
> I'm not really surprised that people are killing people because I have been in a shooting before, almost kind of died, but it didn't happen. My four-year-old sister was almost hurt, but I pulled me, pulled my brother and my sister to safety and me too, I was able to do it."

Eleven-year-old Tyler sitting with her was also hard at work making posters: "I really like Mighty Writers programme because they get us to focus on a bunch of topics that they don't really let kids talk about, and tomorrow we are going to go to a protest against gun violence," she told me as she wrote slogans. "Some of us are going to give speeches [at the protest]. I wrote some quotes and I think my favourite one is: 'Bullets are not school supplies' and 'America, love your kids not your guns'."

Tyler, who has been attending Mighty Writers since she was five, says her mum signed her up as soon as she could. "I guess I could say I really enjoyed it because we wrote books and we wanted to get our writing published. It was really fun and I made some friends, and then my mum took me back during the school year and I worked on many cool workshops. I think that really boosted my confidence because I was doing a lot at the time going to a new school," she added.

Tyler explained that she had a passion for writing and felt that between writing, storytelling and public speaking, she would be able to tell her own stories for a living thanks to the programme.

> "I love to write and I'm a public speaker, so doing this speech is really good and I think will be a great thing for my resume. It's definitely helped me because this is where I get a lot of my writing done. I want to be a movie writer/director. And I also want to still be a public speaker and an actress. So technically, yes, still a writer."

Being able to write about social issues, ones that affect the community, was important, Tyler said.

> "I love this topic so much because a lot of kids are dying every day in gun violence, and the NRA, the government is not going to do anything about it. So, we can do something about it. Yes, I love doing big topics like this. But I also do love sci-fi writing and I love doing, like, a bunch of imaginary stuff. But I mostly love big topics like this."

Before I left, Amelia Long, a volunteer at Mighty Writers for six years, said providing an environment where youngsters felt their voices mattered, that their experiences mattered and that their stories mattered made all the difference.

"I think it's been an opportunity for them to express some of the experiences that they've had. And some of the things that they hear on the news. We've had a conversation earlier this week where I asked, where do you hear about or see gun violence. And we had answers from the news, the radio, to on my block, in my neighbourhood, at school. So, they are aware of these things happening, and having a chance to actually speak up about them and have adults take their opinions and their knowledge seriously on it is I think invaluable."

Amelia's assessment echoed that of Lizzie Hodgson of Think Nation, who told me how through contact with scores of young people all over Britain, it was clear that poverty and all the interrelated issues that come with it leave profound impressions. Being able to talk about it and express themselves is a crucial factor in how poverty will be seen – and how policies are enacted – in the future. As Lizzie puts it: "By giving young people the platform to not only share their ideas on how we can change the poverty stigma, but also know that they are being listened to, and even acted on, is hugely important."

When it comes to dominant portrayals of poverty and the intersecting issues that impact on people's lives every single day, stories (often patently false ones) have been deployed with great effect to cement negative stereotypes and buoy regressive policies. Leveraging alternative stories anchored in lived experience and drowning out the toxic narrative is a solid foundation to build from. Nevertheless, to construct a new narrative, one built to last, requires coherence, cooperation and a fresh strategic approach. In order for this to happen, we need to follow George Lakoff's advice – we need to communicate our own set of frames, in our own language, anchored in our own values.

10

Altered images: constructing a new narrative

"Beware – always – of the person who believes that their own good fortune is entirely of their own making, while ascribing the misfortune of others to a want of intellect or morals."
Stephen McGann, actor

"The fortunate man is seldom satisfied with the fact of being fortunate. Beyond this, he needs to know that he has a right to his good fortune. He wants to be convinced that he 'deserves' it, and above all, that he deserves it in comparison with others ..."
Max Weber, philosopher and sociologist

Fighting the good fight: emerging pathways to change

Something utterly unexpected occurred at the start of 2019. And it occurred in the most unlikely, yet perfect, of places. At the annual World Economic Forum in the Swiss Alps town of Davos, renowned as a shindig for the super-rich to schmooze, back slap, and brag about being concerned with the social good and the environment and then, with zero sense of irony, jump into their private jets to fly off and accumulate yet more billions, one of the panels went viral. On his first visit to the event, 30-year-old Rutger Bregman, a Dutch historian and author of the book *Utopia for Realists: How We Can Build the Ideal World*,[1] suddenly found himself catapulted onto the international media stage (he was branded a 'folk hero' by Vox[2]) when he launched into an off-piste, pre-prepared riff about taxing the rich. The panel was about inequality but Bregman felt compelled to address, as he told *The Washington Post*, 'the elephant in the room' – a room stuffed with the world's wealthy.[3] "I hear people talking the language of participation and justice and equality and transparency," he told the audience. "But then almost no one raises the real issue of tax avoidance. And of the rich just not paying their fair share. It feels like I'm at a firefighters conference and no one is allowed to speak about water."

Even watching the clip on YouTube[4] you can almost feel the oxygen leave the room. "This is not rocket science," Bregman continued. "We can talk for a very long time about all these stupid philanthropy schemes, we can invite Bono once more, but come on, we got to be talking about taxes. That's it. Taxes, taxes, taxes. All the rest is bullshit, in my opinion."[5]

When Bregman's comments were challenged from the audience by the chief financial officer of Yahoo, Ken Goldman, declaring that the panel was "one-sided", that poverty around the world was being reduced, and remarking that the US had a low unemployment rate, another panellist responded and her comments went viral too. Winnie Byanyima, Executive Director at Oxfam International, recounted stories of workers in appalling conditions – some having to wear diapers because they weren't permitted toilet breaks for example – telling Goldman in no uncertain terms that the "quality" of jobs matter, not just whether someone is in work. "These are not jobs of dignity," Byanyima said.

Never before have I had such a strong feeling that the zeitgeist is really shifting and now you can talk about things that were simply not possible just a couple of years ago.
Rutger Bregman, author, *Utopia for Realists*

Both Bregman and Byanyima struck a nerve with a lot of people when a video from the event ended up being viewed millions of times within days and sparking intense mainstream media interest, including from Fox News.[6] Such a simple, unexpected and audacious guerrilla assault on the ideology underpinning global inequities in a place like Davos, was news.

For many viewers of the video clip there was undoubtedly a degree of indulgent satisfaction watching Bregman and Byanyima make their points so fluently and precisely right at the beating heart of elite global capitalism. However, their core sentiments, their core *message* – the importance of *fairness* and *fair play* and *dignity* – have been the threads of common values stitching together many social justice movements over the years and certainly among an array of protest movements and opposition actions since the global financial crisis. They were sentiments – despite a backdrop of right-wing populism – apparent throughout 2019 in the US. Among the most visible were bold proposals including that the wealthy pay more in tax, from politicians like Elizabeth Warren and Alexandria Ocasio-Cortez,[7] and Bernie Sanders' brand of democratic socialism and sustained exhortations that the system is 'rigged' in favour of the rich at the expense of the poor and middle class, all of which had garnered real traction, especially with younger people.[8] Such was the impact and resonance of presidential hopefuls Warren and Sanders' proposals, in fact, that prominent billionaires set about trying to defend themselves against the prospect of paying a bit more tax to mitigate soaring inequality. Pointing to assertions by Jamie Dimon, chief executive of JP Morgan Chase, that Warren 'vilifies successful people', economist and former US Labor Secretary in the Clinton Administration Robert Reich put it in *The Guardian* in November 2019 as follows: 'Billionaires are wailing that wealth tax proposals by Elizabeth Warren and Bernie Sanders are attacks on free market capitalism. Rubbish.'[9]

Also joining the chorus of complaining billionaires was brokerage founder Charles Schwab. Appearing on Bloomberg TV, he suggested that Warren's wealth tax was "wrong directed" and, positioning himself as the ubiquitous self-made man, said: "I came from really nothing and had plenty of incentive to create what we've created."[10]

And another was Facebook founder Mark Zuckerberg, who reacted to Sanders' contention that billionaires should not exist. He contended that billionaires were mostly "people who do really good things and kind of help a lot of other people. And you get well compensated for that."[11]

That billionaires in 2019 were bemoaning the fact that they might have to hand over a bit more to society did not happen just because high-profile politicians were coming up with plans, however. Their newly found victimhood came on the back of a decade's worth of fightback. In the US and in the UK by 2019 there were indications that more radical, progressive solutions – such as Medicare for All[12] and a Green New Deal[13] on one side of the Atlantic and overtures towards Universal Basic Income (UBI)[14] on the other – that would have been widely dismissed as outlandish just a few years before could now be put on the policy table.

Indeed, from the protest movement Occupy a decade earlier, to the anti-austerity efforts[15] in the UK in subsequent years, and from the emergence in America of wages and labour initiatives such as Fight for $15,[16] grassroots momentum for change was flourishing. Meanwhile, the organisation Patriotic Millionaires,[17] a group of self-declared 'traitors to our class' high-net-worth Americans campaigning about the concentration of wealth in the US and advocating for a fairer tax system, the urge to reject a status quo of tax avoidance, evasion and 'socialism for the rich' and push for better pay and jobs for workers, emerged in the decade-long aftermath of the crash and as inequality deepened.[18]

And, while it's true that Republicans in Congress continued to douse their corporate paymasters with tax cuts and the Conservatives in Britain (while paying lip-service to clamping down on tax evasion) still pursued tax cuts for the rich,[19] there were also notable and substantive successes for workers and their allies. Minimum wage hikes introduced in numerous cities and states across America[20] were one example, while in Britain the Labour Party advocated for more progressive taxation and toyed, for instance, with piloting UBI if elected.[21] Visible and large-scale strikes such as those by teachers and air traffic controllers[22] in the US and by fast food workers[23] and 'gig economy' Uber drivers in both countries lent yet further fuel to an engine of insurgence among the 'precariat' and lowest paid.[24]

And, as we saw in Chapter 7, the majority of the US public was broadly in tune with and open to a more progressive line of thinking on issues like raising the minimum wage, with polling showing they wanted taxes on the rich to be raised,[25] while in 2018 support for more tax and public spending among Brits reached a 15-year high.[26]

That our collective understanding of poverty and inequality had been shifting for a while, especially in the US with its excessive disparities of wealth and in a UK hellbent on mimicking it, is not in doubt. Zeitgeist-defining bestselling books focused on inequality, such as *The Spirit Level: Why More Equal Societies Almost Always Do Better* by British scholars Richard Wilkinson and Kate Pickett,[27] and *Capital in the Twenty-First Century*[28] by the French economist Thomas Piketty,[29] helped pave the way for a more nuanced appreciation of the factors giving rise to gross inequality and poverty, and their consequences.

Meanwhile, moves towards placing poverty in a wider rights-based context provided for a further recalibration of our understanding. As Robert Walker writes in his book *The Shame of Poverty*,[30] seeing poverty through the prism of rights, underlined by for example UN declarations such as the UN Millennium Development Goals to eradicate extreme poverty and halve the number of people living on a $1 a day globally by 2015, changes things.

'The language of rights broadens the focus of poverty from material inadequacy to social and power relationships, and embraces a way in which people in poverty are treated,' Walker points out.

> It also creates an affirmative agenda based on dignity and respect.... It also acknowledges the importance of dignity, not only in the context of setting poverty lines and minimum social protection provisions, but also in the delivery of benefits and services, and in the rhetoric of public debate, both giving people in poverty a voice and avoiding the language of denigration that is often so evident in the political construction of poverty.

Taken together, these developments present fertile terrain for a direct and effective challenge to the dominant narrative on poverty and, as a result, the structural causes of that poverty.

A month after the Davos incident, in a discussion between Bregman, Byanyima and the American journalist and author of *Winners Take All: The Elite Charade of Changing the World*,[31] Anand Giridharadas, the role of narrative and language in the context of inequality and poverty – and what was altering about it – was a focal point. And in a good way. It wasn't enough to be 'anti' things that were harming the poorest, they argued, we also have to be *for* something; we need fresh ideas and, crucially, we need to use the sorts of stories, language and framing that resonates with people when talking about those ideas. Fatalism is not an option. Take the following extract from their conversation. It is worth quoting because they make the case so well – in plain, conversational, positive language.[32]

> "**Byanyima:** I don't know whether the left has been sleeping but there has been a dominant narrative that has remained quite unchallenged in the media. This narrative suggests that there is no connection between the super-rich and abject poverty, that you can keep getting richer and richer and this has nothing to do with people getting poorer. And it wasn't always like that...
>
> **Giridharadas:** The idea of the narrative is so important. I think that what you both found yourselves in the middle of in Davos, and what I found myself on my book tour over the last few months, and what politicians such as Alexandria Ocasio-Cortez have found themselves in the middle of, is the growing challenge to a kind of bullshit narrative around wealth and poverty, access and power; it's completely wrong and fraudulent, and it's now crashing down...
>
> **Bregman**: I agree. I think that for a very long time politicians on both the left and the right have believed that most wealth is created at the top....

What Winnie pointed out very well in Davos is that most real wealth is actually created at the bottom…

When, after the financial crash of 2008, it became obvious that neoliberalism was founded on a huge amount of bullshit, the problem was there seemed to be no alternative. The left was against a lot of things: austerity, homophobia, racism, the establishment. But you also need to know what you are *for*."

Of the language deployed by the world's wealthy at Davos, and a topic his book elucidates in detail, Giridharadas had this to say:

"… there are terms such as 'social impact' and 'social venture capital' and 'impact investing'. They are ways of encouraging us not to use words like 'power' and 'justice' and 'dignity'.

Bregman: One thing I've been doing is using a different kind of language, one that centres on basic income for everyone and higher taxes for the rich. Often people on the left use the language of care, or they say something is just immoral or this is unjust. And yes, there is a certain part of the population that is receptive to this language. But there is another part of the population that doesn't really like that language. Also, impoverished people never like being talked down to. One thing to do is take back the win-win language and use it for something else. For example, doing something about poverty – there's a lot of research that shows eradicating poverty is an investment that pays for itself.

Byanyima: Stories are my biggest weapon … people respond to stories very strongly.

Bregman: Never before have I had such a strong feeling that the Zeitgeist is really shifting and now you can talk about things that were simply not possible just a couple of years ago.

Giridharadas: I come to this conversation so optimistic about the power of ideas and books right now. I feel like what we are witnessing is a profound cultural turning point in relation to these issues, caused by activists, artists, and writers who are changing what the public wants by telling honest stories."

Rewriting the rules: disrupting the dominant message on multiple fronts

Giridharadas and co were in good company. As the journalist Andy Beckett wrote in the early summer of 2019,[33] for the first time in decades there appeared to be the emergence of a viable new economic approach on the left that, instead of reacting to neoliberalism, was 'trying to construct a new kind of left-wing economics', with new thinkers emerging and collaborating, seeing opportunities to engineer a fairer society that weren't there before.

Beckett writes:

> A huge political space has opened up. In Britain and the US, in many ways the most capitalist western countries, and the ones where its problems are starkest, an emerging network of thinkers, activists and politicians has begun to seize this opportunity.

When it comes to efforts aimed specifically at targeting the poverty narrative, in the course of working on my regular *Guardian* column, 'Lesson from America', and building Project Twist-It, I came across many people and organisations working hard to plot a course towards a new, non-toxic narrative – and with different narrators. Ideas and initiatives were cropping up all over the place in America and Britain with the sort of momentum and serendipity suggestive of this being no happy accident. And, they spanned a mixture of macro and micro approaches, academic, activist and artist. Some had a primary interest in changing the language and narrative around poverty and for others, for example the Poor People's Campaign,[34] it was an indispensable aspect of their work on social justice, including the ongoing battle for racial justice.

Many of these efforts were intertwined directly with developing ideas and movements focused on how to build a better, fairer society and how to foster compassion and empathy as engines for social change. Nothing about the work I encountered was in the abstract – all had an eye on practical, broader social change. Many of those working in the space in Britain and America by 2019 were small and grassroots with a focus on communities, while others, including academics and activists, were concentrating on a bigger canvas.

> **"I call these the 'I Didn't Do it Alone' stories."**
> Chuck Collins, author, talking to Project Twist-It

In the US, Chuck Collins, author of *Born on Third Base: A One Percenter Makes the Case for Tackling Inequality, Bringing Wealth Home, and Committing to the Common Good*,[35] and director of the Program on Inequality and Common Good at the Institute for Policy Studies, was one of the people at the forefront of the pivot towards focusing on upending the dominant narrative. As a first principle, Collins told me in 2019, he had come to believe that we require a "unified narrative of wealth and poverty" that explains the structural intersection of the two, that *de-individualises* the portrayal of rich and poor, and overturns the notion of "deservedness" to which so many people cling. As the dominant narrative currently stands, it "serves the interests of powerful elites who are interested in individualising the causes of structural poverty", while a tendency to focus on poverty as a discrete issue, "sometimes keeps the frame of vision and conversation focused on 'fixing' poverty", he explained of his thinking.

In *Born on Third Base*, a book which draws on Collins' own upbringing in a secure and well-off environment (in his youth Collins gave away his entire trust fund to charity) to tell the story of how being born to advantage begets advantage through multiple generations, he argues that we need "a more accurate narrative of wealth creation". As he told me later, "I grew up in the richest 1 per cent and … I've got a pretty good list of the 101-plus ways that intergenerational advantage works."

"There is, for example, a fair amount of amnesia when it comes to people remembering how they got to where they are. In *Born on Third Base* I lift up the stories of people who society would view as wealthy and successful and amplify the part of their stories where they disclose the family and government help that made their situation possible. I call these the 'I Didn't Do it Alone' stories. We need to listen to one another's stories – which requires attention, openness, even vulnerability. Practising story-telling has been personally important [for] me to understand the power of narrative and counter-narrative. I think it is one of the ways that we can rewire our brains (and open our hearts) to one another's stories."

It might seem at first as if Collins is being overly optimistic and asking for quite a lot, bearing in mind how tightly the rich hold on to their wealth and adhere to their justifications for accumulating yet more. Why, for example, would those who benefit from the system and the narrative that has served them so well and which makes them feel good about themselves willingly shed their sense of deservedness and accept a narrative that shows they had advantages others did not, or had benefited from 'social investment' such as schooling and infrastructure? Or that they weren't in fact successful purely as a result of hard graft and natural gifts? Wouldn't most of us like to think that hard work and talent reap rewards, and take some personal credit for it? It's a very human, and understandable, impulse after all. As philosopher and sociologist Max Weber wrote over a century ago:

> The fortunate [man] is seldom satisfied with the fact of being fortunate. Beyond this, he needs to know that he has a right to his good fortune. He wants to be convinced that he 'deserves' it, and above all, that he deserves it in comparison with others ...[36]

Yet, as Collins' extensive research has shown, there are already rich people, like those at Patriotic Millionaires, who are willing to upend the wealth creation side of the narrative (and are doing so vocally) by calling out structural and systemic inequities and acknowledging the advantages they benefited from, such as inheritance and low taxes, while asking to be taxed more. Consider Abigail Disney, heiress to a fortune from the media empire of the same name, who reacted to the news that the Walt Disney Co's CEO made 1,424 times more than the median employee in 2018 (his total compensation for the year was $65.6 million), while company staff working at Disneyland in California were struggling to get by on low wages by suggesting that perhaps pay rises for regular workers should be a priority. Speaking at an event on 'humane capitalism', Disney called the CEO's remuneration "insane".

She said: "So there's a point at which there's just too much going around the top of the system into this class of people, who – I'm sorry this is radical – have too much money."[37]

Meanwhile in June 2019 Disney was one of more than a dozen billionaires in the US, including George Soros and Facebook co-founder Chris Hughes, to publicly call to be taxed more to address inequality in an open letter addressed to '2020 presidential candidates'.[38] It came just two months after Ray Dalio, founder of the world's biggest hedge fund, Bridgewater, declared that the gap between rich and poor was a 'national emergency' in an 8,000-word blogpost on the networking site, LinkedIn: 'Why and how capitalism needs to be reformed'.[39]

Mentioning that a number of Democratic contenders already supported a wealth tax on the very rich, the June open letter read:

America has a moral, ethical and economic responsibility to tax our wealth more. Polls show that a moderate tax on the wealthiest Americans enjoys the support of a majority of Americans—Republicans, Independents, and Democrats. We hope that candidates for president will also recognize the force of the idea and join with most Americans in supporting it.

Writing that even the modest increase in tax on the most wealthy they were proposing would bring in a significant amount of revenue – an estimated $3 trillion over ten years – to help counter major issues like the climate crisis, they added:

> That a moderate tax on a miniscule number of Americans could raise so much revenue simply reflects historic levels of wealth among America's richest. The top 1/10 of 1 per cent of households now have almost as much wealth as all Americans in the bottom 90 per cent.

Significantly, the letter frames its proposals in a language of the common good. For example, the authors write that a wealth tax 'is an economic winner' for America, that it will 'make Americans healthier' by addressing inequalities that make people unhealthier, that it is 'patriotic' and will 'strengthen American freedom and democracy', and that 'it is fair'.

And, in June 2019, the billionaire entrepreneur Eli Broad, whose own life story embodies much of what people would associate with the American Dream and the Land of Opportunity as the child of immigrants who went on to extraordinary success, wrote in a similar vein in *The New York Times* advocating for a wealth tax. Broad wrote:

> There's a story we like to tell about American capitalism. Ours is a country that prizes merit, rewards risk and stands apart in its commitment to the collective success of open markets and the free flow of capital. We are a nation of strivers who can pull ourselves up by our bootstraps with the right combination of grit and determination.
>
> That's the tale we love to tell and hear. But take it from a person who has found himself on the fortunate side of that narrative: This story is incomplete. For most people, our system isn't working.
>
> I simply believe it's time for those of us with great wealth to commit to reducing income inequality, starting with the demand to be taxed at a higher rate than everyone else …. I can afford to pay more, and I know others can too. What we can't afford are more

shortsighted policies that skirt big ideas, avoid tough issues and do little to alleviate the poverty faced by millions of Americans. There's no time to waste.

Chuck Collins contends that there are options at our disposal for reframing the conversation – altering the messages around poverty in a way that more people might be open to hearing. Referencing Patriotic Millionaires, he explained:

> "One way we have found to disrupt these stories and myths of deservedness is to supplant them with true stories of how wealthy and 'successful' people have gotten help – family and government assistance – that has made their own individual wealth and opportunity possible."

(When we spoke, Collins was working on his next book: *Disrupting Narratives of Deservedness: Changing the Stories that Justify Economic and Racial Inequality*.)

> **"Don't I have a responsibility to pay back the society that has made everything possible for me? Don't I have an obligation – a duty – to ensure that other kids, who grew up poor like I did, should have the same opportunities for education and employment?"**
> Martin Rothenberg, tech entrepreneur and millionaire

In his 2018 book *Is Inequality in America Irreversible?*[40] Collins suggests that while the barriers to change are significant, they are not insurmountable, and that central to this is deploying stories that are truthful, which don't fall into the trap of using the frames of reference that are defensive or rely purely on statistics to get a point across, and which also offer people a sense of hope and possibility moving forward. 'While data-based messages are motivating for some constituencies, they don't always connect with people who hold powerful stories that explain and justify inequality.'

In a nod to Silicon Valley's fondness for the term 'disruption', Collins argues that disrupting the narrative is exactly what's called for. In the book, he relays the story of tech millionaire entrepreneur, Martin Rothenberg, who while at a press conference to defend the estate tax[41] literally upended expectations when he spoke in favour of it. The estate tax which, like inheritance tax in Britain, has a bucketload of powerful supporters who – very successfully – frame it as some kind of raid on people's hard-earned piggybanks, was niftily rebranded by Republicans as a 'death tax'.[42] Despite affecting a miniscule number of estates (and only those with significant fortunes), even the most modest calls to increase its reach elicit fury among people unaffected by it. Rothenberg, who grew up in poverty, told the conference:

> "My wealth is not only a product of my own hard work. It also resulted from a strong economy and lots of public investment in others and me. Someone else paid for the scientific foundations of technological knowledge I was working on [at college] – and to train my future employees in this knowledge. So, should I pay the estate tax? Of course I should! Don't I have a responsibility to pay back the society that has made everything possible for me? Don't I have an obligation – a duty – to ensure that other kids, who grew up poor like I did, should have the same opportunities for education and employment?"

Collins has been a researcher and advocate too long to suggest there are easy answers – but he does think, like Bregman and others seem to, that when it comes to the poverty narrative we might just be on the cusp of a real shift. He suggests that during what is undoubtedly a time of regressive political upheaval, in many ways the seeds for an adjustment have been sown and are beginning to take root. "I think the currency of these stories is weakening," he says of the deservedness tropes that prop up the narrative.

> "They remain incredibly powerful. But the more we expose them as fallacies and untrue representations of people's lives, the less hold they have over our

brains. I think progressives have a 'we're in it
together' commonwealth story, we need to build a
healthy commonwealth, we need to invest in public
institutions and things that lift up everybody. Those
are powerful stories.**"**

**"This is not just about having a voice, it's about finding a way
to use our voice that will hold politicians to account for the
very real impact that their decisions have on people's lives."**
Tracey Herrington, Thrive Teesside

Among many organisations working at a grassroots level that
I encountered through PTI, challenging the poverty narrative
had quickly become integral to efforts aimed at changing policy
or public attitudes. One example in Britain is the evolution of
Poverty Truth Commissions (PTCs).[43] As with the emergence
of the Poor People's Campaign in the US (which oversaw a
'Truth Commission on Poverty' of its own in New York City in
2017),[44] the poverty truth movement is evidence of a grassroots
and growing aspiration to systematically push change from below
by people who were 'experts by experience' in order to actively
shape policymaking that impacted on poorer and marginalised
people on the ground – while simultaneously presenting a
narrative to counter the culture of blame and shame.

The poverty truth 'model' starts from the premise that
people with lived experience (called 'commissioners') should
be at the heart of local decision-making. The exact nature of
each commission varies from place to place but all start from
a foundation of working collectively and in conjunction with
civic and business groups on issues that affect their everyday lives.
Representation in public and political life is key to the approach,
with 'commissioners' at the centre. Echoing a perspective I have
come across regularly in many years of writing on disability rights
and which has roots in a number of international liberation
movements, the guiding ethos 'Nothing About Us Without
Us' couldn't be clearer.[45]

The first commission, formed in Scotland in 2009 (known
as the Poverty Truth Community from 2019),[46] helped inspire
others, including one in the city of Leeds in the north of

England that launched in 2014.[47] By the summer of 2019 two 'commissions' (the model *is not* about consultation) had taken place in Leeds with another being planned in the city. Tellingly, the Leeds commission adopted a focus on presenting an alternative to the portrayals popularised by 'poverty porn' like *Benefits Street* and it also worked on a bid to work with Truevision Yorkshire to make the film *Fighting Shame*. As the Leeds Poverty Truth Commission put it, shifting perceptions was a central part:

> It is hoped that the project deepens understanding of the difficult and entrenched issues of poverty, improve perceptions and challenge stereotyping, and lead to better decision making by the city's leaders across business, public and voluntary sectors.

Daniel Edmiston, a lecturer in social policy and sociology at the University of Leeds, has been working with the Leeds commission on a project to "distil some of the key lessons of the poverty truth model", the hope being that it could help inform others wishing "to amplify the voice and influence of marginalised citizens".

The most recent Leeds commission "also launched a '*Humanifesto*'[48] to challenge the dehumanising effects of poverty and public perceptions around it", Edmiston points out. "This can be an empowering and transformational experience that instils a sense of common belonging and purpose that challenges 'welfare' myths and poverty stigma."

As these contributors to the *Humanifesto* put it:

> "People think poverty is having no money. It isn't. It's having no love and respect." **Geoff**

> "Hell is not a lifestyle choice." **Nick**

> "A host of legalities and policies erected barriers that trapped me into positions of poverty." **Howard**

And there was Poverty2Solutions,[49] also in the UK, which drew on the voices and input of people with lived experience to explore (as its title implies) solutions emanating from those people. Formed in 2016 from three groups, ATD Fourth World, Dole Animators and Thrive Teesside – all of which were working in the same space of poverty and representation – Poverty2Solutions explicitly aimed to draw on the expertise of its members to highlight key problems related to poverty, reach out to other organisations to collaborate and to campaign 'to try and make sure the voices of people in poverty are better heard in policy and media debates'.

Crucially, as Tracey Herrington at Thrive Teesside put it: "This is not just about having a voice, it's about finding a way to use our voice that will hold politicians to account for the very real impact that their decisions have on people's lives."

The social enterprise Sound Delivery was also actively carving out a space for people's voices and views on poverty to counteract the tendency for poorer people to be talked *about*. An organisation focused on storytelling, it supports the telling of stories through events, audio and other platforms across the UK. PTI hosted some of the organisation's content, including extracts from a landmark 'Being the Story' event in London which showcased people like Steve Arnott,[50] a low-paid warehouse worker and living example of the shift-working 'precariat' with a passion for music who, against great odds, set up a 'beats bus' – a mobile recording studio – to build confidence among young people in the English city of Hull, and who was featured in Sean McAllister's film, *A Northern Soul*.

Sound Delivery also hosted a performance from the play, *Can you hear me from up here?*. This featured the stories of people living in public housing tower blocks addressing what it's like to live in one but also directly tackling attitudes to people living in social housing, the prejudices and stigma they experience, as well their dreams, hopes and aspirations. Inspired by the fire at Grenfell Tower in West London where 72 people lost their lives and hundreds more their homes and loved ones, *Can you hear me from up here?* was part of a wider initiative in the North West of England, On Top of the World,[51] founded by One Housing Association and the Manchester Royal Exchange Theatre. It was yet another potent example of communities and artists collaborating to push back against the negative portrayals of people in poverty and in public housing.

As we saw in earlier chapters, the rhetoric and language around poverty and the related issue of austerity have come under ever-greater scrutiny. This has partly been driven by scholars and researchers seeking to explore the topic in greater depth as poverty and inequality in the US and the UK has garnered more attention – but also increasingly as individuals on the receiving end have fought to have their voices heard. Against this backdrop, discussion about language and 'framing' of poverty – including in the media – has generated a range of responses and recommendations.

For example, the initiative Rethinking Poverty, part of the Webb Memorial Trust,[52] which among other things probes thinking and policy around poverty in Britain and beyond, published a number of articles touching on the subject of shifting language and narrative. Acting as a sort of umbrella hub for ideas and discussions, the project's website provides a window into the state of play on proposals for what we need to do to alter how we talk about poverty. For example, a 2019 article[53] by Manny Hothi, Director of Policy at Trust for London, put forward the argument that rather than temper or moderate the language we use to expose poverty and counter existing perceptions, we should be tougher about it. The article argues that anti-poverty advocates should learn from the hard-hitting, no-holds-barred language adopted by Philip Alston in his UN reports. And, pointing to shifts in tone among environmental campaigners that have pushed the climate crisis to the top of the mainstream political agenda (arguably exemplified by Greta Thunberg's school climate strikes, Extinction Rebellion and David Attenborough on the BBC turning towards a more hard-hitting take on the climate), Hothi suggests that the time for being 'measured and polite' about big societal threats including poverty and inequality has passed.

'The angry and exasperated tone' of Alston's UK report is both important and necessary, the article asserts. 'It could be argued that the tone is counter-productive, that it lets those who deny there is an urgent problem off the hook by allowing them to claim the report is "too political", as the government has already done.' Had the report been written in a less decisive and conclusive manner, Hothi insists: 'I am in no doubt that it would have been received in the same way that the countless reports on the state of UK poverty have been: denial that there is a problem and the assertion that absolute poverty is falling.'

Another area where I became aware of moves being made to address issues around language and poverty portrayal was within the media. As one of the primary conduits for propagating the tropes that bolster the narrative around poverty, this is arguably one of the most important fronts for potentially overturning it. It's a tough one when the media in both the UK and the US is concentrated in the hands of a few owners or overtly right-leaning as with Rupert Murdoch's Fox News, and when local press, independent or otherwise, has been decimated in the digital era. However, as numerous articles and writers referenced in this book attest (and something I hope my own journalism has been testament to), there are abundant examples of ongoing reporting and portrayals of poverty that do not align with the dominant narrative or which directly refute the underlying assertions about the poor subscribed to by purveyors of that narrative. Nevertheless, because these have so far not been enough to drown out the shaming and blaming of the poorest, especially among pundits, dedicated initiatives in Britain and America have emerged in the second decade of the 21st century to encourage more responsible, informed reporting.

In the US, the Economic Hardship Reporting Project (EHRP)[54] was established with the clear intention 'to change the national conversation around poverty and economic insecurity'.[55] The organisation, founded in 2012 in the wake of the Great Recession and inspired by the reporting projects launched during the Great Depression by Franklin D. Roosevelt's New Deal,[56] actively seeks to publish works – narrative features, documentary, photo essays – 'that put a human face on financial instability', in conjunction with a variety of media outlets. It conscientiously works with a diverse pool of reporters (approximately 68 per cent women and 31 per cent minorities) and promotes geographic diversity (for example reporting from rural areas), including work by writers who are struggling financially. As the writer

Sarah Smarsh has pointed out, the make-up of the people doing the job of journalism matters immensely if the fullness of the experience of poverty and marginalisation are to be reported.[57] This is a central characteristic of the EHRP approach:

> Our writers and photographers, some of whom may be on the brink of poverty themselves, tell intimate, heart breaking and sometimes shocking stories originating from their own communities.

Rightly, its work has been recognised by the industry, including with an Emmy Award. From articles on evictions and homelessness, to immigrant struggles, insecure retirement, environmental devastation and deprivation in rural areas, as well as the fundamental yet often ignored connection between poverty and incarceration and between poverty and race, the project has produced an impressively informed and sometimes extremely moving body of work that features stories across the spectrum of American life. And, it has the people at the sharp end of poverty where they should be – at the centre of those stories – without ever resorting to stereotypes.

"It needed to come from other people who'd experienced poverty."

Journalist Rachel Broady talking to Project Twist-It about how the UK National Union of Journalists developed guidelines for reporting poverty

Journalist Rachel Broady grew up in poverty in the UK. After the financial crash she found herself out of work and living on unemployment benefits "for quite a long time". In response, she wrote a blog, *Unemployed Hack*. "Just doing what you do as a journalist to try and find your way through things, you start writing," Broady told me. Growing up in poverty is, she added: "... always a threat at your door, there's always the recognition that you could go there again, but I think I'd forgotten the living everyday reality of it."

When the coalition government of Conservatives and Liberal Democrats was elected and austerity began to be rolled out,

Broady says she became "more acutely aware of what was going on in the media and how it was being used to justify these quite brutal changes to social security – or the welfare system as they prefer to call it". She decided to do something about it. The outcome, after working with over 20 people with lived experience of poverty, anti-poverty organisations and young people at a local media project in the North West of England to make a film about why fair and accurate reporting of poverty is important, was the National Union of Journalists (NUJ) Reporting Poverty Guidelines.[58]

'Our media is saturated with stereotypes and misinformation creating a persistent persecution of the poor. Derogatory language describes those in receipt of benefits. Misunderstandings lead to unfair representation,' Broady writes in the guidelines report. The reporting guidelines highlight the pitfalls and traps that reporters can fall into: for example, using language like 'scrounger' as if it were neutral, or perpetuating myths such as the scale of people cheating the system.

Among some of the guidelines for journalists are:

- Reminders to deal in facts, not supposition
- Advice on how to avoid stereotypes
- Guidance on how to interview respectfully based on a person's circumstances
- Using statistics responsibly.

Comments from people who fed into the development of the guidelines include:

> "Don't contribute to the idea that there are deserving and undeserving poor people – no one wants or deserves to live in poverty."

> "Words hurt. Reports can exacerbate problems and increase hate crimes."

The NUJ's guidelines won't satisfy, or even appeal to, everyone and, of course, some reporters might be amenable to the guidelines yet find themselves in a newsroom where they are under pressure to produce 'click bait' or content that suits their editor's or organisation's ideological standpoint.

Nevertheless, the NUJ guidelines, like much of the work going on to acknowledge the role of stereotyping and stigma around poverty, are a starting point at least. They are evidence of change. And, as Rachel Broady told me, while people from poorer backgrounds are hugely underrepresented among the ranks of journalists: "I do think there are very many opportunities now for journalists to engage with the people they're writing about."

Another grassroots initiative emerged in Britain to make it easier for journalists and people with experience of poverty to connect. The charity On Road Media[59] works to increase accurate and sensitive representation of marginalised groups, for example transgender people and victims of domestic abuse. In 2018/19 it undertook a new project to train people who have lived experience of poverty to work as spokespeople on the topic and to connect with journalists and television producers, including on dramas and soaps which have the power to reach millions of people from diverse backgrounds and with differing points of view.

Thinking different: the beginning of the end for the dominant poverty narrative?

In April 2019 the deputy head of communications at Amnesty International, Thomas Coombes, wrote a blog titled: 'Five Ways to Change the Narrative from Fear to Hope'.[60] In it Coombes argued that 'civil society' is so busy 'exposing the world's most terrible suffering' that hope is rarely communicated, thereby 'fatally undermining' the potential for positive change. What was needed, he argued, was for people to be shown not just the problem, but that an alternative is possible. 'The starting point for a narrative strategy that leads to tangible impact is being able to actually articulate the changes we want to see,' Coombes suggested, in a comment that echoed the arguments of Bregman and co. But, more than this, he pondered: 'We will always use facts and research to make our case, but we can no longer avoid asking ourselves: "What is the emotion you want to trigger in your audience? Can you give the anticipation of feeling good later?'"

Coombes proposed a 'Five-step approach' that he called 'Hope-based Communications.'

The steps were:

1. Sell the solution before documenting the problem.
2. Offer opportunity instead of threat.
3. Celebrate what you stand for instead of criticising what you oppose.
4. Tell stories that show people as everyday heroes, not victims.
5. Make people feel hope, not fear.

Coombes' relatively straightforward – you could call them commonsense – suggestions were indicative of a developing ecosystem of ideas and thinking around how issues, especially social issues like poverty, are framed and communicated to a wider public. Facts matter, of course, but it's what we do with them that we need to think about.

In this vein in 2016 in the US, for example, a new organisation emerged with the explicit goal of shifting narratives. The aptly named Narrative Initiative (NI)[61] was established to work across a range of issues with an explicit mission to: 'catalyse durable narrative change in order to make equity and social justice common sense'. The organisation, founded by a collaboration between the Ford Foundation and Atlantic Philanthropies, and which provides a bridge between multiple interested groups and disciplines, including grassroots organising, art, research and political advocacy, is yet another example of a possible sea-change in thinking around the power of narratives – including how they are deployed to undermine progressive change with such toxic precision. NI is especially interested in what it terms 'deep narratives' characterised (as with the dominant poverty narrative) by pervasiveness and intractability. It was formed to be part of and support what it identified as 'an emerging field of narrative change practitioners, researchers and trainers'.

It's not that the concept of narrative change is something new, the organisation acknowledges, but that there could be advantages from connecting often disparate efforts to benefit each other, including in the realm of poverty and inequality. That it announced its launch just a couple of weeks prior to the presidential election result of November 2016 only made it feel all the more timely and necessary. Its founding report, *Toward New Gravity*, explained:

> Sparked by the recognition that pervasive and systemic narratives permeate every aspect of our daily lives, animate our popular culture and influence our politics, the multi-year collaboration was designed to support social justice leaders, advocates and organizers to better understand and deploy the power of narrative to build fairer, more inclusive societies.

The report also referenced a quote from Margaret Thatcher on taking power in 1981 that provided a telling window into her thinking at the time "it isn't that I set out on economic policies; it's that I set out really to change the approach, and changing the economics is the means of changing that approach," Thatcher had said back then. "If you change the approach you really are after the heart and soul of the nation. Economics are the method; the object is to change the heart and soul."

Back in the UK almost 30 years later, the New Economics Foundation had been doing significant work in the area of framing the economy.[62] Its work on austerity,[63] for instance, unpicked how that particular narrative had quickly been exploited by those in power to become established as the 'dominant story' of the era and how it proved so potent and resilient with the help of metaphors that painted the previous Labour government as having 'maxed out' the nation's 'credit card', making it necessary to 'tighten our belts' through cuts. The NEF report concluded:

> Appealing to values increases the chance people will engage with and respond to what you say, because they are things we hold in common, that resonate at a deep emotional level. And, just like frames, values

are like muscles: the more we appeal to a value, the stronger it becomes.

Its austerity analysis showed how the creation of a set of key tactics made this possible, including:

- A **strong story**: consistent, memorable, full of vivid images and emotional metaphors and a story simple enough to be readily understood and retold.
- A story with a **clear plot** that involved challenge and choice. Namely, the challenge in austerity was tackling national debt, and 'hard choices' had to be made. The choice was to be 'skivers' or 'strivers' and whether to work or 'do nothing'.
- A story with **compelling characters** – heroes and villains. The heroes were 'those who work hard and play by the rules'.
- A story with a **moral** that gave birth to a slew of easily digestible metaphors.
- A story that connected with people's **values**.

In the 21st century we've heard a lot about 'winning hearts and minds', usually in the context of war, but as America and Britain have become more politically polarised, and as marginalised groups including the poorest are hurt and stigmatised by this, we need to be open to new strategies – new ways of connecting with people. If we are repeatedly told that everything is binary, that it's about 'them and us', that fear supersedes hope, then we all lose. Many of us may be sceptical of efforts to change narratives or use communications science to alter 'messaging'. It can seem shallow, manipulative even. But in reality it's critically important. From 2016 with Trump in America and Brexit in Britain we've witnessed the brutally effective power of misinformation, of lies and manipulation, of framing vital social issues from immigration to poverty in a way that engenders hostility and shuts down conversations. Framing is one of the most precious tools we have in the box to potentially turn this ship around, and when it comes to the entrenched poverty narrative, the groundwork has already begun.

Fifteen years after the American cognitive scientist George Lakoff first published his landmark book on framing, *Don't Think of an Elephant: Know Your Values and Frame the Debate*,[64] which could be used as a manual by anyone with progressive ideas attempting to shift public narratives, Coombes was one of many communications practitioners in the non-profit and charitable sectors grappling with how the most pervasive narratives can be overturned and the role that framing has to play in this. The sort of long-term shifts in public opinion needed to consign entrenched problems and ideas to the dustbin of history were not going to be achieved purely through raising awareness or 'naming and shaming', he – rightly – argued. Framing is central to stewarding through a change in perception and a change in attitudes.

When we successfully reframe public discourse, we change the way the public sees the world.
George Lakoff, author, *Don't Think of an Elephant: Know Your Values and Frame the Debate*

In Lakoff's book *Thinking Points: Communicating Our American Values and Vision*,[65] among the many missteps (or 'traps') he identifies that are frequently made by progressives attempting to bring about social change, was: 'The No Framing Necessary Trap'. Lakoff writes:

> Progressives often argue that "truth doesn't need to be framed" and that "the facts speak for themselves". Rather, we need to understand that: People use frames – deep-seated mental structures about how the world works – to understand facts. Frames are in our brains and define our common sense. It is impossible to think or communicate without activating frames, and so which frame is activated is of crucial importance. Truths need to be framed appropriately to be seen as truths. Facts need a context.

Another framing-related trap Lakoff identifies is 'The Spin Trap'. Some progressives, he wrote, fall for the idea that 'clever spin and catchy slogans' ('surface framing') can win public support. However, surface framing alone is 'meaningless without the sort of "deep" framing' that appeals to values and deep moral convictions. Slogans are all well and good, he suggests, but not if they are expected to do all the heavy lifting and are not partnered with deeper frames, 'progressive values and principles' that 'must be in place before slogans can have an effect...'.

Likewise, he cautions against other assumptions; for example, that highlighting a list of issues or policies or programmes as having merit is the same thing as communicating a set of values, or that 'policy speak' or jargon (however earnest or factually accurate) translates as something meaningful. Pointing the finger of blame where it belongs and exposing how bad policies affect people is crucial in any fight to push poverty up the agenda; however, Lakoff argues that just countering lies with the truth tends not to work:

> Simply correcting a lie with a truth is not enough. We must reframe from our moral perspective so that the truth can be understood. This reframing is needed to get our deep frames into the public discourse. If enough people around the country honestly, effectively and regularly express a progressive vision, the media will be much more likely to adopt *our* frames.

When the word *tax* is added to *relief*, the result is a metaphor: Taxation is an affliction.
George Lakoff, author, *Don't Think of an Elephant: Know Your Values and Frame the Debate*

Throughout his work Lakoff provides numerous examples in the US political landscape of framing at work by conservatives. Take tax 'relief'. He shows how, from the day that George Bush Jr entered the White House, the phrase 'tax relief' was ubiquitous. 'It was repeated almost every day thereafter, was used by the press in describing his policies, and slowly became so much a part of the public discourse that liberals started using it.' He adds:

> Think of the framing of *relief*. For there to be relief, there must be an affliction, an afflicted party, and a

reliever who removes the affliction and is therefore a hero. When the word *tax* is added to *relief*, the result is a metaphor: Taxation is an affliction….This is a frame.

There are many, many more examples of framing being deployed effectively by the right. Think 'pro-life' with its implication that 'pro-choice' equals 'anti-life'. And, as Lakoff also correctly pinpointed, journalists – even liberal ones – all too easily adopt the language and frames set by conservatives without necessarily understanding their impact and influence.

'When we successfully reframe public discourse, we change the way the public sees the world,' Lakoff wrote in *Don't Think of an Elephant*. 'We change what counts as common sense.'

When it comes to framing from a progressive standpoint, there is another factor (and one Lakoff writes extensively about) to bear in mind: that the right in Britain and America have expertly and deftly employed framing to push their narratives across multiple issues, making the fight to overcome it a challenging one.

As we've seen already in this book, they have used framing to great effect with poverty and 'welfare', and in the UK around justifying austerity. We have also seen how conservatives in the US (and increasingly so in Britain) have put huge amounts of money and energy into building institutions that will propagate their narratives to support their goals and values. And, as Lakoff also points out, they have systematically ensured that framing – even of issues where the 'truth' might seem self-evident to most – cements an array of conservative narratives and language in the public discourse and consciousness. For example, he details how Frank Luntz,[66] whose work in conservative politics is legendary 'persuaded conservatives to stop talking about "global warming" because it sounded too scary and suggested human agency'. Instead, Lakoff writes, 'he brought "climate change" into our public discourse on the grounds that climate sounded kind of nice … and change just happens…'. Luntz himself explained his approach to PBS Frontline in an interview:[67] "Eighty per cent of our life is emotion, and only 20 per cent is intellect. I am much more interested in how you feel than how you think."

Cartoon © Paul Brook, Joseph Rowntree Foundation

Reframing is tough to do, it takes time and requires consistent and repetitive communication of those frames so they can trigger a response or 'be activated', to use the jargon. But, as Lakoff points out – it works. Conservatives have proved it. How else could something as oxymoronic as 'clean coal' end up being so widely reported in the Trump era?

> **"The good news is that ... culture does, has, always has changed. And the really good news is that it doesn't do so on its own. It does so in response to the stories that we tell."**
> Nat Kendall Taylor, CEO, FrameWorks Institute, talking to Project Twist-It

Cartoon © Paul Brook, Joseph Rowntree Foundation

One bright spring day in 2018 I made my way to the FrameWorks Institute in Washington DC.[68] The compact, colourful offices had the buzzy, focused feel of a West Coast tech start-up, but this was an organisation with a different kind of nerd quality – 'social science for social change' being one of its straplines – and with almost two decades of work on framing social issues in the US and elsewhere ranging from early child development to public health under its belt. The non-profit think tank, headed by Nat Kendall Taylor, an expert in psychological anthropology and communications science, is like a kind of framing ideas factory, drawing on multi-disciplinary research that is then used to help social change organisations reframe their messages to appeal to a wider constituency and, as its website puts it, 'build public will and further public understanding' of their specific issue.

I'm meeting with Nat to learn more about the work he's been doing in Britain on reframing poverty.[69] Three years earlier the organisation began working with the Joseph Rowntree Foundation (JRF), one of Britain's oldest anti-poverty charities (it now classifies itself as a 'social change' organisation), first on ascertaining *how* the British public thought about poverty and then devising a strategy for reframing the issue. JRF was interested in how the dominant narratives around poverty – the persistent individualising of it – were holding back public support for action that could tackle the issue and was seeking out fresh ideas on how that could be altered. "The toxic master narratives and negative public thinking about people in poverty are a barrier to getting action on poverty in the UK," is how the charity's Deputy Director of Advocacy and Public Engagement, Abigail Scott Paul, summed up the challenge. "We need to work harder to create a new narrative infrastructure where hopeful narratives that chime with people's values can permeate through and become the norm."

Nat explained the work as: "Getting a deeper understanding of the way people make sense of the issues of poverty. And then coming up with a set of frames and a story to put to them in that tends to assail and shift those understandings over time."

The historically deeply ingrained association of "individual choice and individual responsibility" with poverty is a tough obstacle to overcome, he conceded.

> "Even people you would think politically would be more progressive, the degree to which people are willing to hold individuals responsible completely and exclusively, unequivocally responsible for their outcomes, is I think striking."

Nat told me he was somewhat surprised by the degree to which the British public subscribed or were amenable to the individual-is-to-blame perception of poorer people when compared with the US, where the notion of a Welfare State hasn't ever really taken root. I can't say that it surprised me. In the modern era the UK has typically looked towards America and not Europe; and from Thatcher to austerity it has sought to emulate its historically welfare-hostile Atlantic cousin. The dominant poverty narrative sits comfortably within the politics of both countries.

The FrameWorks team reached a number of conclusions in the British context about what the public thought about poverty and identified a set of 'cultural models' to define those that could help with the construction of alternative frames to counteract them. These cultural models were 'shared assumptions and patterns of thinking' prevalent across the population. For example, there is one model where poverty is understood to be about 'nonnegotiable needs' like food and shelter, with everything else being 'wants' or luxuries, something that undermines support for a robust benefits system. Another is the 'self-makingness' model, where people attribute poverty to poor choices and level of motivation.

According to the FrameWorks research, a new story that could effectively challenge the dominant cultural models – the components of the dominant poverty narrative – would incorporate a story that:

• Makes a moral case for tackling poverty and ties it to values like compassion
• Uses unexpected messengers as well as messengers that embody these values
• Explains how the economy restricts and restrains people in poverty, or channels them into poverty
• Uses examples to show that poverty exists and to demonstrate characteristics and impacts
• Shows how we all rely on public systems and paints a clear picture of what these look like
• Counters fatalism with clear solutions that make a tangible difference.

The need for a new narrative that can appeal to a broad spectrum of people across our societies is abundantly clear. That it could have a huge impact on the fight for a fairer, socially just system where opportunities to escape impoverishment and eliminate poverty stigma is a goal the majority of people could get behind is not in doubt. That there is an expanding effort to bring this change about should provide us with some much-needed hope.

Nat had this to say:

> "There's good news and bad news. The bad news is that this culture stuff that we are talking about is … really strong and it's pernicious and it's deep and it is durable. I mean individualism ain't nothing new, it's been around and it's been reinforced for a long time. So that's the bad news, like this stuff doesn't change on a dime, it's not capricious. The good news is that

... culture does, has, always has changed. And the really good news is that it doesn't do so on its own. It does so in response to the stories that we tell. "

A final note from the author: lessons learned

Over the years I have learned much from my personal experience of poverty, from reflecting on it, from understanding that to be poor is not an inevitability or due to personal flaws. I have learned about letting go of the shame I carried about being poor as a young person. Through research and my work as a reporter I have learned a great deal about the bigger picture, about the real causes and consequences of poverty and inequality, and I have learned from other people with similar experiences of impoverishment that what we have to say matters. How we are affected by the forces around us counts. And, I have learned, we can make a difference.

While working on this book and on Project Twist-It, I have come to understand a bit more about how we got to where we are, who put us here, where we need to get to, and how we might build a new narrative that helps address the structural causes of poverty and steers us towards a greater consensus on how we can tackle the inequality that holds us back.

SOME OF THE THINGS I LEARNED ABOUT POVERTY:

• One person in poverty is one person too many.

• Extreme poverty and inequality in America and Britain are due to structural causes. They are the result of a political choice that is causing millions to suffer – but – neither is inevitable and they are *fixable*.

• For decades a narrative has been deployed that has been successful at convincing whole swathes of society that being poor is a 'lifestyle choice', and this has helped prevent the emergence of a fairer society.

- Poverty affects every aspect of life from how long we get to live, to self-esteem, to our children's futures. This is not something anyone would wish upon themselves or their family.

- The facts about poverty matter, but they need to be put in context and framed in a way people can understand and which appeals to our sense of justice and compassion.

- Shaming is one of the primary tools for keeping people poor, and from fighting back.

- People *are now* fighting back regardless. Solutions are within our reach.

- The voices and stories of those of us with first-hand experience of poverty should be central to challenging the status quo and to creating an alternative narrative about the poorest.

- Storytellers of all kinds can help us achieve this.

- To win the fight against poverty and to overturn the dominant poverty narrative we will need focus, resources and a robust network of allies.

- It is up to *all of us* to make this happen.

As Rutger Bregman wrote in *The Guardian*:[70] 'What we need is a narrative that speaks to millions of ordinary people. It all starts with reclaiming the language of progress.'

We *can* rewrite the rules. We *can* flip the script. And we will.

One last story

It's 12 February 2019. I was on my way back home from the writers' space where I'd been working on this book for the previous six months with four more to go. It hadn't been the most productive of days and I was berating myself for not having written as much as I should or as well as I could have. Then I met Leticha. She was driving me home in an Uber and we got talking. Leticha asked what my job was and I began telling her about this book and how hard I was trying to write something that mattered so much to me personally and how I wanted to do justice to the people I had met, and to my own story.

I told her about some of the people I'd met along the way; about June Cigar and her extraordinary story of homelessness and fighting for her dignity, about the kids at Mighty Writers and The Warren and at Beatbox Academy who were making their voices heard, about the artists and writers who were giving up their time to help us fight poverty and the poverty narrative. I told her about how people were sharing their stories with me in the hope that collectively we could take down some of the stereotypes about people who are poor, about people on the margins. She began to cry.

We pulled over and Leticha, who came to the US from Mexico as a child with her mother, told me her story. She told me about her mother, an undocumented immigrant living in Southern California who for years had worked tirelessly for a wealthy family that had taken her for granted, exploited her and paid her next to nothing for working long days, year in, year out. "My mother finally left them," Leticha told me. "Six months ago. I was so proud of her for doing that." She told me of how, because of her mother and because of the poverty and struggles of poorer people she saw around her every day, she'd campaigned for a local politician in the hope of bringing about change for undocumented people and their children but how, in the world of Trump and his repressive immigration stance, speaking up had become so much harder than before.

"We need to tell our stories," Leticha said, tears streaming down her cheeks. As she looked over her shoulder at me sitting in the back, I put my hand on her shoulder to let her know that she was heard. We talked a bit about our childhoods, about what we had in common. And we took some deep breaths and looked each other in the eye. "Thank you for doing what you are doing," she said to me. And we held hands for a moment.

Before getting out of the car I said to Leticha that I too believed that we need to tell our stories – and keep telling them – if we are ever to have a chance of knocking down the barriers to progress that poor and low-income people face every day.

She nodded. "Yes. Yes. We must do that. It's the only way."

Notes

Front matter

1   https://narrativeinitiative.org/wp-content/uploads/2019/05/
    TheNarrativeInitiative_TowardNewGravity.pdf

Introduction

1   https://www.fdrlibrary.org/address-text
2   Seabrook, Jeremy (2013) *Pauperland: Poverty and the Poor in Britain*.
    London: C. Hurst & Co.
3   Throughout the book, I use 'Britain'/'British' in a loose sense,
    synonymously with 'the United Kingdom', ie also encompassing
    Northern Ireland.
4   https://www.msn.com/en-us/news/poverty/poverty-in-america/ss-
    BBPx94d. https://www.jrf.org.uk/data
5   https://www.telegraph.co.uk/news/newsvideo/7858570/Norman-
    Tebbit-my-father-got-on-his-bike-to-look-for-a-job.html
6   https://www.dailymail.co.uk/news/article-6817711/Comic-Relief-
    TV-ad-Corbyn-BBC-accused-breaching-neutrality.html
7   https://atd-uk.org/2019/05/31/ruth-lister-the-art-of-ignoring-the-
    poor/
8   https://inequality.org/facts/. https://inequality.org/facts/wealth-
    inequality/; https://www.theguardian.com/inequality/2019/feb/26/
    uk-income-inequality-benefits-income-ons
9   https://read.oecd-ilibrary.org/economics/intergenerational-social-
    mobility-in-oecd-countries_eco_studies-2010-5km33scz5rjj#page27;
    https://www.theguardian.com/news/2018/oct/19/the-myth-of-
    meritocracy-who-really-gets-what-they-deserve
10 Numerous reports have shown that, even when inequality is on the
    political agenda and the 'elites' are the target of voters venting their
    frustrations via Brexit and Trump, the proportion of those from wealthy,
    privately educated backgrounds and elite colleges dominate the top
    professions and populate the top of those professions. Even when
    people from working-class backgrounds make it to the 'professions' they
    earn less than their counterparts from wealthier backgrounds: https://
    www.theguardian.com/society/2019/jun/25/britains-top-jobs-still-in-
    hands-of-private-school-elite-study-finds; see also: 'The Class Ceiling:
    Why it pays to be privileged', https://www.classceiling.org

11   https://www.theguardian.com/politics/2018/sep/28/us-groups-raise-millions-to-support-rightwing-uk-thinktanks

12   https://www.theguardian.com/commentisfree/2019/nov/10/billionaires-warren-sanders-wealth-tax-bezos-dimon-cohen

13   https://www.researchgate.net/publication/311277334_Living_with_and_responding_to_the_'scrounger'_narrative_in_the_UK_Exploring_everyday_strategies_of_acceptance_resistance_and_deflection

14   https://www.npr.org/sections/codeswitch/2013/12/20/255819681/the-truth-behind-the-lies-of-the-original-welfare-queen

15   Garrett, Paul Michael (2017) *Welfare Words: Critical Social Work & Social Policy*, London: Sage. As Garrett also wrote about in his book, the term 'underclass' got a reboot during the London Riots of 2011 with multiple news outlets and politicians revelling in the term to describe those who were on the streets. And it wasn't just tabloid newspapers, the usual culprits at lobbing around denigrating terms for the poor and unemployed: even the BBC got in on it: https://www.bbc.com/news/uk-14488486

16   https://www.brookings.edu/blog/up-front/2014/12/01/social-programs-that-work/

17   https://www.thoughtco.com/who-really-receives-welfare-4126592

18   https://itep.org/the-nations-income-inequality-challenge-explained-in-charts/

19   https://www.theguardian.com/society/2019/jun/19/weak-pay-rises-and-dearer-housing-fuel-jump-in-working-poor-says-ifs

20   https://www.resolutionfoundation.org/media/press-releases/child-poverty-risks-hitting-record-levels/

21   https://www.vox.com/policy-and-politics/2019/6/26/18744304/ceo-pay-ratio-disclosure-2018. In the UK, a survey of executive pay in 2018 by the High Pay Centre found that between 2016 and 2017 the median remuneration leapt by 11%, while that for full-time workers went up by just 2%. When the mean was calculated – accounting for two major outliers where bosses were given extremely large pay rises – the jump was 23% in executive pay over the same period: http://highpaycentre.org/pubs/high-pay-centre-cipd-executive-pay-survey-2018

22   https://www.cnn.com/2019/02/15/tech/amazon-federal-income-tax/index.html

23   https://www.independent.co.uk/news/business/news/youth-jobs-gap-poor-children-unemployment-inequality-a8883131.html; https://www.gov.uk/government/news/class-privilege-remains-entrenched-as-social-mobility-stagnates

24   https://www.thenation.com/article/persistent-precarity/; https://college.unc.edu/2018/08/kalleberg/. Chakraborty debunks the idea of a 'graduate premium' in the UK at: https://www.theguardian.com/commentisfree/2016/apr/19/degree-graduates-low-pay-high-debt-students

25   https://www.theguardian.com/us-news/2019/jun/24/student-debt-us-elections-explained-bernie-sanders

26   https://www.projecttwistit.com/jameelajamil

27 https://prospect.org/article/new-gilded-age-its-everywhere; https://
www.washingtonpost.com/opinions/2018/12/28/we-are-living-
new-gilded-age-proves-it/?utm_term=.8363034a2e37; https://www.
washingtonpost.com/us-policy/2019/02/08/wealth-concentration-
returning-levels-last-seen-during-roaring-twenties-according-new-
research/?utm_term=.16729d0f1a77. The bank UBS's 'Billionaires
Report' reported in 2017 that billionaires globally had increased
their combined wealth by a one fifth in the previous year to a record
$6 trillion: https://www.ubs.com/global/en/about_ubs/art/2018/
billionaires-report.html
28 Walker, Robert (2014) *The Shame of Poverty*, Oxford: Oxford University
Press.
29 https://www.theguardian.com/news/2019/sep/09/inequality-is-it-
rising-and-can-we-reverse-it
30 https://www.theguardian.com/inequality/2019/may/14/britain-risks-
heading-to-us-levels-of-inequality-warns-top-economist
31 https://www.projecttwistit.com/dannydorling
32 https://www.independent.co.uk/news/health/nhs-privatisation-
contracts-virgin-care-richard-branson-jeremy-hunt-a8134386.html;
https://www.mirror.co.uk/news/politics/new tory-health-chief-
voted-12897188
33 https://www.amazon.com/Britain-America-Special-Relationship-
Seminar/dp/1138800015
34 https://onlinelibrary.wiley.com/doi/abs/10.1111/1467-856X.00101
35 https://read.oecd-ilibrary.org/economics/intergenerational-social-
mobility-in-oecd-countries_eco_studies-2010-5km33scz5rjj#page27
36 O'Hara, Mary (2014) *Austerity Bites*, Bristol: Policy Press.
37 www.projecttwistit.com

Part I

1 https://www.theguardian.com/society/2018/oct/10/gordon-brown-
halt-universal-credit-rollout

A short prologue

1 https://en.wikipedia.org/wiki/The_Troubles
2 Northern Ireland and parts of Belfast continue to have high rates
of poverty: https://www.theguardian.com/commentisfree/2010/
jul/14/belfast-riots-ardoyne-poverty-deprivation; https://www.
jrf.org.uk/report/poverty-northern-ireland-2018; https://www.
thedetail.tv/articles/child-poverty2; http://www.irishnews.com/
news/northernirelandnews/2018/01/24/news/one-in-three-
children-growing-up-in-poverty-in-some-parts-of-ni-according-to-
report-1239888/
3 https://inequality.stanford.edu/sites/default/files/increase-income-
segregation.pdf; https://www.geog.ox.ac.uk/research/transformations/
gis/papers/dannydorling_publication_id4161.pdf

Chapter 1

1 https://www.channel4.com/news/un-probes-uk-poverty-amid-benefits-shake-up

2 https://its.law.nyu.edu/facultyprofiles/index.cfm?fuseaction=profile.overview&personid=19742

3 https://www.ohchr.org/EN/NewsEvents/Pages/DisplayNews.aspx?NewsID=23881&LangID=E

4 https://www.theguardian.com/society/2019/mar/08/not-just-schools-five-public-service-areas-struggling-with-cuts?CMP=share_btn_tw; https://www.theguardian.com/society/2019/mar/08/nhs-bosses-benefit-stress-driving-mental-health-care-demand?utm_source=dlvr.it&utm_medium=twitter

5 One of the groups found to be disproportionately impacted by austerity were people from black and minority ethnic backgrounds, according to the UN: https://www.theguardian.com/business/2019/jun/14/austerity-has-fuelled-racial-inequality-in-the-uk-says-un-expert; see also O'Hara, Mary (2014).

6 https://www.nytimes.com/2018/11/13/world/europe/un-extreme-poverty-britain-austerity.html

7 Alston's critiques of governments have ranged from the cruelty of austerity in Brazil to the treatment of women in Saudi Arabia and calling the US to account for health problems with cholera in Haiti: https://www.theguardian.com/world/2017/dec/01/un-extreme-poverty-america-special-rapporteur

8 O'Hara, Mary (2014).

9 People from minority ethnic groups in the UK are more likely to live in poverty than their white counterparts and earn less when in work: http://www.irr.org.uk/research/statistics/poverty/; https://www.independent.co.uk/news/uk/home-news/racial-inequality-uk-racial-disparity-audit-government-report-theresa-may-bme-black-ethnic-minority-a7992016.html. Studies show that, both systemically and causally, people from minority ethnic groups experience discrimination and racism: https://www.theguardian.com/uk-news/2018/dec/02/revealed-the-stark-evidence-of-everyday-racial-bias-in-britain; https://www.theguardian.com/world/2019/jan/17/minority-ethnic-britons-face-shocking-job-discrimination?CMP=share_btn_tw. In addition, as Brexit unfolded and (as with the US) white nationalism was on the rise, an increase in racism was reported in the UK: https://www.theguardian.com/politics/2018/may/11/uk-has-seen-brexit-related-growth-in-racism-says-un-representative

10 Disabled people across the UK were especially affected by austerity policies that took away vital benefits that had been designed to promote full inclusion in society. A number of key supports were cut – including for severely disabled adults and children – that put people at risk of impoverishment and isolation: https://www.theguardian.com/commentisfree/2015/apr/13/tory-austerity-welfare-state-conservative; https://mosaicscience.com/story/life-and-death-austerity/; see also O'Hara, Mary (2014); Cooper, Vickie & Whyte, David (eds) (2017)

The Violence of Austerity, London: Pluto Press. Reports of suicides and attempted suicides soared as more people with disabilities and chronic health conditions were hit by cuts to benefits and a punitive sanctions regime. Following the UN report, this article summed up much of what had happened to disabled people: https://inews.co.uk/opinion/the-un-report-into-austerity-captured-a-key-shift-in-how-disabled-people-are-treated-and-amber-rudd-is-going-to-ignore-it/. In addition, in 2019 there were fresh calls for social media companies to take action on hate crime activity on social media after 40% of disabled people surveyed reported experiencing some form of hate crime online: http://disabilityhorizons.com/2019/05/nearly-40-of-disabled-people-we-surveyed-experienced-hate-crime-online/

11   https://cpag.org.uk/news-blogs/news-listings/un-poverty-rapporteurs-findings-are-wake-call

12   https://leftfootforward.org/2019/06/open-letter-when-the-un-calls-out-poverty-in-the-uk-the-government-must-listen/

13   Earlier in the year Rudd had been forced to resign her position as Home Secretary – one of the most senior in the UK Cabinet – for an immigration approach that produced one of the biggest scandals of the then government around the treatment of Windrush generation migrants from the Caribbean: https://www.theguardian.com/politics/2018/apr/29/amber-rudd-resigns-as-home-secretary-after-windrush-scandal. Seen as part of a wider 'hostile environment' for immigrants, the government was exposed for deporting people who were entitled to live in the UK to the Caribbean: https://www.theguardian.com/uk-news/windrush-scandal

14   https://www.independent.co.uk/news/uk/politics/11-ways-iain-duncan-smith-made-life-harder-for-the-most-vulnerable-people-in-britain-a6941116.html

15   https://www.theguardian.com/society/2018/nov/20/un-poverty-expert-philip-alston-amber-rudd

16   https://www.independent.co.uk/news/uk/politics/amber-rudd-un-poverty-work-pensions-secretary-dwp-department-commons-a8641501.html. Amber Rudd also has form on labelling people on benefits in a negative light. In 2013, Ms Rudd said in an interview with the *Financial Times*: "You get people who are on benefits, who prefer to be on benefits by the seaside. They're not moving down here to get a job, they're moving down here to have easier access to friends and drugs and drink.": https://www.ft.com/content/97b6f7e6-ad46-11e2-b27f-00144feabdc0?source=aw&awc=9060_1542911903_f87ae99b1112f121b5b5da8c1633ebcd

17   https://www.theguardian.com/society/2018/nov/20/un-poverty-expert-philip-alston-amber-rudd

18   https://www.huffingtonpost.co.uk/entry/brexit-minister-kwasi-kwarteng-dismisses-un-report-on-child-poverty_uk_5bf142f7e4b07573881f317b

19   https://www.bbc.co.uk/sounds/play/m00017b6

20   https://www.dailymail.co.uk/debate/article-2005677/Family-breakdown-driven-single-mothers-benefits-absent-fathers.html

21   https://www.theguardian.com/society/2018/aug/06/universal-credit-
      flaws-leaving-families-debt-child-poverty-action-group. Universal
      Credit was a flagship reform to the benefits system whose original
      principal – merging a number of existing benefits and reduce complexity
      in the system and increase incentives to work – was something welcomed
      by most charities working on issues around poverty. However, as
      implementation began, criticisms, including in how the new system
      was rolled out and administered, emerged. When flaws were pointed
      out, including by some Conservative MPs, the government responded
      with some adjustments, including shortening the built-in 42-day wait
      period for a first payment to 25 days. Nevertheless, many critics called
      for the roll-out to be paused. See   https://www.theguardian.com/
      society/2018/jan/25/universal-credit-benefits-scheme-iain-duncan-
      smith

22   https://www.theguardian.com/society/2018/nov/20/un-poverty-
      expert-philip-alston-amber-rudd

23   https://www.channel4.com/news/un-probes-uk-poverty-amid-
      benefits-shake-up

24   https://www.theguardian.com/commentisfree/2018/nov/18/the-
      guardian-view-on-poverty-in-britain-not-just-shocking-but-shameful

25   http://www.cpag.org.uk/content/un-poverty-rapporteur's-findings-
      are-wake-call; https://www.unicef.org.uk/press-releases/unicef-uk-
      responds-to-the-report-on-uk-child-poverty-from-the-un-special-
      rapporteur/; https://www.jrf.org.uk/press/un-special-rapporteurs-
      visit-shows-need-tackle-poverty-here-and-now; https://wbg.org.uk/
      blog/government-must-take-urgent-action-on-poverty/

26   http://socialmetricscommission.org.uk

27   https://www.theguardian.com/society/2018/sep/16/what-is-the-new-
      uk-poverty-measure-and-why-is-it-needed.

28   https://www.theguardian.com/commentisfree/2015/jul/02/david-
      cameron-abolishes-poverty-poor

29   The 12% in 'persistent poverty' means they had spent all or most of the
      past four years below the breadline.

30   https://www.ifs.org.uk

31   https://www.resolutionfoundation.org/publications/the-living-
      standards-outlook-2019/

32   https://www.jrf.org.uk/press/over-one-and-a-half-million-people-
      were-destitute-uk-2017

33   https://www.theguardian.com/society/2018/may/22/benefit-
      sanctions-found-to-be-ineffective-and-damaging; https://www.
      theguardian.com/society/2018/feb/18/disabled-people-million-
      benefit-sanctions-since-2010; https://www.economist.com/
      britain/2018/08/09/benefit-sanctions-may-do-more-harm-than-good;
      https://www.independent.co.uk/news/uk/home-news/benefit-
      sanctions-universal-credit-dwp-report-study-no-evidence-a8577061.
      html; https://www.independent.co.uk/news/uk/home-news/benefit-
      sanctions-increasing-poverty-and-pushing-people-into-survival-crime-
      finds-report-a8363831.html

34   See: O'Hara, Mary (2014); also: Cooper, Vickie & Whyte, David (eds) (2017).
35   https://www.jrf.org.uk/press/over-one-and-a-half-million-people-were-destitute-uk-2017
36   See: O'Hara, Mary (2014); https://news.sky.com/story/universal-credit-fuelling-epidemic-of-suffering-foodbank-charity-claims-11570131
37   https://www.channel4.com/news/charities-overwhelmed-by-food-bank-users-amid-universal-credit-rollout
38   https://www.trusselltrust.org/news-and-blog/latest-stats/end-year-stats/
39   https://www.theguardian.com/society/2019/jan/10/appoint-minister-for-hunger-to-tackle-uk-food-insecurity-mps-urge?CMP=share_btn_tw
40   https://www.theguardian.com/global-development/2018/jan/30/food-insecurity-a-third-of-poorest-households-skip-meals-survey-finds
41   https://www.theguardian.com/society/2019/mar/24/food-banks-are-no-solution-to-poverty
42   https://www.bbc.com/news/uk-england-york-north-yorkshire-47143425
43   https://www.globalcitizen.org/en/content/beauty-banks-hygiene-poverty-toiletries-sali-hughe/
44   https://www.globalcitizen.org/en/content/girl-guides-period-poverty-badge-girlguiding/
45   https://www.bloodybigbrunch.com/about; http://redboxproject.org; see also https://www.bloodygoodperiod.com
46   https://www.theguardian.com/global-development/2019/mar/05/uk-pledges-2m-to-help-end-stigma-and-shame-of-period-poverty
47   https://www.theguardian.com/society/2019/mar/13/government-hammond-to-provide-free-sanitary-products-in-secondary-schools. In August 2018, the Scottish government had become the first in the world to make sanitary products available free to all pupils and students at schools, colleges and universities: https://www.globalcitizen.org/en/content/scotland-free-menstrualproducts-low-income-women/
48   https://www.theguardian.com/society/2019/mar/03/period-poverty-free-tampons-hospitals
49   https://www.mirror.co.uk/news/politics/shameless-tories-use-food-banks-13731692
50   https://www.theguardian.com/society/2018/nov/28/spending-cuts-uk-human-rights-obligations-report?CMP=share_btn_tw. This report came on the back of a series of damning publications by the EHRC the previous year pinpointing numerous ways the government's austerity strategy and cuts hurt the poorest and most vulnerable, including disabled people: https://rightsinfo.org/government-cuts-shut-disabled-people-society-says-new-report/; https://www.huffingtonpost.co.uk/entry/disabled-people-left-behind-equality-and-human-rights-commission_uk_58dab203e4b0cb23e65be5f2; https://www.independent.co.uk/news/uk/home-news/tory-welfare-reforms-hit-poor-vulnerable-hardest-study-a8058176.html

51 https://www.trusselltrust.org/wp-content/uploads/sites/2/2019/06/SoH-Interim-Report-Final-2.pdf

52 https://www.theguardian.com/society/2019/nov/05/welfare-changes-key-factor-rising-poverty-food-bank-use-study-finds

53 https://www.trusselltrust.org/2019/11/13/april-sept-2019-foodbank-figures/

54 https://www.theguardian.com/society/2019/nov/13/more-people-than-ever-turning-to-food-banks-charity-says

55 O'Hara, Mary (2014).

56 https://www.independent.co.uk/news/health/tory-austerity-deaths-study-report-people-die-social-care-government-policy-a8057306.html

57 https://truepublica.org.uk/united-kingdom/dwp-forced-to-admit-more-than-111000-benefit-deaths/

58 https://bmjopen.bmj.com/content/7/11/e017722

59 https://www.theguardian.com/politics/2019/jun/01/perfect-storm-austerity-behind-130000-deaths-uk-ippr-report.

60 As expected, the government was in denial about the conclusions of the EHRC report. A spokesperson responded this way to the report: "We reject this analysis, which doesn't include recent announcements such as the five-year NHS settlement or the increase in universal credit work allowances. The report also predicts future spending but the spending review next year will set out government plans beyond 2019–20. The Treasury, and other government departments, always considers how our policies will affect people of different incomes and those with protected characteristics such as race, religion and disabilities."

61 https://www.jrf.org.uk/work/in-work-poverty; https://www.theguardian.com/society/2018/nov/06/working-people-help-budget-poor-jobs?CMP=share_btn_tw

62 https://www.jrf.org.uk/income-and-benefits. In addition, the independent Institute for Fiscal Studies concluded in March 2018: 57% of people in poverty are children or working-age adults living in a household where someone is in paid work; up from 35% in 1994–95: https://www.ifs.org.uk/publications/11696. This means that poverty is far more sensitive to the plight of low-earning working households than used to be the case. In-work poverty has become one of the most important challenges we face.

63 https://www.jrf.org.uk/report/budget-2018-tackling-rising-tide-work-poverty

64 https://assets.publishing.service.gov.uk/government/uploads/system/uploads/attachment_data/file/652973/The_Great_Escape_-_Report.pdf

65 https://www.jrf.org.uk/report/uk-poverty-2018. The charity defines the poverty line as being when households earn less than 60% of the median income, adjusted for size and type of household. The average median income for UK households after housing costs was £425 [$535] a week (£22,100 [$27,800] a year) in 2016–17.

66 https://www.gov.uk/national-minimum-wage-rates. In the UK, the National Minimum Wage is the minimum pay rate set by the

government, which applies to all workers. It is set at a sliding scale according to age, with apprentices paid a lower rate. The National Living Wage is the minimum pay rate for workers over the age of 25. The Living Wage, on the other hand, is the suggested minimum hourly rate set by the Living Wage Foundation, which is based on the real cost of living (and is, therefore, higher in London than in other areas); see https://www.livingwage.org.uk/

67 https://www.childrenssociety.org.uk/sites/default/files/the-future-of-familyincomes-embargo-23-2-16.pdf

68 https://www.jrf.org.uk/report/uk-poverty-2018

69 https://www.bbc.com/news/education-46457454

70 https://www.theguardian.com/society/2018/dec/05/130000-homeless-children-to-be-in-temporary-lodgings-over-christmas?CMP=Share_iOSApp_Other

71 https://www.theguardian.com/society/2019/jun/19/london-rough-sleeping-hits-record-high-with-18-rise-in-2018-19

72 https://www.bigissue.com/latest/more-than-22000-young-people-are-at-risk-of-homelessness-this-christmas/

73 There have been similar incidents in the US of attacks on homeless people, some of abject cruelty. Some followed the viewing of TV programmes that demonise the poor and destitute. See Pimpare, Stephen (2008) *A People's History of Poverty in America*. New York: The New Press; Chapter 2, pp 62–3.

74 https://www.channel4.com/news/attacks-on-homeless-people-triple-in-just-five-years; https://www.standard.co.uk/news/crime/hull-homeless-attack-shocking-moment-thug-drop-kicks-tent-as-two-people-sleep-inside-a4013841.html

75 https://www.theguardian.com/society/2018/dec/15/people-are-dragged-out-of-tents-attacks-on-homeless-soar-up-to-30%

76 https://metro.co.uk/2019/06/20/homeless-man-dies-another-fighting-life-tent-set-fire-10022168/?ito=article.amp.share.top.twitter

77 https://www.theguardian.com/society/2018/dec/19/homeless-people-violent-attacks-alcohol-easy-prey-liverpool

78 https://www.bbc.com/news/av/uk-england-london-47360552/water-thrown-at-homeless-man-at-sutton-station

79 https://www.theguardian.com/politics/2009/oct/04/david-cameron-bullingdon-club

80 https://www.mirror.co.uk/news/uk-news/bullingdon-club-initiation-ceremony-claim-1725912

81 https://www.independent.co.uk/news/uk/home-news/homeless-woman-jailed-begging-complained-north-wales-a8889786.html

82 https://www.theguardian.com/society/2019/mar/20/sleepers-to-be-offered-stab-proof-coats-that-turn-into-sleeping-bags.

83 https://www.theguardian.com/society/2019/oct/01/homeless-deaths-in-2018-rise-at-highest-level-ons. Drugs were a major reason for the rise in deaths, with some working in the homeless sector saying cuts to drugs and alcohol services had played a part in making people more vulnerable.

84   https://www.telegraph.co.uk/news/2019/10/01/record-rise-homeless-people-dying-ons-figures-show-amid-opioid/

85   https://www.theguardian.com/society/2019/mar/28/poverty-increases-among-children-and-pensioners-across-uk

86   https://www.theguardian.com/business/live/2019/mar/14/spring-statement-austerity-low-income-families-philip-hammond-public-finances-business-live?page=with:block-5c8a1f54e4b0cf92e5a56c7e#block-5c8a1f54e4b0cf92e5a56c7e. The benefits freeze was also an issue for Labour, which faced criticism relating to it, for example, by not making a commitment in its 2017 manifesto to end the freeze: https://www.independent.co.uk/news/uk/politics/labour-benefit-policy-jeremy-corbyn-john-mcdonnell-universal-credit-welfare-conservative-a8610721.html

87   https://www.theguardian.com/commentisfree/2019/mar/30/observer-view-malign-ideas-driving-child-poverty-haunt-brexit-debate

88   https://www.theguardian.com/politics/2019/jun/21/more-than-half-of-tory-members-would-ruin-party-over-brexit

89   https://www.theguardian.com/education/2019/mar/15/schools-have-become-fourth-emergency-service-for-poorest-families?CMP=Share_AndroidApp_Tweet. A damning report from the headteachers union, the Association of Schools and College Leaders (ASCL), concluded in March 2019 that schools had become 'the fourth emergency service' as a result of austerity in England and Wales, having to give out food parcels and even clothing and laundry services.

90   https://www.theguardian.com/society/2018/dec/17/many-pupils-in-england-hungry-and-badly-clothed-say-teachers; https://www.theguardian.com/education/2019/may/20/a-national-shame-headteachers-voice-anger-about-pupils-hunger; https://www.independent.co.uk/news/education/education-news/child-poverty-austerity-headteachers-schools-clothes-food-work-hungry-pupil-a8823236.html; https://www.weforum.org/agenda/2019/02/children-are-so-hungry-in-one-british-town-they-are-eating-from-bins/

91   https://www.theguardian.com/society/2018/jul/25/holiday-hunger-shame-government-childrens-clubs

92   https://www.theguardian.com/society/2019/apr/19/newborn-baby-deaths-may-be-on-rise-among-poorest-in-england

93   https://bmjopen.bmj.com/content/9/10/e029424

94   https://www.theguardian.com/society/2019/jun/23/why-is-life-expectancy-falling; https://www.theguardian.com/society/2019/mar/07/life-expectancy-slumps-by-five-months; https://www.actuaries.org.uk/news-and-insights/media-centre/media-releases-and-statements/longer-term-influences-driving-lower-life-expectancy-projections

95   https://www.bbc.co.uk/news/education-46457454

96   https://undocs.org/A/HRC/41/39/Add.1

97   Ryan, Frances (2019) *Crippled: Austerity and the demonization of disabled people*. London: Verso.

98   https://www.theguardian.com/politics/2019/may/22/un-report-compares-tory-welfare-reforms-to-creation-of-workhouses

99   https://www.theguardian.com/politics/2019/may/22/amber-rudd-to-lodge-complaint-over-un-austerity-report

100   https://www.theguardian.com/society/2019/may/24/un-poverty-expert-hits-back-over-uk-ministers-denial-of-facts-philip-alston?CMP=share_btn_tw

101   https://www.itv.com/news/2019-11-03/universal-credit-and-state-pension-to-rise-in-april/

102   https://www.theguardian.com/politics/2018/dec/14/gordon-brown-didnt-think-see-child-poverty-again-in-my-lifetime-universal-credit

Chapter 2

1   https://www.theguardian.com/commentisfree/2018/nov/14/un-austerity-destroying-lives-philip-alston-poverty-uk

2   https://www.thoughtco.com/creation-of-britains-welfare-state-1221967

3   https://theweek.com/articles/781320/how-republicans-sugarcoat-american-poverty

4   https://www.theguardian.com/society/2017/dec/15/america-extreme-poverty-un-special-rapporteur

5   https://www.nytimes.com/2018/11/13/world/europe/un-extreme-poverty-britain-austerity.html

6   https://newsarchive.ohchr.org/EN/NewsEvents/Pages/DisplayNews.aspx?NewsID=10658&LangID=E The report by the then UN rapporteur Magdalena Sepulveda, which highlighted many areas of concern, including planned cuts to welfare provision in the wake of the financial crisis, was nowhere near as damning as the later UK and US reports from Alston.

7   http://undocs.org/A/HRC/38/33/ADD.1

8   As with any publication that references poverty statistics, the Rapporteur's report acknowledged that there are issues around defining poverty and therefore with measurements of poverty levels. There are competing definitions of poverty in the US and elsewhere and, depending on which is referenced, the top-line figures for how many people are poor can alter. The use of 'selective' statistics that bolster a cause or point of view or policy are commonplace in politics but poverty measures can be especially contentious. For a historical perspective on this, a good start would be *Poverty and Shame: Global Experiences*, which sets the controversies around definitions in an international and historical context: Chase, Elaine & Bantebya-Kyomuhendo, Grace (eds) (2014) *Poverty and Shame: Global Experiences*. Oxford: Oxford University Press. The companion volume is Walker, Robert (2014). See also: https://www.vox.com/2015/9/16/9337041/supplemental-povertymeasure; https://www.irp.wisc.edu/resources/how-is-poverty-measured/. The UN report summarises much of the core controversy in the US thus: There is considerable debate over the extent of poverty in the United States, but the present report relies principally upon official government

statistics, especially from the US Census Bureau. It defines and quantifies poverty in America based on "poverty thresholds" or official poverty measures, updated each year. These thresholds have been present since President Lyndon B. Johnson's war on poverty in the 1960s and use set dollar-value thresholds that vary by family size and composition to determine who is in poverty. Following much criticism of the official poverty measures, the Census Bureau developed a 'supplemental' poverty measure, which is preferred by many experts. According to the official poverty measures, in 2016, 12.7% of Americans were living in poverty, according to the supplemental poverty measure, the figure was 14%.

9   https://www.vox.com/policy-and-politics/2018/12/18/18146253/ tax-cuts-and-jobs-act-stock-market-economy. The tax cuts ushered in by the Republican Congress in 2017 were framed by Trump administration officials and others as something to be lauded. For example, Treasury Secretary Stephen Mnuchin declared that the tax plan would "pay for itself" (it didn't) and would cut the deficit by trillions of dollars. Yet, by October 2018, the federal deficit had jumped 17% year-on-year to $779bn. Meanwhile, while middle-class Americans saw modest tax cuts, the wealthy and corporations enjoyed a windfall and shareholders were showered with stock buy-backs.

10   https://www.theatlantic.com/politics/archive/2017/03/why-work-requirements-in-medicaid-wont-work/520593/; https://www.americanprogress.org/issues/poverty/news/2018/01/12/444953/trumps-medicaid-work-requirements-put-least-6-3-million-americans-risk-losing-health-care/

11   https://www.theatlantic.com/politics/archive/2017/03/why-work-requirements-in-medicaid-wont-work/520593/

12   https://www.theguardian.com/us-news/2018/jun/01/us-inequality-donald-trump-cruel-measures-un

13   https://www.americanprogress.org/issues/poverty/news/2018/06/04/451543/latest-hud-proposal-exacerbate-housing-insecurity-crisis/. Already slim federal support for housing came under attack by the administration, championed by the Housing Secretary Ben Carson. Analysis by the Center for American Progress of the dangers of further reductions in support for people on low incomes for housing concluded: 'Affordable housing is becoming harder and harder for US families to find and keep. In 2016, for example, landlords filed an average of roughly four evictions per minute. Within the past year, more than one-quarter of US residents had trouble covering their housing costs. Today, nearly 4.7 million households—which include almost 4 million children—rely on federal rental assistance programs. But even as the need for this assistance grows, only about 1 in 4 of the eligible lowest-income renters actually receives federal support.'

14   https://www.theguardian.com/us-news/2017/dec/01/senate-republicans-reform-bill-us-tax-code; https://www.cbpp.org/topics/tax-reform.

15   http://inequality.stanford.edu/sites/default/files/Pathways-SOTU-2016-2.pdf. The report notes that, while the UK comes closest to the US out of the 'liberal' welfare regimes, the US is an extreme

outlier. It states: 'It is of course well-known that the liberal welfare regimes found in Anglophone countries (i.e., Australia, Canada, United Kingdom, U.S.) are inequality-producing machines. Can we understand the U.S. profile as simply the expected profile of an Anglophone liberal welfare economy? The simple answer: No.... The U.S. occupies an extreme position even relative to the four Anglophone countries, with the implication that the U.S. is a liberal regime "on steroids." Although the United Kingdom has a poverty and inequality profile that, among the Anglophone countries, comes closest to that of the U.S., even relative to this benchmark the U.S. has a distinctively anemic safety net and a distinctively unequal distribution of wealth'.

16   It is worth noting that the UN report draws on official US Census Bureau data on poverty: https://www.census.gov/topics/income-poverty/poverty/guidance/poverty-measures.html.

17   https://www.theguardian.com/us-news/2018/jun/01/us-inequality-donald-trump-cruel-measures-un. Senator Brooker introduced a Bill to Congress in October 2018, the American Opportunity Accounts Act, proposing that lower income youngsters be given a 'nest egg' at the start of their lives to use towards things like college tuition, as a step towards breaking out of generational poverty: https://www.booker.senate.gov/?p=press_release&id=861

18   https://www.nytimes.com/2018/06/19/us/politics/trump-israel-palestinians-human-rights.html

19   https://www.independent.co.uk/news/world/americas/us-extreme-poverty-numbers-un-nikki-haley-trump-a8417001.html

20   https://www.washingtonpost.com/news/wonk/wp/2018/06/25/trump-team-rebukes-u-n-saying-it-overestimates-extreme-poverty-in-america-by-18-million-people/?utm_term=.a6039bd8aac9

21   https://usun.state.gov

22   https://foreignpolicy.com/2018/08/02/internal-documents-show-how-trump-administration-state-department-misled-public-on-poverty/

23   https://www.foxnews.com/politics/harsh-anti-trump-un-human-rights-report-on-us-extreme-poverty-cherry-picks-data-assumptions-examination-shows

24   https://www.washingtonpost.com/news/wonk/wp/2014/01/08/everything-you-need-to-know-about-the-war-on-poverty/?utm_term=.2fca16ef5c2a

25   https://www.nytimes.com/2018/07/16/opinion/republican-war-on-poverty.html. Four years earlier, Republican congressman and Speaker of the House, Paul Ryan, who had made it one of his personal missions to undermine the safety net even further and was at the forefront of pushing the rhetoric of dependency and entitlement as a means to cut programmes, was promoting the idea that the War on Poverty had failed, so therefore the thing to do was cut support for the poor even further.

26   https://medium.com/@OffKilterShow/trumps-poverty-denial-4c258d46e654

27   https://www.forbes.com/sites/eriksherman/2018/08/04/trump-administration-tries-to-deny-u-s-poverty-with-misleading-numbers/#c66740a6daa9

28   https://www.politico.com/agenda/story/2019/04/25/food-assistance-programs-snap-funding-000894. SNAP (the Supplemental Nutrition Assistance Program, formerly foodstamps) was under repeated attack during the Trump administration. The rhetoric used to justify cuts often drew on the argument that programmes were too expensive to run as well as fostering 'dependency'. Yet, time and again, the evidence showed that such narrow interpretations of the value and effect of programmes such as SNAP were misleading. In their April 2019 *Politico* article, 'How real families use foodstamps', academics Sarah Brown, Sinikka Elliot and Joslyn Brenton point out that the logic underpinning increased work requirements for claimants didn't stand up. Their research, they explained, found that 'for many of the families we studied, getting a job did not mean they could feed their families'.

29   https://www.politico.com/agenda/story/2019/09/04/poverty-safety-net-benefits-000944

30   https://www.cbpp.org/press/statements/trump-administration-floating-changes-to-poverty-measure-that-would-reduce-or. Parrott explained that this was because using a lower measure of inflation like the chained CPI to adjust the poverty line each year would make the eligibility thresholds for various programs that serve people in need lower and lower over time.

31   See: https://talkpoverty.org/2019/05/08/trumps-plan-lower-poverty-redefining-explained/ for more on the proposed changes to the poverty measure. And here: https://theshriverbrief.org/the-war-on-people-who-are-poor-55638fe3e79c

32   https://www.theguardian.com/us-news/2019/jun/16/federal-minimum-wage-record-no-increase-since-2009?CMP=Share_iOSApp_Other. In 2019, the Federal Minimum Wage marked a grim anniversary – 10 years without an increase, a record. At $7.25 an hour, had it matched inflation over the same time period it would have risen by 18%, which would still be far off the call for a $15 minimum wage.

33   https://foreignpolicy.com/2018/08/02/internal-documents-show-how-trump-administration-state-department-misled-public-on-poverty/

34   https://geneva.usmission.gov/2018/06/22/country-concerned-statement-in-response-to-sr-alstons-country-report-on-the-united-states/

35   https://www.theatlantic.com/politics/archive/2018/06/donald-trumps-poverty-problem/563960/

36   https://en.wikipedia.org/wiki/William_Barber_II

37   https://forwardjustice.org/forward-together-moral-movement

38   https://www.poorpeoplescampaign.org

39   https://thinkprogress.org/more-than-100-arrested-nationwide-for-rallying-for-health-care-and-environmental-protection-e949287534c5/

40   https://www.poorpeoplescampaign.org/wp-content/uploads/2018/04/PPC-Audit-Full-410835a.pdf

41   Former vice president Joe Biden ran into trouble when he referenced the PPC's research and misquoted statistics that the IPS and PPC had been using on their campaign. Biden wrongly combined figures by the researchers indicating the number of Americans in poverty with the number on 'low income' and at risk of falling into poverty to produce a blunt figure for the overall number of people living in poverty. *The Washington Post* spoke to poverty scholars immediately to clarify what had been quoted. See this article for a good summary of the debate on poverty definitions and official poverty calculations: https://www.washingtonpost.com/politics/2019/06/20/joe-bidens-claim-that-almost-half-americans-live-poverty/?utm_term=.6d74d45efa4f

42   https://www.vox.com/policy-and-politics/2019/6/18/18683811/poor-peoples-campaign-2020-democrats-biden-sanders-warren

43   https://ips-dc.org/wp-content/uploads/2019/06/PPC-Moral-Budget-2019-report-Key-Findings.pdf

44   http://indianyouth.org/american-indian-life/poverty-cycle

45   https://www.theguardian.com/us-news/flint-water-crisis

46   https://ips-dc.org/souls-of-poor-folks/

47   In absolute terms, White people make up 42.5% of this population (17.3 million), and the next two largest groups are Latinx (11.1 million) at 27.4%, and Black Americans (9.2 million) at 22.7%.

48   According to Children International, 1 in every 7 children in the US will be born into poverty: https://www.children.org/global-poverty/global-poverty-facts/facts-about-poverty-in-usa. Children in the US experience higher poverty rates than most developed nations. Only Greece, Israel, Turkey and Mexico have higher child poverty rates: https://data.oecd.org/inequality/poverty-rate.htm. Studies show that child poverty has longstanding implications for the welfare and wellbeing of children who experience it and analysis shows that the US could take action that would reduce its status as an outlier in this area: https://www.academicpedsjnl.net/article/S1876-2859(16)00027-9/fulltext

49   Households led by Native women had the highest poverty rates (42.6%), followed by those headed by immigrant women (almost 42%), Latinx women (40.8%), Black women (38.8%) and White women (30.2%). LGBTQ people are disproportionately represented among the poor as well: https://ips-dc.org/souls-of-poor-folks/

50   A National Law Center on Homelessness and Poverty (NLCHP) report published in 2017 concluded that the number of homelessness 'encampments' had increased 'dramatically' around the US – up from 19 reported in 2007 to 274 in 2016: https://nlchp.org//wp-content/uploads/2018/10/Tent_City_USA_2017.pdf. In a separate 2017 report, the NLCHP concluded that HUD's 'Point in Time' count underestimated the numbers of homeless people, in part because the methodology fails to take into account the transitory nature of homelessness: https://nlchp.org//wp-content/uploads/2018/10/HUD-PIT-report2017.pdf

51   https://money.cnn.com/2018/05/17/news/economy/us-middle-class-basics-study/index.html

52   https://www.unitedwayalice.org

53 https://www.cbsnews.com/news/almost-half-of-americans-cant-pay-for-basic-needs/

54 https://www.npr.org/2019/01/14/685124785/federal-workers-struggle-to-stretch-their-money-as-shutdown-lingers; https://www.npr.org/2019/01/16/685645520/federal-employees-moonlight-to-pay-the-bills

55 https://scorecard.prosperitynow.org/findings

56 https://www.theguardian.com/business/2019/feb/02/america-record-job-growth-economics-wage-stagnation?CMP=Share_iOSApp_Other; https://www.epi.org/blog/a-close-look-at-recent-increases-in-the-black-unemployment-rate/

57 https://money.cnn.com/2018/05/22/pf/emergency-expenses-household-finances/index.html

58 https://groundworkcollaborative.org/wp-content/uploads/2019/11/The-Costs-of-Being-Poor-Groundwork-Collaborative.pdf

59 The long history of discrimination in housing – and the nature of segregation – in America is a key element in the landscape of US poverty and in entrenching inequalities. As many researchers, writers and activists have pointed out, even efforts to level the playing field slightly, such as fair housing laws, have met with repeated acts of sabotage while multiple, intersecting factors serve to restrict progress: https://www.theguardian.com/commentisfree/2019/jan/24/housing-market-racism-persists-despite-fair-housing-laws?CMP=Share_iOSApp_Other. As pointed out by Keeanga-Yamahtta Taylor, author and assistant professor in the Department of African American Studies at Princeton in this *Guardian* article, residential segregation in America on race grounds is far from a thing of the past while the fallout of the financial crisis served to exacerbate existing inequalities and discrimination in the housing market for people of colour, including being denied mortgages at much higher rates than white counterparts.

60 When there was an uptick in wages alongside encouraging unemployment figures in April 2019 many were quick to celebrate – and for good reason. Nevertheless, the underlying structural issues around pay and the types of employment people could find still stood: https://inequality.org/great-divide/reality-behind-surging-economy/

61 It's worth pointing out that the US is the *only* country in the entire world not to have ratified the UN Convention on the Rights of the Child, which, in essence, protects the economic and social rights of children.

62 https://www.ers.usda.gov/topics/food-nutrition-assistance/food-security-in-the-us/key-statistics-graphics.aspx#insecure

63 https://www.feedingamerica.org/sites/default/files/research/hunger-in-america/hia-2014-executive-summary.pdf

64 https://www.feedingamerica.org/hunger-in-america

65 https://theshriverbrief.org/child-poverty-should-be-a-nationaloutrage-df7b74edbc0f

66 https://www.huffpost.com/entry/child-poverty-in-america-is-indefensible_b_59f21fabe4b06acda25f485c

67   https://www.washingtonpost.com/news/wonk/wp/2018/02/12/
      trumps-budget-hits-poor-americans-the-hardest/?utm_
      term=.78c1506e8078
68   https://www.newyorker.com/news/our-columnists/the-white-houses-
      new-budget-exposes-donald-trumps-lies-about-protecting-medicare-
      and-medicaid
69   https://www.politifact.com/truth-o-meter/promises/trumpometer/
      subjects/medicaid/
70   https://www.nytimes.com/2019/04/17/opinion/disability-budget-
      cuts-trump.html?smid=tw-nytopinion&smtyp=cur
71   https://www.washingtonpost.com/news/wonk/wp/2018/02/12/
      trumps-budget-hits-poor-americans-the-hardest/?utm_
      term=.78c1506e8078
72   https://slate.com/news-and-politics/2007/10/who-s-afraid-of-
      socialized-medicine.html.
73   There are exceptions. There is in England a charge of £9 ($11) per
      item for those able to pay for prescriptions (although not across the
      whole of the UK) – with charges reduced for multiple items with a
      pre-payment certificate.
74   https://www.theguardian.com/us-news/2019/nov/14/health-
      insurance-medical-bankruptcy-debt?CMP=Share_iOSApp_Other
75   https://www.theguardian.com/commentisfree/2018/jul/03/nhs-
      religion-tories-health-service
76   https://www.theguardian.com/society/commentisfree/2019/nov/05/
      nhs-precious-ill-us-big-pharma-costs-healthcare
77   https://www.theguardian.com/society/2019/mar/22/patients-nhs-
      long-waiting-time-watchdog-national-audit-office
78   https://www.independent.co.uk/news/health/brexit-latest-eu-nursing-
      shortage-hospital-social-care-nhs-a8618976.html
79   https://www.kingsfund.org.uk/publications/what-does-public-think-
      about-nhs
80   Medicare is the federal health insurance programme for: people who are
      65 or older; certain younger people with disabilities; and people with
      end-stage renal disease (permanent kidney failure requiring dialysis or a
      transplant, sometimes called ESRD): https://www.medicare.gov/what-
      medicare-covers/your-medicare-coverage-choices/whats-medicare
81   Medicaid is a means-tested programme that provides healthcare for
      low-income people in the US. Medicaid is the largest source of funding
      for medical and health-related services for people with low incomes
      in the US, providing free health insurance to 74 million low-income
      and disabled people (23% of Americans) as of 2017. See https://
      en.wikipedia.org/wiki/Medicaid
82   https://www.healthcare.gov/glossary/affordable-care-act/
83   https://www.usatoday.com/story/news/nation/2019/05/09/
      health-insurance-1-1-million-more-americans-lost-
      coverage-2018/1140304001/
84   https://www.cnbc.com/2019/02/11/this-is-the-real-reason-most-
      americans-file-for-bankruptcy.html

85   https://www.theguardian.com/us-news/2019/jun/27/us-hospitals-lawsuits-medical-bills?CMP=Share_iOSApp_Othe

86   https://www.americanprogress.org/issues/healthcare/news/2018/12/20/464562/conservatives-using-courts-attack-health-care-americans/

87   https://www.kff.org/health-reform/issue-brief/pre-existing-conditions-and-medical-underwriting-in-the-individual-insurance-market-prior-to-the-aca/

88   https://www.cdc.gov/nchs/nhis/index.htm

89   https://www.nytimes.com/2018/01/02/upshot/us-health-care-expensive-country-comparison.html?nytapp=true

90   https://www.thebalance.com/causes-of-rising-healthcare-costs-4064878

91   https://www.healthsystemtracker.org/chart-collection/infant-mortality-u-s-compare-countries/#item-infant-mortality-higher-u-s-comparable-countries; see also discussion of rising infant mortality in England at p 48. In 2018, another UK statistic sent out ominous signs of the path the country was taking when, 'unprecedented' in modern British history, life expectancy flatlined: www.dannydorling.org/?p=6506

92   https://www.cnbc.com/id/100840148

93   https://ips-dc.org/wp-content/uploads/2018/04/PPC-Audit-Full-410835a.pdf

94   https://khn.org/news/under-trump-number-of-uninsured-kids-rose-for-first-time-this-decade/

95   https://www.cnn.com/2019/10/30/politics/us-children-health-insurance/index.html

96   https://www.kff.org/medicaid/issue-brief/key-issues-in-childrens-health-coverage/

97   Multiple studies affirm that access to good healthcare from an early age promotes health, educational and other attainment later in life: https://theshriverbrief.org/child-poverty-should-be-a-national-outrage-df7b74edbc0f; https://www.childpovertyusa.org; https://www.cypsc.ie/_fileupload/Documents/News%20and%20Events/The%20Impact%20of%20Early%20Childhood%20on%20Future%20Health,%20FPHM%20RCPI,%20May%202017.pdf; https://www.ncbi.nlm.nih.gov/pmc/articles/PMC3652568/; https://academic.oup.com/heapro/article/30/suppl_2/ii102/643035. It is not surprising then that in the US, children with health coverage fare better throughout their lives than those without.

98   O'Hara, Mary (2014).

99   Chase, Elaine & Bantebya-Kyomuhendo, Grace (eds) (2014); Walker, Robert (2014).

100 https://www.childpovertyusa.org/our-kids-our-future.

101 https://www.thenation.com/article/child-poverty-us-2020-half-plan/ https://campaignforchildren.org/take-action-child-poverty-reduction-act-of-2017/

Part II

1 https://www.moneysorter.co.uk/calculator_inflation2.html#calculator
2 Families with children received a small cash benefit, or 'allowance' for each child each week. Child benefits in general evolved over time but when I was a teenager it was a 'universal' benefit that all families received regardless of income: https://revenuebenefits.org.uk/child-benefit/policy/where_it_all_started/

Chapter 3

1 https://www.youtube.com/watch?v=8bkBoAcPIQ0
2 Among the many pathologies spread about the poor – stupidity is a common one. As Stephen Pimpare (2008, p 10) writes, 'I'm not stupid, I'm just poor. People don't seem to get the difference."
3 https://www.merriam-webster.com/dictionary/the per cent20American per cent20dream
4 There are many studies on the political potency of the concept of meritocracy, but see this article as a pertinent introduction: https://www.theguardian.com/news/2018/oct/19/the-myth-of-meritocracy-who-really-gets-what-they-deserve
5 https://ig.ft.com/sites/business-book-award/books/2016/shortlist/makers-and-takers-by-rana-foroohar/; https://www.theatlantic.com/business/archive/2012/09/the-truth-about-makers-and-takers-we-are-all-the-takers/262601/
6 http://eprints.lse.ac.uk/55289/1/Chauhan_Representations-of-poverty-in-British-newspapers_2014.pdf
7 https://www.tandfonline.com/doi/abs/10.1080/09627251.2011.550156?src=recsys&journalCode=rcjm20
8 https://www.secretentourage.com/motivation/10-things-only-poor-people-do/
9 https://inequality.org
10 For a detailed historical perspective on the portrayal of poverty and the poor throughout American history and how it acts as a precursor to today's conceptualisation of poverty and deservedness, the academic and author Stephen Pimpare's books and articles are a great launching point. In *A People's History of Poverty in America* (2008), Pimpare offers an expansive analysis of the historical treatment of the poorest people in the US. He is particularly persuasive in his examination of how the poorest have been repeatedly blamed for their circumstances while simultaneously being infantilised or punished by welfare structures driven by either pity and condescension or by morality-based requirements for better behaviour and 'supplication'. None of this, he points out, has fostered the dignity of the people in need of help or focused on what people say they actually want – good jobs that pay a decent wage and a benefits system that supports rather than judges them – and it has served to reinforce stereotypes around dependency-by-choice.
11 Chuck Collins, interviewed by Mary O'Hara for Project Twist-It. The full interview is at https://www.projecttwistit.com/chuck-collins

12   https://www.thebritishacademy.ac.uk/sites/default/files/98p251.pdf. Northern Ireland historically had a higher unemployment rate than the rest of the UK, a situation exacerbated by The Troubles. In 1989 it was a record 9% higher than in the UK generally.

13   https://www.margaretthatcher.org/document/106689

14   https://www.theguardian.com/global/2017/may/09/enemies-state-tory-project-shrink-public-services-schools-health-inspectors-book-dismembered

15   http://blogs.lse.ac.uk/politicsandpolicy/the-politics-of-reason-post-war-consensus/

16   https://www.bbc.com/news/business-47190525. One of the best encapsulations of the austerity variant of the poverty narrative was from the New Economics Foundation, in September 2013 (see: https://neweconomics.org/2013/09/framing-the-economy): "Well-framed, well-crafted and often repeated, the austerity story is the dominant political narrative in Britain today. The Coalition has an economic narrative that is the textbook definition of a powerful political story. They have developed a clear plot, with heroes and villains, and use simple, emotional language to make their point clear. Repeated with remarkable discipline over several years, their austerity story has gained real traction with the British public. The government has successfully framed all economic debates on its own terms, but what is most powerful about their narrative is how resilient it is to different circumstances. If the economy is strong the medicine is working; if the economy is weak we need more medicine."

17   https://www.projecttwistit.com/heejungchung

18   https://www.theguardian.com/politics/2013/apr/12/thatcher-britain; https://www.theguardian.com/politics/2012/dec/28/margaret-thatcher-role-plan-to-dismantle-welfare-state-revealed

19   https://www.bbc.com/news/uk-politics-45356189. A favourite tactic among Conservatives in the UK in the 1980s (especially those with a libertarian bent) was to decry what they referred to as the 'Nanny State' – a conceptualisation of government as inappropriately interfering in people's personal lives on everything from car and food safety to taxation and spending.

20   https://www.bbc.com/news/business-37751599

21   https://www.theguardian.com/commentisfree/2019/may/15/inequality-britain-social-injustice-beveridge-report?CMP=share_btn_tw

22   http://evonomics.com/rise-of-neoliberalism-inequality/

23   https://www.theguardian.com/books/2016/apr/15/neoliberalism-ideology-problem-george-monbiot

24   https://www.theguardian.com/commentisfree/2011/nov/07/one-per-cent-wealth-destroyers

25   http://content.time.com/time/specials/packages/article/0,28804,1877351_1877350_1877322,00.html

26   https://workinprogress.oowsection.org/2016/02/03/rising-us-income-inequality-was-fueled-by-reagans-attacks-on-unions-and-continued-by-clintons-financial-deregulation

27   O'Hara, Mary (2014).

28   https://assets.publishing.service.gov.uk/government/uploads/system/uploads/attachment_data/file/762141/fraud-and-error-stats-release-2017-2018-final-estimates.pdf. The total level of benefits overpayment in the UK due to fraud in 2017/18 was estimated at 1.2%: https://www.bbc.co.uk/news/election-2017-39980793. In this article on foodstamp (SNAP) fraud in the US in 2016, Forbes cites a rise in levels of fraud (which is defined widely to include swapping foodstamps for money), but notes that 'the fraud identified in 2016 amounted to a mere 0.9 per cent of the total. That was up from 0.5 per cent in 2012': https://www.forbes.com/sites/simonconstable/2018/04/04/the-facts-about-food-stamp-fraud/#209e9ec3f880

29   https://www.washingtonpost.com/archive/business/1987/05/26/yuppie-investors-put-money-where-their-life-styles-are/8fadcb78-d13b-40fa-86dc-533465ff14b7/

30   https://www.commentarymagazine.com/articles/bonfire-vanities-30-years-later/

31   https://en.wikipedia.org/wiki/Gordon_Gekko

32   https://www.nytimes.com/1987/04/26/business/feeling-poor-on-600000-a-year.html

33   https://www.telegraph.co.uk/news/uknews/11347454/Mother-and-daughter-weigh-a-total-of-43-stone-and-get-34k-a-year-handouts-but-refuse-to-diet.html

34   'Bru' was a commonly used shorthand for the unemployment office where people 'signed on' every week to declare their employment status. This would then activate a payment of the 'dole' – a colloquial term for unemployment benefits at that time.

35   http://etheses.whiterose.ac.uk/12565/1/26Mar2016_The%20final.pdf

36   https://www.newamerica.org/weekly/edition-135/rise-and-reign-welfare-queen/

37   https://journals.sagepub.com/doi/10.1177/0044118X96027004002

38   See Cash Carraway's book, *Skint Estate*, for a raw and brutally honest depiction of how single mothers in poverty and battling the benefits system and low pay in Britain today are told they are 'a stain' on society: Carraway, Cash (2019) *Skint Estate: A memoir of poverty, motherhood and survival*. London: Ebury Press.

39   https://www.telegraph.co.uk/active/9767768/Campaign-of-fear-needed-to-deter-girls-from-becoming-teenage-mothers-Thatcher-minister-said.html

40   https://www.margaretthatcher.org/document/101830

41   http://news.bbc.co.uk/2/hi/uk_news/197963.stm. Even after she was ousted from power, Thatcher was still touting single mothers as a problem. In 1998 during a speech in Kentucky she suggested they should be handed over to religious orders so that the children could be 'brought up with family values": https://www.newamerica.org/weekly/edition-135/rise-and-reign-welfare-queen/

42   https://www.independent.co.uk/news/uk/home-news/promiscuous-scroungers-or-loving-parents-teenage-mums-fight-back-1877268.html

43   https://www.dailymail.co.uk/news/article-28860/UK-tops-league-teenage-pregnancy.html; https://www.beds.ac.uk/knowledgeexchange/news

44   http://etheses.whiterose.ac.uk/12565/1/26Mar2016_The%20final.pdf

45   The targeting of single mothers has a long history. For example, in the Victorian era – when there were also hysterical concerns raised about welfare distributed by parishes being too generous and making people idle – especially single mothers – the Royal Commission into the operation of the Poor Laws reported: 'The effect has been to promote bastardy; to make want of chastity on the woman's part the shortest road to obtaining either a husband or a competent maintenance; and to encourage extortion and perjury' (see https://www.bbc.com/news/uk-politics-33256084).

46   https://warwick.ac.uk/fac/cross_fac/iatl/reinvention/issues/volume11issue1/frampton/

47   https://www.huffingtonpost.co.uk/entry/boris-johnson-women-column-specatt_uk_5ddee7e2e4b0d50f329bd4af?guccounter=1

48   https://www.theguardian.com/politics/2019/dec/04/boris-johnson-claimed-children-of-working-mothers-more-likely-to-mug-you

49   https://www.nytimes.com/2018/02/10/opinion/sunday/single-mothers-poverty.html

50   https://abcnews.go.com/blogs/headlines/2013/05/teen-moms-photo-banned-from-high-school-yearbook/

51   https://thinkprogress.org/too-often-teen-mothers-receive-shame-instead-of-support-805b5fa8d9d/

52   https://www.colorlines.com/articles/teen-moms-look-support-find-only-shame

53   https://niemanreports.org/articles/the-welfare-queen-experiment/

54   https://robertreich.org/post/171361714715

55   https://www.cnn.com/2019/06/19/politics/arthur-laffer-curve-medal-of-freedom-donald-trump/index.html; https://www.npr.org/2019/06/19/733779337/from-a-napkin-to-a-white-house-medal-the-path-of-a-controversial-economic-idea

56   https://www.thoughtco.com/us-economy-in-the-1980s-1148148

57   https://www.newamerica.org/weekly/edition-135/rise-and-reign-welfare-queen/

58   https://www.nytimes.com/1976/02/15/archives/welfare-queen-becomes-issue-in-reagan-campaign-hitting-a-nerve-now.html

59   Edin, Kathryn J. and Shaefer, H. Luke (2015) *$2 a Day: Living on Almost Nothing in America*. New York: Houghton Mifflin Harcourt.

60   The Brookings Institution offers a good summary of the law's main components: https://www.brookings.edu/research/welfare-reform-and-immigrants/

61   At a state level in the years that followed the reforms, some of the most egregious efforts to simultaneously deny people access to government programmes and vilify and shun them were experimented with or

proposed. The law provided an extra ideological springboard for one of the most controversial: 'drug-testing' of TANF applicants.

62   https://www.newamerica.org/weekly/edition-135/rise-and-reign-welfare-queen/

63   To learn more about how the welfare queen myth, and the poor in general, have been portrayed in film in America see: Pimpare, Stephen (2017) *Ghettos, Tramps and Welfare Queens: Down and Out on the Silver Screen*, New York, Oxford University Press.

64   https://www.newamerica.org/weekly/edition-135/rise-and-reign-welfare-queen/

65   https://www.cnbc.com/2016/09/01/wearing-brown-shoes-could-lose-you-a-banking-job-in-uk.html

66   https://www.theguardian.com/commentisfree/video/2019/mar/21/brexit-breakdown-anywhere-but-westminster-a-big-day-in-the-north-video

67   http://www.digitaljournal.com/article/318903. Limbaugh made his remark in response to presidential candidate, Mitt Romney, who said, when running against President Barack Obama, that he didn't worry about the poor because they had a safety net. Liberal commentators responded that the safety net was actually riddled with holes; while, on the right, what was left of the net was once again pilloried for encouraging laziness.

68   https://dod.defense.gov/News/Article/Article/881729/veteran-homelessness-drops-nearly-50-percent-since-2010/

69   https://www.washingtonpost.com/news/wonk/wp/2017/10/09/why-so-many-veterans-go-hungry-and-the-vas-new-plan-to-fix-it/?utm_term=.80ebe586a749

70   https://www.ohchr.org/EN/NewsEvents/Pages/DisplayNews.aspx?NewsID=22533

71   https://talkpoverty.org/basics/

72   https://talkpoverty.org/basics/. The National Center for Children in Poverty (NCCP) documented in a fact sheet that among America's poor children, 4.2 million are White (10%), 4 million are Latino, (27%) 3.6 million are African American (33%), 400,000 are Asian (12%), and 200,000 are American Indian (40 per cent). 'Contrary to some stereotypes about America's poor,' the NCCP reported, 'at least one-third of the 13 million children living in poverty are white. The notion held by many Americans that poverty is not a white problem is simply false.'

73   Pimpare, Stephen (2008).

74   Abramsky, Sasha (2013) *The American Way of Poverty: How the Other Half Still Lives*. New York: Nation Books.

75   https://www.bls.gov/opub/mlr/2017/article/history-of-child-labor-in-the-united-states-part-2-the-reform-movement.htm

76   See O'Hara, Mary (2014).

77   Shildrick, Tracy (2018) *Poverty Propaganda: Exploring the Myths*. Bristol: Policy Press. For a compelling distillation of the antecedents to today's obsession with categorising poorer people as deserving or undeserving in the UK context and how moral judgements have been repeatedly

made by governments in the construction of portrayals of the poor and, by extension, more punitive welfare provision – most recently in the wake of the economic crisis of 2008, see Serana Romano's paper, 'Idle paupers, scroungers sand shirkers, past and new social stereotypes of the undeserving welfare claimant in the UK, where she demonstrates how earlier constructions of poverty that depicted the poor as undeserving entrenched negative attitudes and legitimised policies that harmed the poorest, including through criminalising and imprisonment: http://www.social-policy.org.uk/wordpress/wp-content/uploads/2015/04/18_romano.pdf.

78   Patrick, Ruth (2016) 'Living with and responding to the "scrounger" narrative in the UK: exploring everyday strategies of acceptance, resistance and deflection', *Journal of Poverty and Social Justice*, 24: 3, pp. 245–259.

79   https://www.projecttwistit.com/karendolan

80   https://www.nbcnews.com/politics/2016-election/trump-s-worst-offense-mocking-disabled-reporter-poll-finds-n627736

81   Often attributed to Winston Churchill, the special relationship has been referenced ad-nauseam (mainly by the British after they were forced to come to terms with a declining empire and still be seen as internationally significant) and regarded as having reached a high point with Thatcher and Reagan): https://www.theguardian.com/politics/2019/apr/28/britain-america-history-special-relationship-highs-and-lows-churchill-to-trump. The relationship has often been a source of mockery with the British depicted in numerous cartoons as being a hapless 'poodle' to the Americans: https://www.cartoonstock.com/directory/u/us-uk_relations.asp

82   http://markblyth.com. Blyth describes himself this way: "I was born in Dundee, Scotland, in 1967. I grew up in relative poverty, in a very real sense a 'welfare kid'. Today I'm a professor at an Ivy League university in the USA. Probabilistically speaking, I am as extreme an example of intragenerational social mobility as you can find anywhere."

83   https://www.projecttwistit.com/markblyth

84   On UK media ownership see: https://www.mediareform.org.uk/media-ownership/who-owns-the-uk-media. Three companies own 83% of the UK newspaper market: News UK (owned by News Corp – Richard Murdoch); Daily Mail Group (owned by Viscount Rothermere); and Reach (formerly known as Trinity Mirror). The billionaire Barclay brothers, Sir David and Sir Frederick Barclay, own Telegraph Media Group. For Forbes, Kate Vinton identified the 15 billionaires who own America's news media: https://www.forbes.com/sites/katevinton/2016/06/01/these-15-billionaires-own-americas-news-media-companies/#1a42f4f4660a

85   See this article by George Monbiot for some background on the forces at play and how the US and the UK are ever-more connected in an anti-state mission: https://www.theguardian.com/commentisfree/2018/dec/07/us-billionaires-hard-right-britain-spiked-magazine-charles-david-koch-foundation.

86 https://www.theguardian.com/books/2019/feb/07/rutger-bregman-winnie-byanyima-anand-giridharadas
87 https://object.cato.org/sites/cato.org/files/serials/files/cato-journal/1996/5/cj16n1-1.pdf
88 https://www.opendemocracy.net/en/dark-money-investigations/revealed-how-uk-s-powerful-right-wing-think-tanks-and-conse/
89 https://mainlymacro.blogspot.com/2018/08/how-bbc-balance-and-bad-think-tanks.html; http://www.grahamscambler.com/greedy-bastards-dark-money-think-tanks/
90 https://www.geos.ed.ac.uk/homes/tslater/mythofbrokenbritain_slater.pdf
91 As Daniel Silver, Becky Clarke, Amina Lone and Patrick Williams write in Discover Society: 'In 2006 the CSJ identified the five pathways to poverty: family breakdown, educational failure, worklessness and dependency, addiction and serious personal debt. The pathways are a tautology that not only reverses social causation, they also individualise the causes of poverty within a stigmatising 'underclass' framework that deftly rejects the wider structural inequalities that create and (re)produce poverty and inequality.' (https://discoversociety.org/2014/05/06/the-centre-for-social-justice-decision-based-evidence-making-to-punish-the-poor/).
92 Pimpare, Stephen (2008), p 12.

Chapter 4

1 https://ips-dc.org/souls-of-poor-folks/
2 https://www.theguardian.com/books/2013/jun/15/iain-banks-the-final-interview
3 http://www.cc.com/video-clips/zq2rpw/the-colbert-report--poor--in-america
4 https://www.heritage.org/poverty-and-inequality/report/air-conditioning-cable-tv-and-xbox-what-poverty-the-united-states
5 https://en.wikipedia.org/wiki/Great_Society.
6 https://www.theguardian.com/politics/2019/mar/22/dwp-document-refers-to-benefit-claimant-as-lying-bitch
7 https://www.moneyadviceservice.org.uk/en/articles/personal-independence-payment-an-introduction
8 https://www.rightsnet.org.uk/forums/viewthread/14271
9 See O'Hara, Mary (2014) for examples; also the work of Dr Frances Ryan at https://differentprinciples.wordpress.com/
10 Local papers in the UK, such as *The Liverpool Echo*, which pursued the Stephen Smith story, despite being under financial pressure as they also are in the US, have often done a sterling job in highlighting the impact of government cuts and welfare reforms on individuals and families, including contemptuous treatment by the government: https://www.liverpoolecho.co.uk/news/liverpool-news/devastating-numbers-show-just-how-15728239; https://www.manchestereveningnews.co.uk/news/greater-manchester-news/northern-cities-been-hammered-austerity-15739876; https://www.manchestereveningnews.co.uk/

news/greater-manchester-news/woman-59-battling-multiple-sclerosis-16361334

11   https://www.theguardian.com/society/2019/mar/18/misleading-dwp-letter-causing-ill-and-disabled-people-to-lose-benefits

12   https://www.theguardian.com/society/2019/feb/12/man-wins-fit-for-work-appeal-seven-months-after-his-death

13   https://www.independent.co.uk/news/uk/politics/theresa-may-fit-to-work-assessment-women-suicide-benefits-disability-a8577306.html

14   https://www.independent.co.uk/news/uk/home-news/pip-waiting-time-deaths-disabled-people-die-disability-benefits-personal-independence-payment-dwp-a8727296.html

15   https://www.imdb.com/title/tt5168192/

16   https://www.imdb.com/title/tt8359816/

17   https://www.theguardian.com/society/2019/apr/21/stephen-smith-liverpool-seriously-ill-emaciated-man-denied-benefits-dwp-dies

18   Stephen's case was far from an anomaly. See here for another example, this time of a 69-year-old man with six months to live being told by the DWP that he had to reapply for his benefits: https://www.mirror.co.uk/news/uk-news/man-6-months-live-devastated-16224193

19   https://www.gov.uk/employment-support-allowance. ESA was controversial from the get-go and its many flaws had been repeatedly flagged up by disabled people. New problems with its administration emerged on a regular basis: https://www.independent.co.uk/news/uk/home-news/disability-benefits-dwp-backpay-employment-support-allowance-a8588621.html. When 200,000 more disabled people were thrust into poverty (according to the government's own figures published in April 2019), disability activists pointed out the role that cuts to disability benefits had played: https://www.disabilitynewsservice.com/number-of-disabled-people-in-poverty-rose-by-200000-in-one-year-says-dwp/

20   https://www.liverpoolecho.co.uk/news/liverpool-news/weighing-six-stone-barely-able-15762870

21   https://www.gov.uk/government/statistics/mortality-statistics-esa-ib-and-sda-claimants

22   https://metro.co.uk/2019/11/18/man-drops-dead-job-centre-queue-declared-fit-work-11174319/

23   https://www.theguardian.com/society/2015/feb/04/jobcentre-adviser-play-benefit-sanctions-angela-neville

24   https://jech.bmj.com/content/70/4/339. This paper confirmed that Work Capability Assessments have a negative impact on mental health for those assessed or reassessed, concluding that 'The programme of reassessing people on disability benefits using the Work Capability Assessment was independently associated with an increase in suicides, self-reported mental health problems and antidepressant prescribing. This policy may have had serious adverse consequences for mental health in England, which could outweigh any benefits that arise from moving people off disability benefits.'

25   The DWP has increasingly outsourced benefits assessments to private companies, with three companies earning £50m per month between

them in July 2018: https://www.thecanary.co/trending/2018/07/26/
the-dwp-just-revealed-the-eye-watering-millions-it-paid-out-to-
private-companies/. Private contractors conducting the assessments
have been frequently criticised for using untrained staff to carry out
assessments, for prioritising profits and performance targets over
achieving the right decision and for the fact that a high proportion
of appeals against assessment decisions are decided in favour of the
claimant – further reinforcing the argument that the initial assessment
decisions are taken without due care: https://www.independent.co.uk/
news/uk/politics/private-companies-fit-for-work-assessments-benefits-
atos-capita-a7496881.html. In March 2019, Amber Rudd, Work and
Pensions Secretary, announced plans to involve more private providers
in the assessment process: https://www.benefitsandwork.co.uk/
news/3889-more-private-firms-to-to-get-slice-of-pip-and-wca-cake

26   Blyth, Mark (2013) *Austerity: The History of a Dangerous Idea*. New York:
Oxford University Press.

27   https://www.theguardian.com/books/2013/jun/15/iain-banks-the-
final-interview

28   Shildrick, Tracy (2018).

29   https://b.3cdn.net/nefoundation/a12416779f2dd4153c_2hm6ixiyj.pdf

30   https://www.theguardian.com/commentisfree/2018/feb/16/anguage-
austerity-economic-policy

31   As Paul Krugman noted in 2015: '… scare talk about debt and deficits
is often used as a cover for a very different agenda, namely an attempt to
reduce the overall size of government and especially spending on social
insurance. This has been transparently obvious in the United States,
where many supposed deficit-reduction plans just happen to include
sharp cuts in tax rates on corporations and the wealthy even as they take
away healthcare and nutritional aid for the poor. But it's also a fairly
obvious motivation in the UK, if not so crudely expressed. The "primary
purpose" of austerity, the *Telegraph* admitted in 2013, "is to shrink the
size of government spending" – or, as Cameron put it in a speech later
that year, to make the state "leaner … not just now, but permanently":
https://www.theguardian.com/business/ng-interactive/2015/apr/29/
the-austerity-delusion

32   Ryan, Frances (2019) *Crippled: Austerity and the demonization of disabled
people*. London: Verso.

33   In 2011, Louise Casey was appointed as the first 'Troubled Families
tsar', heading up the Troubled Families programme launched earlier
that year by Prime Minister David Cameron. The initiative was much
criticised, with one report claiming that it had had little discernible
impact, despite its c£450m annual budget: https://www.localgov.co.uk/
Troubled-Families-tsar-defends-programme-amid-controversy/41884

34   Research shows that the numbers of large families claiming benefits
are miniscule, while intergenerational poverty within families hovers at
around just 0.5% of UK households: https://www.theguardian.com/
news/datablog/2012/nov/20/benefits-stigma-newspapers-report-
welfare

35 https://www.telegraph.co.uk/news/politics/david-cameron/9354163/David-Camerons-welfare-speech-in-full.html

36 For a history of and background to tax credits in the UK see: https://revenuebenefits.org.uk/tax-credits/policy/research/where-it-all-started/

37 https://www.itv.com/news/2013-04-05/david-cameron-backs-george-osborne-over-philpott-benefits-row/

38 https://www.theguardian.com/politics/2013/apr/05/pm-osborne-linking-philpott-welfare; see also O'Hara, Mary (2014), pp. 95-6.

39 Duncan Smith was at the centre of the austerity rollout in its formative years. He was notorious for deflecting criticism – and as I learned from those on the frontline all around the country, his welfare reforms caused untold harm and distress. As one welfare advice officer, Nick Dilworth, told me in 2014 of what he was seeing as reforms kicked in: "People are coming in with multiple problems....You get grown men crying. What you see are broken lives. It means we are seeing people for whom all you can do is give short-term answers like food-bank vouchers. Then your problem as a frontline worker is, 'how am I supposed to solve this?'": https://www.theguardian.com/society/2014/sep/30/welfare-rights-shame-iain-duncan-smith-nick-dilworth-reform

40 https://www.theguardian.com/politics/2013/may/09/iain-duncan-smith-benefits-cap-statistics

41 Iain Duncan Smith also gained notoriety for his claim in 2013 that he could live off £53 a week (the amount one benefit claimant was left with after housing costs): https://www.telegraph.co.uk/news/politics/9964767/Iain-Duncan-Smith-I-could-live-on-53-per-week.html. After a petition demanding that he prove this claim gained over 300,000 signatures, he responded by calling the petition a "stunt" and claimed that he knew what it was like to "live on the breadline": https://www.bbc.co.uk/news/uk-politics-22006841

42 https://www.theguardian.com/society/2014/sep/30/welfare-rights-shame-iain-duncan-smith-nick-dilworth-reform

43 https://www.dailymail.co.uk/news/article-2237199/The-poor-risks-benefit-says-welfare-minister-slams-dreadful-system.html

44 https://www.theguardian.com/books/2013/sep/18/jk-rowling-government-poor-people

45 https://www.gingerbread.org.uk/what-we-do/about-gingerbread/staff-and-supporters/our-supporters/

46 https://www.politics.co.uk/news/2013/09/11/michael-gove-poor-to-blame-for-food-banks

47 Rafael Behr, 'Shirkers v strivers', *New Statesman*, 29 November 2012, https://www.newstatesman.com/politics/politics/2012/11/shirkers-v-strivers. See also Zoe Williams, 'Skivers v strivers: the argument that pollutes people's minds', *The Guardian*, 9 January 2013, https://www.theguardian.com/politics/2013/jan/09/skivers-v-strivers-argument-pollutes

48 See O'Hara, Mary (2014)

49 Lancaster, Simon (2018) *You are not Human: How Words Kill*. London: Biteback Publishing.

Notes

50 https://www.independent.co.uk/news/uk/politics/corbyn-european-social-democrats-reject-austerity-neoliberalism-warning-a8432511. html

51 As Paul Krugman wrote: 'It has been astonishing, from a US perspective, to witness the limpness of Labour's response to the austerity push. Britain's opposition has been amazingly willing to accept claims that budget deficits are the biggest economic issue facing the nation, and has made hardly any effort to challenge the extremely dubious proposition that fiscal policy under Blair and Brown was deeply irresponsible – or even the nonsensical proposition that this supposed fiscal irresponsibility caused the crisis of 2008-2009': https://www.theguardian.com/business/ng-interactive/2015/apr/29/the-austerity-delusion

52 http://eprints.lse.ac.uk/55289/1/Chauhan_Representations-of-poverty-in-British-newspapers_2014.pdf

53 Jenna Sloan, 'Help us stop £1.5bn benefits scroungers', *The Sun*, 12 August 2010: https://www.thescottishsun.co.uk/archives/news/39299/help-us-stop-1-5bn-benefits-scroungers/

54 Ben Riley-Smith, 'Disability hate crime: is "benefit scrounger" abuse to blame?', *The Guardian*, 14 August 2012: https://www.theguardian.com/society/2012/aug/14/disability-hate-crime-benefit-scrounger-abuse. In 2018 police figures revealed a one-third increase in disability hate crime over the previous year (https://www.independent.co.uk/news/uk/disability-hate-crime-rise-latest-figures-united-response-a8583751. html), while figures released in early 2019 revealed there had also been a one-third increase in online disability hate crime over the previous year: https://www.theguardian.com/society/2019/may/10/online-hate-against-disabled-people-rises-by-a-third. See also the 2018 survey by disability charity Scope, 'The disability perception gap': https://www.disabilityrightsuk.org/news/2018/may/scope-report-highlights-negative-public-attitudes-towards-disabled-people

55 Cited in Walker, Robert (2014), p 167.

56 https://www.dailymail.co.uk/news/article-2132997/The-skiving-capitals-Britain-Brentwood-tops-list-55-reassessed-incapacity-benefit-claimants-fit-work.html

57 Cited in Shildrick, Tracy (2018), p 26.

58 https://www.mirror.co.uk/news/uk-news/benefits-cheat-who-couldnt-dress-14982386

59 Walker, Robert (2014), p 167.

60 Walker, Robert (2014), p 168.

61 See Jones, Owen (2012) *Chavs: The Demonization of the Working Class*. London: Verso. For contemporary, accessible analysis of how reality television, defines and demeans certain sectors of the working classes, including people on benefits see Wood, Helen and Skeggs, Beverley (eds) (2011) *Reality Television and Class*. British Film Institute. Also Johnson, B. and Forrest, D. (2017) *Social Class and Television Drama in Contemporary Britain*. London: Palgrave, https://www.palgrave.com/gb/book/9781137555052

62 https://en.wikipedia.org/wiki/Jeremy_Kyle. The show – cancelled in May 2019 – regularly attracted upwards of one million viewers in its morning slot on ITV.

63 https://en.wikipedia.org/wiki/Trisha_Goddard_(TV_series)

64 https://www.indy100.com/article/the-nine-most-jeremy-kyle-topics-in-the-history-of-the-jeremy-kyle-show--WJGRJcyKeb

65 https://www.theguardian.com/commentisfree/2019/may/15/jeremy-kyle-cruelty-guests-death-show-tv?CMP=Share_iOSApp_Other; https://metro.co.uk/2019/05/18/the-jeremy-kyle-shows-popularity-showed-we-are-a-society-lacking-in-kindness-9585235/

66 http://news.bbc.co.uk/2/hi/entertainment/7011962.stm

67 https://www.theguardian.com/media/2019/may/14/jeremy-kyle-show-ruined-life-guest-speaks-out

68 https://www.theguardian.com/media/2019/may/13/jeremy-kyle-show-suspended-after-death-of-guest

69 Johnson, B. and Forrest, D. (2017).

70 https://en.wikipedia.org/wiki/Benefits_Street

71 Tyler, Imogen (2013) *Revolting Subjects: Social Abjection and Resistance in Neoliberal Britain*. London: Zed Books, pp 162–63.

72 Jones, Owen (2012).

73 https://journals.sagepub.com/doi/abs/10.1177/1749975517712132?journalCode=cusa

74 https://en.wikipedia.org/wiki/Poverty_porn

75 https://www.channel4.com/news/benefits-street-birmingham-channel-4-twitter-row

76 https://www.jrf.org.uk/blog/playing-media's-'poke-fun-people-poverty'-game-gets-us-nowhere

77 https://www.projecttwistit.com/abigail-scott-paul

78 https://www.theguardian.com/tv-and-radio/2018/sep/13/the-mighty-redcar-review-proper-heartwarming-film-making

79 https://www.theguardian.com/politics/2019/nov/03/tory-candidate-francesca-obrien-wrote-people-benefits-street-should-be-put-down

80 https://www.projecttwistit.com/abigail-scott-paul

81 Also see the blog by Tanya Lawson, a person with lived experience of poverty from the north east of England, who outlines how *Skint Britain* distorts the reality of people like her struggling to get by: https://www.jrf.org.uk/blog/we-need-more-flexible-system-support-people-low-incomes#UniversalCredit

82 https://interestingengineering.com/15-examples-anti-homeless-hostile-architecture-that-you-probably-never-noticed-before

83 https://nypost.com/2016/01/17/poor-door-tenants-reveal-luxury-towers-financial-apartheid/; https://www.theguardian.com/society/2018/nov/25/poor-doors-developers-segregate-rich-from-poor-london-housing-blocks

84 https://www.theguardian.com/cities/2019/mar/25/too-poor-to-play-children-in-social-housing-blocked-from-communal-playground

85 http://paullewismoney.blogspot.com

86 McAllister's film toured the UK in cinemas (funded by JRF as part of its Talk Poverty umbrella – the same initiative funding Project Twist-It)

and was broadcast on mainstream television to overwhelmingly positive reviews. The film follows warehouse worker Steve Arnott as he attempts to get a business idea of bringing music on a 'beats bus' to kids in disadvantaged areas off the ground in the city of Hull in the North East of England. In one article the British Film Institute even posited, 'Why *A Northern Soul* challenges TV's war on the poor': https://www.bfi.org.uk/news-opinion/news-bfi/interviews/northern-soul-sean-mcallister

87 https://en.wikipedia.org/wiki/Jack_Monroe
88 As William Keegan rightly argued in *The Observer* newspaper, by 2019 the force and fallout of austerity had caught up with the Conservatives, as evidenced in disastrous 2019 local elections results: https://www.theguardian.com/business/2019/may/05/austerity-not-failure-to-deliver-brexit-behind-tory-election-losses
89 https://www.theguardian.com/politics/2017/jan/08/theresa-may-tories-party-social-justice-speech; https://www.independent.co.uk/voices/theresa-may-social-mobility-michael-gove-speech-brexit-capitalism-a8353916.html
90 https://www.theguardian.com/membership/2018/apr/20/amelia-gentleman-windrush-immigration
91 https://leftfootforward.org/2018/07/social-justice-campaigns-are-furious-at-the-government-after-tories-ditch-inequality-talks/
92 https://www.bbc.com/news/uk-politics-42212270
93 https://www.buzzfeed.com/alexspence/may-burning-injustices-analysis?utm_source=dynamic&utm_campaign=bfsharecopy
94 https://www.thetimes.co.uk/edition/news/tory-party-orders-mps-to-ditch-rhetoric-on-burning-injustices-cpfjklr95?utm_source=newsletter&utm_campaign=newsletter_119&utm_medium=email&utm_content=119_31.07.2018 per cent20Red per cent20Box per cent20Mugged per cent20(1)&CMP=TNLEmail_118918_3848392_119
95 https://twitter.com/sketchaganda/status/1153957622376218629

Chapter 5

1 https://www.theguardian.com/society/commentisfree/2017/may/02/lunch-shaming-battle-against-child-poverty
2 https://fns-prod.azureedge.net/sites/default/files/SNOPSYear1.pdf
3 https://www.nytimes.com/2017/04/30/well/family/lunch-shaming-children-parents-school-bills.html
4 https://www.americanbar.org/groups/young_lawyers/publications/tyl/topics/access-to-education/incentives-behind-lunch-shaming.html
5 http://www.frac.org/blog/end-school-lunch-shaming. The *New York Times* article (see n 3 above) points out that even where anti-shaming policies are in place, schools still have the problem of dealing with unpaid meals debt: 'But feeding hungry children whose families have meal debt does not solve the problem for schools, which still must grapple with paying the bill. In 2016, the School Nutrition Association published a review of almost 1,000 school lunch programs, finding that nearly 75 per cent of districts had unpaid meal debt.'

6   https://www.upi.com/Top_News/US/2019/06/19/Rep-
    Ilhan-Omar-introduces-bill-to-stop-school-lunch-shaming-
    practices/5151560977485/
7   https://www.nbcnews.com/news/us-news/minnesota-school-threw-
    out-hot-meals-students-over-15-lunch-n1081106
8   As was pointed out at the time, and many times since, Obama attracted
    criticism for action not taken to hold bankers fully accountable for the
    catastrophe. He also faced criticism both for his stimulus not being big
    enough: https://www.truthdig.com/articles/its-been-10-years-since-
    banks-were-bailed-out-and-people-were-sold-out/ –, and for being
    excessively big: https://www.abc.net.au/news/2017-01-18/barack-
    obamas-economic-legacy-might-be-judged-well-by-history/8191220
9   https://www.abc.net.au/news/2017-01-18/barack-obamas-economic-
    legacy-might-be-judged-well-by-history/8191220
10 https://prospect.org/article/economic-crisis-black-and-white
11 https://www.ft.com/content/687c0184-aaa6-11e8-94bd-
    cba20d67390c
12 It should be noted of course that, when politically expedient during
    his presidential campaign, Trump pledged not to go after social security
    including Medicaid and Medicare (especially bearing in mind how
    many older Republican voters access them): yet once in power, as
    with everything else he did, he reversed course in the blink of a tweet:
    https://www.vox.com/policy-and-politics/2017/1/25/14376014/
    trump-social-security-medicare-mulvaney
13 https://tobereadbooks.com/5-books-that-explain-the-tea-party-
    movement/
14 It has been convincingly argued that the integration of the Tea Party's
    more extreme ethos and individuals like Sarah Palin and those who won
    elections for the GOP as members into the Republican Party played
    a major role in the populist takeover that set the stage for Trump and
    his excesses: https://www.washingtonpost.com/opinions/the-gops-
    dysfunction-all-started-with-sarah-palin/2015/10/25/bdd34892-7442-
    11e5-8248-98e0f5a2e830_story.html?utm_term=.ebc95ae84f0b
15 Pimpare, Stephen (2008).
16 https://thehill.com/opinion/campaign/401820-what-happened-to-
    the-tea-party
17 https://www.pbs.org/newshour/nation/stimulus-bill-turns-5-years-
    old-still
18 https://journalistsresource.org/studies/politics/elections/tea-party-
    movement-2010-midterm-elections/
19 As Sasha Abramsky (2013, p 47) noted, 'Tea Party activists, energised
    by the 2010 midterm elections, proposed cutting a startling $9 trillion
    from federal spending during a 10-year period.' One suggestion included
    eliminating the Departments of Education and of Housing and Urban
    Development.
20 http://www.cnn.com/2010/OPINION/04/15/dennis.tea.party.goals/
    index.html
21 https://www.irp.wisc.edu/publications/focus/pdfs/foc121b.pdf. In his
    paper, 'The Origins of "Dependency": Choices, confidence or culture',

Notes

David T. Ellwood, Professor of Public Policy at the Kennedy School for Government, writes: "It's hard to miss the profound shift in emphasis and tone that has occurred in poverty discussions over the past 10–15 years. He notes that one of the major right-wing think tanks, The American Enterprise Institute, as part of its 'Working Seminar on the Family and American Welfare Policy, focused its report almost entirely on the problem of 'behavioural dependency', and he continues: 'The transformation of the debate is extraordinary, for a focus on dependency represents more than a change of terms. It represents and implicit shift in behavioural models.'

22 https://www.npr.org/2016/01/23/464068087/how-sarah-palin-paved-the-way-for-donald-trump

23 https://www.nytimes.com/2018/04/13/opinion/paul-ryan-donald-trump-republicans.html

24 https://www.salon.com/2015/06/12/fox_news_big_welfare_lie_gets_demolished_the_shiftless_moocher_meme_is_one_big_myth/

25 https://www.colorlines.com/articles/why-tea-party-lawmakers-are-trying-conflate-poverty-and-drug-addiction

26 https://www.americanprogress.org/issues/economy/news/2011/12/09/10832/drug-testing-america/

27 https://www.whsv.com/content/news/508826082.html

28 https://www.politico.com/story/2018/02/01/welfare-reform-gop-paul-ryan-382591. Paul Ryan was repeatedly criticised for wrapping his welfare proposals in language that framed programmes being seen as 'entitlements' by users who failed to take personal responsibility. He also faced scepticism within his own party for pushing too hard during a congressional election year.

29 https://www.limaohio.com/opinion/columns/280348/rebecca-vallas-chicken-little-meets-the-welfare-queen

30 https://www.nytimes.com/2011/12/01/us/we-are-the-99-percent-joins-the-cultural-and-political-lexicon.html

31 https://www.cnn.com/2012/09/21/opinion/spalding-welfare-state-dependency/index.html

32 https://www.heritage.org/welfare/report/the-2012-index-dependence-government

33 https://www.nationalreview.com/corner/tragedy-dependency-culture-david-french/

34 https://www.silive.com/opinion/columns/2013/11/the_entitlement_culture_is_mak.html

35 https://www.dailysignal.com/2011/07/09/president-obama-admits-welfare-encourages-dependency/

36 https://www.foxnews.com/politics/study-number-of-able-bodied-adults-on-food-stamps-doubled-after-stimulus-change

37 https://www.foxnews.com/opinion/why-welfare-mimimum-wage-make-it-harder-for-poor-americans-to-succeed

38 Garrett, Paul Michael (2017), p 52, quoting Sandford F. Schram in *Becoming a Footnote* (2013). SUNY Press.

39 https://www.washingtonpost.com/outlook/2018/10/23/daniel-patrick-moynihan-isnt-hero-we-need-age-trump/?utm_term=.08018eaae53e

40 https://www.washingtonpost.com/news/the-fix/wp/2013/03/04/why-mitt-romneys-47-percent-comment-was-so-bad/?utm_term=.9dd28f8c84da

41 https://www.washingtonpost.com/politics/decision2012/leaked-videos-show-romney-dismissing-obama-supporters-as-entitled-victims/2012/09/17/5d49ca96-0113-11e2-b260-32f4a8db9b7e_story.html?utm_term=.cafb5fc224ab

42 https://www.epi.org/blog/raising-the-federal-minimum-wage-isnt-just-the-right-thing-to-do-for-workers-its-also-good-for-the-economy/

43 Cited in Abramsky, Sasha (2013).

44 Abramsky, Sasha (2013).

45 https://www.newsweek.com/donald-trump-tax-welfare-food-stamps-1420037?fbclid=IwAR2Q7YVj4RREpH_lm4guRLcB9NwSMGFXW5hni6Pf2toZsdq31rrA78sr8q8

46 https://www.vanityfair.com/news/2018/09/the-left-behind-trump-voter-has-nothing-more-to-tell-us?verso=true

47 Trump, in his love affair with executive orders, even issued one to compel his millionaire cabinet to come up with ways to cut welfare spending and toughen eligibility criteria: https://www.whitehouse.gov/presidential-actions/executive-order-reducing-poverty-america-promoting-opportunity-economic-mobility/

48 https://newrepublic.com/article/146859/media-abetting-gops-war-welfare. Jaffe also points out how, in a rare departure from the general trend, Politico showed how it could and should be done with its headline: 'Behind Trump's plan to target the federal safety net'. In the article it said: 'Under the banner of welfare reform, the administration is eyeing changes to healthcare, foodstamps, housing, and veterans programmes.'

49 https://www.wsj.com/articles/after-push-on-taxes-republicans-line-up-welfare-revamp-next-1512469801

50 https://www.theguardian.com/media/2016/oct/13/liberal-media-bias-working-class-americans

51 https://www.mediamatters.org/blog/2013/09/18/the-real-consequences-of-terrible-journalism/195942

52 http://www.rollcall.com/news/clash_over_nutrition_program_expected_to_focus_on_who_deserves_food_aid-227643-1.html?zkPrintable=true

53 https://insider.foxnews.com/2017/11/09/marco-rubio-tax-code-shouldnt-encourage-welfare-over-work

54 https://www.foxbusiness.com/politics/trumps-2020-budget-and-the-benefits-of-moving-more-americans-from-welfare-to-work

55 https://www.foxnews.com/opinion/newt-gingrich-mary-mayhew-hope-for-those-trapped-in-welfare-dependency-thanks-to-trump

56 https://www.foxnews.com/opinion/its-time-to-overhaul-welfare-the-right-way-heres-how

57   "We think it's important to get people from welfare into work. We have a welfare system that's basically trapping people in poverty and effectively paying people not to work and we've got to work on that": Paul Ryan, (then) Speaker of the House of Representatives, December 2017, defending his plan to cut anti-poverty programmes and social security benefits, https://www.chicagotribune.com/news/nationworld/politics/ct-republican-welfare-cuts-20171206-story.html

58   https://www.politico.com/magazine/story/2018/03/09/trump-wealthiest-cabinet-members-217336. And this is only the cabinet. In a way, Trump was merely following a pattern of rapid wealth growth in Congress. By 2018, 51% of US Congress members were deemed millionaires with the cumulative net worth of senators and representatives jumping by a fifth in two years: https://www.rollcall.com/news/hawkings/congress-richer-ever-mostly-top

59   https://www.npr.org/2017/05/25/530068988/ben-carson-says-poverty-is-a-state-of-mind

60   https://www.washingtonpost.com/news/wonk/wp/2017/05/22/trump-to-poor-americans-get-to-work-or-lose-your-benefits/?noredirect=on&utm_term=.7ac30e31cf54

61   https://www.usatoday.com/story/opinion/2018/12/20/usda-secretary-sonny-perdue-snap-benefit-reform-workers-welfare-column/2343066002/

62   https://www.washingtonpost.com/business/economy/commerce-secretary-doesnt-understand-why-unpaid-federal-workers-use-food-banks/2019/01/24/866d3100-1fe4-11e9-8e21-59a09ff1e2a1_story.html?utm_term=.d908e8ec0926

63   https://www.washingtonpost.com/business/economy/commerce-secretary-doesnt-understand-why-unpaid-federal-workers-use-food-banks/2019/01/24/866d3100-1fe4-11e9-8e21-59a09ff1e2a1_story.html?utm_term=.d908e8ec0926

Chapter 6

1   https://atd-uk.org/projects-campaigns/understanding-poverty/

2   https://www.nbc.com/the-good-place

3   See the PTI filmed interview with Jameela: https://www.projecttwistit.com/jameelajamil

4   https://milescorak.files.wordpress.com/2012/05/poor-relatively-speaking-sen.pdf

5   https://en.wikipedia.org/wiki/Adam_Smith

6   https://milescorak.files.wordpress.com/2012/05/poor-relatively-speaking-sen.pdf

7   Seabrook, Jeremy (2013), which gives an historical analysis of the perception of poverty and the poor in England and how the vilification and maltreatment of the poorest has strong roots built over centuries.

8   Seabrook, Jeremy (2014) 'Why shame is the most dominant feature of modern poverty', *The Guardian*, 30 September 2014: https://www.theguardian.com/commentisfree/2014/sep/30/shame-modern-poverty-poor-people-tory-welfare-cuts

9   Shildrick, Tracy (2018); Pimpare, Stephen (2008).

10   Seabrook, Jeremy (2014) 'Why shame is the most dominant feature of modern poverty', *The Guardian*, 30 September 2014.

11   https://www.merriam-webster.com/dictionary/shame

12   https://socialprotection.org/discover/blog/psycho-socio-consequences-poverty—-why-it's-important-talk-about-shame

13   Walker, Robert (2014).

14   https://atd-uk.org/projects-campaigns/understanding-poverty/

15   Ronson, Jon (2015) *So You've Been Publicly Shamed*. London: Riverhead Books.

16   Chase, Elaine and Bantebya-Kyomuhendo, Grace (eds) (2014); Walker, Robert (2014).

17   http://www.benbaumberg.com/files/2016 per cent20JSP per cent20stigma per cent20paper per cent20final.pdf

18   Walker, Robert (2014).

19   https://socialprotection.org/discover/blog/psycho-socio-consequences-poverty—-why-it's-important-talk-about-shame

20   Chase, Elaine and Bantebya-Kyomuhendo, Grace (eds) (2014); Walker, Robert (2014).

21   Patrick, Ruth (2016) 'Living with and responding to the "scrounger" narrative in the UK: exploring everyday strategies of acceptance, resistance and deflection', *Journal of Poverty and Social Justice*, 24: 3, pp 245–259.

22   Chase, Elaine and Walker, Robert (2012) 'The Co-construction of Shame in the Context of Poverty: Beyond a Threat to the Social Bond', *Sociology*, 47(4), pp. 739–754, doi: 10.1177/0038038512453796.

23   Walker, Robert (2014).

24   http://www.lse.ac.uk/News/Latest-news-from-LSE/2018/08-Aug-2018/Television-shows-that-glamourise-wealth

25   https://www.forbes.com/sites/taxanalysts/2014/03/14/where-is-the-outrage-over-corporate-welfare/#4ce5cfe527dd

26   https://www.aljazeera.com/news/2019/02/2020-democratic-presidential-candidates-190225202457543.html

27   https://inequality.org/great-divide/billionaire-bonanza-2018-inherited-wealth-dynasties-in-the-21st-century-u-s/

28   Even when politicians do moot tax rises, these have tended to be couched in language aimed at allaying fears of anything like a significant increase.

29   https://www.brookings.edu/blog/up-front/2019/03/14/americans-want-the-wealthy-and-corporations-to-pay-more-taxes-but-are-elected-officials-listening/

30   There have been some notable exceptions to this, especially in the US since the election of Donald Trump. See Chapter 4.

31   https://opportunityagenda.org/explore/resources-publications/window-opportunity-ii/income-inequality-equal-opportunity

32   http://www.pewresearch.org/fact-tank/2018/10/04/partisans-are-divided-over-the-fairness-of-the-u-s-economy-and-why-people-are-rich-or-poor/

33   Leslie McCall (2013) *The Undeserving Rich: American beliefs about inequality, opportunity and redistribution,* Cambridge University Press.

34   http://www.bsa.natcen.ac.uk/media/39285/bsa35_key-findings.pdf

35   There has been some research that shows younger people in very wealthy families are rejecting the 'deservedness' narrative of wealth that their elders ascribe to: https://www.mcall.com/opinion/mc-opi-american-meritocracy-myth-20190621-rlekpyv2wjbz5lr7lo6or3greu-story.html

36   https://www.latimes.com/projects/la-na-pol-poverty-poll/

37   Lauter wrote: 'Asked why antipoverty efforts have failed, more than half of Americans said the main problem was that programs were poorly designed. Among poor people, however, about 3 in 10 said the problem was that programs had not been given enough money to succeed.'

38   https://www.jrf.org.uk/report/attitudes-different-generations-welfare-system

39   The JRF research suggests that negative media coverage and the rhetoric of politicians towards poverty have a role to play in shifting attitudes but that the dramatic change over time can't be put down entirely to this: 'The most significant factor, however, is the 'period effect': the change in attitudes across society over time. There is a lack of evidence to justify the argument that political rhetoric or newspaper reporting have brought about this change, though both are likely to have contributed to negative perceptions of welfare.'

40   http://natcen.ac.uk/our-research/research/british-social-attitudes/

41   The survey found that the proportion of people agreeing with this statement had fallen since 2015, but it was still higher than in 2001 when those agreeing that strong welfare benefits caused dependency was 39%. A particularly encouraging finding from the 2017 survey was the possibility of a softening of attitudes on government cuts. At the start of austerity in 2011, 42% of people felt cutting benefits would damage too many people's lives – down from 58% ten years earlier. However, the study found a 'sharp rise' in the proportion of people less willing to accept that cutting benefits wouldn't cause harm, saying this highlighted 'a possible tipping point in public attitudes towards welfare spending cuts'.

42   https://www.theguardian.com/commentisfree/2018/sep/18/rich-britons-inequality-poverty-social-wealth

43   https://www.theguardian.com/society/2018/oct/04/increasing-number-of-britons-think-empathy-is-on-the-wane

44   https://www.theguardian.com/society/2018/oct/04/increasing-number-of-britons-think-empathy-is-on-the-wane

Part III

1   The 11+ still exists in some parts of the UK and remains extremely controversial for a number of reasons, including that it favours children from better-off backgrounds. Paying private tutors is commonplace, providing an unfair advantage over poorer kids. One study in 2018 found that 70% of children who were tutored secured a grammar school place, with just 14% of those not tutored achieving entry:

https://www.independent.co.uk/news/education/education-news/parents-private-tutors-tax-grammar-school-places-children-entrance-tests-ucl-a8268406.html

2 The use of 'College' in the school's name, I would come to realise, reflected its unusual and bold ambitions for the girls who went there – the vast majority of whom were from low income and poor backgrounds. For more on St Louise's, see Rae, John (2013 [2001 hb]) *Sister Genevieve: An Inspirational Teacher at the Heart of the Troubles.* London: Thistle Publishing.

3 https://en.wikipedia.org/wiki/Education_in_Northern_Ireland

4 Sister Genevieve (Mary) O'Farrell was a legend in West Belfast for her unshakeable faith in her school, which she headed for 25 years, in us, and in our capacity to overcome poverty given the right support and encouragement: https://www.theguardian.com/world/2002/jan/21/gender.uk. Also, see 'Sister Genevieve: A courageous woman's triumph in Northern Ireland by John Rae': https://www.goodreads.com/author/show/53814.John_Rae

5 https://www.telegraph.co.uk/news/2019/04/30/oxbridge-should-consider-poor-pupils-one-b-two-cs-a-level-place/

Chapter 7

1 https://www.projecttwistit.com/billie-jd-porter

2 https://www.projecttwistit.com/markbrown

3 https://www.theguardian.com/commentisfree/2019/mar/11/universal-credit-spring-statement-benefits. The respected Institute for Fiscal Studies head, Paul Johnson, explains in this article how a 'disruptive' change to the UK benefits system – Universal Credit – will impact one in three working households in some capacity. He points out that tens of millions are spent on working-age benefits with people relying on them to keep their heads above water while millions are in poverty in a low-wage, low-skill economy. Wages are habitually so low that most of the money given in benefits 'now goes to households with someone in paid work. A system originally designed largely to support those out of work for a limited period has become one that supports the low-paid and the sick and disabled for long stretches of their lives.' Structural and system factors much wider than the benefits system are at play, he stresses. 'Nearly 60% go to households where someone is in paid work but not earning enough to achieve an adequate standard of living. The big problem here is not just low pay, but the lack of progression. For too many people, low-paid work is not a stepping stone to better pay, it is a trap.'

4 www.theguardian.com/commentisfree/2018/sep/13/zero-hours-contracts-unions-john-mcdonnell-labour-market; https://www.cbsnews.com/news/low-wage-work-really-is-a-dead-end-for-millions/

5 https://www.projecttwistit.com/voices

6 https://blogs.lse.ac.uk/politicsandpolicy/going-after-welfare-cheats-misses-the-bigger-picture/

7   https://www.newamerica.org/weekly/edition-174/myths-waste-fraud-and-abuse/

8   https://blogs.lse.ac.uk/politicsandpolicy/going-after-welfare-cheats-misses-the-bigger-picture/

9   https://ips-dc.org/report-billionaire-bonanza-2018/

10   Pimpare, Stephen (2008), p 11.

11   Land, Stephanie (2019).

12   https://www.psychiatrictimes.com/special-reports/addressing-poverty-and-mental-illness

13   https://www.theguardian.com/society/2018/jul/23/shelter-warns-of-leap-in-working-homeless-as-families-struggle

14   https://england.shelter.org.uk/professional_resources/policy_and_research/policy_library/policy_library_folder/people_living_in_bad_housing_-_numbers_and_health_impacts; https://www.theguardian.com/society/2019/apr/13/trapped-britain-new-slums-poverty-austerity-social-housing?CMP=Share_iOSApp_Other

15   https://www.generationrent.org

16   https://www.theguardian.com/environment/2019/may/21/us-pollution-incinerators-waste-burning-plants-report?CMP=Share_iOSApp_Other; https://www.theguardian.com/environment/2019/jun/27/us-air-pollution-north-east-mid-atlantic-analysis-union-concerned-scientists?CMP=Share_iOSApp_Other

17   The latest book from Harriet Washington sheds new light on this in the US, especially as it relates to race: *A terrible thing to waste: Environmental Racism and Its Assault on the American Mind* (Little, Brown; July 23); https://www.theguardian.com/us-news/2019/apr/15/were-not-a-dump-poor-alabama-towns-struggle-under-the-stench-of-toxic-landfills?CMP=Share_iOSApp_Other

18   https://www.theguardian.com/us-news/2019/apr/04/new-york-south-bronx-minorities-pollution-inequity?CMP=Share_iOSApp_Other; https://www.epa.gov/sites/production/files/2015-09/documents/webpopulationrsuperfundsites9.28.15.pdf

19   https://theconversation.com/welcome-to-britain-a-land-where-jobs-may-be-plentiful-but-are-more-and-more-precarious; https://www.nytimes.com/2018/09/11/magazine/americans-jobs-poverty-homeless.html; https://econofact.org/employment-and-poverty

20   https://www.nelp.org/wp-content/uploads/2015/03/BrokenLawsReport2009.pdf

21   https://nypost.com/2017/10/28/loan-sharks-are-preying-on-the-citys-poorest-residents/; https://www.theguardian.com/society/2018/apr/03/crackdown-payday-loans-predatory-lending-mental-health-poverty

22   http://fortune.com/2019/01/29/americans-liquid-asset-poor-propserity-now-report/

23   http://www.cpag.org.uk/content/problems-benefits-system

24   http://time.com/5090112/infant-mortality-rate-usa/; https://www.washingtonpost.com/national/health-science/a-shocking-number-of-us-women-still-die-from-childbirth-california-is-doing-something-

about-that/2018/11/02/11042036-d7af-11e8-a10f-b51546b10756_
story.html?utm_term=.905cb99796d6

25   https://www.children.org/global-poverty/global-poverty-facts/facts-
about-poverty-in-usa

26   https://www.who.int/mental_health/policy/development/1_
Breakingviciouscycle_Infosheet.pdf

27   O'Hara, Mary (2014).

28   Wilkinson, Richard and Pickett, Kate (2009) *The Spirit Level: Why
Greater Equality Makes Societies Stronger.* New York: Bloomsbury.

29   Wilkinson, Richard and Pickett, Kate (2018) *The Inner Level: How
More Equal Societies Reduce Stress, Restore Sanity and Improve Everyone's
Well-being.* New York: Allen Lane.

30   https://uccs.ucdavis.edu/events/the-hidden-injuries-of-childhood-
poverty-the-impact-of-class-stigma-stereotypes-and-bias

31   https://uccs.ucdavis.edu/events/event-files-and-images/copy_of_
Bullock.UCSac.2017.pdf

32   https://psychology.ucsc.edu/about/people/faculty.php?uid=hbullock

33   http://www.psychchange.org/psychologists-against-austerity.html. In
particular, Psychologists against Austerity identified what they termed as
'five ailments' related to austerity. These were: humiliation and shame,
fear and distrust, instability and insecurity, isolation and loneliness, and
being trapped and powerless.

34   https://psychagainstausterity.wordpress.com/psychological-impact-of-
austerity-humiliation-shame/

35   The English county of Kent has some of the wealthiest towns in the
whole of the UK, yet areas of poverty are spread around the county:
https://www.kentlive.news/news/kent-news/most-deprived-districts-
kent-poverty-896329; https://www.kentonline.co.uk/dover/news/
one-in-four-children-in-118325/

36   http://thepsychreport.com/research-application/featured-research/
the-cognitive-burden-of-poverty/

37   http://science.sciencemag.org/content/341/6149/976

38   http://thepsychreport.com/essays-discussion/scarcity-excerpt-
mullainathan-shafir/

39   Mullainathan, Sendhil and Shafir, Eldar (2013) *Scarcity: Why having too
little means so much.* London: Allen Lane.

40   http://thepsychreport.com/essays-discussion/scarcity-excerpt-
mullainathan-shafir/

41   https://www.projecttwistit.com/markbrown

42   https://en.wikipedia.org/wiki/Hand_to_Mouth:_Living_in_
Bootstrap_America

43   Tirado, Linda (2014) *Hand to Mouth: Living in Bootstrap America.* New
York: Penguin Random House: https://www.theguardian.com/
books/2014/sep/24/hand-to-mouth-review-linda-tirado-poor-poverty

44   https://www.projecttwistit.com/lindatirado

45   Hudson, Kerry (2019) *Lowborn: Growing Up, Getting Away and Returning
to Britain's Poorest Towns.* London: Chatto & Windus.

Chapter 8

1   https://www.scotsman.com/lifestyle-2-15039/culture/edinburgh-festivals/fringe-society-boss-upper-class-increasingly-dominating-the-arts-1-4786178

2   McGarvey, Darren (2017) *Poverty Safari: Understanding the Anger of Britain's Underclass*, Edinburgh: Luath Press.

3   https://www.theguardian.com/news/ng-interactive/2019/jan/25/fighting-shame-women-leeds-tell-stories-fighting-poverty

4   de Waal, Kit (2019) *Common People: An Anthology of Working-Class Writers*. Unbound.

5   Hudson, Kerry (2019).

6   Carraway, Cash (2019).

7   Tirado, Linda (2014).

8   Desmond, Matthew (2016) *Evicted: Poverty and Profit in the American City*. New York: Crown Publishing.

9   Land, Stephanie (2019).

10   https://www.nytimes.com/2018/09/10/books/review/sarah-smarsh-heartland.html

11   https://gcgh.grandchallenges.org/challenge/voices-economic-opportunity

12   https://www.projecttwistit.com/

13   https://psycnet.apa.org/record/2006-22926-000; https://www.who.int/mental_health/policy/quality_rights/mht_article_quality_rights.pdf?ua=1; http://stephenhinshawauthor.com/books/the-mark-of-shame/

14   https://www.newstatesman.com/economics/2012/11/scroungers-fraudsters-and-parasites-how-media-coverage-affects-our-view-benefit-cl

15   https://www.sciencedirect.com/science/article/pii/S0016718514000372

16   Miller, Joshua and Schamess, Gerald (2000) 'The Discourse of Denigration and the Creation of "Other"', *The Journal of Sociology and Social Welfare*, 27:3, pp 39–62, is interesting on the wider area of denigration of disadvantaged groups.

17   Lakoff, George (1990) *Don't Think of an Elephant: Know Your Values and Frame the Debate*. Vermont: Chelsea Green Publishing.

18   Hatcher, Daniel L. (2016) *The Poverty Industry: The Exploitation of America's Most Vulnerable Citizens*. New York: NYU Press.

19   https://www.theguardian.com/society/2012/oct/24/us-anti-poverty-campaigner-lim-miller

20   Miller, Mauricio L. (2016) *The Alternative: Most of What You Believe about Poverty is Wrong*. North Carolina: Lulu Publishing Services.

21   The FII's approach is to champion the strengths of low-income people and communities, rather than concentrate on perceived deficits that need fixing.

22   https://phys.org/news/2018-01-good-storytelling-base-modern-society.html; https://time.com/5043166/storytelling-evolution/

23   https://b.3cdn.net/nefoundation/a12416779f2dd4153c_2hm6ixryj.pdf

24   https://www.projecttwistit.com/blog/2018/10/22/compelled-to-tell
25   Snaith, Mahsuda (2017) *The Things We Thought We Knew*. London: Doubleday.
26   https://www.projecttwistit.com/janetowendriggs
27   https://www.piecebypiece.org
28   http://into-action.us
29   The Skid Row Housing Trust offers a good summary of this area of LA, its origins and evolution: http://skidrow.org/about/history/
30   https://www.theatlantic.com/politics/archive/2018/02/welfare-reform-tanf-medicaid-food-stamps/552299/
31   https://endhomelessness.org/homelessness-in-america/homelessness-statistics/state-of-homelessness-report/
32   https://invisiblepeople.tv/tent-cities-in-america/
33   http://www.latimes.com/opinion/editorials/la-ed-homeless-crisis-overview-20180225-htmlstory.html
34   https://www.dailynews.com/2019/01/26/gentrification-is-failing-in-los-angeles/
35   https://www.cbsnews.com/news/los-angeles-hidden-homeless-priced-out-cbsn-originals/
36   https://www.nytimes.com/2018/05/07/us/california-economy-growth.html
37   https://news.stanford.edu/2018/09/27/students-document-poverty-california-research-study/
38   https://www.census.gov/content/dam/Census/library/publications/2016/demo/p60-258.pdf. The Supplemental Poverty Measure takes account of differences in costs of living among states including for housing and health costs. It is a favoured measure among researchers who argue that it is a more accurate reflection of poverty: https://www.politifact.com/california/statements/2017/jan/20/chad-mayes/true-california-has-nations-highest-poverty-rate-w/. The Census Bureau's Official Poverty Measure uses income levels (the official threshold for a two-adult, two-child family was $24,036 in 2015): https://www.census.gov/library/publications/2016/demo/p60-256.html; see also https://www.politifact.com/california/statements/2017/jan/20/chad-mayes/true-california-has-nations-highest-poverty-rate-w/
39   https://www.history.com/topics/great-depression/hoovervilles
40   To their credit, Californians were beginning to respond to the homelessness crisis by 2018, including by agreeing to be taxed more to direct much-needed cash towards the crisis, but the problem was profound even with some steps being taken. In addition, during 2019 Democratic lawmakers in the state were pushing the new governor, Gavin Newsom, to up safety net spending: https://www.politico.com/states/california/story/2019/05/21/democratic-lawmakers-prepare-to-push-newsom-on-safety-net-spending-1025563
41   https://www.couragecampaign.org/

Chapter 9

1   https://www.bac.org.uk/content/39748/young_people__learning/homegrown_1229/perform_your_own_music/bac_beatbox_academy

2   https://thinknation.co

3   https://www.thewarren.org

4   https://www.projecttwistit.com/thewarren

5   https://www.projecttwistit.com/alternativecensus

6   https://www.channel4.com/programmes/the-undateables

7   https://en.wikipedia.org/wiki/Greta_Thunberg

8   http://www.dannydorling.org/?p=6695

9   https://arts-emergency.org/news/panic-report/

10   https://www.woodenarrow.org/about

11   http://youngactors.org.uk/socks/

12   https://levile.co.uk/2018/05/14/council-in-me-2018-by-wale-legacy/

13   https://levile.co.uk/2018/05/14/council-in-me-2018-by-wale-legacy/

14   https://mightywriters.org

15   https://www.projecttwistit.com/mightywriters

16   https://podcasts.apple.com/us/podcast/write-on-project-twist-it/id1458816181

Chapter 10

1   Bregman, Rutger (2017) *Utopia for Realists: How We Can Build the Ideal World*. London: Little Brown.

2   https://www.vox.com/future-perfect/2019/1/30/18203911/davos-rutger-bregman-historian-taxes-philanthropy

3   https://www.washingtonpost.com/business/2019/01/31/an-angry-historian-ripped-ultra-rich-over-tax-avoidance-davos-then-one-was-given-mic/?utm_term=.88392d1618c3

4   https://www.youtube.com/watch?v=r5LtFnmPruU

5   In the UK in November 2019 tax avoidance by the rich was yet again in the news: https://www.theguardian.com/business/2019/nov/05/thousands-of-uks-richest-people-exploiting-loophole-to-cut-tax-rate

6   An interview with Tucker Carlson on Fox News went awry, ending with Carlson telling Bregman to 'go fuck yourself' after an exchange where Bregman said the channel's hosts were millionaires funded by billionaires: https://www.vox.com/2019/2/20/18233556/tucker-carlson-rutger-bregman-nowthis-dutch-historian

7   https://www.newyorker.com/magazine/2019/06/24/can-elizabeth-warren-win-it-all. Warren, who already had a reputation for taking on vested interests and highlighting inequality and economic unfairness, notably in banking, made inroads in her presidential nomination bid with a series of specific policies that resonated with a significant portion of the population founded on, as Sheelah Kohlatkar in *The New Yorker* observed, "... a pragmatic advocate for the middle class, someone who can bring systemic reforms to education, health care, and democracy itself." Alexandria Ocasio-Cortez, who was also registering with a slew of policy stances including Medicare for All and a Federal Jobs

Guarantee plus, became known as a figurehead of the Green New Deal. Along with Sanders, Ocasio-Cortez and Warren were pushing policies on the left thought unbroachable in the mainstream in recent years. Sanders' successes in the Democratic primaries for the 2016 presidential election were an early precursor to the landscape altering – and one which he was driving. When in 2019 Sanders accused Trump and the Republican Party of "hypocrisy" for their attacks on his ideology, he invoked Franklin Roosevelt as a model to follow – framing, much as Warren was beginning to do – the fight against poverty and inequality as an American fight – and he quoted Martin Luther King's prescient observations that the US "has socialism for the rich, rugged individualism for the poor": https://www.theguardian.com/us-news/2019/jun/12/bernie-sanders-2020-vision-fdr-democratic-socialism?CMP=Share_iOSApp_Other

8   https://www.washingtonpost.com/opinions/warrens-push-for-a-wealth-tax-could-be-a-game-changer/2019/01/29/a6beced4-232a-11e9-90cd-dedb0c92dc17_story.html

9   https://www.theguardian.com/commentisfree/2019/nov/10/billionaires-warren-sanders-wealth-tax-bezos-dimon-cohen

10   https://www.bloomberg.com/news/articles/2019-11-12/charles-schwab-joins-chorus-of-billionaires-opposing-wealth-tax

11   https://www.theguardian.com/commentisfree/2019/oct/21/mark-zuckerberg-plea-biillionaire-class-anti-democratic?CMP=Share_iOSApp_Other; https://time.com/5735384/capitalism-reckoning-elitism-in-america-2019/

12   https://www.motherjones.com/kevin-drum/2019/03/heres-how-to-fund-medicare-for-all/

13   https://www.gp.org/green_new_deal

14   https://www.theguardian.com/society/2019/jun/12/sheffield-council-backs-universal-basic-income-trial?CMP=Share_iOSApp_Other. UBI has been much debated with advocates in a number of countries arguing in its favour. In 2018 the city of Sheffield in England was poised to become one of the first UK cities to trial it after the council formally gave the idea its support. Significantly, the Sheffield proposal was championed by a grassroots group of activists and researchers, UBI Lab: https://www.ubilabsheffield.org/resources

15   O'Hara, Mary (2014), pp 193–204.

16   https://fightfor15.org

17   https://patrioticmillionaires.org

18   Such shifts are not unique to Britain and America, of course. The Gilets Jaunes in France for example have proven a persistent fightback against rising inequality in that country: https://www.theguardian.com/world/2018/dec/03/who-are-the-gilets-jaunes-and-what-do-they-want

19   https://www.bbc.com/news/uk-politics-48577579; https://www.independent.co.uk/news/uk/politics/boris-johnson-tax-cuts-poverty-family-tory-leadership-contest-government-a8965921.html

20   http://www.ncsl.org/research/labor-and-employment/state-minimum-wage-chart.aspx

21   https://www.theguardian.com/society/2019/may/12/labour-would-trial-universal-basic-income-if-elected-john-mcdonnell-says

22   https://www.nytimes.com/2019/02/19/us/teachers-strikes.html?login=email&auth=login-email

23   https://www.vox.com/policy-and-politics/2019/5/23/18637050/mcdonalds-workers-strike-presidential-democrats; https://www.theguardian.com/commentisfree/2019/jan/29/air-traffic-controllers-defeated-trump?CMP=Share_iOSApp_Other

24   https://www.bbc.com/news/business-45734662; https://www.cnbc.com/2019/05/07/uber-lyft-drivers-to-go-on-strike-over-low-wages-and-benefits.html; https://en.wikipedia.org/wiki/Precariat

25   https://news.gallup.com/poll/232484/slim-majority-says-middle-class-pays-fair-tax-share.aspx?g_source=link_newsv9&g_campaign=item_247052&g_medium=copy; https://news.gallup.com/opinion/polling-matters/247052/americans-long-standing-interest-taxing-rich.aspx. High-profile drives by progressive politicians such as AOC and Bernie Sanders to increase the top rate of tax or introduce a 'wealth' tax appeared to be resonating widely with the public.

26   https://uk.reuters.com/article/uk-britain-politics-tax/support-in-uk-for-more-tax-and-spending-at-15-year-high-survey-idUKKCN1M03AQ

27   Wilkinson, Richard and Pickett, Kate (2009) *The Spirit Level: Why Greater Equality Makes Societies Stronger*. New York: Bloomsbury; https://www.equalitytrust.org.uk/resources/the-spirit-level

28   Piketty, Thomas (2017) *Capital in the Twenty-First Century*, trans. Arthur Goldhammer. USA: Harvard College.

29   https://en.wikipedia.org/wiki/Thomas_Piketty

30   Walker, Robert (2014).

31   Giridharadas, Anand (2018) *Winners Take All: The Elite Charade of Changing the World*. Knopf Publishing.

32   https://www.theguardian.com/books/2019/feb/07/rutger-bregman-winnie-byanyima-anand-giridharadas

33   https://www.theguardian.com/news/2019/jun/25/the-new-left-economics-how-a-network-of-thinkers-is-transforming-capitalism

34   https://www.poorpeoplescampaign.org/

35   https://www.chelseagreen.com/product/born-on-third-base/

36   Weber, Max (1948) 'The Social Psychology of the World Religions', in *Max Weber: Essays in Sociology*, H.H. Gerth and C. Wright Mills (eds). London: Routledge, p 271.

37   https://www.washingtonpost.com/nation/2019/04/22/disneys-ceo-made-times-much-his-employees-an-heir-disney-fortune-thinks-thats-insane/?utm_term=.6ac8636ffd70

38   https://int.nyt.com/data/documenthelper/1342-wealthtaxletter-june2019/1852b1968e8e0d52b1a0/optimized/full.pdf#page=1

39   https://www.linkedin.com/pulse/why-how-capitalism-needs-reformed-parts-1-2-ray-dalio/

40   Collins, Chuck (2018) *Is Inequality in America Irreversible?*. London / Medford: Polity Press.

41 https://americansfortaxfairness.org/tax-fairness-briefing-booklet/fact-sheet-the-estate-inheritance-tax/. A similar fight about inheritance tax is ongoing in the UK: https://www.ft.com/content/d38fb112-46df-11e8-8ee8-cae73aab7ccb

42 https://thehill.com/policy/finance/427328-senate-republicans-reintroduce-bill-to-repeal-the-estate-tax

43 https://www.faithincommunityscotland.org/poverty-truth-commission/

44 https://nytruthcommission.org/introduction

45 https://www.edgehill.ac.uk/i4p/files/2018/03/Learning-from-Developing-Poverty-Truth-Commission.pdf

46 https://thirdforcenews.org.uk/tfn-news/poverty-truth-commission-becomes-a-movement-for-change

47 http://www.leedspovertytruth.org.uk

48 https://www.projecttwistit.com/s/LPTC_HuManifesto_2018_NEW.pdf

49 https://www.poverty2solutions.org

50 https://www.projecttwistit.com/sound-delivery

51 http://beingthestory.org.uk/speakers/on-top-of-the-world

52 https://www.rethinkingpoverty.org.uk/contact-us/. The Webb Memorial Trust, founded by the social reformer Beatrice Webb in 1947, was wound down in 2017 and Rethinking Poverty is part of its legacy.

53 https://www.rethinkingpoverty.org.uk/rethinking-poverty/reporting-on-poverty-why-the-tone-matters/

54 http://economichardship.org

55 http://economichardship.org/about

56 https://www.pbs.org/wgbh/americanexperience/features/surviving-the-dust-bowl-works-progress-administration-wpa/

57 See: https://longreads.com/2014/11/07/interview-poor-teeth-writer-sarah-smarsh-on-class-and-journalism/?utm_content=buffer8246f&utm_medium=social&utm_source=twitter.com&utm_campaign=buffer/

58 https://www.nuj.org.uk/news/reporting-uk-poverty-new-film-launched/

59 https://www.onroadmedia.org.uk

60 https://www.bond.org.uk/news/2019/04/5-ways-to-change-the-narrative-from-fear-to-hope

61 See https://narrativeinitiative.org for more on NI's work including the report it published after conducting a 'listening tour' of 'over 100 experts, innovators and visionaries from a range of disciplines and communities that intervene at the intersection (and sometimes the edges) of social justice and narrative change': https://narrativeinitiative.org/wp-content/uploads/2019/05/TheNarrativeInitiative_TowardNewGravity.pdf

62 https://neweconomics.org/2018/02/framing-the-economy-2/

63 https://b.3cdn.net/nefoundation/a12416779f2dd4153c_2hm6ixryj.pdf

64 Lakoff, George (2004) *Don't Think of an Elephant: Know Your Values and Frame the Debate*. Vermont: Chelsea Green Publishing.

65 Lakoff, George (2006) *Thinking Points: Communicating Our American Values and Vision*. New York: Farrar, Straus and Giroux.
66 https://en.wikipedia.org/wiki/Frank_Luntz
67 https://www.pbs.org/wgbh/pages/frontline/shows/persuaders/interviews/luntz.html
68 http://frameworksinstitute.org
69 http://frameworksinstitute.org/assets/files/PDF_Poverty/JRFUKPovertyMessageMemo2018Final.pdf
70 https://www.theguardian.com/commentisfree/2016/aug/19/socialism-left-hard-well-morally-superior-right

Selected further reading

Abramsky, Sasha (2013) *The American Way of Poverty: How the Other Half Still Lives*. New York: Nation Books.

Blyth, Mark (2013) *Austerity: The History of a Dangerous Idea*. New York: Oxford University Press.

Carraway, Cash (2019) *Skint Estate: A Memoir of Poverty, Motherhood and Survival*. London: Ebury Press.

Chase, Elaine and Bantebya-Kyomuhendo, Grace (eds) (2014) *Poverty and Shame: Global Experiences*. Oxford: Oxford University Press.

Cooper, Vickie and Whyte, David (eds) (2017) *The Violence of Austerity*. London: Pluto Press.

Edin, Kathryn J. and Shaefer, H. Luke (2015) *$2 a Day: Living on Almost Nothing in America*. New York: Houghton Mifflin Harcourt.

Garrett, Paul Michael (2017) *Welfare Words: Critical Social Work & Social Policy*. London: Sage.

Hudson, Kerry (2019) *Lowborn: Growing Up, Getting Away and Returning to Britain's Poorest Towns*. London: Chatto & Windus.

Johnson, B. and Forrest, D. (2017) *Social Class and Television Drama in Contemporary Britain*. London: Palgrave

Jones, Owen (2012) *Chavs: The Demonization of the Working Class*. London: Verso.

Land, Stephanie (2019) *Maid: Hard Work, Low Pay, and a Mother's Will to Survive*. New York: Hachette Books.

O'Hara, Mary (2014) *Austerity Bites*. Bristol: Policy Press.

Pimpare, Stephen (2008) *A People's History of Poverty in America*. New York: The New Press.

Ryan, Frances (2019) *Crippled: Austerity and the Demonization of Disabled People*. London: Verso.

Seabrook, Jeremy (2013) *Pauperland: Poverty and the Poor in Britain*. London: C. Hurst & Co.

Shildrick, Tracy (2018) *Poverty Propaganda: Exploring the Myths.* Bristol Policy Press.

Tirado, Linda (2014) *Hand to Mouth: Living in Bootstrap America.* New York: Penguin Random House.

Walker, Robert (2014) *The Shame of Poverty.* Oxford: Oxford University Press.

Index

5 Things Newsletter 159–61

A

Abramsky, Sasha 83, 117–18, 338n19
Into Action 244
Affordable Care Act 2010 65, 79
Alston, Philip
  on healthcare in US 77, 79
  on racial poverty stereotyping 116
  report on poverty
    in UK 9–10, 22–5, 50, 56, 289–90
    in US 5, 57–9, 115–17
'Alternative Census' 255, 256–7
American Dream 9, 58, 90, 217, 249
Arnott, Steve 288
art 240–2
ATD Fourth World 179, 288
'audit' of poverty (IPS report) 67, 129
austerity
  Alston on 10, 22, 50
  bankers and 219
  and change in poverty narrative 120–1
  child poverty 25–6, 46, 47
  deaths related to 41
  driving extreme poverty 11, 39
  homelessness 43–4
  institutionalisation of narrative of poverty 132–5
  Labour Party's response to push for 141–2
  links between poverty, mental health and 212
  and loss of income 39

media support for 142–8
narrative 11, 135–42, 296, 326n16
New Economics Foundation's analysis of 295–6, 328n16
a political choice 11, 22, 47, 81
at ten-year mark 4, 50–1, 149–50
welfare policy of 4, **5**, 11, 24–5, 39–41, 46, 47, 50, 81, 132–3

B

baby banks 37
Banks, Iain 129
Barber, William, III 66–7, 68–9, 82
Battersea Arts Centre Beatbox Academy (BBA) 252, 257–62
beauty banks 38
Beckett, Andy 279
Ben-Meir, Alon 74–5
benefits
  accessing 89–90, 133–4, 156–7, 207–8
  assessments 132, 134, 135
  claiming 'dole' 18, 101, 116–17
  drug test requirements 156–7
  fraud 100, 203–4
  freeze on 46
  public attitudes to 109, 189–90
  sanctions 132–3, 134–5, 141
Benefits Street 146–8
Bill and Melinda Gates Foundation 225
billionaires 3
  call for wealth tax on 282–3
  complaining 274–5
  UBS report on 309n27
Bilo, Charlotte 180–1
Black, Rachel 108–9, 109–10

357

Blyth, Mark 124
Born on Third Base 280–1
Bostridge, Carol 34–5, 38
Brady, David 105
Bregman, Rutger 272–3, 305
  in conversation with Giridharadas
    and Byanyima 277–9
Brexit 14, 46–7, 296
British Social Attitudes Survey
  2017 190
  2018 187
Broad, Eli 283–4
Broady, Rachel 291–2, 293
Brown, Gordon 15, 50–1
Brown, Mark 199–200, 216
budget proposals, 2019 White
  House 75–6
Bullingdon Club 44
Bullock, Heather 210–12
Byanyima, Winnie 273
  in conversation with Giridharadas
    and Bregman 277–9
Byrne, Liam 141

C
California 248–9
  homelessness in Los Angeles
    242–50
Cambridge University 110–11,
  230–1
Cameron, David 137, 138–9,
  333n31
Can you hear me from up here? 288–9
Carraway, Cash 223, 327n38
Carson, Ben 170
Carthew, Natasha 238–9
Center for American Progress
  (CAP) 61–2, 122, 151, 156, 157
Center on Poverty and Inequality,
  Stanford University 60, 248
Center on Poverty and Social Policy,
  Columbia University 72
Centre for Social Justice (CSJ) 127,
  128, 140, 331n91
child poverty
  austerity and increases in 25–6,
    46, 47
  "Dickensian picture" 49
  free school meals 47–8, 151–4
  healthcare in US and 80

'The Hidden Injuries of
  Childhood Poverty' report
  210–14
IFS forecast 30
impact on mental health and
  wellbeing 209, 212
increase in infant mortality linked
  to rising 48–9
JFR report 2018 43
racial patterns 116
Resolution Foundation report
  30, 31
statistics
  in UK 23, 29, 30, 31, 42, 46
  in US 70, 74–5, 329n72
stigma and shame of 210, 211
teenagers' reflections 213–14
in working families 25, 31, 43, 46
Child Poverty Action Group
  (CPAG) 25–6
Chung, Heejung 97–8, 109
Cigar, June 193, 242–5, 249–50
climate change 299
Clinton, Bill 108, 109–10
Coalition, Conservative and Liberal
  Democrat 22, 141, 142, 326n16
cognitive 'load' of poverty 214–20
The Colbert Report 129–31
Coleman, Garrie 148
Collins, Chuck 93, 95–6, 280–1,
  284–6
Conservative Party
  Alston on welfare policies of 10,
    22
  austerity narrative 11, 135–42
  politicians justifying austerity cuts
    137–40
  response to UN report on poverty
    26–7
  ten years after start of austerity 4,
    50–1, 149–50
  under Thatcher 97–100, 107, 109
Coombes, Thomas 293–4
Corbyn, Jeremy 142
Corlett, Adam 46
Corn, David 163
Council in Me 264–5
Cruz, Claudia 228, 229
Cuccinelli, Ken 77
Culp-Ressler, Tara 106

culture
  enabling poverty 81–2, 124–8,
    211, 217
  enabling shame and stigma around
    poverty 254
  poverty-shaming in popular 146–8
'culture of dependency' 159–64,
  338–9n21

D

Daily Express 144
Daily Mail 142, 144
Daily Mirror 144
Dalio, Ray 282–3
Davis, Marquis 59–60
deaths
  disabled people 133, 134
  homeless people 45
  infant 48–9
  related to austerity policies 41
Deaton, Angus 8
debt 6, 207
  medical 80
  money lenders 84–5
  school lunch 153, 337n5
Democratic Party
  Limbaugh on 164
  presidential contenders, 2020 3,
    67, 186, 282
  and supporters' attitudes to
    poverty 187
Dennis, Phillip 155–6
deservedness, narrative of 96,
  119–20, 280, 285–6
'deserving' vs. 'undeserving' poor
  97–8, 170, 329–30n77
Desmond, Matthew 223
desperation 201–2
destitution
  definition of 32
  factors tipping people into 32,
    39, 79
  levels of UK 23, 31
  a story in Los Angeles 242–50
dimensions of poverty 179
disabilities, people with
  cuts and sanctions to benefits 76,
    132–3, 332n19
  hate crimes towards 143, 311n10
  Stephen Smith 133, 134
  target for press ire 143, 144

Work Capability Assessments 134,
  135
Disney, Abigail 282
disruption of dominant poverty
  narrative 279–93
Dolan, Karen 121–2, 123
'dole,' claiming 18, 101
  toxic narrative of people 116–17
Domokos, John 112
Dorling, Danny 8–9, 125–6
Downey, Gloria 200–1
drug testing for benefits 156–7
Duncan Smith, Iain 127, 140, 178

E

Economic Hardship Reporting
  Project 290–1
Edmiston, Daniel 287
education 110–11, 194–6, 230–1
Ellwood, David T. 340n21
empathy 190–1
Equality and Human Rights
  Commission (EHRC) report
  2018 39, 41
experiences of poverty *see* poverty,
  lived experiences of

F

financial crash 2008
  fuelling poverty narrative after
    151–8
  shaming in Trump's time, post-
    164–6
  shaming post-crash, pre-Trump
    159–64
financial precariousness of
  households 55, 60, 71–2, 171,
  262
Finnigan, Ryan M. 105
'Five Ways to Change the Narrative
  from Fear to Hope' 293–4
food insecurity
  in Britain 33–4, 85–7
  in US 63, 73–4, 115, 202
foodbanks 33–4
  expansion into other essential
    products 37–8
  Gove on 140–1
  rising demand for 39–40
  in school holidays 47
  workers and volunteers 34–7

foodstamps (now known as SNAP)
5, 54, 59, 115, 118, 168, 171, 202,
206, 320n28, 327n28
Foreign Policy magazine 64
Fox News 161, 168, 169, 171, 273,
290
FrameWorks Institute 301–4
framing 296–300
conservatives' expert use of
299–300
Lakoff on 297–9
of poverty in US and UK 124–5
reframing poverty in UK 301–4
Frampton, Hetty 103–4
fraud, welfare benefits 100, 203–4
free school meals 47–8
'lunch shaming' 151–4
Freud, Lord 140
fundamental attribution error 182–3
furloughed government workers
71, 171

G

Garland-Olaniran, Sheilah 88, 101,
177
Garnham, Alison 25–6
Garrett, Paul Michael 161–2
Gilliam, Franklin D., Jr. 107
Gingrich, Newt 118, 169
Giridharadas, Anand, in conversation
with Byanyima and Bregman
277–9
Glackin, Jon 45
Glubenkian Theatre, Canterbury
252
Goldman, Ken 273
Gooch, Andrew 253–4
Gove, Michael 140–1
The Guardian 7, 26, 39, 44, 50, 98,
136–7, 144, 151, 190, 216, 231,
274, 305
guidelines on reporting on poverty,
NUJ 291–3
guilt 177, 178, 198, 201

H

Haley, Nikki 60, 61
hard work, belief in 187–8, 211,
217, 249, 281
Harris, John 112
Hayward, Andrew 45

health
poverty and impact on 207, 208–9
healthcare
in UK 8–9, 78
in US 65, 77
interplay with poverty 79–80
'socialised medicine' 77
uninsured children 80
Heritage Foundation 129, 130, 160
Hernandez, Sylvia 200, 202
Herrington, Tracey 286
Hodgson, Lizzie 256–7
Holbourne, Zita 240–1
Holland, Joshua 126, 127
homeless
deaths 45
experiences in US 53–6, 242–50
poems and songs about 253–4,
265
statistics 44, 70, 246
Trump administration's position
on 62–3
in UK 43–5
verbal and physical attacks on
44–5, 149
veterans 115
Hothi, Manny 289
housing
discrimination 73
new developments 149
poverty and sub-standard 18, 207
subsidies 59, 76
see also public housing
Hubgen, Sabine 105
Hudson, Kerry 219–20
Humanifesto 287
humiliation 18, 20, 101, 178, 204,
205–6, 210, 212
hygiene essentials 37–8

I

immigrants
access to benefits in US 76–7
'hostile environment' for 150
undocumented 306
incomes
attributed to hard work 187–8
austerity policies and loss of 39
disparities between worker and
executive pay 5, 282

stagnation in Britain 30–1
see also wages
individualism 98, 124, 211, 217, 280, 302
infant mortality 48–9, 80, 208–9
inflation inequality 72
Institute for Fiscal Studies (IFS) 5, 8, 30
Institute for Policy Studies (IPS) 67, 69–70, 121, 129, 280
Institute for Public Policy research (IPPR) 41
Is Inequality in America Irreversible? 284–6

J
Jaffe, Adi 182–3
Jaffe, Sarah 166–7
Jamil, Jameela 173–5
The Jeremy Kyle Show 145–6
Johnson, Boris 4, 104–5, 150
Joseph, Keith 102
Joseph Rowntree Foundation (JRF) 31, 32, 41–3, 146, 147, 190, 301
Jun, Miyang 102, 103

L
labels 3, 93, 256
Labour Party
  benefits freeze issue 316n86
  New Labour's anti-poverty measures 29, 107
  progressive policies 275
  response to austerity 141–2, 335n51
Lakoff, George 233, 296, 297–9
Lancaster, Simon 141–2
Land, Stephanie 205–6, 223–4
Langford, Jodie 253
language
  denigrating 3, 91, 93, 141–2, 146, 278
  framing of issues and use of 299–300
  hard-hitting 289–90
Lauter, David 188–9
laziness 10, 90, 114, 116–17, 122, 127, 159, 174, 188, 198
Leyva, Rodolfo 183–4
life expectancy 49, 208
Limbaugh, Rush 113, 163–4

Lister, Ruth 2
The Liverpool Echo 134
living wage 314–15n66
Loach, Ken 133–4
London School of Economics (LSE) 142–3
lone parents 30, 114, 140
  public attitudes to assistance for 187
  see also single mothers
Long, Amelia 270–1
Los Angeles, homelessness in 242–50
Los Angeles Times 188, 246–7
low wages 25, 42, 64, 160–1, 163, 216–17, 282, 344n3
'lunch shaming' 151–4
Luntz, Frank 299–300

M
Mani, Anandi 214–15
maternal mortality 208
May, Theresa 150
McAllister, Sean 149, 223, 288
McCarthy, Shona 221
McGann, Stephen 272
McGarvey, Darren 'Loki' 222
measurement of poverty
  adjusting US 63–4
  Joseph Rowntree Foundation 316n65
  Social Metrics Commission (SMC) 28–9
  Supplemental Poverty Measure (SPM) 70, 317–18n8, 348n38
  UN Rapporteur's report on issues around 317–18n8
  unrealistic US 71–2
media
  Economic Hardship Reporting Project 290–1
  experiment into impact of materialistic 183–4
  local press 134, 246–7, 331–2n10
  moves to change portrayals of poverty in 290
  national press coverage of poverty 142–5
  NUJ Reporting Poverty Guidelines 291–3
  ownership of 126, 290

On Road Media 293
teenagers' reflections on portrayals
of poverty in 213–14, 262
television shows 129–31, 145–8
transmitting poverty narrative 102,
106, 126, 159–60, 166–9, 175
use of term 'underclass' 3
Medicaid 59, 65, 76, 79, 80
medical debt 80
Medicare 76
mental health, poverty and 208,
209–10
children in poverty 209, 212
and Work Capability Assessments
135
meritocracy 9, 90–1, 211, 217
Mighty Writers 267–71
Miller, Mauricio Lim 235–8
minimum wage
Federal 320n32
in UK 275, 314–15n66
minority ethnic groups in UK
310n5, 310n9
Molina, Tim 248–9
Monbiot, George 98–9, 330n85
money lenders 84–5, 207
Monroe, Jack 149
Moynihan, Daniel Patrick 162
Mullainathan, Sendhil 215
Mulvaney, Mick 170
Murray, Conrad 260–1
myths 205

N
Narrative Initiative (NI) 294–5
Nat Cen British Social Attitudes
Survey
2017 190, 343n41
2018 187
National Health Service (NHS)
8–9, 78
National Union of Journalists
(NUJ) Reporting Poverty
Guidelines 291–3
neoliberalism 97–101, 278
Neville, Angela 134–5
New Economics Foundation 136,
238, 295–6
The New York Times 105, 152, 164,
283–4
Newkirk, Vann R., II 64–5

Nieman Lab, Harvard University
106–7
A Northern Soul 149, 288

O
Obama, Barack 79, 154, 163, 164,
224
The Observer 46, 47
Ocasio-Cortez, Alexandria 274
Occupy Movement 158
Off-Kilter 61–2
On Road Media 293
Osborne, George 139
Owen-Driggs, Janet 241–2

P
Parrott, Sharon 64
Patrick, Ruth 120–1, 181–2
Patriotic Millionaires 275, 281–2,
284
'Paul' 266–7
Pelosi, Nancy 171
period poverty 38
Personal Independence Payments
(PIP) 132, 133
'personal responsibility' 124, 157,
163, 190
Personal Responsibility and Work
Opportunity Reconciliation Act
(PRWORA) 108
Pew Research Center 187, 188, 210,
211
Piece by Piece 242
Pimpare, Stephen 52, 117, 128, 131,
197, 205, 325n2, 325n10
poems 253–4
political choice
of austerity 11, 22, 47, 81
of poverty 4, 22, 47, 81, 107
Poor People's Campaign (PPC)
66–9, 88, 221, 228, 229, 233,
279, 286
Porter, Billie J.D. 197–8
Portes, Jonathan 41
poverty, lived experiences of 52–6,
172, 197–203
of author 16–17, 18–20, 47–8,
84–7, 101, 194–6, 204, 229
voices of people with 234–42
willingness to talk about 226–32

young people 173–5, 198–9,
213–14, 266–7
challenging fatalistic assumptions
258–61
poverty measurement *see*
measurement of poverty
poverty narrative 1–3, 10, 11, 51, 77,
81–2, 89–97, 330–1n61
beginning of end for 293–304
challenging 221–6, 233–4
changing, emerging pathways to
272–9
disrupting dominant 279–93
and entrenchment of poverty
121–3
fabricating myths to suit 102–10
fuelling, after 2008 financial crash
151–8
infiltrating everyday existences
112–14
institutionalisation under austerity
132–5
to maintain status quo 241, 280
media transmitting 102, 106, 126,
159–60, 166–9, 175
observations on toxic 112–19
personal realisation of 96–7
post-crash, pre-Trump 159–64
racism in 116
role of shaming in sustaining 178
Romney and 162–3
similarities between US and
Britain in approach 7–10, 80–2,
124–8
think tanks and 126–8
in Trump's time 164–72
unified narrative of wealth and
280
'us' and 'them' 122–3
writers, artists and film makers and
alternative 222–4, 263–5, 288–9
young people challenging 254,
258–62
'poverty porn' 145–9, 214, 223, 262
poverty propaganda 119–23, 126,
1315
poverty trap 21–6, 206–8
Poverty Truth Commissions (PTCs)
286–7
Poverty2Solutions 288

propaganda, poverty 119–23, 126,
131
Psychologists for Social Change/
Psychologists Against Austerity
(PAA) 210, 212
public attitudes 109, 183–91, 212
public housing
Can you hear me from up here?
288–9
Council in Me 264–5
experiences of living in 84,
239–40
media portrayals of 240
Purdue, Sonny 171

R
race
and attitudes to poverty 189
food insecurity by 73–4
poverty rates by 70, 116
racism and poverty 3, 73, 101, 108,
116
Reagan, Ronald 99, 107–8
Spitting Image puppet 88–9
Republican Party
denial of poverty in era of Trump
60–5
opposition to healthcare
programmes 79, 80
poverty narrative 122, 156, 157,
164–6
support for tax cuts 58, 60
and supporters' attitudes to
poverty 187, 188
Tea Party movement 155–7, 158
Trump cabinet members on
poverty 170–2
welfare policies 4–5, 58–9, 63–5,
75–7, 122, 123, 157–8, 165–6
Resolution Foundation 5, 30–1, 46
Rethinking Poverty 289
Riccione, Christine 52–6
rights-based context for poverty 276
Roach, Louisa 265–6
Rodrigues, Antonio 263
Romano, Serana 330n77
Romney, Mitt 157, 162–3
Ronson, Jon 179
Roosevelt, Eleanor 7
Roosevelt, Franklin D. 1, 154
Ross, Wilbur 171–2

Rothenberg, Martin 284, 285
Rowling, J.K. 140
Rudd, Amber 26, 50
Ryan, Paul 156, 319n25, 339n28, 341n57

S
safety net *see* social safety net
sanctions, benefit 132–3, 134–5, 141
Sanders, Bernie 76, 274
sanitary products 38
Saunders-Browne, Kieton 263–4
Schumer, Chuck 171
Schwab, Charles 274
Scott Paul, Abigail 146, 147–8, 302
Seabrook, Jeremy 1, 176, 177
Sen, Amartya 175–6
Shafir, Eldar 215
Shah, Nadine 265
shame, definition 177
shaming and blaming of poor 81–2, 121–2, 124–6, 172, 173–5, 191, 212, 305
    children 151–4, 210, 211
    leaving its mark 180–3
    making sense of shame 175–80
    in popular culture 146–8
    role in sustaining poverty narrative 178
    under Trump 164–6
Shildrick, Tracy 119–20
Shittu, Wale 264–5
single mothers 142
    history of targeting 328n45
    households below poverty line 70
    media demonisation of 143
    myth of 'welfare queens' 3, 102–10
    Thatcher on 327n41
    see also lone parents
Skid Row, Los Angeles 245–8
Skint Britain 146, 147, 148
Slater, Tom 127–8
Slevin, Jeremy 62
Smarsh, Sarah 15, 167–8, 185, 224, 240, 291
Smith, Harry Leslie 21
Smith, Stephen 133, 134
Snaith, Mahsuda 239–40
social capital 111
social media 95, 148, 171, 254

Social Metrics Commission (SMC) 28–9
social safety net 3–4
    charity providing 15, 74
    gaps in UK 22, 23, 37–41, 81
    Limbaugh on 113, 164
    public support for a stronger 187, 212
    Ryan on 156
    shredding of US 74–7, 123, 170, 246, 320n28
    similar efforts in UK and US to discredit 56, 57
Socks 264
'The Souls of Poor Folk' 67, 69, 129
Sound Delivery 288–9
speaking out against poverty 221–6
    voices of people with lived experiences of poverty 234–42
    willingness to talk publicly 226–32
'special relationship' 9, 80–2, 124–8
The Spectator 104
Spitting Image 88–9
Sprague, Aleta 108–9, 109–10
Spriggs, William 154
Stanford Center on Poverty and Inequality 60, 248
The State of Hunger report 39
statistics, poverty
    child poverty
        in UK 23, 29, 30, 31, 42, 46
        in US 70, 74–5, 329n72
    homelessness 44, 70, 246
    in UK 23, 29
        'working poor' 42
    in US 57, 70
        California 248
        race 116
Statue of Liberty 77
stereotypes 92–3, 94, 116–17
    in media 143, 167–8
    racial 116
stigma of poverty 181–3
    for children 210–11
    young people exploring ways to smash 252–7
storytelling 238–40
    alternative 263–5
    'I Didn't Do it Alone' stories 281
    Sound Delivery focus on 288–9

structural causes of poverty 6, 72–3,
185, 206–7, 212, 304
poverty narrative and concealing
of 81, 121, 128, 280
student debt 6
suicides 133, 135
The Sun 143, 145
Supplemental Nutrition Assistance
Program (SNAP) *see* foodstamps
(now known as SNAP)
Supplemental Poverty Measure
(SPM) 70, 317–18n8, 348n38

T
tax
avoidance 273, 275
cuts 58, 60, 186
estate tax 285
public opinion on 276
'relief' 298–9
rises, mooting 345–6n28
wealth tax on very rich 274–5,
282–3
Taylor, Nat Kendall 300, 302, 303–4
Tea Party 155–7, 158
teenage parenthood 102–3, 105–6
television shows 129–31, 145–8
televisions 130, 214, 229
Thatcher, Margaret 97, 98, 99–100,
107, 109, 295, 327n41
Theoharis, Liz 221, 228
think tanks 3, 126–8
The Colbert Report satire 129–31
Thinking Points 297–9
ThinkNation 252, 256
Tilford, Simon 190
Tirado, Linda 52, 193, 216–18, 223
Trisha 145
trolls 95
Trump, Donald 296
budget proposals 75–6
cabinet 170–2
cultural demonisation of people
123
denial of poverty in era of 60–5
election of 154
poverty shaming 164–6
tax cuts 58, 60, 186
Trussell Trust 33, 39, 40, 47
Tutu, Desmond 21

U
UN Special Rapporteur on
Extreme Poverty and Human
Rights 5, 56–7
UK report 22–6, 50, 56
response to 26–8, 50
tone of 289–90
US report 5, 57–60, 72–4, 77,
115–17
response to 60–5
unemployment 96, 97, 136, 161–2,
180–1
United Way Alice Project (ALICE)
70
Universal Basic Income (UBI) 275
Universal Credit 27, 28, 39, 50

U
Vallas, Rebecca 62–3, 71–2, 122–3,
151, 156, 157–8
veterans 115
voices of people with lived
experiences of poverty 234–42

W
wages 5, 163
living 315n66
low 25, 42, 64, 160–1, 163,
216–17, 282, 344n3
minimum 275, 314–15n66,
320n32
stagnation in Britain 30–1
see also incomes
Walker, Robert 88, 144–5, 178, 183,
191, 276
Waller, Vince, Jr. 78
Walsh, Holly 35, 36–7
The Warren 253–4
Warren, Elizabeth 3, 274
wealth
adulation for 82, 100–1, 254
attributed to personal effort 90,
95–6, 187–8
creation 277–8
hoarding of 186, 204
inequality 8, 23, 58, 60, 190
narrative of 2–3, 10, 90, 95–6,
280–1, 284
privilege and entitlement 110, 172
redistribution of 65–6, 178
tax proposals 274–5, 282–3,

of US Congress members 341n58
see also billionaires
Webb Memorial Trust 289
Weber, Max 272
welfare 'dependency' 109, 156,
   159–64, 165, 190
welfare policy
   of austerity 4, 5, 11, 24–5, 39–41,
      46, 47, 50, 81, 132–3
   under Bill Clinton 108, 109–10
   similarities in US and UK
      approach 9, 80–1
   under Thatcher 97
   of Trump administration 4–5,
      58–9, 63–5, 75–7, 123, 157–8,
      165–6
'welfare queens' 3, 102–10
Whitaker, Tim 268–9
Whitenstall, Tracey 27
Williams, Zoe 136–7
Wood, Jimmy 114
Woods, Kat 218–19
Work Capability Assessments 134,
   135
'working poor' 5–6, 24, 51, 70–2
   appalling working conditions 273
   benefits 46, 344n3
   child poverty rates 25, 31, 43, 46
   foodstamps 320n28

increase in numbers of 41–3
in thankless, insecure jobs 204,
   207, 216–17
World Economic Forum, Davos
   272–4
World Health Organization 208,
   209
writing project 267–71

Y

young people
   'Alternative Census' 255, 256–7
   BBA 252, 257–62
   challenging narrative of poverty
      254, 258–62
   live event to 'smash stigma of
      poverty' 252–7
   lived experiences of poverty
      173–5, 198–9, 213–14, 266–7
   Mighty Writers 267–71
   personal journeys and challenges
      266–7
   power of storytelling 263–5
   priorities to tackle stigma of
      poverty 254

Z

Zuckerberg, Mark 274–5

Made in the USA
Columbia, SC
26 March 2020